T…
East … …ies

Transnational Modern Languages

Transnational Modern Languages promotes a model of Modern Languages not as the inquiry into separate national traditions, but as the study of languages, cultures and their interactions. The series aims to demonstrate the value – practical and commercial, as well as academic and cultural – of modern language study when conceived as transnational cultural enquiry.

The texts in the series are specifically targeted at a student audience. They address how work on the transnational and the transcultural broadens the confines of Modern Languages; opens an extensive range of objects of research to analysis; deploys a complex set of methodologies; and can be accomplished through the exposition of clearly articulated examples.

The series is anchored by *Transnational Modern Languages: A Handbook*, ed. Jenny Burns (Warwick) and Derek Duncan (St. Andrews), which sets out the theoretical and conceptual scope of the series, the type of research on which it is based and the kinds of questions that it asks. Following on from the *Handbook*, the series includes a text for the study of the following Modern Languages:

Transnational French Studies, ed. Charles Forsdick (Liverpool) and Claire Launchbury (Leeds)

Transnational German Studies, ed. Rebecca Braun (Lancaster) and Benedict Schofield (King's College London)

Transnational Spanish Studies, ed. Catherine Davies (IMLR) and Rory O'Bryen (Cambridge)

Transnational Italian Studies, ed. Charles Burdett (Durham) and Loredana Polezzi (Cardiff)

Transnational Portuguese Studies, ed. Hilary Owen (Manchester/Oxford) and Claire Williams (Oxford)

Transnational Russian Studies, ed. Andy Byford (Durham), Connor Doak (Bristol) and Stephen Hutchings (Manchester)

Transnational East Asian Studies, ed. Kevin N. Cawley (Oxford) and Julia C. Schneider (Cork)

Transnational East Asian Studies

edited by

Kevin N. Cawley and Julia C. Schneider

LIVERPOOL UNIVERSITY PRESS

First published 2023 by
Liverpool University Press
4 Cambridge Street
Liverpool
L69 7ZU

British Library Cataloguing-in-Publication data
A British Library CIP record is available

ISBN 978-1-80207-729-2 (HB)
ISBN 978-1-80207-730-8 (PB)

Typeset by Carnegie Book Production, Lancaster
Printed in the UK by CPI Group (UK) Ltd, Croydon CR0 4YY

Contents

Figures

Chapter 2

Chapter 4

Chapter 7

Chapter 8

Contributors

Nadeschda Bachem is an assistant professor in Korean Studies at the Institute of Oriental and Asian Studies, University of Bonn. She received her PhD in 2018 from SOAS, University of London, with a thesis entitled "Remnants of Empire: Colonial Memory in Japanese and South Korean Short Fiction, 1953–1972". Her research focuses on comparative South Korean and Japanese literature, postcolonial theory, and gender studies.

Adam Cathcart is Lecturer in Chinese History at the University of Leeds and is the co-editor of *Decoding the Sino-North Korean Borderlands* (Amsterdam University Press, 2021). His articles have appeared in *Twentieth-Century China, China Quarterly* (Gordon White Prize), and across the gamut of Korean studies journals. He has previously taught at Queen's University Belfast, run courses at Sichuan University in Chengdu, and given guest lectures at University College Cork. His research in Yanbian was supported by Academy of Korean Studies grants (AKS-2013-R11 and AKS-2015-R49).

Kevin N. Cawley is Senior Lecturer in Korean Studies and Director of the Irish Institute of Korean Studies since 2011. He is a founding member of the Society for the Study of Pre-Modern Asia at the University of Oxford, where he has been a visiting fellow (at Wolfson College) and is also an editor of Korean Philosophy for the Stanford Encyclopedia of Philosophy. He is the author of *The Religious and Philosophical Traditions of Korea* (Routledge, 2019), which examines Korea's intellectual history with a significant focus on Buddhism and Neo-Confucianism. He has published widely on different aspects of Korean studies in a variety of leading peer-reviewed journals such as *Translation Studies, Acta Koreana, Asian Ethnicity,* and *History* *of Education*, and authored multiple book chapters, generally drawing on contemporary critical theory.

Yu-Wen Chen is Professor of Chinese Studies at the University of Helsinki (Finland) and Hosting Professor of Asian Studies at Palacky University (Olomouc, Czech Republic). She is one of the editors of the *Journal of Chinese Political Science*. Chen represents Finland in Horizon 2020's COST ACTION: China in Europe Research Network. She is the academic liaison for the University of Helsinki at the Nordic Centre in Fudan University and at the Nordic NIAS Council. She has held academic positions at Nazarbayev University, University College Cork, and Academia Sinica.

Jamie Coates is Lecturer in East Asian Studies at the University of Sheffield. Trained as an anthropologist, he uses ethnographic, historical, and media-text approaches to explore the relationships between technology, mobility, and identity in urban Northeast Asia. He is currently investigating how media and migration change local imaginaries in the Sino-Japanese context. His works include "The Cruel Optimism of Mobility" in *positions: Asia Critique*, "So Hot Right Now: Reflections on Virality and Sociality from Transnational Digital China" in *Digital Culture and Society*, and the ethnographic film "Tokyo Pengyou" in the *Journal of Anthropological Films.*

Jennifer Coates is Senior Lecturer in Japanese Studies at the School of East Asian Studies, University of Sheffield. She is the author of *Making Icons: Repetition and the Female Image in Japanese Cinema, 1945–1964* (Hong Kong University Press, 2016). Her current ethnographic research project focuses on early post-war film audiences in Japan.

James H. Grayson is Emeritus Professor of Modern Korean Studies in the School of East Asian Studies at the University of Sheffield. He is an anthropologist and an ordained Methodist minister. He served with the Methodist Church in the Republic of Korea from 1971 to 1987, when he joined the staff at Sheffield. He has written extensively on religion in Korea (particularly Christianity and folk religion) and on the historic and contemporary folklore of Korea. He has authored *Korea: A Religious History* (Routledge Curzon, 1989; 2nd ed. 2002) and *Myths and Legends from Korea: A Compendium of Ancient and Modern Materials* (Routledge, 2001). He has a particular research interest in the process by which religions spread across cultural boundaries. This was the focus of his doctoral research, which was published as *Early Buddhism and Christianity in Korea: A Study in the Emplantation of Religion* (Brill, 1985).

Sarah Hanisch is an interdisciplinary migration scholar who works at the intersection of anthropology, African studies, and Chinese studies. She holds a PhD in Chinese Studies and an MA in Global Studies. Her main research interests are the lived experiences of migrants in the Global South, and the relationship between migration, broader transformations, and state projects. She has conducted extensive field research in China, Taiwan, Lesotho in South Africa, and Tanzania. Her research has been published in both academic and non-academic outlets.

Aya Homei is Lecturer in Japanese Studies at the University of Manchester, where she specialises in the history of population science, women in medicine, family planning in global health and overseas development assistance, and gerontological sciences in East Asia, with a focus on modern Japan. She has acted as guest editor of two special journal issues: "Critical Approaches to Reproduction and Population in Post-War Japan" (*Japan Forum*, 2021) and "Population Control in Cold War Asia" (*East Asian Science, Technology and Society*, 2016). Her most recent book, *Science for Governing Japan's Population*, is forthcoming in 2022 with Cambridge University Press.

Julia Marinaccio holds a PhD in China Studies from the University of Vienna and a Master's in Political Science from the National Chengchi University in Taipei. Her research addresses environmental governance and political transnationalism in China and Taiwan. She is currently a postdoctoral fellow at the Department of Foreign Languages, University of Bergen.

Marco Milani is Assistant Professor at the Department of Arts, University of Bologna. Previously, he has been a lecturer at the School of East Asian Studies, University of Sheffield, a postdoctoral fellow at the Korean Studies Institute, and a lecturer at the School of International Relations, University of Southern California. He has also held teaching positions at the Hankuk University of Foreign Studies and been a visiting research fellow at the Institute for Peace and Unification Studies (South Korea) and at the Leiden Institute for Area Studies (Netherlands). He has published numerous articles and book chapters on North and South Korea's foreign policy, contemporary Korean history, and inter-Korean relations. He is co-editor of *The Korean Paradox: Domestic Political Divide and Foreign Policy in South Korea* (Routledge, 2019).

Lei Qin was Assistant Adjunct Professor in Modern Chinese Studies at University of California, Los Angeles from 2018 to 2020, having previously lectured at University College Cork. She taught a wide range of topics on modern China, from history, society, and politics to culture and literature, which find an interdisciplinary coexistence in her research. Her current research focuses on early twentieth-century cultural politics and political communication with a transnational perspective.

Julia C. Schneider is Lecturer in Chinese History at the Department of Asian Studies at University College Cork. She holds a joint PhD in Modern Sinology from the universities of Ghent and Göttingen and an MA in Classical Sinology from Heidelberg University. From 2014 to 2019, she was Akademische Rätin at the Department of East Asian Studies, University of Göttingen. Her book *Nation and Ethnicity* (Brill, 2017) won the Foundation Council Award of the University of Göttingen. Her research interests are in historiography, the history of ideas, and ethnohistory in Qing and Republican times, as well as Jurchen and Manchu studies. She has edited several special issues and books and published articles in journals such as the *Journal of Asian History* and *Global Intellectual History*.

Allan C. Simpson specialises in contemporary South Korean queer-identified literature, especially short story and novel fiction, and poetry. He has studied the posthumous works of the poet Ki Hyeongdo; his MA compared the poetry of Hwang Inch'an with a short story by Lee Eunmi; and his doctoral thesis was on the novels of author Kim Hyena. His areas of research interest include queer theory and class studies.

Carlotta Sparvoli is Associate Professor at the University of Venice. In 2012, she was awarded a PhD from the University of Ca' Foscari Venice and won a six-month research grant within the Taiwan Fellowship Program. From 2012 to 2015, she conducted postdoctoral research at the University of Parma. From 2016 to 2019, she served as Director of the MA programme in Teaching Chinese to Speakers of Other Languages at the School of Asian Studies of University College Cork (Ireland). Her most recent publication is "The Expression of Modality in Classical Chinese: Notions, Taxonomy and Distinctive Features", *Oxford Research Encyclopedia of Linguistics*. She serves on the editorial board of the journal *Chinese as a Second Language Research* (De Gruyter Mouton), and is also active as a reviewer and external examiner for several academic journals and institutions.

Barbara Wall is an associate professor in Korean Studies at the University of Copenhagen. She has a BA in Japanese Studies and Classical Chinese from Heidelberg University, an MA in Confucian Studies from Sungkyungkwan University, Seoul, and a PhD in Korean Literature from Ruhr-University Bochum. Her main research interests are the circulation, translation, and adaptation of literary narratives in Korea, Japan, and China. Now she is working on her first book, in which she experiments with digital tools to visualise and create story universes like *The Journey to the West*. Her articles have appeared in journals such as *Acta Koreana*, *Journal of Japanese and Korean Cinema*, and *International Journal of Communication*.

Till Weingärtner is a lecturer in Contemporary East Asian Studies (Japan) and the director of the Centre for Advanced Studies in Languages and Cultures (CASiLaC) at University College Cork. Since his student days his research has primarily focused on Japanese comedy and film. During his postgraduate research on Japanese comedy at Kansai University (Osaka), he tried his hand at stand-up comedy, even winning an award and hosting a local radio show with his Japanese comedy partner. These experiences in the Japanese entertainment industry had a big impact on his research, and he remains interested in performance, not only from an academic perspective but also organising performances for Japanese artists and occasionally performing himself in Japanese, German, and English.

Introduction

The Value of Transnationalism in the Study of East Asia

Kevin N. Cawley and Julia C. Schneider

In *Minor Transnationalism*, Lionnet and Shih (2005, 5) discuss the growth of transnational studies as "a new field of inquiry" that was starting to emerge, particularly in the social sciences, but linked to new theories related to globalisation. This might lead one to think that "transnationalism" is something new, or something that can only be applied to modern contexts and texts/multimedia. This discussion of the transnationalism in relation to modern events in East Asia is something observed and analysed in most literature regarding transnationalism. A special issue of *The Journal of American-East Asian Relations* (16.3, 2009) brought together a selection of articles on transnationalism to explain geopolitical shifts since the Second World War linked to race and multiculturalism. Recent handbooks on the topic also examine East Asia as having become interconnected through trade and cultural exchanges over the past few decades, topics discussed in *Transnational Trajectories in East Asia* (2015). Following this trend of describing transnationalism as a recent phenomenon emerging during the twentieth century, *Transnational Convergence of East Asian Pop Culture* (2021) focused on popular culture as a space for investigating transnational interactions relating to pop music.

This book then broadens the discussions on transnationalism and highlights its potential for interdisciplinarity, while demonstrating how it should not be delimited as a theoretical framework to only examine recent discourses; it has collected a series of more longitudinal studies to highlight that transnationalism is something that has value when examining the past, just as much as when examining the present. The past and the present continually interact with the potential to always shape the future. Artificially erected borders, which appear on maps and globes, fail to consider the ways people in diverse regions live and practise their everyday lives, existing beyond boundaries. Humans have always been on the move, they have never been homogeneous; they have always interacted and interbred, and they have evolved together, not apart. This is of course nothing new, and definitely not "modern", irrespective of how one interprets that term.

Though the nation-state is a recent creation, the peoples of East Asia have long had clear ideas on their own sociopolitical identities but also been keenly aware of important imported cultural influences, while relying heavily on intertrading in these proto-cosmopolitan environments. Even from the tenth century Koreans acknowledged that while they had drawn on Buddhism and Confucianism from China, they had adapted it to their own specific context, aware that they were distinctively different peoples, as emphasised by King T'aejo (r. 918–943) in the "Ten Injunctions" (訓要十條, K. *Hunyo sipcho*) he left to guide the state, considered by some as a form of proto-nationalism (Duncan, 1998). Proto-nationalist sentiments have been identified in the Chinese Song Dynasty (960–1279), too, mainly in reaction to constant military threats from the north and north-east by Khitan and Jurchen khans and emperors. This led the Song elites to a heightened feeling of Chinese superiority in view of these semi-nomadic and nomadic peoples whom they considered barbarian, but to whose military superiority they had to submit (Trauzettel, 1975).

As Hendry and Underdown explain, these "processes" of human migration, interacting, and exchange are "visible in fossil, genetic and archaeological records" (2012, 139). In this sense, people have always been involved in a process of change and transformation. Indeed, the prefix "trans-", coming from Latin, embodies this process and can mean (among other things): across, beyond, change, transfer. Hence, transnationalism can be viewed as a way to overcome the problematics of the concepts of methodological nationalism, "national", "nationality", and indeed "nationalism", as concepts of identity and spatiality as well as concepts temporally situated in modernity. As a methodology, transnationalism does not assume the national and thus also overcomes the shadows that modern nationalisms tend to cast over the past, rejecting the validity and meaningfulness of "the national", "nationality", and "nationalism" for the study of history. It will help students to look beyond these very loaded terms and encourage them to see beyond and across borders, and to examine how ideas have been used and transformed in different contexts. The presupposition of methodological nationalism, that is, that "the nation-state is the natural and necessary form of society in modernity" and therefore the main unit of analysis in social sciences, but also in the humanities, has been rejected by many scholars (Chernilo, 2006). However, the national has nevertheless remained a strong influence in these fields. In their diversity, the chapters in this book show how the paradigm of nationalism can be overcome meaningfully and result in rich studies of the present and the past, which will be useful for students from many different disciplines.

Elie Kedourie (1960, 9) defined nationalism as a "doctrine that holds that humanity is naturally divided into nations, [and] that nations are known by certain characteristics which can be ascertained". In the eighteenth century, national consciousness or "nation-ness" developed among the "Creole Pioneers" in the Americas and then the French revolutionaries (Anderson, 2006 [1983], xiii, 47–48). Over the course of the nineteenth and twentieth centuries, the normative conceptualisation of nations and nation-states—that national borders should follow divisions between people that are naturally determined, historically real, and objectively definable—has become deeply rooted in many people's perceptions of the geopolitical world. Moreover, nationalism and its manifestation as (nation-)state borders have deeply shaped academic disciplines. This is true for disciplines that focus on analysing contemporary times like social and political sciences as well as contemporary history when national state borders are becoming increasingly impermeable as control mechanisms become more sophisticated. However, national state borders also cast their shadows into the past and to times when they did not even exist. This comes to the fore in history-related disciplines that tend to focus on the unit of the nation-state even if they address (pre-)nation-state times. This is also true for East Asian studies, which is subdivided into three "national" disciplines, Chinese, Korean, and Japanese studies.

The framework of nationalism has been so influential that the (re)-introduction of the concept of transnationalism now indeed seems to be something "new", bringing back to light notions of the ongoing normality of human migration, interaction, and exchange that for most of human history have in fact been the norm. Applied in historical studies, transnationalism therefore refers not only to a premodern trans-"statism", but to the acknowledgement in general that modern nation-state borders cannot be assumed for premodern times. A transnational approach is thus almost unavoidable when analysing those times. However, it is equally important to keep the realities of ongoing processes of migration, interaction, and exchange in mind when analysing and researching modern phenomena. In contemporary studies, the concept of transnationalism serves as a lens that acknowledges and emphasises that exchange and interaction are crucial factors in our world despite ever-increasing advances in technology that allow states to control their borders and restrict access.

This lens of transnationalism is particularly important in the case of East Asian studies due to a deep-rooted and often unconscious nationalist approach. Eric Hobsbawm, an otherwise strong proponent of the modernist-constructivist paradigm of nationalism, erroneously claimed that China,

Korea, and Japan are "among the extremely rare examples of historic states composed of a population that is ethnically almost or entirely homogenous" (1990, 66). These states, Hobsbawm continues, "exist, more or less, within their historic frontiers". The nationalist assumption of age-old homogenous East Asian nations had originally been asserted by East Asian nationalists and intellectuals (Perdue, 2005; Schneider, 2017, 21). They perceived of their own ethnic identity as truly "primordial" nations with long and unchanging histories. Moreover, Sinologists, Koreanists, and Japanologists themselves supported and strengthened the idea of East Asian primordial or at least perennial nations. The multicultural, transnational, and ever-changing character of East Asia has been downplayed or downright ignored. Therefore, today East Asian studies can only benefit from bringing the transnational focus back into the picture and "rescuing history", but also religious and cultural studies as well as political and social sciences, "from the nation" (Duara, 1995). Our volume therefore combines studies from different disciplines that deal with East Asia, and that apply transnational as well as transdisciplinary approaches and methodologies.

In recent years, as Jung emphasises, "The indigenization of modern Western culture and the sharing of cultural proximity have become driving forces of creating [East] Asianness, and the combination of these forces enables cultural products to travel across the various Asian countries" (2011, 22). Iwabuchi also relates this to "the emergence of [an] Asian capitalist sphere" where countries, such as Japan, cannot delimit their products "within clearly demarcated national boundaries" (2001, 202). This is also most definitely the case for Korean pop music, known as K-pop which "has been dynamically circulated in the bigger popular culture market beyond Asia" (Jung, 2011, 170). However, this cultural transnationalism is not new in East Asia, especially where languages are concerned. For example, Chinese, Korean, and Japanese were all deeply linked through Chinese characters, in which even the elite scholars of Korea wrote until the end of the nineteenth century. While the Japanese still use Chinese characters, known as Kanji, Koreans use their own alphabet now, Han'gŭl. Nevertheless, Korean academic texts used mixed scripts—Han'gŭl and Hanja (as the Chinese characters are known in Korea)—until very recently, despite the creation of Han'gŭl dating to the fifteenth century. Jieun Kiaer highlights how "Korea and Japan, under the umbrella of the Chinese cultural sphere, have both a sociocultural and linguistic heritage", adding that "roughly 57% of Korean vocabulary is Sino-Korean and derived from Chinese" (2018, 2). China has clearly exerted a very strong cultural influence beyond the modern boundaries of the region, shaping the history of ideas there on many levels. Michel de Certeau (1997, 103) illustrates the various ways in which culture "intervenes": developing stratified societies, the creation of cultural works, religious and philosophical worldviews, modes of behaviour, as well as things acquired and communicated through language. In this sense, East Asia can be understood when examined through a transcultural lens, which is at the heart of transnationalism, where geographic boundaries recede and are more symptoms of the modern "nation-state". The interactions between China, Korea, and Japan go back almost two millennia. By the seventh century, Korean missionaries were bringing Sinitic Buddhism and culture to Japan. In turn, Japan and Korea were sending diplomatic envoys and embassies to China around this period (Hudson, 1964, 344), transforming the culture and institutions of their own countries, transplanting cultural modes of being transnationally. These institutions and cultural interactions did not come about because of war or invasion, and Hudson (1964, 344) notes that they did not come about by conquest, but rather because Sinitic culture was admired and China's neighbours sought to partake of it. This is very different from the Western conquests, where even missionaries forced their religion and white god on various indigenous peoples.

This book will help students of East Asian studies, which is one of the fastest-growing disciplines in recent years. As an example, Korean could only be studied in ten universities in the United States in 1975, but by the early 2000s over 130 universities were offering Korean as a language option. *Transnational East Asian Studies* will introduce students to the transnational, sociopolitical, and intellectual interactions that have shaped diverse East Asian territories, today part of the modern states of China, Korea, Taiwan, and Japan, from the past up to the creation of modern states in the colonial periods, and transformation of the region under industrialisation, decolonisation, war, and revolution in the twentieth and twenty-first centuries. This book can serve as a core text for introductory lectures and courses to East Asian studies, taking the field beyond the national to the transnational. At the same time, it invites students to move beyond disciplinary to transdisciplinary approaches to study and analyse East Asia, by bringing the advantages of the meaningful combination of literary, religious, and cultural studies, history, philosophy, social and political sciences to the fore. It will deal with many themes that are important to develop a comprehensive and coherent understanding of the transcultural complexity and richness of the region, overturning entrenched modern nationalistic narratives that delimit the vast array of interactions that have taken place over the centuries, shaping the region.

Apart from introducing students to transnational and transdisciplinary approaches to East Asia, *Transnational East Asian Studies* exemplifies that the study of languages and the usage of original source texts are crucial for a thorough understanding of their respective areas and thus highly relevant for all so-called area studies. Together with the other volumes in the Transnational Modern Languages (TML) series, this book adheres to the principles of the series' anchor, *Transnational Modern Languages: A Handbook* (Burns and Duncan, 2022) and demonstrates that languages do not follow nation-state borders, and mostly do not even divide or unify cultures and societies, but that languages need to be understood as simultaneously overlapping and diverging with other types of human identities like cultures and societies. The transcultural usage of languages in the East Asian context, particularly but not exclusively the Chinese literary language, enables scholars of the three traditional East Asian disciplines of Chinese studies (Sinology), Korean studies (Koreanology), and Japanese studies (Japanology) to research and analyse social and political developments, literary and cultural exchanges, and philosophical and religious influences across and beyond modern and premodern state borders. As this book shows, such transnational, transregional approaches are not merely a subdiscipline of Chinese, Korean, and Japanese studies but form a fundamental research approach that is crucial to understanding East Asia.

Organisation of the Book

The 16 chapters in this book cover a wide array of disciplines in the humanities and social sciences, from Confucian philosophy to transnational security in East Asia, and from the premodern to the contemporary. While each chapter provides an original contribution to its respective field, *Transnational East Asian Studies* demonstrates the potential of the transnational lens to examine and understand East Asia by bringing together such diverse chapters that all apply this lens to their particular field. They put the transnational into the context of related concepts (migration, hybridity, flows, colonialism, universalism, etc.) and thus broaden its analytical usefulness and applicability.

Part I of this book, "Cultures Crossing Borders", draws together chapters that look at how historically ideas, beliefs, and all other aspects of culture have crossed borders, drawing different peoples together through a transnational *modus vivendi*. The communication of intellectual ideas in the region through the use of literary Chinese further connected the region transculturally, reinforced by the common language used to disseminate Confucian, Buddhist, and Daoist ideas. It demonstrates how transnationalism can be used as a methodology to think about the effects of Confucianism and Buddhism beyond their country of origin. It furthermore looks at how "classical" works of literature are not as "fixed" and static as we might like to think, but rather have been transformed through their own varying receptions in East Asia, from the past to the present, the "original" source shaped by factors that are beyond the written word.

Kevin N. Cawley's chapter, "Confucianism and Becoming-in-the-World: A Transnational *Modus Vivendi*", examines how ideas both philosophical and religious have historically shaped the cultural traditions in East Asia through transnational iterations, not delimited by territorial borders. It discusses the different ways in which philosophy and religion were traditionally interrelated and intellectually intertwined in the region, unlike in the West where they still remain quite separate (diverging) disciplines. Next, the trajectory of Confucianism from its origins in China to its transplantation in Korea are outlined, leading to the emergence of Neo-Confucianism, later used *de rigueur* in Korea for political purposes to overturn the Koryŏ dynasty (918–1392) and to found the Chosŏn dynasty (1392–1910). Cawley underscores how this philosophy transformed and hierarchically curtailed social and gender relations, an effect which still reverberates in modern Korean society, and across the entire region.

In "Diffusion and Transnationalism: 'Emplantation' and the Crossing of Cultural Boundaries", James H. Grayson illustrates how "transnationalism" provides an excellent opportunity to consider the theoretical issues involved in the transmission of culture or aspects of culture across the boundaries of cultural spheres, and within the "internal" boundaries of cultural spheres. He draws on his own theory of "emplantation", widely used by scholars of religion in East Asia, which provides a model for explaining the process of the diffusion or transmission of culture, specifically the cross-cultural transmission of religion. The transmission of Buddhism from the Indian culture world into the Chinese culture world over a 700-year period from the first to the seventh century is used as a case study to illustrate both the periodisation of the process of cultural transmission and the social, political, and cultural factors which impede or assist in the process of such diffusion.

Carlotta Sparvoli examines one of the great classics in Chinese, the *Romance of the Three Kingdoms* (*Sanguo yanyi* (三國演義), attributed to Luo Guanzhong (羅貫中), 1330?–1400?). Her study sheds light on the specific depiction of war and heroism in this paradigmatic Chinese narrative. It highlights how this Chinese classic underlines a concept of war extraneous to the fascination of warfare found in Western epics, showing that the Chinese notion of *epos* privileges the virtues of strategy and intelligence over heroism and military prowess. It also describes how, from being a subject of historical accounts, this story was transformed into a fictional construction, retracing the process along which the text was turned into an identitarian event in the "construction of memory" of the Middle Kingdom to the point of being celebrated in the colossal pan-Asian movie production *Red Cliff* (2008).

Barbara Wall's chapter deals with *The Journey to the West*, one of the most popular narratives in East Asia. One of the best-known versions of *The*

Journey comes from a Chinese novel, *Xiyouji* (西遊記), written at the end of the sixteenth century. *The Journey* owes its popularity in large part to the uncountable versions that exist across various times, cultures, and media. Indeed, one of the most popular variations today might be the Japanese adaption *Dragonball*. This study will focus on a group of often overlooked religiously didactic variations that use *The Journey* as a missionary medium, including relief images on the pagoda of the Kyŏngch'ŏn Temple from the fourteenth century, wall paintings in the Maitreya Hall of T'ongdo Temple from the eighteenth century, and the lion dance of Pungsan Mask Dance from the twentieth century. This chapter will help students to understand the interwovenness of literature and religion in premodern Korea and to become familiar with the transnational circulation of transmedia storytelling.

Part II, "Nation, Empire, and Beyond", combines chapters that emphasise transcultural, translingual, and transnational East Asian identities, both modern and premodern. They pay special attention to the question of how state power is challenged by transnational factors, approaches, mechanisms, and exchanges (Chapters 5 and 7) and how states but also individuals deal with the realities of transnational identities (Chapters 6 and 8).

In "Postcolonial Theory in East Asian Studies", Julia C. Schneider analyses how the concept of colonialism has been used to refer to and analyse the conquest history of the Qing empire in recent decades. She questions whether colonialism, being normativised by an experience that originally assumed a European "centre" that conquers, subjects, and exploits a non-European "periphery", can be meaningfully transplanted to a non-European historical context, particularly to the transcultural ruling elite of the Qing empire and the people conquered by the Qing. She demonstrates the problems that derive from such a conceptual transfer by examining Qing conquests under the lens of postcolonial theory and of transcultural/transnational understandings of Qing identity.

Nadeschda Bachem shows how Japan's colonialism affects South Korean identities up to the present. In her chapter, "Multilingualism as a Tool of Resistance against Homogenising National Narratives", she uses the story "I Love You" (아이러브유, K. *Ai rŏbŭ yu*, 1962) by South Korean writer Pak Sunnyŏ as a prism to investigate the struggle with a transcultural identity that was forced upon Koreans growing up under Japanese colonial rule before 1945. Bachem reveals how South Koreans who were faced with Japanese colonial propaganda and assimilation strategies in their childhood and youth try to come to terms with their pre-1945 categorisation as inferior citizens of a Japanese colonial empire, trying to reinvent themselves as a nation of the newly founded South Korean state and at the same time manifesting a clear colonial dichotomy of Japanese perpetrators versus Korean victims.

Qin Lei discusses the neglected topic of the China-centred transnational internationalist movement that was initiated by Willi Münzenberg and his circle in "Conjuring a Battling China". Münzenberg's left-wing popular front campaign existed throughout the 1920s and 1930s. The dominant narrative of Republican China usually focuses on the civil war between nationalists and communists. Lei, however, discloses other actors in this setting. She focuses on how media for working-class readers of Weimar Germany influenced the image of China as a newly awakened nation willing to fight for its revolutionary renewal. This image travelled back to China, and Lei scrutinises how Chinese members of the Communist International, but also Chinese left-wing intellectuals in general responded to it.

In the last chapter of Part II, "*Fanxiang Toupiao* 返鄉投票", Julia Marinaccio addresses the issue of the procedural and institutional obstacles that Taiwanese emigrants face when wanting to exercise their right to vote from abroad. Marinaccio uses the voting of the Taiwanese community in Vienna in the 2020 presidential elections as a case study. In the absence of a system of postal voting, Taiwanese voters must return to Taiwan physically to cast their ballots, which means that they face high travel costs and need substantial time resources. In her study, Marinaccio analyses how Taiwanese emigrants *de facto* deal with the absence of an external voting system, focusing on processes, actors, and practices in the mobilisation of emigrant voters.

Part III, "Transnationalism in Popular Cultures", brings together a series of chapters that explore transnationalism through the media of modern popular cultures, by examining cinema and music from Korea, Japan, and Taiwan, as well as the language of queer identity in South Korea and its representation in popular culture there.

Till Weingärtner's chapter examines the transnational work of Yang Yonghi, one of the most prolific "*Zainichi* Korean" film-makers in Japan (*Zainichi* Korean refers to North and South Korean nationals who live in Japan). First, it looks at Yang's documentary *Dear Pyongyang* (ディア・ピョンヤン, J. *Dia Pyonyan*, 2006), which examines the impact on her father of his decision to send his three sons to live in North Korea in 1971 and his family's relationships, giving us insight into her family's life and their visits to North Korea. The film also succeeds in revealing many of her father's inner conflicts as a diligent activist for North Korea. Next, Weingärtner analyses Yang's feature film *Our Homeland* (かぞくのくに J. *Kazoku no kuni*, 2012), which reflects her personal family history through the setting of a fictional family. *Our Homeland* depicts the re-encounter of a young *Zainichi* Korean woman with her brother, who had been sent to live in North Korea and is now allowed a short visit to his family in Japan. The chapter further analyses several key issues, including the theme of family, language, the issue of the fatherland, and Yang's own national identity, working in Japan.

In "Re-Presenting Sino-Japanese Relations through *Flavors of Youth*", Jamie Coates and Jennifer Coates initially note how the relationship between China and Japan is often represented as typified by conflict, tension, and difference. They then identify how the Sino-Japanese context is also a transnational field of creative collaboration, co-production, and shared reception of texts that often emphasise popular cultural continuities shared between the two countries. Taking *Flavors of Youth* (詩季織々, J. *Shiki ori ori*, 肆式青春, C. *Si shi qing chun*, by Li Haoling, Jiaoshou Yi Xiaoxing, and Takeuchi Yoshitaka, 2018) as a key text that exemplifies recent developments in Sino-Japanese creative collaboration, they identify an emphasis on shared emotional states and affective commonalities between everyday China and Japan. *Flavors of Youth* was developed by Japanese production studio CoMix Wave Films and the Chinese animation company Haoliners Animation League as a co-production for Netflix and StudioCanal. At the industry level, it draws attention to the transnational production of animation styles that were once imagined as distinctly Japanese, and represents the rise of collaborations within the Northeast Asian media industry.

Allan Simpson's chapter, "Translation/Transplantation of Queer in South Korea", explores the extent to which South Korean translations and transplantations of Anglosphere linguistic and acronymic identities, such as queer and LGBT, have been adopted in South Korean activist and artistic (literary) contexts, while also drawing on the works of writer Kim Hyena, whose novels problematise "being queer" in South Korea. He questions whether such Korean translations and transplantations demonstrate similar homonormative tendencies as they do in North American, European, and other contexts? Therefore, this chapter also explores the different uses of non-heteronormative language, and especially the increasing debate as to whether or not Asian contexts should adopt English-originated queer language at all. In grassroots activism specifically, more globalised queer terms are deployed than local terms. On academic, legal, and activist fronts, there seems to be more of a mixture of globalised and locally translated terms, reflecting the important way that transnationalism can be a useful methodology to examine these important issues.

Yu-Wen Chen examines the colonial influence of Japan in Taiwan through its manifestations in Taiwan's cinema and popular music. A transnational approach is useful for understanding this colonial influence and its effects on Taiwan's film and pop music industries. This influence on the music industry can be seen in the *enka* performance style, evoking sorrow, while Taiyupop (Taiwanese-language pop) was influenced by *enka* and, later,

Mandopop's (Mandarin-language pop) sadness paradigm. This paradigm is also evident in Taiyupian (Taiwanese-language film), which is itself influenced by Japanese cinema. Chen shows how Japanese films have had a much greater influence on the technology, styles, and themes of Taiyupian than Mandarin films. However, transnational influences can sometimes create difficulties in distinguishing the Japanese influence. She also shows how it is possible that the Japanese influence was interrupted in a particular political context at a specific time. In the final part of her chapter, she suggests that film can be a better medium for exploring Taiwan's relationship with its former coloniser simply because it can explore content more deeply than song lyrics. Japanophilia, rather than Japanophobia, is more often aroused by these artistic presentations.

Part IV, "Transnationalism in Global East Asia", embeds East Asia in the world and addresses concepts of global transnationalism in different settings. In "A Gateway to Exciting Opportunities? The Lives of African Migrants Inside and Outside Taiwan's University Campuses", Sarah Hanisch explores African student migration to Taiwan based on interviews, document analysis, and group discussions. Due to a shared experience of colonialisation and struggles for independence in the Global South, Asia is a popular destination for students from Africa. However, Hanisch shows that although African students in Taiwan are heterogenous and have different socio-economic backgrounds, they all face limited professional opportunities in Taiwan after graduation, and she explores how they deal with those limitations.

Aya Homei addresses the integration of family planning into global health programmes that particularly targeted Asia in the 1960s and 1970s. In her chapter, "Transnationalism and Medical Cooperation in Family Planning in East Asia (1950s–1970s)", Homei demonstrates how twentieth-century population studies indicated a correlation between demographic patterns on the one hand and economic and social development on the other, and how transnational health organisations suggested to use family planning as a means to modify the latter in East Asia. She uses the Asian Parasite Control Organization as an example to show how inter-Asian medical cooperation gained momentum and finally replaced support from outside Asia.

In his chapter "From Liberation to the Great Leap Forward", Adam Cathcart scrutinises how the People's Republic of China dealt with the transnational identity of Chinese Koreans, that is, ethnic Koreans who had migrated to the Republic of China during Japanese colonial rule over Korea. Those who did not return to the Koreas in the late 1940s came to be considered an exceptionally loyal "model minority" by the Chinese Communist Party (CCP) in the 1950s. However, with the implementation of the Second Five-Year-Plan, also called the "Great Leap Forward", in 1958, the CCP began to suspect ethnic

Korean intellectuals of adhering to "local nationalism". Cathcart analyses the assimilationist strategies the CCP used to address this perceived threat to national unity in a region deeply relevant to national security.

In the final chapter, "The New Challenges of Transnational Security in Twenty-First-Century East Asia: The Case of North Korea", Marco Milani focuses on the difficulties East Asian countries have with applying transnational security approaches. Transnational security gained importance after the end of the Cold War due to emerging issues such as terrorism, migration, climate change, etc. However, so far East Asian countries have not yet managed to apply a security policy that fully embraces transnational approaches. Using North Korea as a case study, Milani analyses how weak transnational cooperation, a general strategic mistrust related to historical controversies, and a general focus on national instead of transnational security present major challenges to transnational security in East Asia.

References and Further Reading

Anderson, Benedict. 2006 [1983]. *Imagined Communities: Reflections on the Origin and Spread of Nationalism*. Rev. ed. London: Verso.

Burns, Jennifer, and Derek Duncan (eds.). 2022. *Transnational Modern Languages: A Handbook*. Liverpool: Liverpool University Press.

Chernilo, Daniel. 2006. "Methodological Nationalism and Its Critique". In *The SAGE Handbook of Nations and Nationalism*, edited by Gerard Delanty and Krishan Kumar, 129–40. London: SAGE.

De Certeau, Michel. 1997. *Culture in the Plural*, translated by Tom Conley. Minneapolis: University of Minnesota Press.

Duara, Prasenjit. 1995. *Rescuing History from the Nation: Questioning Narratives of Modern China*. Chicago: University of Chicago Press.

Duncan, John. 1998. "Proto-Nationalism in Premodern Korea". In *Perspectives on Korea*, edited by Sang-oak Lee and Duk-soo Park, 198–221. Sydney: Wild Peony Press.

Hendry, Joy, and Simon Underdown. 2012. *Anthropology: A Beginner's Guide*. London: One Publications.

Hobsbawm, Eric John. 1990. *Nations and Nationalism since 1780: Programme, Myth, Reality*. Cambridge: Cambridge University Press.

Hong Seok-Kyeong, and Dal Yong Jin (eds.). 2021. *Transnational Convergence of East Asian Pop Culture*. London: Routledge.

Hudson, Geoffrey Francis. 1964. "China and the World: A Summary of Intellectual and Artistic Influences". In *The Legacy of China*, edited by Raymond Dawson, 340–363. Oxford: Oxford University Press.

Iwabuchi, Koichi. 2001. "Uses of Japanese Popular Culture: Trans/Nationalism and Postcolonial Desire 'Asia'". *Emergences* 11 (2): 199–222.

Jung, Sun. 2011. *Korean Masculinities and Transcultural Consumption*. Hong Kong: Hong Kong University Press.

Kedourie, Elie. 1960. *Nationalism*. London: Hutchinson University Library.

Kiaer, Jieun. 2018. *The Routledge Course in Korean Translation*. London: Routledge.

Lionnet, Françoise, and Shih, Shu-mei. 2005. "Introduction: Thinking through the Minor, Transnationally". In *Minor Transnationalism*, edited by Françoise Lionnet and Shu-mei Shih, 1–23. Durham, NC and London: Duke University Press.

Perdue, Peter C. 2005. "Where Do Incorrect Political Ideas Come From? Writing the History of the Qing Empire and the Chinese Nation". In *The Teleology of the Modern Nation-State: Japan and China*, edited by Joshua A. Fogel, 174–199. Philadelphia: University of Pennsylvania Press.

Schneider, Julia C. 2017. *Nation and Ethnicity: Chinese Discourses on History, Historiography, and Nationalism (1900s–1920s)*. Leiden: Brill.

Soysal, Yasemin Nuhoğlu (ed.). 2015. *Transnational Trajectories in East Asia: Nation, Citizenship, and Region*. London: Routledge.

Trauzettel, Rolf. 1975. "Sung Patriotism as a First Step toward Chinese Nationalism". In *Crisis and Prosperity in Sung China*, edited by John W. Haeger, 199–214. Tucson: University of Arizona Press.

Part I

Cultures Crossing Borders

1

Confucianism and Becoming-in-the-World

A Transnational *Modus Vivendi*

Kevin N. Cawley

Introduction

Confucianism has historically shaped the lives of people in East Asia through transnational interactions, not delimited by territorial borders, but reinvigorated by moving across and beyond them, connecting people as a result, shaping who they become. Ong emphasises how "transnationality [...] alludes to the *trans*versal, the *trans*actional, the *trans*lational and the *trans*gressive aspects of contemporary behaviour" (1999, 4). I would also argue that transnationalism can work as a prism through which we examine the reverberations of the past in the present, especially where ideas and ideologies stemming from religion and philosophy are concerned, shaping how different members of society were supposed to act and interact, particularly the elite who often manipulated and transgressed their own rules. This chapter will begin by discussing Confucianism as a way of "Becoming-in-the-World" for those Asian countries where its ideas were traditionally interrelated and intellectually intertwined with local sociopolitical systems. Next, the trajectory of Confucianism from its origins in China to its transplantation in Korea will be outlined, where we find interactions with other traditions that had deep roots there, including Buddhism, which had been supported by the royal family on the peninsula. It will then detail how Confucianism was eventually recalibrated in China during the Song dynasty (960–1279), especially through the writings of the philosopher Zhu Xi (1130–1200), leading to the emergence of Neo-Confucianism, later used *de rigueur* in Korea for political purposes to overturn the Koryŏ dynasty (918–1392) and to establish the Chosŏn dynasty (1392–1910). The Chosŏn dynasty is considered by some to be the closest thing to an ideal Confucian state, and Coogan underscores how, "in education, bureaucracy, principles of government, and high culture, the Koreans reproduced a model Confucian civilization" (2005, 329).

Of course, "ideal" and "model" depend on whose experience of living in such a Confucian state one considers: its huge numbers of slaves would definitely have had different thoughts on this, and they would probably not have considered their treatment to be "civilised". What we can take from this though is that Confucianism was responsible for shaping one's *modus vivendi* in its different transnational forms, which also reflect its cultural translations into different contexts, with Korea being the focus of this chapter. It transformed and hierarchically arranged society, seriously curtailing social and gender relations, enforcing certain rites of passage, and shaping how one used language to assert one's own place and others' in terms of seniority or social position. For all intents and purposes, Confucian culture imposed itself upon one's personhood reinforced through tradition and education, shaping the person one "could" become, with women forced to follow the rules that men made for them, reinforced through moral primers that privileged male members of their family.

The Confucian *Way* of Becoming-in-the-World

Chinese civilisation has been extremely important in Asia, and its culture has exerted great influence on non-Chinese peoples, such as the Koreans, Vietnamese, and Japanese. Hudson underscores that:

> The most important distinguishing feature of this civilisation was the use of the Chinese script and the study of Chinese classical literature that went with it. Not only did Korea, Vietnam, and Japan use the Chinese written language as a vehicle of culture much as Latin was used in western Europe in the Middle Ages, but they stocked their own languages with words and phrases borrowed from Chinese [...] As a result of their acquisition of Chinese written characters, the educated class in these countries [...] was open to the influence of the ideas which it expressed; thus the Confucian conceptions of society and government [...] were spread abroad beyond the borders of China itself. (1964, 340–341)

Each of the traditional "Three Teachings" of China, in the form of Confucianism, Daoism (sometimes "Taoism"), and Buddhism, were transmitted in their Chinese version, not using Sanskrit or Pali, making an "indelible imprint on Korea, Vietnam and Japan" (Dawson, 1964, 341–342). A particularly important term, *Dao* 道, often translated as "the way", is used by these teachings (in particular Daoism and Confucianism), in the sense of a guide or pathway to help human beings become the best versions of themselves. In all three traditions, it recognises our innate good nature and perfection, as well as the potential to develop and change for the better, contrasting greatly with Christian teachings on original sin. In their "philosophical translation" of *The Analects of Confucius*, Ames and Rosemont Jr. describe *dao* as a "way of living in the world", or, "a way of becoming [human]" (1999, 45–46). The Confucian *way*, drawing on the Chinese textual sources, the subject of this study, is largely grounded in traditions handed down from one's ancestors and predecessors, shaping their "Being-in-the-World". This phrase is drawn from Martin Heidegger's *Being and Time* (2008), and depicts how "Being" (*Dasein*) is inextricably intertwined with tradition—imbedded in it without preparation—without time to adjust. In Asian Confucian cultures, but particularly in Korea, "Being" is thrust into a Confucian tradition where even one's social interactions are organised and prescribed, even if one follows Buddhism and/or other traditional religions (or none at all).

Being, in the Heideggerian sense, encompasses thinking and acting, and how these are shaped by the world around us, taught and reinforced through tradition. Heidegger emphasises that Being "falls prey to the tradition [...] tradition thus becomes master [...] in such a way that what it 'transmits' [...] becomes concealed" (2008, 42–43). We, therefore, are embedded within the tradition we find ourselves thrust into, and we inevitably interpret from the point of view of a consciousness which has been shaped, but also contaminated, by tradition. *Traditio*, the Latin origin of "tradition", means a handing down, which can be teachings and sayings, but also expectations. In Chinese (and Korean), the word for tradition stems from two Chinese characters, 傳統 (C. *Chuantong*, K. *Chŏnt'ong*): 傳, meaning to pass on, hand down, or to spread, and 統, meaning to unite or to unify. This clearly means that people are united by traditions and conventions that are handed down, sometimes without being questioned. Heidegger (2008, 191) notes that we interpret based on what we have in advance (*Vorhabe*), in what we see in advance (*Vorsicht*), and also a way of conceiving ideas, fore-conceptions (*Vorgriff*). In a sense, our understanding if shaped by the influence of our historical circumstances and the values and traditions that are emphasised and privileged at a given time. Gadamer goes so far as to suggest that "Understanding is, essentially, a historically effected event" (2006, 299). He delineates how people's historical consciousness is shaped by the historical effects in which their individual consciousness is situated. Therefore, their ideas reflect the general historical consciousness of their era, and so these ideas unconsciously reveal the effects of their tradition as it is part of the historical process generated by its effects, in this case individuals are shaped by Confucian ideology, reinforced by the state and buttressed through laws, for good or for bad. This ideology was largely critical of other religious traditions such as Shamanism, Buddhism, and Daoism, and argued that humans should depend on themselves and their own inherent abilities to solve their problems (social and personal), ruling out the need for help from gods or deities. In this context, it might make better sense to discuss one's own "Becoming-in-the-World", where Being is considered more as a journey, with Confucianism providing a path*way*.

This path*way* is safeguarded by the Confucian texts that shaped the tradition as a whole, starting with the Five Classics, which predate Confucius himself, though he is considered to have edited them and added his own commentaries to them. The Five Classics comprised (1) the *Yijing* (易經) [Book of Changes], (2) the *Shujing* (書經) [Book of Documents], (3) the *Shijing* (詩經) [Book of Poetry], (4) the *Liji* (禮記) [Records of Rites], and (5) the *Chunqiu* (春秋) [Spring and Autumn Annals]. Originally, there were Six Classics, as the *Yuejing* (樂經) [Classic of Music] was included among the ancient Classics, but as it was lost by the Han dynasty (202–220 CE), we now usually refer to the Five Classics. It was during the Han period that Vietnam and Korea were initially influenced by Confucian culture, starting to study these ancient "classics" (經, C. *Jing*, K. *Kyŏng*). Interestingly, a similarity exists between the Latin root of "text" and the Chinese root of the word for the classical "texts" (經). Both words contain the concept of weaving fabric: *textus* in Latin comes from the verb for "weaving", or the pattern of weaving, while in Chinese, the radical (糸, C. *Mi*) of the word used to describe the classical texts, *jing*, also contains this idea, meaning "thread". Both entail the idea of threading together different ideas like a fabric—in a sense, weaving lessons and teachings from the past into new readers and students. Therefore, one could add that the Confucian tradition reveres and honours the past and its past "sage" rulers: it is not concerned with seeking to introduce radical new changes. Moreover, the tradition that is known as Confucianism in the West is known as *Ruxue* in Chinese (儒學, K *Yuhak*) [the study of the scholars (the Ru)], or *Rujiao* (儒教, K. *Yugyo*) [the teachings of the scholars], which further underpins this appreciation of the past. Even Confucius was careful to clarify that "Following the proper way, I do not forge new paths; with confidence I cherish the ancients" (Ames and Rosemont, 1999, 111). This legacy of esteeming the past would be reflected in Korea's adaptation of Confucianism.

Religious and Philosophical Transnationalism

Ideas and ideologies travel and can take root in places beyond the borders of the state where they first emerged. As such, religious and philosophical traditions have always been transnational, linking states and peoples, by what

Gadamer, who has been influenced by Heidegger, describes as their "historically affected consciousness (*wirkungsgeschichtliches Bewußtsein*)" (2006, 301). Gadamer (2006, 266–269), again commenting on Heidegger, notes that our interpretations begin with foresights and fore-conceptions whose authority is grounded in the force of those traditions, and so meaning is generated through the sociohistorical fore-structures embedded in religious and philosophical traditions. Korea, due to its close geographical proximity to China, easily adopted and acculturated the intellectual and spiritual trends of its neighbour. The "Three Teachings", in the form of Buddhism (which was already a transnational translation of its original form), Confucianism, and Daoism, had already become integrated within Korean society to varying degrees by the fifth century CE. From this point until modern times, and despite the invention of a phonetic script, Han'gŭl (also written Hangeul), in the fifteenth century, nothing rivalled Chinese as the literary language of the educated class (Dawson, 1961, 344–345). During the Three Kingdoms period (c. 57–668), Koguryŏ (高句麗), Paekche (百濟), and Silla (新羅) were rival states seeking control of the peninsula, as well as cultural supremacy to validate their political control, and they all received influences from Chinese civilisation, which linked them (see Grayson, 2002, 22–52). However, the *Annals of Koguryŏ*, found in the *History of the Three Kingdoms* (三國史記, K. *Samguk Sagi*), note that "Confucianism and Buddhism both are on the rise but the teachings of [Daoism] are not yet widespread [year 643] and we have not yet acquired what is known as 'Daoist Practitioners of the World'" (Kim, 2012, 221). Notably, not only had Buddhism already been adapted by all three states by this point, but Korean missionaries had spread the religion, along with Confucianism and Chinese characters, to Japan, as recounted in Japanese sources like the *Kojiki* (古事記) [Record of Ancient Matters] and the *Nihon Shoki* (日本書紀) [Chronicles of Japan], both dating from the early eighth century (see Cawley, 2019, ch. 2). In particular, the importance of Paekche missionaries is stressed by Grayson, who underscores the important contributions of Koreans to the development of Japan's culture, not only in terms of religion, but also the "sophisticated art and architecture of the Chinese world, notably the Northern Wei style", adding that Korea was "the principal transmitter and active agent in the early development of Japanese Buddhist civilization" (2002, 33). In Europe at the same time, Irish monks were spreading Christianity on the British Isles and mainland Europe in a similar transnational manner. In Chapter 2 of the present volume, Grayson also examines the transnational diffusion of Buddhism looking at different contexts in East Asia.

Confucianism, by aligning itself with the Chinese state bureaucracy and law, was particularly influential, helping to bolster Korea's own cultural and political supremacy, especially *vis-à-vis* Japan at this point. Koguryŏ had already set up a centre for Confucian studies in 372, known as the *T'aehak* (太學) [literally meaning "Great Learning"], as well as other private schools known as *kyŏngdang* (扃堂), which literally means "literary hall" (where the classics were studied). Later, after Silla had aligned itself with the powerful Chinese Tang dynasty (618–907) to unify the peninsula in 668 (marking the start of the Unified-Silla period until 935), a centralised Confucian college was set up in 682 known as the *Kukhak* (國學, meaning "National" Academy), illustrating how Koreans felt that Confucianism was now not something uniquely Chinese, but something prestigious that had become an integral part of their own cross-cultural identity, contributing to their own nation's (國, K. *kuk*) educational identity, which focused on the study of Chinese characters and Chinese texts. The *Kukhak* was set up by the Minister of Rites "to train and educate members of Silla's expanding officialdom in the Confucian classics and rituals" (Kim, 2013, 252 n. 7). In both cases, these institutions emphasised the study of the Five Classics, the *Analects* of Confucius, and the *Classic of Filial Piety* (孝經, C. *Xiaojing*, K. *Hyogyŏng*, J. *Kyūjitai*), making Confucianism central to the state and integral to its educational system, which was primarily accessible only to the sons of the elite until the end of the nineteenth century (Grayson, 2002, 74).

Neo-Confucian Transnationalism

Li points out that the most "serious challenge to the supremacy of Confucianism was an alien religion called Buddhism" (1965, 155): "alien" because it had not originated in China. Buddhist ideas had penetrated China around the middle of the first century CE, and the original texts received from India had to be translated from Sanskrit into Chinese. During the initial Sinicisation period of these imported texts, many Buddhist ideas were conveyed by drawing on the vocabulary from Daoist texts, such as the *Daodejing* (道德經, also written as *Tao Te Ching*), attributed to the philosopher Laozi who probably lived during the fourth century BCE (Fung, 1983, 260). This contributed to quite a different feel to the Chinese form of Buddhism that emerged, and which would go on to take root in East Asia. We have already seen that these ideas had spread to Korea and were transmitted from there to Japan—all using the Chinese sources. During the eighth and ninth centuries, under the Tang dynasty, Buddhism had been embraced by the masses and received munificent patronage, far outstripping the prestige of the Confucians by that point (Chan, 1963, 336; Creel, 1971, 190–191). However, by the end of the dynasty Buddhism had lost its patronage, spurred by the Confucian scholars who criticised the economic impact of the Buddhists' many monasteries draining revenue from the state, but also their political and economic abuses, and failure to adhere to their own moral codes. Buddhism could not compete on a pragmatic level with the new surge of interest in Confucianism, which could remedy sociopolitical failings, as precursors to Neo-Confucianism were delighted to point out (Creel, 1971, 203; Li, 1968, 184–185; Fairbank and Goldman, 1999, 83–85).

Han Yu (768–824), along with his disciple Li Ao (died c. 844), are generally seen as the precursors to Neo-Confucianism, especially their focus on the ideas of human nature from Mencius, the most important Chinese philosopher after Confucius, who would become a central figure of Neo-Confucian philosophy, particularly in Korea (see Chan, 1963, 452–455). Han Yu also wrote one of the first critiques of Buddhism, though largely based on what he considered to be its rejection of the concrete impact of the "social relationships" of Confucianism in "this world", contrasting them with Buddhist shortcomings of Being-in-the-World, critical of their focus on afterlives and reincarnation (De Bary and Bloom, 1999, 583–585). This newly revitalised interest in Confucianism would grow exponentially during the Song dynasty, particularly with the writings of "The Five Sages of Song": Shao Yong (1011–1077), Zhou Dunyi (1017–1073), Zhang Zai (1020–1077), and the two brothers Cheng Hao (1032–1085) and Cheng Yi (1033–1107). More important though, was the contribution of Zhu Xi (also Chu Hsi) (1130–1200), who edited and synthesised the ideas in their texts he agreed with: in 1178, when he compiled *Jinsilu* (近思錄) [Reflections of Things at Hand] with Lu Zuqian (1137–1181), there were only Four Sages. Shao had been discarded for his association with Daoism, as well as his lack of focus on self-cultivation (Chan, 1987, 122–124; Tillman, 1992, 114–118).

Wing-Tsit Chan comments that, "NO ONE has exercised greater influence on Chinese thought than [Zhu Xi], except Confucius, Mencius, Lao Tzu, and Chuang Tzu" (1963, 588; original emphasis). Ames and Rosement, Jr. emphasise how "Zhu Xi's commentaries [...] became definitive of the [Neo-Confucian] tradition from the early fourteenth through the twentieth centuries" (1999, 17), and this influence also extended to Korea, becoming deeply rooted there, to such a degree that one could risk death for disagreeing with or challenging those "orthodox" interpretations. Zhu was also responsible for the very significant redirection of the Confucian tradition away from its original sources in the Five Classics, when in 1190 he published four other texts together for the first time and called them the Four Books, a title which has stayed with them until the very present: *Lunyu* (論語) [The Analects], *Daxue* (大學) [The Great Learning], *Zhongyong* (中庸) [The Doctrine of the Mean], and *Mengzi* (孟子) [The *Mencius*]. The Great Learning and The Doctrine of the Mean were originally chapters in the *Liji* [Record of Rites]. By 1313 these texts, with Zhu's commentaries, "were the basic texts in civil service examinations and in school education" (Chan, 1987, 130). They would remain the focus of Confucians and the basis of the state exam system until 1912, assuring that Zhu's ideas modified the future reception of these texts, which were also accepted as orthodoxy in Korea. Chan points out that "they have exercised far greater influence on Chinese life and thought in the past six hundred years than any other Classic" (1963, 589).

Just as had happened in the transition between the Tang to Song dynasties in China, marked by the promotion of Neo-Confucianism and the demise of Buddhism, a similar ripple effect also reverberated in Chosŏn Korea, which was particularly restrictive and challenging for women in the upper strata of society to a much greater extent than during the previous Koryŏ dynasty (918–1391). This gendered sociopolitical transition was also encoded in the national "Grand Code for State Administration", known as the *Kyŏngguk taejŏn* (經國大典), legally determining one's status, while formally legitimising the subjugation of females to males by the late fifteenth century.

Confucian Social Mechanisms and Indoctrination Manuals for Women

Gadamer's reading of Heidegger shows the effects of history governed by philosophical tradition on the social consciousness. Chosŏn Korea makes a good case study to illustrate this important point. Gradually, Neo-Confucianism supplanted the Buddhist tradition, usurping its effects on Becoming-in-the-World, a "world" that would be Confucianised. This even meant extirpating certain Buddhist rituals, replacing them with Confucian ones, undermining Shamanism, and eventually slaughtering thousands of Catholics in the nineteenth century for threatening to undermine its authority, suggesting that Catholic values eroded the norms and *bienséances* of a moral Confucian society (Cawley, 2015). In her essay in *A Companion to Gender History*, Vivian-Lee Nyitray describes how, "With the founding of the [Chosŏn] dynasty (1392–1910) came profound social change, occasioned in great measure by the suppression of Buddhism and the adoption of Confucianism as state ideology" (2006, 281). This is not dissimilar to the renaissance of Confucianism witnessed in China during the Song dynasty (960–1279), a period which also oversaw greater regulation of the lives of women and the spread of deforming foot-binding practices in Chinese society, further restricting women to the private realm (Nyitray, 2006, 279).

In Chosŏn, one's very being was rigidly demarcated by one's hereditary social status: *yangban* (elite aristocratic class); *chungin* (the middle people who had some technical training, such as translators/interpreters/doctors); *yangin/sangmin* (commoners, who bore the brunt of the taxes); and finally the *ch'ŏnmin* (base people, including everyone from slaves (*nobi*) to shamans and butchers) (Deuchler, 1992, 12–13, 310 n. 27, 377 n. 25). The leading Confucian scholars had largely been preoccupied by "moral" metaphysical debates, but were not particularly interested in the "*problematik* of slavery [...] although to a large degree, the wealth that supported their literati lifestyle and that ungirded their educational institutions depended on the labor of *nobi*" (Hejmanek, 2011, 141). Hejmanek (2011, 140–141) notes that some Korean scholars, such as Yi Ik (1681–1763), did criticise the system of hereditary slavery, which notably did not exist in China, but at the same time they did not set their slaves free as early converts to Catholicism did some decades later. One's interpersonal "Becoming-in-the-World" was further calibrated through "Five Cardinal Relationships" (五倫, C. *wulun*, K. *oryun*). Each relationship was related to a particular virtue, reinforcing a delimiting social mechanism where superiors and inferiors learn their place, again stemming from the *Mencius* (3A:4):

> between father and son there should be affection; between ruler and minister there should be righteousness; between husband and wife there should be attention to their separate functions; between old and young there should be proper order; and between friends there should be faithfulness. (Chan, 1963, 69–70)

Marriage was supposed to culminate in the birth of a son, reflecting one's filial duty to create male offspring, emphasised in the *Mencius* (4A:26): "There are three ways you can fail to honour your parents, and the worst is to have no heir" (Hinton, 1999, 137). In Chosŏn (as was the case in China), the family created by marriage was considered the basis of social life and linked to the very important Confucian rituals for the ancestors (祭祀, K. *Chesa*), performed by the eldest son who would also inherit the patrilineal estate. Men, too, were yoked into this state apparatus of control through heteronormative marriages. Cornelius Osgood notes that one of the few ways to "escape" it was by becoming a monk, and that a male was considered to be "a boy in the community until he does so", though pointing out that "Marriage under the old Korea system was almost as certain as death" (1950, 103).

Nyitray comments on the transformation of women's lives on the Korean Peninsula from the previous Koryŏ dynasty, underscoring how the "state apparatus of civil control chipped away at women's historical rights and privileges of inheritance, of mobility and action outside the home, and of their legal status as wives and mothers" (2006, 281). In *The Confucian Transformation of Korea: A Study of Society and Ideology* (1992), Deuchler examines the agnatic implications of the Chosŏn dynasty in great detail (see especially ch. 3). She highlights how this societal system differed from that of China, describing it as "a uniquely Korean interpretation and adaptation of the Confucian model" used to create a rigidly structured and stratified society (Deuchler, 1992, 289). Deuchler points out the ways in which social mobility was delimited, particularly for women, but also for sons not born of the primary wife—such sons were not permitted to sit the civil service exams or to perform rituals to the ancestors—while acknowledging that this was not the case in China, where secondary sons were less marginalised due the fact that Chinese lineages were "more loosely structured" (1992, 288). Nevertheless, it is a fact that Confucianism, when used as a state ideology, could negatively impact the lives of men, too. It could hinder their own Becoming-in-the World, and if they were not the "pure" sons of the primary wife, their potential was seriously curtailed. This injustice-of-birth is clearly captured in an important work of fiction written in Han'gŭl dating from the second half of the Chosŏn period, which provides an insightful yet scathing social critique of Confucian *yangban* society: *The Story of Hong Gildong* (홍길동전) (see Minsoo Kang's translation, 2016). The main protagonist, despite being quite brilliant, is prohibited from sitting the civil service exams, and thus prevented from advancing in society, as he is the son of a concubine. He soon takes matters into his own hands, abandoning all social expectations, which leads him into many adventures in this entertaining tale that anyone interested in Korea should read (hence no spoilers here). The tale reflects how one is not even considered part of the father's line of descent if not a "legal" son of the primary wife: in such cases, the men are also victims of uncontrollable circumstances, though not nearly as much as the women who were often sequestered in the home.

Sue Spall notes how oppositional pairs have been used to construct two groups of people in societies: one "muted" and one "dominant" (1989, 92). The group that is not represented publicly is the "muted" group. In this Confucian context, this is women, who were confined inside the home, enforced by the *naewaebŏp* (內外法), the inner-outer law. Han Hee-sook suggests that this was "based on the notion of rigid gender roles, in which men were considered to be the '*wae*' while women were the '*nae*' [resulting in] the imposition of behavioural codes that restricted men's sphere to matters outside of the house, and conversely, women's to internal family matters" (2004, 114–116). Lee Sang-wha (2005) is deeply critical of the remodelling of patriarchal patterns of behaviour validated by Confucian scholars through the (mis) application of the metaphysics of yin (陰, pronounced *ŭm* in Korean) as weak (and muted), and yang (陽) as strong (and dominant), linked to the social functions of women as passive and men as active: originally yin and yang refer to two aspects of the same thing (the sunny and shaded side of a hill), hence masculinity and femininity are not exclusively related to males or females, but to different qualities both possess.

This delimiting moral system also emphasised chastity as the female virtue *par excellence*, while men could frequent prostitutes, or "female entertainers" (*kisaeng*), and father children with several women, as well as spread venereal diseases. Instructional texts for women reinforced reductive and formalised "correct rules of female behaviour" or *yŏbŏm* (女範). *The Confucian Four Books for Women* (Pang-White, 2018) consisted of texts dating from the Han, Tang, and Ming dynasties, and was first circulated in the early seventeenth century in China, but was also widely available in Korea and Japan from the seventeenth century. These books, which were written by women, "were considered a very important collection of four didactic texts for the education of women", and consisted of (1) Lessons for Women, (2) Analects for Women, (3) Teachings for the Inner Court, and (4) Short Records of Models for Women (Pang-White, 2018, 3). The representation of women in these texts was shaped by the expectations of Zhu Xi, who recommended certain texts to women "so that they can become virtuous models for their children, relatives and villagers" (Pang-White, 2018, 12). Of great importance was *Zhu Xi's Family Rites* (朱熹家禮, C. *Zhuxi jiali*, K. *Chuja karye*), which linked personal self-discipline with the rigid application of propriety and "virtue" of women, also advocated in his magnum opus *Reflections on Things at Hand* (近思錄, C. *Jinsilu*, K. *Kŭnsarok*). Both works were immensely influential in Korea.

Michael J. Pettid (2011) argues that the discourse surrounding "virtuous women" (*yŏllyŏ*), and "un-virtuous women" (*pul-yŏllyŏ*) heightened in Korea after the Japanese invasions of the late sixteenth century, when many Korean women were raped by Japanese soldiers, or their reputations sullied through association with men from outside their own family. To reinforce Confucian values for women, Koreans had long been producing their own didactic guidebooks such as *Instructions for the Inner Quarters* (內訓書, K. *Naehunsŏ*) written by Queen Sohye (1437–1504). One of the most important was the *Illustrated Guide to the Three Bonds* (三綱行實圖, K. *Samgang haengsil-to*), first published in 1434. This is a collection of tales that highlight Confucian virtues in practice, using examples from China mostly, but also from Korea, and was repeatedly edited and supplemented throughout the Chosŏn dynasty (discussed in detail in Oh, 2011). The three bonds honed in on three of the Five Relationships: (1) loyalty between subject and ruler; (2) distinction between husband and wife; and (3) filial piety to parents (Pettid, 2011, 50). This effectively shaped who the individual could/would "become" through this process of heteronormative existential conditioning, where one's being-in-the-world was tied up in this process of becoming. Later, this same work was also translated into the vernacular script, "thus enabling it to reach a wider audience", highlighting he *trans*lational aspect of *trans*nationalism (Pettid, 2011, 55). Furthermore, an updated version was printed in 1617 under the title *Tongguk sinok samgang haengsil* (New and Expanded Korean Conduct of the Three Bonds), offering guidance for "becoming-virtuous" Confucian women. This text embodies the transnational linguistic context of these primers, and Pettid highlights how the accounts were written in:

> both literary Chinese and *han'gŭl* script [...] accompanied by an illustration depicting the noteworthy [virtuous] activity. The composition of the work allowed it to reach a wide audience: literary Chinese for *yangban* literati, *han'gŭl* script for those with less education such as women, commoners, and children, and illustrations for the illiterate. (2011, 55)

Furthermore, such texts, highlighting the important roles that individuals play as part of an interconnected society, also reflect the "moral individualism" of Confucianism, as it is described by De Bary (1985). Lee also comments on the fact that Confucianism "stresses the initiative of every person for undertaking the lifelong process of self-cultivation and self-realization"; however, he also emphasises that this individuality is inextricably linked with "mutual cooperation [...] A person is only human if he/she performs his/her fitting role(s) in the network of interpersonal relationships" (2006, 397), but I would add that these roles always reinforce heteronormativity. Lee, drawing on Heidegger's ideas, notes that in the Confucianist mode, "Being" is always "being-with" (*Mitdasein*), linked to the "sense of relatedness and interdependence of human beings", whereby, just as in Heidegger's work, *Dasein* "is a happening (*Geschehen*) or a process" (2006, 396–403). This process ties in with the idea of one's "becoming" outlined in this chapter, whereby the conditions for one's existence is shaped by the tradition, and what the tradition chooses to hand down or to teach us through specific texts, which already embody the ideological conditions for this "be-coming" process of who we can eventually become.

Conclusion

Thinking about Confucianism in terms of transnationalism, and transnationalism's inherent link with the translational, offers us an interesting way to think about the process of Becoming-in-the-World, when considered from an East Asian Confucian perspective. This chapter has focused primarily on the interaction between China and Korea in terms of ideas shared predominantly though the use of Classical Chinese and a corpus of religio-philosophical texts: the Five Classics, the Four Books, but also the *Four Books for Women* and other Korean manuals to instruct one on the process of "becoming" a heteronormative Confucian member of society. Anna Sun refers to this as "a gradual process that involves ritual practices, academic education, and moral self-cultivation, as well as the participation in certain Confucian social institutions" (2013, 120). She also highlights how in "the case of Korea, here the connection between ancestral rituals and Confucianism seems to be much more pronounced" (2013, 118). This indissociable connection to the past (bound up in traditions that have been handed down), orients Koreans' sense of who they are, and to some degree also shapes who they will become, again, tied up with being-with-others as part of a dynamic process. This "traditional" process has been restrictive for women, to say the least, and their bodies have been bound up in their relationships with men. This has only recently been challenged by them as part of the transnational (and inherently) translational #MeToo movement (K. #미투; C. #我也是), which is deeply *trans*gressive to Confucian patriarchal norms, to return to Ong's ideas expressed at the start of this chapter. Even in Korea, where Confucianism is still considered to be very deeply imbedded within the various sociopolitical apparatus of the state and used to shape the process of "becoming", it is being challenged and transformed by more recent sociopolitical transnational reverberations, whereby one's becoming is also seeing a noticeable shift. This shift now permits a plurality of "becomings", no longer delimited and restricted by heteronormative patriarchal constructs, but rather opening them up to other (im)possibilities of becoming-in-the-world, where being-with-others has been radically re-envisaged in a more equitable way, but a way that remains long.

References and Further Reading

Ames, Roger T., and Henry Rosemont, Jr. 1999. *The Analects of Confucius: A Philosophical Translation*. New York: Ballantine.

Cawley, Kevin N. 2015. "Dangerous Women in the Early Catholic Church in Korea". In *Religious Transformation in Modern Asia*, edited by David W. Kim, 76–97. Leiden: Brill.

——. 2019. *Religious and Philosophical Traditions of Korea*. New York: Routledge.

Chan, Wing-Tsit. 1963. *A Sourcebook in Chinese Philosophy*. Princeton: Princeton University Press.

——. 1987. *Chu Hsi and His Thought*. Hong Kong: The Chinese University Press.

Coogan, Michael D. 2005. *Eastern Religions: Hinduism, Buddhism, Taoism, Confucianism, Shinto*. London: Duncan Baird.

Creel, Herrlee. 1971. *Chinese Thought from Confucius to Mao Tse-tung*. Chicago: University of Chicago Press.

De Bary, William Theodore (ed.). 1967. *Reflections on Things at Hand: The Neo-Confucian Anthology Compiled by Chu Hsi and Lü Tsu-Ch'ien*. New York: Columbia University Press.

——. 1985. *The Rise of Neo-Confucianism in Korea*. New York: Columbia University Press.

De Bary, William Theodore, and Irene Bloom (eds.). 1999. *Sources of Chinese Tradition*, Vol. 1. New York: Columbia University Press.

Deuchler, Martina. 1992. *The Confucian Transformation of Korea: A Study of Society and Ideology*. Cambridge, MA: Harvard University Press.

Fairbank, John K., and Merle Goldman. 1999. *China: A New History*. Cambridge, MA: Harvard University Press.

Fung Yulan. 1983. *A History of Chinese Philosophy, Vol. 1: The Period of the Philosophers (from the Beginnings to Circa 100 B.C.)*, translated by Derek Bodde. Princeton: Princeton University Press.

Gadamer, Hans-Georg. 2006. *Truth and Method*, translated by Joel Weinsheimer and Donald G. Marshall. New York: Continuum Publishing Group.

Grayson, James H. 2002. *Korea: A Religious History*. London: Routledge Curzon.

Han, Hee-sook. 2004. "Women's Life during the Chosŏn Dynasty". *International Journal of Korean History* 6: 113–160.

Heidegger, Martin. 2008. *Being and Time*, translated by John Macquarrie and Edward Robinson. New York: Harper Perennial.

Hejtmanek, Milan. 2011. "Devalued Bodies, Revalued Status: Confucianism and the Plight of Female Slaves in Late Chosŏn Korea". In *Women and Confucianism in Chosŏn Korea: New Perspectives*, edited by Youngmin Kim and Michael J. Pettid, 137–149. New York: SUNY Press.

Hendry, Joy, and Simon Underdown. 2012. *Anthropology*. London: Oneworld Press.

Hinton, David (trans.). 1999. *Mencius*. Washington, DC: Counterpoint.

Hudson, Geoffrey Francis. 1964. "China and the World: A Summary of Intellectual and Artistic Influences". In *The Legacy of China*, edited by Raymond Dawson, 340–363. Oxford: Oxford University Press.

Kang, Minsoo (trans.). 2016. *The Story of Hong Gildong*. New York: Penguin.

Kim Pusik. 2012. *The Koguryŏ Annals of the Samguk Sagi*, translated by Edward J. Shultz and Hugh H. W. Kang. Seoul: The Academy of Korean Studies Press.

——. 2013. *The Silla Annals of the Samguk Sagi*, translated by Edward J. Shultz, Hugh H. W. Kang, and Daniel C. Kane. Seoul: The Academy of Korean Studies Press.

Lee, Kwang-Sae. 2006. *East and West: Fusion of Horizons*. Paramus: Homa & Sekey.

Lee, Sang-wha. 2005. "Patriarchy and Confucianism". In *Women's Experiences and Feminist Practices in South Korea*, edited by Chang Pilwha and Kim Wun-Shil, 67–117. Seoul: Ehwa Woman's University Press.

Li, Dun J. 1965. *The Ageless Chinese*. London: J. M. Dent and Sons.

Lionnet, Françoise and Shu-mei Shih (eds.). 2005. *Minor Transnationalism*. Durham, NC: Duke University Press.

Nyitray, Vivian-Lee. 2006. "Confucian Complexities: China, Japan, Korea and Vietnam". In *A Companion to Gender History*, edited by Teresa A. Meade and Merry E. Wiesner-Hanks, 273–284. Oxford: Blackwell.

Oh, Young Kyun. 2011. "Printing the *Samgang haengsil-to* 三綱行實圖 (Illustrated Guide to the Three Relationships), a Premodern Korean Moral Primer". *East Asian Publishing and Society* 1(1): 1–38.

Ong, Aihwa. 1999. *Flexible Citizenship: The Cultural Logics of Transnationality*. Durham, NC: Duke University Press.

Osgood, Cornelius. 1951. *The Koreans and Their Culture*. New York: Ronald Press.

Palais, James. 1996. *Confucian Statecraft and Korean Institutions*. Seattle: University of Washington Press.

Pang-White, Ann A. 2018. *The Confucian Four Books for Women: A New Translation of the Nü Sishu and the Commentary of Wang Xiang*. Oxford: Oxford University Press.

Park Ilpong (trans.). 1987. *Sohak* (小學) [The Lesser Learning]. Seoul: Yukmunsa.

Pettid, Michael J. 2011. "Confucian Educational Works for Upper Status Women in Chosŏn Korea". In *Women and Confucianism in Chosŏn Korea: New Perspectives*, edited by Youngmin Kim and Michael J. Pettid, 49–70. Albany: SUNY Press.

Rule, Paul A. 1986. *K'ung-Tzu or Confucius: The Jesuit Interpretation of Confucianism*. London: Allen & Unwin.

Spall, Sue. 1989. "Gynocriticism". In *Feminist Readings: Feminists Reading*, edited by Sara Mills and Lynne Pearce, 83–121. Virginia: Harvester Wheatsheaf.

Sun, Anna. 2013. *Confucianism as World Religion: Contested Histories and Contemporary Realities*. Princeton: Princeton University Press.

Tillman, Hoyt Cleveland. 1992. *Confucian Discourse and Chu Hsi's Ascendancy*. Honolulu: University Hawai'i Press.

2

Diffusion and Transnationalism

"Emplantation" and the Crossing of Cultural Boundaries

James H. Grayson

Diffusion and Cultural Transmission

Marvin Harris, in the landmark book *The Rise of Anthropological Theory* (1969), devotes an entire chapter, chapter 14, to "Diffusionism" to debunk the idea of diffusion as a viable scholarly explanation. He writes that "the attempt to explain cultural differences and similarities by appealing to the non-principle of diffusion" is fundamentally a sterile theory, a non-theory (Harris, 1969, 377). And yet, the transmission of material and social culture from one society to another, from one culture to another, from one cultural sphere to another, is a widely recognised fact both historically and in contemporary times. For example, the Ecclesiastical History Society dedicated its conferences in 2015 and 2016 to the "translation" of Christianity—its adaptation to changed cultural circumstances. The papers from these conferences were published as *Translating Christianity* (Ditchfield, Metheun, and Spicer, 2017). In this book, dedicated to the concept of "transnationalism", there is an excellent opportunity to reconsider the theoretical issues involved in the transmission of culture or aspects of culture across the boundaries of cultural spheres, and within the "internal" boundaries of cultural spheres.

Ralph Linton in *The Tree of Culture* (1959) devotes two chapters to "Processes of Cultural Change" and "Cultural Evolution". He suggests that cultural change, the adoption by one culture of a new cultural element, follows a fourfold process of (1) the presentation of the new cultural element, (2) the acceptance or rejection of the new cultural element, (3) the modification of the new cultural element to the cultural context of the receiving culture, and (4) the elimination of the older cultural element whose functions have been taken over by the new cultural element. He comments that there has to be at least one innovator who invents something or borrows something from another culture (Linton, 1959, 41–43). He then considers the factors which might affect the acceptance of the new cultural element, among which are the congruity of the new element "with the pre-existing value system of the society" and the "importance of the innovator's social status in determining a society's acceptance or rejection of new things". One final observation which he makes is that the elimination of older cultural elements is not necessarily complete or total (Linton, 1959, 44–46).

Linton is probably the first anglophone scholar to outline the *stages* in the process by which new cultural features are adopted into a sociocultural system, but he did not give a detailed discussion of *how* this process of change took place. Although the second stage—the acceptance or rejection of the new cultural element, is the crucial stage, he says little about how acceptance might occur other than that it might have to do with its utility, its congruence with existing cultural elements, or the prestige of the innovator.

Linton's reflections on cultural transmission derive from his interest in smaller-scale societies, and individual cultural elements—particularly elements of material culture. In *The Tree of Culture*, Linton writes extensively about prehistoric culture complexes and six historic/contemporary cultural complexes, or "cultural spheres". Nonetheless, his concept of culture change/transmission appears to be modelled on the transmission of small-scale examples of material culture and the behavioural complexes associated with them. His model does not appear to consider complex cultural traditions, such as a system of religious belief and practice, and so, his discussion is largely descriptive and lacks detail about the process of the transmission of a culture complex such as a religion.

Linton's description of cultural change and cultural adoption is not complex enough to describe the transmission of complex cultural elements—such as a set of religious beliefs and practices, and how the transmission of these complex elements occurs in large-scale societies with a deep historical record. Linton's model of cultural transmission gives many hints and suggestions but is not nuanced enough to explain the diffusion of a "religion" from one complex and sophisticated culture to another.

As a Methodist missionary and anthropologist living and working in south Korea in the 1970s and 1980s, I wanted to understand why Protestantism was growing so rapidly there. Linton's model provided some clues but, as mentioned, it was inadequate for examining a society with the historical depth and cultural complexity of Korea. Another source of inspiration was an article by E. M. Pye (1969) who outlined a concept of the "transplantation of religion" (both the transmission of religious traditions and the revival of existing traditions) as comprising three stages of contact, adjustment, and reclarification. However, this idea is only outlined, and not developed in any detail. In my own research, drawing on some of the ideas of Linton and Pye, I developed a model for explaining the process of religious transmission called the theory of emplantation. My research examined the transmission of Buddhism from the Indian culture world into the Chinese culture world from the first to the seventh centuries, a period long enough to enable us to see both the processual periods of cultural transmission, and the social, political, and cultural factors which impeded or assisted the process of diffusion.

The theory of emplantation indicates that a successfully transmitted religion goes through a series of three stages before "emplantation"—its rooting in the soil of a culture different or alien to the one in which it originated. There are also five factors affecting the acceptance or rejection of a new religious tradition:

(1) the resolution of contradictions between core values of the religion and the receiving society,

(2) the achievement of tolerance or acceptance by the ruling elite,

(3) the resolution of linguistic barriers to understanding the core teachings of the religion,

(4) the resolution of any conflicts between the new religion and pre-existing traditions, and

(5) more broadly, those political conditions which might predispose the acceptance or rejection of the new religion.

One specific issue considered was the chronological sequence in which these issues were faced and resolved. I concluded that this model of the transmission of religious beliefs and practices had wider relevance to the broader issue of the transnational diffusion of culture (Grayson, 1985, 13–15).

Crossing the Boundaries of Cultural Spheres: Transmitting Buddhism from India to China

Buddhism had spread along trade routes from the subcontinent into Central Asia, becoming well established in the oasis city states by the first century BCE. By the first century CE, Buddhism was present in the Han empire of China (漢, 206 BCE–220 CE) in the Central Asian expatriate commercial communities, but its greatest growth took place following the dissolution of the Han empire into a series of (often ephemeral) states north and south of the Yangtze River. Many of the northern states were ruled by peoples from

Central Asia, and known to the Chinese as "barbarians" (胡, C. *hu*). This state of political disunion continued until 581 with the establishment of the Sui dynasty (隋, 581–618) and its long-lived successor, the Tang dynasty (唐, 618–906) (Ebrey, 2010 [1996], 60–135; Zürcher, 2007 [1959]). An examination of Buddhism from its introduction in the first century until the beginning of the Tang, when it had achieved unparalleled religious, intellectual, and artistic influence, shows that its development passed through three distinct phases: "Phase 1: Contact and Explication", "Phase 2: Penetration", and "Phase 3: Expansion". Phase 1 could be further subdivided into subphases: "A: Contact" and "B: Emplantation"; Phase 3 could also be subdivided into subphases "A: Growth and Contention" and "B: Supremacy" (see Fig. 1).

The General Pattern	**Phase 1** Contact & Explication		**Phase 2** Penetration	**Phase 3** Expansion	
	Subphase A Contact	Subphase B Emplementation		Subphase A Growth & Contention	Subphase B Supremacy
The Specific Patterns					
The Slow Penetration Pattern	**Phase 1**		**Phase 2**	**Phase 3**	
The Rapid Conversion Pattern			**Phase 2**	**Phase 3**	

Fig. 1. Model of the growth of missionary religions.

I found that in the first phase, there were three tasks which had to be achieved:

(1) the acquisition of the Chinese language and the explication of essential Buddhist concepts,

(2) the resolution of conflicts between the core values of Chinese civilisation and Buddhist philosophy and religious beliefs, and

(3) the achievement of the toleration of Buddhism by the political elite.

When propagators of Buddhism (not necessarily clerics or formal "missionaries") first came to China, a knowledge of both the spoken and written languages was essential in order to introduce the radically new ideas of the

Buddhist tradition. Linguistically the languages of India and of Central Asia are unrelated to Chinese, and there were no cultural-linguistic connections between them at this point. Linton refers to this stage as one of "presentation", but it is clear that the simple presentation of a new cultural element or complex of culture is not enough. What it is, why it is important or significant, and how it will improve on the existing state of affairs needs to be explained and promoted. Thus, knowledge of the everyday, general language was not enough. Knowledge of the specialised vocabulary and the ideas of Chinese philosophical discourse was essential if Buddhist religious and philosophical concepts were to be made comprehensible to an intellectual class familiar with the discourse of Confucianism and the other philosophical traditions (Grayson, 1985, 3–5; Zürcher, 2007 [1959], 18–56).

However, my research also showed that a simple knowledge of sophisticated Chinese vocabulary and the character of Chinese philosophic discourse would not have been enough in themselves to create the conditions enabling the widespread diffusion of Buddhism. There was an essential contradiction between the core values of Confucian China and Indian Buddhism, which had to be resolved before significant strides could be made. This finding corresponds to Linton's idea of the congruence of a new cultural element to the existing culture.

At the core of Buddhist monastic practice was the requirement for "clerical" Buddhist followers to leave their family to join a monastic establishment in which they would pursue their individual course towards "liberation", being freed from attachment to the things of this world. Nothing like a monastery had ever existed in Chinese culture. Leaving one's family, going to live in a monastic community, and joining an alternative family made up of unrelated people, struck at the core of Confucian thinking about familial relationships. Filial piety (孝, C. *xiao*; K. *hyo*), the reverent attitude towards one's parents and senior members of the family, was the chief moral pillar of family relationships and society. Indeed, the very term for becoming a monastic Buddhist is *chujia* (出家), "leaving the family". Removing oneself from the family was tantamount to rejecting *xiao* and would have been seen as destroying *the* core element of the structure of society (Zürcher, 2007 [1959], 280–285).

Over the next centuries, Buddhist missionaries worked hard to resolve this issue by claiming that Buddhist monastics took up monastic life to spiritually benefit their families. Buddhist clerics developed an ancestral ritual to parallel the Confucian ancestral ceremony *dishi* (祭祀). Thus, by providing a resolution to the clash of values and practice, by showing that Buddhism actually supported the Confucian value of filial piety, Buddhism could spread beyond a small circle of curious and interested individuals. Referring to the model for emplantation, this process of resolution formed the key task of

Subphase B, rooting Buddhism in the soil of Chinese culture (Zürcher, 2007 [1959], 280–285). Cawley has examined the role of Confucianism in depth in Chapter 1, showing its sociocultural effects in East Asia.

In the East Asian diplomatic world of the middle of the first millennium, cultural exchange was used to cement relationships between different kingdoms. The so-called "barbarian" rulers of the northern kingdoms used Buddhism to establish diplomatic relations with the ancient kingdoms of Korea and Manchuria by sending monks and nuns, Buddhist scriptures, and Buddhist statues, effectively transmitting Buddhism to these nations (Grayson, 2002, 24–36).

It is clear from this historic record that the key factors in the transmission of Buddhism were the acquisition of language and the resolution of conflicts of values. No new religious tradition could make headway if there was a lack of general or specialised linguistic knowledge, or without resolution of conflicts of values. However, the historical evidence also shows that the transmission of Buddhism into these various states was made easier if powerful political or socially significant figures expressed an interest or tolerance of Buddhism. Although confirming an observation made by Linton, this aspect was not essential as the evidence also shows that even in circumstances of intolerance, the religion grew.

When the three issues of language, value conflict resolution, and sociopolitical toleration had been achieved, Buddhism became emplanted—rooted in the cultural soil of these "Chinese" states. Once this had been achieved, the second phase of transmission, "Penetration", occurred with Buddhism rapidly penetrating into the cultural soil of China. By the beginning of the third phase, "Expansion", Buddhism had come to challenge the prior traditions of philosophy, religion, art, and architecture, and by the end of the 700-year period was pre-eminent in all of these areas.

There was a significant variation in the pattern of the transmission of religious belief and practice—the "Rapid Conversion Pattern". The general pattern of transmission, the "Slow Penetration Pattern", was a lengthy, steady explication and adaptation of Buddhist teaching and practice to the soil of Chinese culture, typified by the states established south of the Yangtze River from the third century. These states were governed by elites who had fled south of the river following the collapse of the Han Dynasty in the early third century due to invasion by peoples from central and northern Asia. Buddhism grew in the south because it was promoted by many "refugees" who, bringing their faith and learning with them, cultivated and spread the doctrines and practices of Buddhism. Southern Buddhism had a strong and widespread popular base which provided stability and continuity for greater growth (Grayson, 1985, 5–9).

This is not true in the north. Buddhism in northern China was promoted by the rulers (who were seen as "barbarians" by the Chinese elite) because it was a universalistic teaching which could bind together the two disparate ethnic communities. Consequently, the promotion of Buddhism there depended on the patronage or favour of the ruler, the emperor (Grayson, 1985, 9–10). Arthur Wright (1959, 54–57, 62), in discussing the close relationship between the northern imperial courts and the Buddhist establishment within their territories, refers to the relationship as a Buddhist form of the Caesaro-papism typical of the relationship between the emperors of the Byzantine empire and the Orthodox Church.

The immediate acceptance by the emperor and the court effectively eliminated the first stage of our model, "Contact and Explication", allowing the process to move straight to the stage of "Penetration". Dependence on patronage meant that when a new emperor ascended the throne, or there was a dynastic change (often the case during the Period of Disunion), the policy towards Buddhism could change. Immediate acceptance and immediate rejection in changed circumstances exemplifies the "Acceptance and Rejection Syndrome". The "Rapid Penetration" model is inherently unstable, and raises a question about Linton's comment on the importance of the prestige of the "innovator", the person who introduces a new cultural element into a society. Clearly the prestige of the emperor and the imperial court aided initial growth, but it is equally clear that the widespread support of a new doctrine by elite and non-elite members of a society provided a more stable basis for growth and continuity. Simple promotion of a new cultural element by an elite member of a society is not in itself sufficient for long-term growth and stability (Grayson, 1985, 10–13).

The third stage in the model is Phase 3, "Expansion", which has two subphases "Growth and Contention" and "Supremacy". In this phase, Buddhism became an established feature in both North and South China, but was stronger and more stable in the south. Tracing the history of southern Buddhism throughout the fourth, fifth, and sixth centuries, certain conflicts stand out. First, as a result of the substantial presence of Buddhism on the religious and cultural horizon, there were movements to reject Buddhism as being "un-Chinese" by both Daoists and Confucianists. Buddhism was said to be a debased form of either Daoism (if the attack was led by Daoists) or Confucianism (if the attack was led by Confucianists). This argument was called the *huahu* theory (化胡) [converting the barbarians], and claimed that either Laozi or Confucius went to India and "converted" the barbarians to their teaching; now the "barbarians" were bringing back a debased form of Chinese teachings (Zürcher, 2007 [1959], 37–38). Possibly the first Daoist text to assert this theory is the *Huahu jing* (化胡經) [Scripture on the Conversion of the Barbarians], composed by Wang Fu (王浮) around the year 300. This text claims that the Daoist philosopher Laozi went to India to teach his doctrines there (Zürcher, 2007 [1959], 290–320). A further attack made by the Confucianists was that Buddhism undermined *xiao*, filial piety, the single most important and visible sign of which was an individual's performance of the ancestral rituals. To counter this claim of impiety, the Buddhists created their own form of ancestral rituals to commemorate deceased relatives (Zürcher, 2007 [1959], 280–285).

The third stage was not just about contention with existing traditions which felt threatened by the "new" doctrine and its practices, and the Buddhist response. It was also about spread and growth. Because Buddhism was well established, rulers and individual Buddhist clerics confidently participated in projects of Buddhist missions (布教, C. *Bujiao*) "spreading the teaching", transmitting Buddhist doctrines and practices beyond their national boundaries. Both the northern and southern states engaged in this work, most notably the empire of Northern Wei (北魏, 386–534), which was substantially responsible for the spread of Buddhism into Manchuria and the Korean Peninsula (Ebrey, 2010 [1996], 95–100, map 98).

Another sign of the spread and depth of Buddhism, both north and south, is the appearance of popular cults devoted to a particular figure in the Buddhist pantheon (Chen, 1964, 275–296). A final positive characteristic of this period is the continued translation and retranslation of Buddhist texts—both scriptures and doctrinal materials, indicating the increasingly sophisticated understanding of the complex ideas of Indian Buddhism. However, the fact that translation occurred over a period of more than 400 years indicates the complexity of transmitting radically different ideas, beliefs, and practices from one cultural world into another (Zürcher, 2007 [1959], 280–285).

"Emplantation" is a model of the process of cultural transmission which helps to understand how a religion from a completely different social, religious, and political context could be successfully transmitted, emplanted, and become dominant in the Chinese religious and philosophical worlds. The model is not predictive, but only a tool for examining the historical facts to see what processes were at work leading to the success of Buddhism in China, a success which the renowned historian of Buddhism in China, Erik Zürcher, referred to in the title of his seminal work, *The Buddhist Conquest of China* (first published 1959). The model does not assume the continued pre-eminence of Buddhism, but only indicates how it came to achieve widespread social and cultural acceptance in Chinese society. My research also demonstrated that this model had a wider application beyond the "Chinese" states, to which we now turn.

Crossing Internal Boundaries: The Transmission of Buddhism from China to Korea

A cultural sphere is an area of the world the territories of which are geographically contiguous, and which shares a high degree of cultural commonality in terms of religion, social mores, art, architecture, and sociopolitical concepts and structures. A cultural sphere usually encompasses a number of different peoples and ethnic groups which share many or most of these cultural features, but which also retain a number of unique cultural features of their own. The term "cultural sphere" implies that there is one area within the sphere which was the source of the cultural complex, and from which this cultural complex diffused or spread. A cultural sphere also implies that the other nations, states, and ethnic groups composing it received this cultural complex by some form of sociocultural transmission.

The theory of emplantation, explaining how a cultural trait or cultural complex is transmitted from one sphere to another, is also useful for describing and explaining the transmission of culture *within* a single cultural sphere. In this section, we will examine the transmission of Buddhism to the three ancient kingdoms of Korea—Koguryŏ (高句麗), Paekche (百濟), and Silla (新羅)—which occupied territory in both Manchuria and the Korean Peninsula (Kim, 2012, 32–121).

From the first to the seventh centuries, the ancient kingdoms began to absorb "Chinese" civilisation, first from the Han empire which lay to their west and then, subsequent to its collapse, from the various states which occupied its former territory. Until the early third century, southern Manchuria and the northern part of the Korean Peninsula were governed by the Han empire under a series of military commanderies, following which the kingdom of Koguryŏ governed the territory. South of Koguryŏ, the central and southern portions of the peninsula were dominated by two kingdoms, Paekche in the south-west (also controlling the vital Han River Valley), and Silla in the south-east (later controlling the valley).

By the fourth century, these states had adopted the sociopolitical culture of Han, including the use of the Chinese writing system, the governmental practices and structures of Han, and the philosophical system which underlay governance, Confucianism (Cawley, 2019, ch. 1). The Confucian system of civil service examinations and the educational system used to prepare candidates to take these exams were adopted later (Kim, 2012, 55–73). These sociopolitical changes could be seen as a process of "modernisation"—to use a mid-twentieth-century term, adopting the culture of what was seen to be the most advanced political entity in the geographical area. This culture was perceived to be a single cultural "package", which included a religious tradition—Buddhism.

From the fourth to the tenth century, from the time of the introduction of Buddhism to its full-blown flourishing, there are six stages of historical development: (1) initial contact, (2) official acceptance, (3) growth and evangelism, (4) penetration, (5) popularisation of Buddhism, and (6) development of the meditative schools. In historic stage 1, Buddhist "missionaries" arrived with the purpose of spreading Buddhist teaching (in Koguryŏ, Paekche, Silla), or were sent as part of a diplomatic measure to solidify relationships between states (Paekche and Silla). In either case, the courts eventually gave formal recognition to the new teachings and promoted them, which is historic stage 2. In historic stage 3, we see the building of great temples, rulers taking Buddhist-style reign names, monks going to China to study, and the sending of "missionaries" to Japan.

In historic stage 4 all of these trends are heightened, indicating that the new religious tradition has become rooted, "emplanted", into the cultural soil of the kingdoms, ready to expand. In historic stage 5, there is growth in the sophistication in Buddhist practice with the appearance of formal schools of Buddhism based upon particular scriptural texts, the numbers of monks travelling on a study pilgrimage to India, and the emergence of popular cults focused on the worship or adoration of specific Buddhist figures. Finally, in stage 6 the several schools of meditative Buddhism appear, collectively called *Sŏn* (禪) in Korean, and known in Chinese as *Chan*, or *Zen* in Japanese (Grayson, 1985, 17–62).

Broadly, these historical stages correspond well to the three phases of the model of emplantation. Historic stages 1 and 2 correspond to Phase 1a of the model, Contact, while historic stage 3 corresponds to Phase 1b, Emplantation. Historic stage 4 directly corresponds to Phase 2 of the model, whereas historic stages 5 (monastic schools, study pilgrimages to India, the development of popular cults) and 6 (development of meditative schools of Buddhist practice) correspond to Phase 3a, Expansion. Thus, in a simplistic way, the historic facts of the transmission of Buddhism from the core of the cultural sphere to the Manchurian/Korean states corresponds well with the phases of the model of emplantation.

However, there are important differences between the transmission of Buddhism from India to China and its transmission within the cultural sphere of "China". First of all, the model when applied to intercultural sphere transmission indicates that two tasks had to be accomplished—the acquisition of the language of the receptor culture and its use in verbal and written transmission, and the resolution of any conflict of values between the two cultural systems. In intracultural sphere transmission such as we have been examining, these tasks had already been accomplished. The Korean states had already acquired the writing system of China, its governmental system and practices, and its sociopolitical philosophy, Confucianism. Because the "Korean" states were "modernising", the prestige of the "Chinese" cultural package enabled the more ready acceptance of Buddhism by the political elites of these states.

Second, in this case study of intracultural sphere transmission there is no example of a substantial conflict between existing religious traditions with the exception of Silla when King Pŏphŭng (法興, r. 514–539) was about to formally adopt Buddhism. But this event was not an example of the resistance by an indigenous, formally institutionalised religious tradition, but a conflict at court (Kim, 2012, 45). What *is* interesting is that there was no process of transforming the traditional or "folk" religious practices into an institutionalised religion with a formally trained clergy, sacred texts, formalised written liturgies, and large religious edifices such as happened in China and Japan. The advent of Buddhism in China led to the emergence of institutionalised "folk" religion, and the schools of religious Daoism. In Japan, the advent of Buddhism led to the institutionalisation of "folk" practices (particularly those associated with the royal house) which became "Shinto" (Kasahara, 2001, 140–145). Again, the institutionalisation of "Korean" folk religious traditions may never have happened because of the prestige of "Chinese" civilisation during the era of "modernisation".

Concluding Remarks

Reflecting on our examination of the transmission of religions across the boundaries of cultural spheres, and within cultural spheres, we have found that there were three phases in this process and that there were five factors influencing the success of the outcome of the transmission. The chronological order of the resolution of issues raised by the five factors was seen to be crucial. In the initial phase, acquiring knowledge of the language and specialist terminology and the resolution of conflicts of values was essential for emplantation. In Linton's model of culture change, stage 2, the acceptance or rejection of a new culture trait, is followed by stage 3, the adaptation of a new trait. My research showed the opposite; for a culture trait or complex to be accepted there must be initial accommodation to the local culture, particularly the resolution of conflicts and differences. Linton also suggested that the acceptance of a new trait may be the result of the prestige of the "innovator". My research has shown that while this was true to a certain exact, it was the prestige of "Chinese" civilisation which enabled the toleration of Buddhism by the elite of the kingdoms in both continental East Asia and in Korea. Although this prestige created favourable conditions for the presentation of Buddhism, it was not a guarantee that Buddhism would be accepted, grow, and expand.

The theory of emplantation provides a model for examining the historical process of cultural or religious transmission, to evaluate the success of that process, and to learn why this transmission was successful or not. An examination of the historical features of the transmission of Buddhism into China and Korea confirms the general outlines and principles of Linton's ideas about culture change, and deepens and enriches it. These long diachronic studies illustrated that, contrary to Harris, processes of cultural diffusion are empirical and contribute to the general anthropological study of culture and society. Diffusion as a concept is neither sterile, nor a non-theory.

References and Further Reading

Cawley, Kevin N. 2019. *Religious and Philosophical Traditions of Korea.* New York: Routledge.

Chen, Kenneth K. S. 1964. *Buddhism in China: A Historical Survey.* Princeton: Princeton University Press.

Ditchfield, Simon, Charlotte Metheun, and Andrew Spicer (eds.). 2017. *Translating Christianity.* Studies in Church History 53. Cambridge: Cambridge University Press/Ecclesiastical History Society.

Ebrey, Patricia. 2010 [1996]. *Cambridge Illustrated History of China.* 2nd ed. Cambridge: Cambridge University Press.

Grayson, James H. 1985. *Early Buddhism and Christianity in Korea: A Study in the Emplantation of Religion.* Leiden: Brill.

——. 2002. *Korea: A Religious History.* Rev. ed. London: Routledge Curzon.

Harris, Marvin. 1969. *The Rise of Anthropological Theory: A History of Theories of Culture.* London: Routledge and Kegan Paul.

Kasahara, Kazuo, ed. 2001. *A History of Japanese Religion.* Tokyo: Kosei.

Kim, Jinwung. 2012. *A History of Korea: From "Land of the Morning Calm" to States in Conflict.* Bloomington: Indiana University Press.

Linton, Ralph. 1959. *The Tree of Culture.* New York: Alfred A. Knopf.

Pye, E. Michael. 1969. "The Transplantation of Religions". *Numen* 16: 234–239.

Wright, Arthur F. 1959. *Buddhism in Chinese History.* Stanford: Stanford University Press.

Zürcher, Erik. 2007 [1959]. *The Buddhist Conquest of China: The Spread and Adaptation of Buddhism in Early Medieval China.* 3rd ed. Leiden: Brill.

3

The Battle of Red Cliffs

From History to Transnational Identity

Carlotta Sparvoli

Red Cliff

In July 2008, the pomp and pageantry of the upcoming Beijing Olympics were heralded by the release of the greatest film epic ever produced in China: *Red Cliff* (赤壁, C. *Chi Bi*) by Hong Kong director Johnny Woo. The plot is inspired by chapters 43–50 of one of the Ming classic novels, the *Romance of the Three Kingdoms* (三國演義, C. *Sanguo yanyi*), hereafter *Romance*, attributed to Luo Guanzhong (羅貫中, 1330?–1400?). The core event is the naval battle that took place in 208 CE at Chi Bi, midway along the Yangtze River, upstream from present-day Wuhan (de Crespigny, 2018, 206 n. 78). It tells how the combined forces of two southern kingdoms, guided by Liu Bei (劉備, 161–223) of Shu and Sun Quan (孫權, 182–252) of Wu, against all odds, routed the mighty fleet of Cao Cao (曹操, 155–220) of the Hans. Under the skilled guidance of Zhou Yu (周瑜, 175–210), the commander of Wu's troops, and thanks to clever stratagems and intuitions of Zhuge Liang (諸葛亮, 181–234), a host of no more than 50,000 men successfully scattered the Han troops, numbered in the hundreds of thousands.

Labelled by the *Xinhua* news agency (2008, n. pag.) as the most expensive Asian-financed film ever, *Red Cliff* appeared almost 100 years after the first film ever produced in China, *Conquering Dingjun Mountain* (定軍山, C. *Dingjun shan*, Beijing, 1905) (Xiao et al., 1999, 128). Both movies were

This study has been carried out as part of the MIUR Excellence Project DIVE-IN *Diversity & Inclusion*, conducted by the Department of Modern Languages, Literatures, and Cultures - Alma Mater Studiorum - Università di Bologna (iniziativa Dipartimenti di Eccellenza MIUR [L. 232 del 01/12/2016]).

inspired by military actions described in the *Romance*; however, unlike *Dingjun shan*, *Red Cliff*'s themes cannot be exhaustively explained in terms of "cultural awareness" (Hu, 2003, 39). Instead, they are related to the occasion offered by Beijing 2008 to project to a planet-wide audience the image of China's "rediscovered power" (Casarini, 2007).

Even though the antagonistic element that characterises the Olympic Games is removed from the most profound aspects of Chinese culture, modern-day China has taken on with the perspective of emerging victorious in the competition among nations (Bergman, 2008). Therefore, the colossal production of *Red Cliff* might be interpreted as a celebration of the new geopolitical role of China. We could infer that a mechanism has been utilised analogous to that of the US film industry, in which the Turnerian myth of the "New Frontier" was consolidated, reinterpreted, and exported around the globe, through western movies—a genre wherein the western frontiers embody a new field of opportunity, a way out of the bondage of the past. In such a framework, the epic tale becomes the object of a mythification process wherein the *secular* is transposed from the *sacred* dimension and celebrates the foundation of an ethnic, cultural, and national identity. However, the fundamental intent of *Red Cliff* is not satisfactorily captured by this interpretative model. Firstly, this pan-Asian production was made to be marketed internationally, meeting diverse audiences' entertainment needs (Lafi Youmans and Means Coleman, 2014, 232). Second, in the movie, power display seems to prevail over the epic celebration. As highlighted in Donald Clarke's review for *The Irish Times*: "the film feels like one of those military strategy [video] games which require the player to tick a dozen boxes before allowing his tiny ships to advance one square forward. For stretches of half-an-hour or more, we get little else but manoeuvres, tactics and the flinging of fireballs" (2009, n. pag.).

It is indeed rather striking to observe that the movie glorifies the battle that marked the Han army's defeat and the Chinese empire's territorial disintegration. Soon after, it was followed by the first interregnum, the Three Kingdoms (220–265), which formed the transition from the ancient empire to medieval China. The story of this event provided the basis of identity-forging writings, such as the *Romance*. One of the great classics of Chinese literature, it has entertained generations of adults and become part of the collective imagination of younger generations around the world, thanks to the adaptation of its plot into role-playing and video games and animated films. For instance, as noted by Hong Junhao (2007, 132–133), *The Battle of the Red Cliffs* videogame was also released in Taiwan, Hong Kong, and Southeast Asia, while in North America 25,000 units were sold in just three months.

In this chapter, I intend to examine the cultural contents being projected by *Red Cliff* and trace the trajectory that transformed the deeds of the Three Kingdoms into a transnational (pan-Asian) theme. I will highlight how these epic narratives support a concept that is foreign to the fascination of war and elaboration of the drama. They instead refer to a particular notion of *epos* that favours the virtues of strategy and intelligence rather than heroism and military prowess. To do this, I will introduce some observations on the specific nature of the Chinese *epos*. I will then review the process through which Red Cliffs battle becomes an identity-creating event in the "memory construction" of the Chinese empire.

The Chinese Epos

To clarify the *epos* that developed around the *Romance*, it is useful to review some "long-held" concepts throughout Chinese history that can be seen already in the literary tradition of pre-imperial China. I will begin with an observation regarding the literary genre. Although the designation of "epic" could apply to the repertory celebrating the passage from the Shang Dynasty (c. sixteenth century–1045 BCE) to the Western Zhou (1045–771 BCE), there are also aspects that render this genre attribution problematic. These writings include content tied to the warrior tradition, but this material seems to be crystallised in historiographic schema. Regarding the "rigidity" of the elaboration of epic material, Keightley states: "The Chinese narratives, when compared with the Greek, are remarkable for the lack of dramatic complexity [...] these are texts that are frequently concerned with how men should act, or how ideally, they did act" (2002, 141).

In other words, the historiographic tradition is imbued with a sort of "written power" which, starting in the second century BCE with the consolidation of Confucian orthodoxy, gained hegemony over historical material (Johnson, 1981, 270–271). At the centre of these epics are not deeds of war, but rather events connected to the legitimacy of establishing a central power. In Chinese *epos* a different conception of *heroism* from that of the Homeric tradition is at play. Namely, tales of heroism unfold in the "successful imposition of Central States culture on a previous state of disorder" (Nylan, 2001, 162). Thus, the mythological connotation is directly attached to the civilising contribution inherent to the Chinese empire.

In addition, again comparatively with Western tradition, it should be noted that, where Greek rationality is formed from its encounter with *mythos*, that of the Middle Kingdom takes on ritual, 禮 *li*, as its foundational concept (Cheng, 2000, 40). If we accept the stipulation that myth and ritual are correlated systems of meaning (Ries, 1982), then *myth* is an exemplary model of all significant activities while *ritual* is a system which, thanks to the mediation of the sovereign, creates harmony and guarantees continuity. Just as *mythos* is connected to *epos* and thus to war, *ritual* is connected to the *cult of sovereignty* and, from there, to the civic sphere.

Therefore, in ancient China, the prominence of the ritual aspect implicates the elaboration of a shared mythology. This is found in the myth of the five predynastic emperors, credited with all the major inventions and discoveries upon which was founded civilisation (water supply, millet cultivation, and writing, to give a few examples). As Cheng (2000, 28) notes, this mythology also has three emblematic heroes. The first two are King Wen and King Wu, whose posthumous names refer to cultural refinement (文, C. *wen*) and warlike power (武, C. *wu*); they embody the two opposite poles in the spectrum of public virtue, namely civic and military accomplishments. The third hero is the Duke of Zhou (the regent of King Cheng), who is the emblem of loyalty and voluntary renunciation of power.

Thus, military power is seen as the proper complement to the civil sphere (the latter is to be understood as culture and good governance). These two dimensions constitute an inseparable dyad, the *wen-wu* dichotomy, a biological and cultural construct encompassing mental and physical attainments and thus shaping a "masculinity ideal throughout Chinese history" (Louie, 2003, 4). The equilibrium between the military and cultural spheres represents the true essence of *Sunzi's Art of War* (孫子兵法, C. *Sunzi bingfa*, fourth century BCE), the famous treatise on the art of war. The virtuous man is, therefore, he who: "holds high the military sphere and nurtures the cultural sphere" (上武, 修文, C. *shang wu, xiu wen*) (Pohl, 2008, 28). In addition, whereas in Western narrative schema the hero fights evil, in the Chinese view, especially in the context of Confucian historiography, the opposing forces are the (legitimate) sovereign (王, C. *wang*) and the usurper (霸, C. *ba*) (Tillman, 2004, 85).

The *wen-wu* regulative ideal is typically performed through the containment of the self; in the military sphere, the latter is shaped into "the containment of war" (Louie, 2003, 5). Consequently, the conception itself of heroism (as inferred from literary sources) has a substantially different connotation from Western archetypes. *A hero is wise* (even more than brave), is loyal to his lord, and, above all, is willing to voluntarily relinquish power when his mission has been completed. The wise king is he who, possessing the cunning of Odysseus (see Raphals, 2018, 191ff.) and the loyalty of Hector, knows how to avoid open conflict, aware that war must first of all be waged against oneself.

The concept of courage itself is therefore charged with other meanings which are especially clear in the context of the Confucian tradition. As Scarpari notes, it is based not so much on physical presence but rather on the inner strength and security deriving from moral integrity. Courage is seen as a natural expression of sensitivity and wisdom and, consequently, "[a]n individual can possess simultaneously the qualities of *renzhe* [humanitarian spirit], *zhizhe* [superior knowledge] and *yongzhe* [courage], but *ren* [sense of humanity] is the primary virtue which must never be lacking" (Scarpari, 1991, 46; my translation).

Finally, whatever the attributes of a hero, it should be remembered that, in a culture that favours the group and not the individual, and which tends to downplay individual egocentric impulses, the ideals of competition must necessarily be of marginal worth. From the pre-imperial Chinese perspective, although common, war was considered a *calamity* (Wohlfart, 2008, 57–68) that the community must avoid at all costs through the art of good governance. In the worst case, when there was no way to overcome human folly, it was necessary to win with as little damage possible (on your side), including through the use of schemes and cunning tricks. Needless to say, what has been said so far should not give the idea that ancient China did not witness the destructive events and massacres that have characterised human history elsewhere (Sawyer, 2007, 16–17).

This concept of war is found in *Sunzi bingfa*, mentioned above. In this work, as in all highly technical texts, emphasis is not placed primarily on the ethics of an action, but rather its *efficacy* and *validity*. The centrality of an ideal that Wohlfart underscores in this passage from *Sunzi bingfa* will thus come as no surprise: "Ultimate excellence lies not in winning every battle but in defeating the enemy without ever fighting" (2008, 62). Moreover, as we will emphasise below, the story of the battle in Chinese literature is characterised by a propensity for plot twists, unexpected turns of events, and spectacular actions. It is not subject to what Hillman calls "the terrible love of war", an allusion to the union of "beauty and violence, terror and love" typical in Western culture (2004, 106). In Chinese literature, war was also separate from the concept of the Sublime, an aesthetic category not only associated with the view of the magnificence of nature, but also, in the words of Edmund Burke, the "strenuous purposes of heroism" (qtd. in Hillman, 2004, 119).

This dark, seductive force unfolds in the classic Greek epic. In the Chinese tradition, instead there is no idealised tension of battle as the ultimate sphere for self-realisation. Although the narration of history by the sages of antiquity includes struggle and duels, these are aspects connected to the fight for political power. The scenario of war is not circumscribed by the arena of Greek tragedy, as there is no tragedy, no nemesis, no catharsis.

These are, then, the essential coordinates of the Chinese *epos* needed to correctly contextualise the transformation that occurred across the various transpositions of the Red Cliffs story.

Finally, to conclude this brief excursus, an important caveat is in order. One might think that the differences between the Chinese and Western heroic ideals might also contribute to accounting for the (dis)similarities in their respective imperial formations. For instance, as instantiated by the premodern Qing territorial conquest and the nineteenth-century European colonial empires. However, as shown by Schneider in this volume, the distinctive features of the Qing empire are better understood outside of the comparison with European normative models. Moreover, even adopting such a dichotomy, a decisive difference between the two rulerships is found in the marked multicultural and multilingual traits of the Qing administration, a feature that is not immediately related to heroic ideals.

The First Accounts of the Battle

The Red Cliffs campaign was first narrated in two versions (de Crespigny, 1991, 9). The first is found in the biography of commander Zhou Yu in *juan* 54 of *Chronicles of the Three Kingdoms* (三國志, C. *Sanguozhi*), hereafter *Chronicles*, by Chen Shou (陳壽, 233–297) with commentary by Pei Songzhi (裴松之, 372–451), who cites third-century sources. The second version was narrated as part of *juan* 65 of the *Comprehensive Mirror for Aid in Government* (資治通鑒, C. *Zizhi tongjian*) by Sima Guang (司馬光, 1019–1086), a monumental account of Chinese history from 403 BCE to 959 CE (for a detailed analysis of the events, see de Crespigny, 1991, 9 n. 24; de Crespigny, 2018, 254–260).

The core of the story, as gleaned from the English version by de Crespigny (2018, 205ff.) of *Zizhi tongjian*, is as follows. The army coming from the north, unprepared for the unhealthy swamp environment and fatigued from the long campaign, arrive at Red Cliffs and make camp on the north-west bank of the river. On the other side, their enemies do not dare to attack. This impasse is broken thanks to the initiative of a subordinate of Zhou Yu, Huang Gai, who sends a message to Cao Cao in which he asks permission to surrender (given troop morale on both sides, this would not seem suspicious) and, in exchange, to provide supplies to his army. Huang Gai prepares ten warships on which are stowed grease-soaked reeds and faggots wrapped in red cloth bearing the dragon standards. He ties a boat with oars to the stern and, once in the middle of the river, he lights a fire and retreats with his men leading his boats while the wind does the rest, pushing the fiery cluster into the enemy fleet.

The battle's description is further enlarged upon in the section generally referred to as "the gathering of heroes" (群英會, C. *Qunying hui*), which comprises chapters 43–50 of the *Romance.* It is precisely thanks to its inclusion in a literary form that this battle (in reality, a herald of the first split in the Celestial Empire), asserted itself as the founding event of historical Chinese identity. At first glance, this might seem bizarre given that there is no unequivocal schema on the basis of which an act of war becomes key in "creating a nation" (see Ranger and Hobsbawm, 1993; Renan, 2018). The trigger could be an episode that marks the attainment of national unity or the halting of the advance of an external threat. But it could also be a major defeat which, in the minds of a people, had the effect of celebrating the spirit of resistance to annihilation (as in the case of the battle for Kosovo). As we will see in the following two sections, this event first became an identity-defining symbol in parallel with the change in perspective that occurred between the *Chronicles* and the *Romance.* With the establishment of the Qing dynasty in 1644 and its translation into Manchu, the *Romance* started its journey to a transnational dimension as will be outlined below, relying on the accounts by Choe (2012) and Gimm (2013). The historical context of an "intrastate battle" marking the collapse of the empire thus offered a powerful catalyst for the Battle of Red Cliffs to be included in the "transnational past" shared by East and Southeast Asian traditions.

From Song Historical Fiction to the Ming Romance on the Loyal and the Worthy

The shift from annalistic accounts to fictional literature has been reconstructed by McLaren (2006), based on a detailed survey of the historiographic sources starting with the Southern Song Dynasty (1127–1279). In a period in which the northern territories were dominated by the Tangut Xia (1038–1227) and the Khitan Liao (916–1125) who, like the Song themselves, claimed to be the true heirs of the Tang (Tillman, 2004, 88), the theme of the struggle of succession narrated in the *Three Kingdoms* was crucially relevant. It thus triggered the debate around the criteria for legitimising imperial power according to the ideal of "proper succession" (正通, C. *zheng tong*). The question then was whether the ability to control territory should be preferred to the contenders' moral virtues (or even to birthright); in the private historical works of the Song, in contrast to the previous historiography, Cao Cao was thus depicted as an evil *usurper* and Liu Bei as a sort of knightly hero and wise Confucian *sovereign* (McLaren, 2006, 309). The deeds of the protagonists were also embedded in a causal chain of events, thus creating a new genre of *historical fiction* called *yanyi* (演義), i.e. "exposition of the meaning" of the story's events (McLaren, 2006, 293).

A Transnational Cultural Past Starting from the Manchu Translation

As highlighted by Choe, Chinese fictional literature played a significant role in the cultural life of the Jurchens in the Later Jin (1616–1636): Nurhaci (努爾哈赤, C. *Nu'erhachi*, 1559–1626) was especially fond of the *Romance* and in 1639 his successor Hong Taiji (or 皇太極, C. *Huang Taiji*, 1592–1643) commissioned the translation of Chinese novels into Manchu, to use them as guides for administration (Choe, 2012, 96ff.). Not only is the translation of the *Romance* considered "one of the most important works in the Sinicization of the Manchus" (Gimm, 2013, 111), it also contributed to the transcultural and multi-ethnic characterisation of Jurchen rule described by Schneider in Chapter 5.

Based on a Ming edition from the Jiajing period (1522–1566) and commonly referred to by the title *Ilan gurun-i bithe*, the Manchu version of the *Romance* was published in 1650, soon after the conquest of Beijing, under the patronage of the prince regent Dorgon (多爾袞, C. *Duo'ergun*, 1612–1650). In parallel to the conquest of Tibet, Xinjiang, and Inner Mongolia, which doubled the territory of China proper, and due to effective Manchu management of multilingualism (Shih, 2011, 712), the *Ilan gurun-i bithe* was also translated into Tibetan, Sibe, and Mongolian (West, 2005).

Finally, in 1703, a trilingual translation, commonly referred to as "the Joseon translation", was published, including the Manchu source text, its Hangŭl transcription, and a Korean vernacular translation (Choe, 2012, 97). This text was one of the textbooks used by Koreans to study Manchu (Gimm, 2013, 112) and played a crucial role in the propagation of the *epos* of the Three Kingdoms in Korea, which in turn, in the early twentieth, contributed significantly in mobilising national consciousness.

As highlighted by Hashimoto (2014, 66ff.), the shared memory stemming from the *Romance* provided the framework for the reception and reconceptualisation of the idea of nation building coming from the West, in a period constellated by the publication of "historical and creative writings on 'the hero'" (英雄, C. *yingxiong*, J. *eiyū*, K. *yŏng'ung*), figures such as Oliver Cromwell (1599–1658) and George Washington (1732–1799). Along these lines, the Italian Risorgimento became a source of inspiration, promoting the idea of "nation building" (建国, C. *jianguo*, J. *kenkoku*, K. *kŏn'guk*), which entered the Korean intellectual as a result of a "mediated translation" conducted through the lens of the shared East Asian tradition of heroism.

The process began in Japan with Hirata Hisashi's (平田久, 1872–1923) *The Three Italian Nation-Building Heroes* (伊太利建国三傑, J. *Itarī kenkoku sanketsu*, 1892); the latter was creatively rewritten by referring to the classic antecedents in Chinese literature by Liang Qichao (梁啟超, 1873–1929) (意大利建國三傑傳, C. *Yidali jianguo san jie zhuan*, 1902–1907). Finally, it was translated into four different Korean versions of which the most influential is Sin Ch'aeho's (1880–1936) 이태리건국삼걸전 (K. *Yit'aeri kŏn'guk samgŏl chŏn*, 1907) (Hashimoto, 2014).

To illuminate the essence of this multilayered adaptation, Hashimoto provides the quotation below from a Korean reviewer of Sin Ch'aeho's translation, wherein the nation-building heroes are paralleled to the *Romance* hero Zhuge Liang:

> The saying goes: "If you do not shed tears after reading the 'Memorial on Sortie' [出師表, K. *Ch'ul sa p'yo*, attributed to Zhuge Liang], you are surely not a loyal subject [...]." So I would say if your blood does not get boiled or your crying does not become loud after reading the *Biographies of the Three Italian Heroes*, you are a wood- or stone-like man. If each of our ambitious people keeps a copy of the *Biography* at his side, and worships it in the morning and dreams about it in the night, there will be a day when he will undertake a patriotic endeavor. (2014, 67–68)

In the following two decades, the literature celebrating heroism, including the heroes of the *Romance*, experienced a surge in popularity: from 1929 to 1931, the *Samguk yŏnŭi* (三國演義) was published in the *Mail sinbo* (每日申報, 1910–1945, Jeong 2014). Just five years later, during the Sino-Japanese War, the *Romance* was revived in the Japanese popularised versions by Yoshikawa Eiji (吉川英治, 1892–1962), the *Sangokushi* (三国志). In the area of its circulation, from the Qing period the *Romance* became part of a transnational literary tradition, which is particularly strong in Vietnam, Korea, and Japan, whose literary traditions are "deeply interrelated through the cultural capital of classical Chinese writing" (Hashimoto, 2014, 131). Importantly, the themes of dynasty legitimation and nation building, within the framework of the "intranational" war among three pretenders to the Chinese throne, became transnationally relevant in the discursive construction of cultural modernity in Asia.

Now we can briefly trace the essential traits of the paradigmatic hero of this shared transnational tradition, as narrated in the Battle of the Red Cliffs section of the *Romance* and as personified in the figure of Zhuge Liang.

The Hero of The Romance of the Three Kingdoms

In the transition from the *Chronicles* to the *Romance*, the narration takes on new elements. The revisionist Song historians declare the need to restore balance between the civil and military spheres; this aspect was also significant in the new characterisation of the individuals involved, in particular

Zhuge Liang (諸葛亮, 181–234, courtesy name Kongming 孔明), diplomat and strategist in the service of Liu Bei, who embodied the ideal of the "general and Confucian sage" as a sort of compensation for the military weakness that characterised China in that era of anxiety and insecure frontiers (Tillman, 2004, 89).

The figure of Zhuge Liang is placed at the centre of the plot as opposed to the Sun clan. He is the hero of the romance, and yet his heroism is not only that of a warrior. His human capabilities and talents are also extolled, and these are even more efficacious when combined with the accidentality of nature. At the centre of the story are two warlords, Zhuge and Zhou Yu, who, although less powerful than their adversary, win the decisive battle thanks to their cunning use of their knowledge of nature (as in the episode of "borrowing the arrows from the enemy" described in the following section).

In the early Ming period (1368–1644), at the dawn of the new Chinese territorial unity, in the rewriting of the past and building of identity, use was made of a paradigm that Ma (1975, 279) defined the "dynasty-building theme", in which the narration is centred on the struggle for reunification of the nation and the creation of a new order.

A trait in the portrayal of Zhuge common to both the *Chronicles* and the *Romance* is his extreme loyalty to his lord who, on his death bed, will entrust his kingdom to him because of the failings of his own son, an aspect that evokes the model of the Duke of Zhou (see Section "The Chinese *Epos*" above). A parallel with the heroes of predynastic tradition is developed in the ensuing tradition by crediting Zhuge with a number of inventions, such as a transport device (木牛流马, C. *muniuliuma*), the semi-automatic crossbow, and even *mantou* (a common recipe for filled steamed bread). Moreover, over the following centuries, Zhuge Liang was canonised as an actual god of war. Shrines dedicated to Zhuge Liang are also found outside of China, such as the Waryongmyo shrine in Seoul.

Heroic Intelligence at the Red Cliffs

As noted in the account of the battle, the victory of Red Cliffs was the result of knowledge of the elements of nature. Fire became a formidable weapon thanks to the wind which, unexpectedly on that day, was blowing towards the river rather than the mountains. Similarly, Zhuge obtained one of his most impressive successes thanks to his ability to correctly foresee the movement of the sky, as exemplified in the exploits recounted in the first half of chapter 46 of the *Romance*. This section is often identified as "Borrowing arrows with straw boats" (草船借箭, C. *Cao chuan jie jian*), a proverb (like many others taken from the story) which means "using wisdom to take advantage of the power and resources of your adversary".

To clarify the meaning of this expression, it is useful to describe the crucial passages of the episode described in the *Romance*. The field commander Zhou Yu, jealous of Zhuge's valour, sets a trap for him. He summons him in the presence of the other soldiers and asks him what might be the best weapon for winning a naval battle. As the commander expected, his aide suggests the use of arrows. Zhou Yu, certain of the impossibility of this mission, orders Zhuge to obtain 100,000 within ten days. Zhuge requests just three and offers this own life if the plan fails. During the first two days, he is completely relaxed and seems unperturbed about his promise, which worries his superiors. Only on the third day does he ask for 20 boats full of straw bundles lined with black cloth. In addition, he asks that a few men be placed on each boat. Towards evening, when the fog descends along the banks of the river, the small fleet is brought in front of the enemy camp. Zhuge commands his men to shout and beat drums. Visibility is very poor and the enemy general, Cao Cao, does exactly what Zhuge expected: he commands his archers to attack the boats. The hero waits until the enemies have shot a sufficient number of arrows and then has his "armada" retreat while Cao Cao, now realising the trick, watches helplessly from the shore.

Not only is Zhuge portrayed here as a Daoist "artist of war", consistent with the idea espoused by Wohlfart (2008, 62–63); more importantly, he would not have succeeded in "borrowing the arrows from the enemy" if the fog had not been foreseen. And wherein lies this propitious intuition? Zhuge, himself, responds to Zhou Yu's advisor, Lu Su:

> 為將而不通天文, 不識地利, 不知奇門, 不曉陰陽, 不看陣圖, 不明兵勢是庸才也。亮於三日前已算定今日有大霧, 因此敢任三日之限。公謹教我十日完辦, 工匠料物, 都不應手, 將這一件風流罪過, 明白要殺我。我命係於天, 公謹焉能害我哉! (*Sanguo yanyi*, 1990, 398)

> A military commander is a mediocrity [...] unless he is versed in the patterns of the heavens, recognizes the advantages of the terrain, knows the interaction of prognostic signs, understands the changes in weather, examines the maps of deployment, and is clear about the balance of forces. Three days ago I calculated today's fog. That's why I took a chance on the three-day limit. Zhou Yu gave me ten days to finish the job, but neither materials nor workmen. He plainly meant to kill me for laxity. But my fate is linked to Heaven. How could Zhou Yu have ucceeded? (Roberts, 2020, 225–226)

A man of action cannot limit himself to knowing military tactics; he must also be able to interpret "heavenly matters" (天文, C. *tian wen*). Specifically, the talents cited by this strategist refer to intelligence and observation. He must "understand" (通, C. *tong*), "be aware" (識, C. *shi*), "know" (知, C. *shi*), "be informed" (曉, C. *xiao*), "observe" (看, C. *kan*), and "have clearly in mind" (明, C. *ming*).

Military success is the epiphenomenon of a set of cognitive actions, from observation to awareness, which are then brought into effect in the battlefield. Talent, intuition, and cunning are at the centre of Zhuge's heroism. But such talent is never used at the expense of loyalty to the throne, as shown by his willingness to give up his own life in the event of failure, because "[t]here is no room for levity in the army" (軍中無戲言, C. *junzhong wu xiyan*) (Roberts, 2020, 222), as the field commander Zhou Yu chastises Zhuge when he declares—almost pompously—that he will be able to accomplish his mission in just three days.

Conclusion

Throughout this excursus, I have tried to briefly reconstruct the trajectory and the themes which allowed the Battle of the Red Cliffs to be projected in the collective memory of East Asia. I focused on the specific portrayal of heroism conveyed by the *Romance* and highlighted the themes that are related to the transcultural elements of Confucianism and Daoism.

Firstly, central to the scene is the battle between good and evil, represented in the paradigm of the conflict between the sovereign (*wang)* and the usurper (*ba*); thus, the antagonists of this saga are seen as different incarnations of the criteria for Confucian legitimacy. Secondly, the ideal of heroism, concentrated in the figure of Zhuge Liang, embodies the Confucian virtues of loyalty and self-sacrifice (modelled on the Duke of Zhou), wisdom, and inventive genius (as for the Confucian kings), united with the efficacy and levity of the Daoist-model artist of war. The figure of Zhuge Liang is the perfect synthesis of cultural refinement (*wen*) and military prowess (*wu*). The talents most emphasised are intelligence and observation of the natural world, that is, the origin of the strategist's providential intuition that ensures success at the Battle of the Red Cliffs. And yet, above and beyond individual worth, the value of alliance with the group and its cohesion remains pre-eminent.

Finally, as shown by focusing on the case of Korea and following Hashimoto's (2014) interpretative model, the transnational theme of the heroic quest for legitimacy was involved in the formation of national identities, mobilising commitment across Far East Asia. In this regard, a powerful catalyst was the glorification of the "loyal subject" (臣子, C. *Chenzi*, J. *Shinshi*,

K. *Sinjia*). In the *Romance*, such a hero offers his life to protect the legitimate king in the face of imminent disaster; in the modern context, he instead strives to build the nation after a historical and prolonged humiliation. These elements, combined with other sources of inspiration from the transnational literature, resonated powerfully to revive civic engagement in the first decades of the nineteenth century.

References and Further Reading

Primary Sources

Ames, Roger T., and D. C. Lau (trans.). 1996. *Sun Pin: The Art of Warfare*. New York: Random House/Ballantine.

De Crespigny, Rafe (trans.). 1969. *The Last of the Han: Being the Chronicle of the Years 181–220 AD as Recorded in Chapters 58–68 of the Tzu-chih t'ung-chien of Ssu-ma Kuang*. Canberra: Australian National University, Centre of Oriental Studies.

Nylan, Michael (trans.). 2020. *The Art of War: Sun Tzu*. New York: W. W. Norton.

Roberts, Moss (trans.). 2020. *Three Kingdoms, A Historical Novel*. Berkeley: University of California Press.

Sanguo yanyi (三國演義) [The Romance of the Three Kingdoms]. 1990. 羅貫中 (Luo Guanzhong) (attributed). 2 vols. Beijing: Renmin wenxue chuban.

Sanguo zhi (三國志) [Chronicles of the Three Kingdoms]. 2018. 羅開玉 (Kaiyu Lou). Shanghai: Shanghai guji chubanshe.

Sunzi bingfa (孫子兵法) [The Art of War of Master Sun]. 2011. 孫子 (Sunzi). Changsha: Hunan renmin chubanshe.

Zizhi tongjian (資治通鑒) [The Comprehensive Mirror for Aid in Government]. 2019. 司馬光 (Sima Guang). Ha'erbin: Beifang wenyi chubanshe.

Secondary Sources

Bergman, Barry. 2008. "Games Aside, the Real Olympic Challenge Is Engaging with China". *UC Berkeley News*, 8 May. https://www.berkeley.edu/news/berkeleyan/2008/05/08_chinasymposium.shtml [accessed 16 July 2022].

Casarini, Nicola. 2008. "Tra mercato e valori". *Affari Internazionali*, 28 March. https://www.affarinternazionali.it/archivio-affarinternazionali/2008/03/tra-mercato-e-valori/ [accessed 16 July 2022].

Cheng, Anne. 2000. *Storia del pensiero cinese*, Vol. 1, translated and edited by Amina Crisma. Turin: Einaudi [original ed.: *Histoire de la pensée chinoise*. Paris: Seuil, 1997].

Choe, Yongchul. 2012. "Manchu Studies in Korea". *Journal of Cultural Interaction in East Asia* 3: 89–101.

Clarke, Donald. 2009. "Red Cliff/Chi Bi". *Irish Times*, 12 June. https://www.irishtimes.com/culture/red-cliff-chi-bi-1.782908 [accessed 16 July 2022].

De Crespigny, Rafe. 1991. "The Three Kingdoms and Western Jin: A History of China in the Third Century AD". *East Asian History* 2: 143–165.

——. 2009. "The Military Culture of Later Han". In *Military Culture in Imperial China*, edited by Nicola di Cosmo, 90–111. Cambridge, MA: Harvard University Press.

——. 2018. *Generals of the South: The Foundation and Early History of the Three Kingdoms State of Wu*. Internet publication, CreativeCommons.

Gimm, Martin. 2013. "The Manchu Translations of Chinese Novels and Short Stories: An Attempt at an Inventory". In *Literary Migrations: Traditional Chinese Fiction in Asia (17th–20th Centuries)*, edited by Claudine Salmon, 93–126. Singapore: Institute of Southeast Asian Studies.

Hashimoto, Satoru. 2014. "Afterlives of the Culture: Engaging with the Trans-East Asian Cultural Tradition in Modern Chinese, Japanese, Korean, and Taiwanese Literatures, 1880s–1940s". Doctoral dissertation, Harvard University.

Hillman, James. 2004. *A Terrible Love of War*. New York: Penguin.

Hong, Junhao. 2007. "From Three Kingdoms the Novel to Three Kingdoms the Television Series: Gains, Losses, and Implications". In *Three Kingdoms and Chinese Culture*, edited by Kimberly Besio and Constantine Tung, 125–141. Albany: State University of New York Press.

Hu, Jubin. 2003. *Projecting A Nation: Chinese National Cinema before 1949*. Hong Kong: Hong Kong University.

Jeong Seonkyung. 2014. "'Maeilsinbo'e beonyeogdoen 'Samgug'yeon'ui'e daehan gochal" (《每日申報》에번역된《三國演義》에대한고찰) [A Study on the Translation of *Romance of the Three Kingdoms* Published Serially in *Mailshinbo*]. *Jung'gug eo'mun hagji* [Chinese Literature Journal] 43: 121–151.

Johnson, David. 1981. "Epic and History in Early China: The Matter of Wu Tzu-hsü". *The Journal of Asian Studies* 40 (2): 255–271.

Keightley, David N. 2002. "Epistemology in Cultural Context: Disguise and Deception in Early China and Early Greece". In *Early China/Ancient Greece: Thinking through Comparisons*, edited by Steven Shankman and Stephen W. Durrant, 114–154. New York: State University of New York Press.

Lafi Youmans, William, and Robin Means Coleman. 2014. "Global Media, Global Cultures: How Do Culture and Globalization Influence Each Other?" In *Intercultural Communication for Everyday Life*, edited by John R. Baldwin, Robin R. Means Coleman, Alberto González, and Suchitra Shenoy-Packer, 227–248. Hoboken: John Wiley & Sons.

Louie, Kam 2003. "Chinese, Japanese and Global Masculine Identities". In *Asian Masculinities: The Meaning and Practice of Manhood in China and Japan*, edited by Kam Louie and Morris Low, 1–17. London: Routledge Curzon.

Ma, Yau-woon [Youyuan]. 1975. "The Chinese Historical Novel: An Outline of Themes and Contexts". *Journal of Asian Studies* 34 (2): 277–294.

McLaren, Anne E. 2006. "History Repackaged in the Age of Print: The *Sanguozhi* and *Sanguo yanyi*". *Bulletin of the School of Oriental and African Studies* 69 (2): 293–313.

Nylan, Michael. 2001. *The Five "Confucian" Classics.* New Haven and London: Yale Press University.

Pohl, Karl-Heinz. 2008. "Kung-fu: Musings on the Philosophical Background of Chinese Martial Arts". In *Philosophieren über den Krieg. War in Eastern and Western Philosophies,* edited by Hans-Georg Moeller and Günter Wohlfart, 17–32. Berlin: Parerga.

Ranger, Terence, and Eric Hobsbawm (eds.). 1993. *The Invention of Tradition.* Cambridge: Cambridge University Press.

Raphals, Lisa. 2018. *Knowing Words: Wisdom and Cunning in the Classical Traditions of China and Greece.* Ithaca and London: Cornell University Press.

Renan, Ernest. 2018. *What Is a Nation? and Other Political Writings,* translated and edited by M. F. N. Giglioli. New York and Chichester: Columbia University Press.

Ries, Julien. 1982. *Le mythe et sa signification: Bible, ethnologie, sociologie, psychanalyse, structuralisme, religion.* Louvain-la-Neuve: Centre d'Histoire des Religions.

Sawyer, Ralph D. 2007. "Chinese Strategic Power: Myths, Intent, and Projections". *Journal of Military and Strategic Studies* 9 (2): 1–64.

Scarpari, Maurizio. 1991. *La concezione della natura umana in Confucio e Mencio.* Venice: Editrice Cafoscarina.

Shih, Shu-Mei. 2011. "The Concept of the Sinophone." *PMLA* 126 (3): 709–18.

Sparvoli, Carlotta. 2010. "La battaglia della Roccia Rossa. Da cronaca a evento identitario". *La Torre di Babele* 6: 99–112.

Tillman, Hoyt Cleveland. 2004. "Textual Liberties and Restraints in Rewriting China's Histories: The Case of Ssu-ma Kuang's Reconstruction of Chu-ko Liang's Story". In *The New and the Multiple: Sung Senses of the Past,* edited by Thomas C. Lee, 61–106. Hong Kong: The Chinese University of Hong Kong.

West, Andrew. 2005. *The Textual History of Sanguo Yanyi: The Manchu Translation.* http://www.babelstone.co.uk/SanguoYanyi/TextualHistory/Manchu.html [accessed 7 April 2021].

Wohlfart, Günter. 2008. "Eternal Peace–Eternal War, Some Remarks on Kant and Sunzi". In *Philosophieren über den Krieg. War in Eastern and Western Philosophies,* edited by Hans-Georg Moeller and Günter Wohlfart, 57–68. Berlin: Parerga.

Xiao, Zhiwei, Zhang Yingjin, and Zhang Yingjin. 1999. *Encyclopedia of Chinese Film.* London and New York: Routledge.

Xinhua News. 2008. "Most Expensive Asian Film, 'Red Cliff', Set to Be Red Hot at Box Office". 10 July.

4

Translation beyond the Written Word

Imagining the Transnational Spread of *The Journey to the West* in East Asia

Barbara Wall

Introduction

The Journey to the West is one of the most popular story worlds in East Asia. One of the most widely referenced versions of *The Journey* comes from a Chinese novel, *Xiyou ji* written at the end of the sixteenth century. It tells the story of the Monkey King, Sun Wukong, who protects the Buddhist monk Tripitaka during his odyssey from China to the Western Heaven in search of the real Buddhist scriptures. Tripitaka is modelled after Xuanzang (c. 602–664), probably the most famous among the Chinese monks who travelled to India "in search of the dharma". The story world of *The Journey* owes its popularity in large part to the countless versions that exist from various times, cultures, and media. One of the most popular versions today might be the Japanese manga *Dragonball*. The Monkey King also appears as Wukong in the popular video game *Fortnite*, and the Japanese TV adaptation *Monkey* from the 1970s not only reached cult status in the UK and Australia but was also broadcast in South America. In this study we imagine that all these different versions of *The Journey* together, regardless of temporal, spatial, or medial differences, form a pool which I call the "story world of *The Journey*".

Many scholars believe that the transnational circulation of a story like *The Journey* starts with the written translation of the "original". Sŏ Hyeŭn (2015), for example, argues that *The Journey* was first translated into Korean before it could spread in Korea in the form of various adaptations. This chapter questions this assumption and imagines the transnational spread of *The Journey* beyond written translations. I do not want to deny the importance of written translations, but I argue that especially in the case of *The Journey* visual translations played a significant role in the transnational spread of the story world. As we will see below, visual translations sometimes even preceded written ones.

This chapter explores the transnational spread of *The Journey* in East Asia by focusing on its circulation in Korea. One of the aims of this study is to free *The Journey* from the narrow spatiotemporal frame according to which it is often reduced to a Chinese novel written at the end of the sixteenth century. Therefore, I consciously refer to the story as *The Journey* and avoid using transcriptions of the title (C. *Xiyou ji*, J. *Saiyūki*, Viet. *Tây du ký*, K. *Sŏyugi*). I intentionally use the abbreviated English title *The Journey* to emphasise that the story persists without regard to the boundaries of periodisation and national literatures. By exploring visual versions from outside of China dating across several centuries, I hope to emphasise not only the transnationality, but also the transtemporality and transmediality of *The Journey.* Although an investigation of all variations of *The Journey* around the world would be an interesting project, the time and resources required for such a project are prohibitive. Here, I will focus exclusively on visual Korean versions of *The Journey.*

Studies of *The Journey* in Korea tend to rely on the old categories from reception studies, which portray Korea as the "receiver" in a rather passive way and emphasise the sixteenth-century novel as the "original" of *The Journey.* Accordingly, Korean versions have tended to be evaluated as confirmation of the extraordinary accomplishments of the alleged original. Major studies of the reception of *The Journey* in Korea include whole books, chapters, and articles by Yi Chaesu (1969), Chŏng Kyubok (1972), Yi Sangik (1992), Isobe Akira (1995), Min Kwandong (2006), Song Chŏnghwa (2010), and Sŏ Hyeŭn (2015). My own research here has benefited greatly from these studies and would not have been possible without them. However, they all focus on written translations or references and regard the Chinese novel from the sixteenth century as the "original" of *The Journey.* I focus on three visual translations and argue that *The Journey* was already circulating in Korea long before the sixteenth century.

Specifically, I analyse relief images on the pagoda of the Kyŏngch'ŏn Temple from the fourteenth century, wall paintings in the Maitreya Hall of T'ongdo Temple from the eighteenth century, and the TV animation *Narara syup'ŏbodŭ*, or *Fly Superboard*, from the 1990s. I chose these three examples that all translate *The Journey* visually because they stem from different centuries, use different media, and transfer *The Journey* into different "webs of meaning". This diversity lends itself to an exploration of the general features of visual translations. What do the three visual translations of *The Journey* have in common despite their diversity? How does their visuality influence the translation process?

I will first provide a short introduction to the story world of *The Journey*, before moving on to the theoretical concept of visual translation and consider how it can be applied as a methodological tool to examine the three visual translations. Finally, the analysis of the three translations will help us better understand how visual translation has contributed to the transnational spread of *The Journey*.

The Story World of *The Journey*

There are multiple versions of the story world of *The Journey*. The first published variation in English is Arthur Waley's *Monkey* (1961 [1942]). A more recent and more comprehensive edition, in four volumes, is Anthony Yu's *The Journey to the West* (2012), which relies on the first standard modern critical Chinese edition published by Bejing's Zuojia chubanshe (作家出版社). The fact that this Chinese edition is again based on more than six different Chinese versions of *The Journey* tells us a lot about the dynamics in the story world. Yu's text is generally considered a translation, but how does one "translate" a story if you have not one specific source text but must deal with a patchwork of several sources? We will come back to this question in the next section. Let us now first see how Anthony Yu tells *The Journey*.

The prologue starts with Sun Wukong's miraculous birth from a stone, describes his career as the Monkey King at Flower-Fruit Mountain, and tells how Patriarch Subhūti teaches him about his supernatural abilities. He defeats every antagonist with the help of his miraculous weapon, the Compliant Rod. Sun Wukong's battle culminates in his fight against all heavenly authorities. When even the Jade Emperor, who reigns in Heaven, sees no way to defeat him, Buddha comes to help and makes a bet with Sun Wukong. He promises to yield to him if the monkey manages to jump out of his palm. Sun Wukong fails and is imprisoned beneath the Five-Phases Mountain for the next 500 years.

In the meantime, Bodhisattva Guanyin begins to search for a pilgrim who can find the real Buddhist scriptures in the West, and he settles on the monk Tripitaka. Taizong, an emperor of Tang China who has just come back from the Underworld, organises a Grand Mass for the chosen monk. Tripitaka can free Sun Wukong from the Five-Phases Mountain, and he offers to do so on the condition that Sun Wukong accompanies and protects him on his journey to the West. The monk controls the monkey by means of a cap that Sun Wukong wears on his head that hurts him whenever he is disobedient. After he encounters and accepts three other disciples, Zhu Bajie, Sha Wujing, and a horse, Tripitaka's odyssey begins. The pilgrims have multiple adventures and finally obtain the Buddhist scriptures.

1: Havoc in Heaven	20: Mountain of Flames
2: Search for Scripture Pilgrim	21: Golden Light Monastery
3: Tripitaka's Childhood	22: Poetry at Brimble Ridge
4: Taizong in Underworld	23: Small Thunderclap
5: Grand Mass	24: Tuluo Village
6: Recruitment of Disciples	25: Scarlet-Purple Kingdom
7: Widow and Three Daughters	26: Cobweb Cave
8: Ginseng	27: Lion-Camel Mountain
9: White-Bone Lady	28: Bhiksu Kingdom
10: Scarlet Purple Kingdom	29: Bottomless Cave
11: Silver Horn and Golden Horn	30: Dharma Destroying Kingdom
12: Black Rooster Country	31: Phoenix-Immortal Prefecture
13: Red Boy	32: Jade-Flower District
14: Dragon King in Black River	33: Gold-Level Prefecture
15: Cart Slow Country	34: Kingdom of India
16: Heaven-Reaching River	35: Squire Kou
17: Great King One-Horn	36: Obtaining the Scriptures
18: Women State	37: Last Ordeal
19: Two Sun Wukongs	38: Return to the East

Fig. 1. Episodes associated with the story world of *The Journey.*

The prologue and acquisition of the Buddhist scriptures at the end serve as a frame, which is filled with multiple episodes. Fig. 1 presents a list of 38 episodes that are associated with *The Journey*. Here, they are listed in the order in which they appear in Yu's translation, but it is important to note that not every version of *The Journey* includes all 38 episodes and not every version tells them in the same order as Yu does in his translation. How is it possible to leave out whole episodes or tell them in a different order? The episodes tend to repeat a similar pattern and thus are somewhat interchangeable: 1. the pilgrims encounter an obstacle (often a monster) → 2. Sun Wukong contrives a plan to overcome it → 3. The obstacle is overcome → 4. The pilgrims happily continue their journey.

This simple repetitive pattern of the episodes makes it easy to leave out whole episodes, to choose among them, and to change the order. Xie Minghun therefore suggests understanding each episode as a “separate unit” (單元, C. *danyuan*) (Xie, 2013, 203) that authors can rearrange as they like. If we think of each episode of *The Journey* as a bead and each version of *The Journey* as a bead necklace, it is up to the authors which beads they select, and in which order they string the beads. Authors may choose to string 38 episodes, others may prefer a shorter necklace and only choose eight episodes, or even fewer. We will now explore how the authors of the three visual translations string the beads, which means we will follow Xie’s suggestion and focus especially on the translation of episodes as separate units.

Visual Translation: Transcoding beyond the Written Word

Translations are traditionally considered to be closer to the original than references, allusions, adaptations, or parodies. As Linda Hutcheon points out, according to most traditional schemes, the criteria of translation are faithfulness and equivalence to the source text (Hutcheon and O’Flynn, 2013, 16), while the primary criterion of adaptation is usually the creativity with which it is adapted to a new context. As Susan Bassnett emphasises in the preface to the fourth edition of *Translation Studies*, though, recent translation theory tends to understand translation as “transcoding”. According to Marion Eggert, transcoding can be compared to the concept of “cultural translation”, referring to the “transfer of ideas, practices, larger or smaller units of interrelated signs, from one cultural context into another” (Eggert, 2020, 6). Based on this approach, the lines between translation and adaptation necessarily become blurred.

In this study we will apply Eggert’s concept of transcoding to explore the dynamics in the story world of *The Journey*. While traditional concepts of translation (lat. *trans* = “across” + lat. *latus* = “side”) suggests that we are transferring an object from one side to another, usually in written form, the concept of transcoding emphasises that the transfer does not necessarily have to take place between two “sides” but can also involve multiple “different webs of meaning” (Eggert, 2020, 10). The three visual translations in this study fit very well into this concept of transcoding, since they do not rely on any one specific original text of *The Journey* that they transfer from one side to another. They rely rather on a patchwork of diverse sources or on “different webs of meaning” in the form of multiple versions of *The Journey*.

The concept of transcoding helps us better understand what happens to objects when they are transferred into new contexts, be it in written, visual, or auditory form. While traditional translation studies tend to compare the original or “source text” to the translation or “target text” to evaluate how faithfully the latter has transferred the original, transcoding studies pay more attention to the transformation of the objects that are transferred into new contexts or new webs of meaning. Transcoding studies therefore make it possible to illuminate the dynamics of translation without the pressure to specify an original. What happens to the objects when they enter a new web of meaning? How do they change their form? How does the visual nature of a translation impact the transfer? And what happens to the contexts?

We will now examine closely the three visual translations to explore how they transfer various elements of *The Journey*. We will not compare them to any alleged original but will rather focus on how *The Journey* became a visual part of a pagoda, a temple wall painting, and an animation. We will especially pay attention to how episodes of *The Journey* are transcoded. Which elements of the episodes are transcoded? Which "beads" or episodes do the authors of the three visual translations choose, and how do they string them to create a new "necklace" or a new version of *The Journey*?

The Journey in Reliefs

The oldest Korean variation of *The Journey* appears in the form of reliefs on the ten-storey stone pagoda of the Kyŏngch'ŏn Temple (1348), which is now preserved in the National Museum of Korea in Seoul. The pagoda is 13.5 m tall and was originally built in Kaep'ung near Kaesŏng, which now belongs to North Korea. After Korea became a Japanese protectorate in 1905, the Japanese occupiers realised the worth of the pagoda, disassembled it, and smuggled it to Japan. After continuous international criticism, the pagoda finally returned to Korea in 1918 and was kept from this time on in the southern peninsula. The pagoda references 18 of the 38 episodes of *The Journey* (see Fig. 1) on 22 relief panels. Since the pagoda was built more than 200 years before the alleged original was written in the sixteenth century, none of the traditional studies on the "reception" of *The Journey* in Korea has mentioned it. This visual translation precedes any written translation in Korea.

The ten storeys of the pagoda depict various Buddhist symbols and narratives derived from Buddhist scriptures. Most of them do not allude to *The Journey*, but 20 panels on the second storey and two panels on the third of the stylobate do. Fig. 2 gives an impression of the height of the pagoda, which suggests that the second and third storeys are at eye level and therefore exactly the part that visitors notice first. It is significant, then, that this key position on the pagoda features not scenes from Buddhist scriptures, but rather a variation of *The Journey*. Some of the panels are easy to decipher, while others are so damaged that identifying the figures and symbols requires guesswork. Luckily, we also have the reliefs of the ten-storey stone pagoda of the Wŏngak Temple, which was built in 1467 as a direct copy of the pagoda of the Kyŏngch'ŏn Temple. The reliefs of the Wŏngak Temple are better preserved and can thus help us to

Fig. 2. The ten-storey pagoda of Kyŏngch'ŏn Temple at the National Museum of Korea (Kaesŏng Kyŏngch'ŏnsa t'ŏ sipch'ŭngsŏkt'ap).

decipher the damaged parts of the earlier pagoda. The Wŏngak Temple pagoda is located in T'apkol Park ("Pagoda Park") in downtown Seoul.

The Korean National Research Institute of Cultural Heritage (Kungnip munhwajae yŏn'guso) and the Cultural Heritage Administration (Munhwajae kwalliguk) provide detailed surveys of both pagodas, including rubbings of the panels. Furthermore, Sin Soyŏn, curator at the National Museum of Korea where the pagoda of the Kyŏngch'ŏn Temple is now preserved, has begun a debate with Xie Minghun and Yŏm Chungsŏp via several scholarly articles; their scholarship focuses on which episodes of *The Journey* we can decipher on the pagodas and how we can read them.

Figure 3 shows which episodes we can find on each panel of the pagoda's second storey and how the episodes are arranged. The numbers indicate the episode numbers as listed in Figure 1.

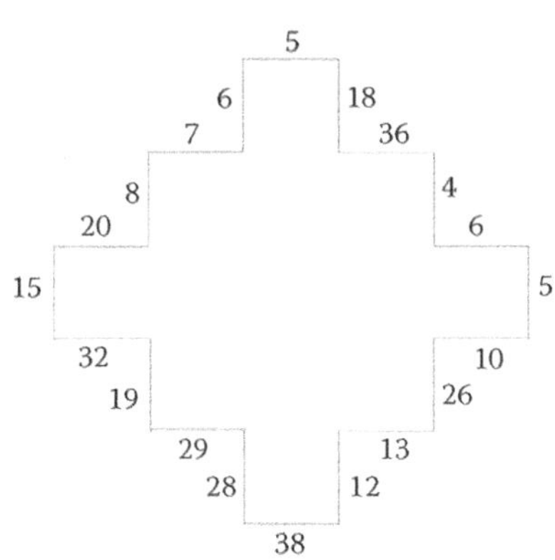

Fig. 3. Arrangement of the episodes on the 20 panels of the second storey of the Kyŏngch'ŏn temple pagoda, compiled by the author.

The pagodas themselves do not mention the title of *The Journey* or any written text related to that story world. We only have the images on 22 panels to determine which episodes the reliefs actually transcode.

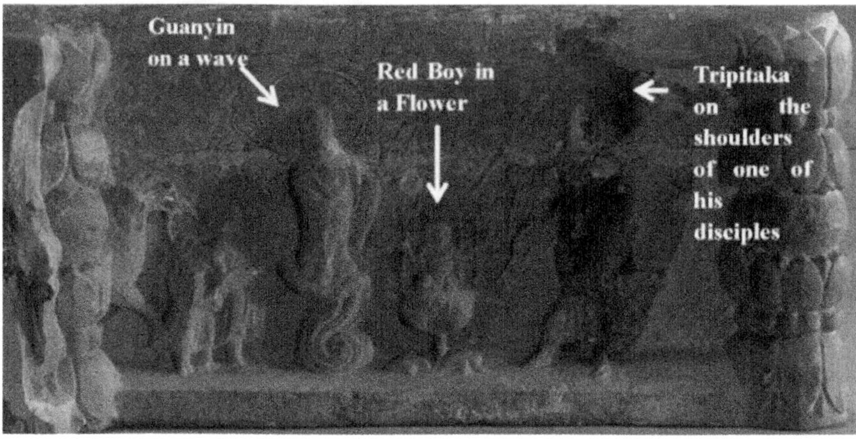

Fig. 4. The "Red Boy" episode on the pagoda of the Kyŏngch'ŏn Temple, https://www.museum.go.kr/site/main/relic/recommend/view?relicRecommendId=16858.

Twenty-two panels on the pagoda activate 18 episodes of *The Journey*, which means there are some episodes which appear on more than one panel. One of the episodes is the "Red Boy" episode (ep. 36), which I will use as an example to show how the pagoda transcodes *The Journey*. In the figure above, we can see that Bodhisattva Guanyin is slightly to the left of the middle, with a halo and riding a wave. On the right is Tripitaka, on the shoulders of one of his disciples. And in the middle, we see the Red Boy sitting in a flower. In the "Red Boy" episode, Guanyin transforms everything into an ocean as part of his strategy to block the Red Boy's attacks and finally to capture him with a thousand-leaf lotus platform that turns out to be made of thousands of swords. What helps us to decode this panel as the "Red Boy" episode is a combination of actants (characters, objects, places) that play a decisive role in the episode, including the Red Boy, Guanyin and Tripitaka, the wave, and the lotus flower. On this panel, as elsewhere on the pagoda, the artists used only one panel to transcode one episode. In Anthony Yu's translation, one episode often occupies more than 50 pages, but the relief artists depicted a key scene of the episode including the main characters, the main objects, and the main places. Since the artists only had one panel to depict a whole episode, they had to distil it to its essence, which we can understand as an early form of what Nancy Miller (2007) calls "snack culture" in her "Minifesto for a New Age".

Accordingly, we can understand each panel as the essence of a single episode. In total, the artists distilled the essence of 18 episodes on the pagoda.

The Journey on Temple Walls

The Journey also appears on wall paintings in the Maitreya Hall of T'ongdo Temple located in Kyŏngsang Province in south-east Korea. We find seven paintings in total that are related to *The Journey*, three on the eastern wall and four on the western wall. Each painting has a title written in Chinese on the pillars on both sides of each painting, indicating the chapter titles we can find in several variations of *The Journey* from the Ming period. In contrast to the Kyŏngch'ŏn Pagoda, where no written text was added to its translation of *The Journey*, the temple wall paintings here provide written pointers that help viewers to decode the images as belonging to the story world of *The Journey*. Ch'oe Mina, curator at the Ulsan Museum, explains that the paintings are loosely based on the images used in Li Zhuowu's Chinese version of *The Journey* from the seventeenth century. Li Zhuowu's version includes 200 images (Ch'oe, 2015, 105).

Fig. 5. "One woman vainly longs for sensual joys": Painting on the eastern wall of the Maitreya Hall at T'ongdo Temple (Munhwajaech'ŏng and Sŏngbo munhwajae yŏn'guwŏn, 2008, 370).

For example, the first painting on the eastern wall to the left has the title "One woman vainly longs for sensual joys" (一姪空懷情慾喜), which alludes to chapter 94 in Li Zhuowu's version, titled "Four priests are feted at the royal garden; one fiend vainly longs for sensual joys" (四僧宴樂御花園,一怪空懷情慾喜). We can observe that the title of the painting only uses the second half of the chapter title from Li Zhuowu's version and changes the character 怪 [fiend] to 婬 [woman]. While this could also simply be a mistake based on the similarity of the Chinese characters, Hong Sŏngch'o (2013, 200) argues that the artist might have wanted to emphasise the fiend's female identity. Chapter 94 of Li Zhuowu's variation is part of the "Kingdom of India" episode (ep. 34) which tells how the king of India plans to marry Tripitaka to his daughter, who turns out to be a demon. When Sun Wukong realises her true identity, the princess begs her royal father to send Tripitaka's disciples out of the court to secure her wedding. The wall painting depicts exactly this scene. We can see a female figure on the right, kneeling and begging with her hands clasped in front of a much taller and bigger person in the centre standing on a round pedestal.

Interestingly, while the pose of the figures matches the scene in *The Journey*, the female figure is not dressed as a princess and in fact resembles the other surrounding officials, which means that the depiction of her in the painting obscures the fiend's female identity, like the Chinese character in the title of Li Zhuowu's variation. Pak Sejin, curator at the museum at T'ongdo Temple, also suggests that the artist might have tried to shed light on the princess' demonic nature by not depicting her as a princess (2013, 68). However we interpret the portrayal of the princess in the painting, the title leaves little doubt that it activates the "Kingdom of India" episode. Like the panels on the pagoda of the Kyŏngch'ŏn Temple, the wall paintings also activate specific episodes of *The Journey* by choosing one representative scene from them, while the written titles might have served as a reading guide for the informed visitor. The paintings also distil the episodes to their essence.

In total, the paintings transcode six episodes: "Taizong in the Underworld" (ep. 4), "Grand Mass" (ep. 5), "Bottomless Cave" (ep. 29), "Dharma-Destroying Kingdom" (ep. 30), "Phoenix-Immortal Prefecture" (ep. 31), and "Kingdom of India" (ep. 34). While each painting uses titles from Li Zhuowu's version of *The Journey* to guide viewers to certain episodes, the paintings themselves transcode the respective episodes visually by depicting one key or essential scene that includes all the main actants. The reliefs on the Kyŏngch'ŏn pagoda and the wall paintings in the Maitreya Hall of T'ongdo Temple support Xie Minghun's suggestion that the episodes should be understood as separate units. Rather than devoting one panel to one character, place, or actant of *The Journey*, the artists decided to devote one panel, or in some cases two, to one episode, which means their visual translations of *The Journey* have a strong focus on episodes. We could even say that the episode becomes the unit of translation.

The Journey as Animation

Now we will jump forward around 600 years in time to one of the most popular adaptations of *The Journey* in South Korea today, the animation *Narara syup'ŏbodŭ* (날아라 슈퍼보드), or *Fly Superboard*. The South Korean channel KBS 2TV aired *Fly Superboard* in five seasons and 54 episodes between 1990 and 2002 with the highest viewer ratings ever recorded for a Korean animated series. *Fly Superboard* basically tells the story of how good wins against evil. Here "good" is, of course, represented by Tripitaka and his disciples Sun Wukong, Zhu Bajie, and Sha Wujing. The whole animation starts with a heavenly voice explaining that the journey will be about "eliminating evil and planting peace" (*agŭl ŏpsaego p'yŏnghwa rŭl simgo*). "Evil" is broadly defined in the series, attached to concepts as diverse as pollution, computer games, and corruption.

Fly Superboard does not mention *The Journey* directly. It is inspired by Hŏ Yŏngman's *manhwa* (漫畫, J. *manga*, C. *manhua*) *Mr. Son* (*Misŭt'ŏ Son*, 1989–1990) whose title refers to the name of Sun Wukong (K. Son Ogong). Across the series, *Fly Superboard* strings ten "beads" or activates the following ten episodes: 1, 6, 7, 9, 10, 11, 12, 16, 19, 20, 26. It does not maintain any previously established order. The first episode presents "Recruitment of the Disciples" (ep. 6). Episode four then tells "Widow and Three Daughters" (ep. 7), and then episode five jumps back to "Havoc in Heaven" (ep. 1). Many episodes of the series reference other episodes from *The Journey* and mix them with actants from other story worlds, including Medusa, King Arthur, the Frog King, or Merlin. This means that *Fly Superboard* combines ten episodes as if they were separate units or "beads" without following any conventional sequential order, while adding elements from other story worlds as it jumps from one episode to the next.

Fig. 6. Mr Son with nunchuks flying on his superboard in *Fly Superboard*, season 1, ep. 3.

This animated series shows how transcoding transforms the objects of translation. The monkey, for example, is called Mr Son. His compliant weapon is not a staff, but nunchuks, and instead of a headband or crown, he wears a helmet that causes him a headache whenever Tripitaka sings a certain song. As Fig. 6 shows, Mr Son does not soar on clouds, but uses the "superboard" to which the title of the animation alludes. The pilgrims do not set out to find Buddhist scriptures; instead, the goal of their journey is simply the elimination of all evil and the establishment of peace. In other words, the animation uses the actants of *The Journey*, but they are transformed to fit a new web of meaning. The same is true of the episodes.

Fly Superboard activates ten of the 38 episodes (see Fig. 1), but does not simply retell episodes of *The Journey* as they are told in any well-known previous text. The animation transcodes the episodes by transferring them into new contexts, and by doing so positions them in a new web of meaning. The second episode of season three, for example, activates "Black Rooster Kingdom" (ep. 12). In Antony Yu's translation of *The Journey* (chs 36–39), the dead king of the Black Rooster Kingdom appears in Tripitaka's dream to ask him for help. The king explains that a Daoist demon showed up in his kingdom and saved it from a severe drought. Once the demon earned the king's trust, however, it murdered him and buried him in a well, then transformed itself into an exact image of the king and began to rule the Black Rooster Kingdom himself. Sun Wukong manages to reveal the truth by reviving the true king with a white jade token that had originally belonged to the king. At the end of the episode, though, it turns out that the Daoist demon was actually a transformation of Bodhisattva Mañjuśrī's lion, sent by Mañjuśrī himself to the Black Rooster Kingdom to punish the king for his arrogance.

While it is not clear here which characters represent good and evil, the animation avoids this ambivalence. In the animated series, the kingdom does not suffer a drought, it instead runs out of oil resources. Similar to Yu's version, a demon (now a demon robot) appears to help at first, but then it kills the king, buries him in a well, and becomes king. In both versions the son of the king, the designated successor, plays a decisive role in revealing the truth. In the series, it is not a white jade token that reveals the true king, but a finger ring on which the Chinese character for "king" (王, C. and K. *wang*) is engraved. While Sun Wukong manages to revive the king in Yu's version, the prince becomes king in the series.

We can clearly recognise the "Black Rooster Kingdom" episode in *Fly Superboard*. The main actants (a suffering kingdom, a king, a demon that kills the king, a king's son, a token) are the same, but they are transformed to match the new code of the animation. While the artists of the Kyŏngch'ŏn pagoda and the wall paintings in T'ongdo Temple mainly used one panel to transcode one episode, *Fly Superboard* tells each episode in sequence and often uses one instalment for one episode. This means that the animation also basically distils each episode to its essence, although the essence of each episode includes more elements than in the case of the pagoda and the temple wall paintings.

Conclusion

The relief images on the pagoda of the Kyŏngch'ŏn Temple from the fourteenth century, the wall paintings in the Maitreya Hall of T'ongdo Temple from the eighteenth century, and the animated TV series *Narara syup'ŏbodŭ* from the 1990s are very different examples of visual translations of *The Journey*. While scholars tend to focus on written translation to explain the transnational spread of such stories, the three visual translations discussed above give an idea of how *The Journey* might have circulated transnationally without necessarily relying on written translations. The fourteenth-century relief images in particular show that visual translations can predate written translations. In general, none of the visual translations is or tries to be a faithful translation of any stable source text. They do not transfer a written source text into a written target text, but rather transfer a combination of episodes from the story world of *The Journey* into new webs of meaning. All three visual translations use episodes as the unit of translation.

I suggested above that we understand the episodes as separate units or beads. In analysing the three visual translations, it becomes clear that the artists behind the visual translations distilled episodes to their essence and used images of episodes from *The Journey* that they transferred into new webs of meaning. More precisely, they tend to use one image or, in the case of the animation, a sequence of images for one episode. These images comprise key scenes from the episodes, and the actants, which include the main characters, objects, and locations of an episode. The images alone, though, do not require the artists to have read a written version of *The Journey*. With the exception of the artists of the temple wall paintings, who added written references to Li Zhuowu's version of *The Journey* on the co-located pillars, there is no evidence that written versions played a role in the transcoding process at all. The artists might have simply been inspired by other visual or auditory versions. This suggests that the direct source for the images might not have been any external version of *The Journey*, but rather the imagination of the artists, imagination built upon their knowledge of the story world of *The Journey* and possibly influenced by multiple versions.

What applies for the artists or the "encoders", also seems to apply to the viewers or the "decoders". While the artists used their imagination to depict

The Journey, the viewers are expected to use their informed imagination to decode the images. While there is of course no guarantee that all viewers are able to decode the images and relate them to *The Journey*, visual translation still seems to facilitate the transnational spread of literary knowledge, since national and linguistic barriers cannot hinder communication based on imagination.

References and Further Reading

Bassnett, Susan. 2014. *Translation Studies*. New York: Routledge.

Ch'oe Mina. 2015. "T'ongdosa Yonghwajŏn ŭi Sŏyugido yŏn'gu" (통도사 용화전 (龍華殿) 의 ≪서유기도 (西遊記圖)≫ 연구) [A Study on the Paintings from *The Journey* in the Maitreya Hall at T'ongdo Temple]. *Munmul yŏn'gu* 28: 93–132.

Chŏng Kyubok. 1972. "Sŏyugi wa Han'guk kososŏl" (서유기와 한국고소설) [The Journey and Korean Classical Fiction]. *Asea yŏngu* 15: 109–151.

Eggert, Marion. 2020. "Cultural Transmutations in Korea's Past and Present. Transcoding, Code-switching and Other Cultural Practices". *Bochumer Jahrbuch zur Ostasienforschung = Bochum Yearbook of East Asian Studies* 43: 5–14.

Hong, Meisun. 2018. *Transforming Monkey: Adaptation and Representation of a Chinese Epic*. Seattle: University of Washington Press.

Hong, Sŏngch'o. 2013. "Chosŏn sidae Sŏyugi ŭi chŏnp'a wa yŏnghyang yŏn'gu – munhŏn kirok kwa sŏyugido rŭl chungsimŭro" (조선시대 (朝鮮時代) ≪서유기 (西遊記)≫ 의 전파 (傳播) 와 영향 (影響) 연구: 문헌기록 (文獻記錄) 과 ≪서유기도 (西遊記圖)≫ 를 중심으로) [A Study on the Circulation and the Influence of *The Journey to the West* during Chosŏn Times: With a Special Focus on Records in Literature and on Paintings]. *Chungguk ŏmun nonch'ong* (中國語文論叢) 56: 183–208.

Hutcheon, Linda, and Siobhan O'Flynn. 2013. *A Theory of Adaptation*. London: Routledge.

Isobe Akira (磯部彰). 1995. *Saiyūki juyōshi no kenkyū* (西遊記受容史の研究) [A study on the reception history of Xiyouji]. Tokyo: Taga shuppan.

Kaesŏng Kyŏngch'ŏnsa t'ŏ sipch'ŭngsŏkt'ap (개성 경천사 터 십층석탑) [The ten-storey pagoda of Kyŏngch'ŏn Temple at the National Museum of Korea]. *E-myujiŏm* (e 뮤지엄). https://tinyurl.com/5h2u67us [accessed 28 July 2022].

Kungnip munhwajae yŏn'guso. 2005–2006. *Kyŏngch'ŏngsa sipch'ŭng sŏkt'ap I–III* (경천사 십층석탑) [The Ten-Storey Stone Pagoda of Kyŏngch'ŏng Temple]. Seoul: Kungnip munhwajae yŏn'guso.

Miller, Nancy. 2007. "Minifesto for a New Age". *Wired*, 1 March. https://www.wired.com/2007/03/snackminifesto/ [accessed 3 January 2021].

Min Kwandong. 2006. "Sŏyugi ŭi kungnye yuip kwa p'anbon yŏngu" (≪서유기≫ 의 국내유입과 판본연구) [A Study on the Introduction of *Xiyouji* in Korea and Its Editions]. *Chungguk sosŏl nonch'ong* (中國小說論叢) 23: 215–240.

Munhwajaech'ŏng and Sŏngbo munhwajae yŏn'guwŏn. 2008. *Han'guk ŭi sach'al pyŏkhwa: sach'al kŏnch'ungmul pyŏkhwa chosa pogosŏ: Kyŏngsang namdo 1* (한국의 사찰벽화: 사찰건축물벽화조사보고서) [Korean Temple Wall Paintings: Report of a Survey on Wall Paintings in Temple Architecture: Southern Kyŏngsang Province 1]. Seoul: Ch'ŏnil munhwasa.

Munhwajae kwalliguk. 1993. *Wŏngaksaji sipch'ŭng sŏkt'ap chosa pogosŏ* (원각사지 십층석탑 (圓覺寺址十層石塔) 실측조사보고서) [Survey on the Wongak Temple Site]. Seoul: Munhwajae kwalliguk.

Pak Sejin. 2013. "T'ongdosa Yongwajŏn pyŏkhwa yŏn'gu" (통도사 용화전 벽화연구) [A Study on the Wall Paintings in the Maitreya Hall of T'ongdo Temple]. MA diss., Dongguk University.

Sin Soyŏn. 2006. "Wŏngaksaji sipch'ŭng sŏkt'ap ŭi Sŏyugi pugak yŏn'gu (원가사지 십층석탑의 서유기 부각연구) [Reliefs of *The Journey* on the Ten-Storey Pagoda of the Wŏngak Temple Site]. *Misulsahak yŏn'gu* 249: 79–112.

——. 2014. "Kyŏngch'ŏnsa sipch'ŭng sŏkt'ap kidanbu tosang yŏn'gu" (경천사 십층석탑 기단부 도상연구) [A Study on the Images on the Stylobate of the Ten-Storey Pagoda of the Kyŏngch'ŏn Temple]. *Ch'ŏnt'aehak yŏn'gu* 17: 127–175.

Sŏ Hyeŭn. 2015. "Chosŏn sidae Sŏyugi ŭi kaejak yangsang kwa kŭ sosŏlsajŏk ŭimi" (조선시대 서유기의 개작양상과 그 소설사적 의미) [Adaptations of *The Journey* in the Chosŏn Dynasty and Their Meaning for the History of Literary Fiction]. *Ŏmullonch'ong* 65: 91–117.

Song Chŏnghwa. 2010. "*Xiyouji* yu dongya dazhong wenhua" (《西游记》与东亚大众文化) [*Xiyouji* and East Asian popular culture]. PhD dissertation, Fudan daxue.

Waley, Arthur. 1961 [1942]. *Monkey*. London: Penguin.

Xie Minghun (謝明勳). 2013. "Hanguo Jingtiansi Yuandai xiyou gushi fudiao tujie (韓國敬天寺元代石塔《西遊》故事浮雕圖解) [An analysis of the relief images from the story Journey to the West on the stone pagoda from the Yuan dynasty at the Korean Kyŏngch'ŏn Temple]". *Chungŏ chungmunhak* (중어중문학) 56: 163–214.

Yi Chaesu. 1969. *Hanguk sosŏl yŏn'gu* (한국소설연구) [A Study on Korean Fiction]. Seoul: Sŏnmyŏng munhwasa.

Yi Sangik. 1992. "Hanguk sosŏl ŭi pigyo yŏngu: Sŏyugi ŭi yŏnghyang ŭl chungsim ŭro" (한국소설의 비교연구: 서유기의 영향을 중심으로) [A Comparative Study on Korean Fiction with Special Focus on the Influence of *The Journey*]. *Tongbang munhak pigyo yŏngu ch'ongsŏ* 2: 369–424.

Yŏm Chungsŏp. 2017. "Kyŏngch'ŏnsa Wŏn'gaksaji t'ap ŭi ch'wigyŏng pujo e taehan chaegŏmt'o: wŏnjaryo wa ŭi ch'ai wa changmyŏn sŏnt'aek ŭi ŭimi rŭl chungsim ŭro" (경천사 · 원각사지탑의 취경부조에 대한 재검토: 원자료와의 차이와 장면선택의 의미를 중심으로) [A New Approach to the Reliefs Portraying the Obtainment of the Scriptures on the Pagodas of the Kyŏngch'ŏng Temple and Wŏn'gak Temple]. *Chonggyo munhwa yŏn'gu* 28: 117–159.

Yu, Anthony C. (trans. and ed.) 2012. *The Journey to the West*. 4 vols. Rev. ed. Chicago and London: The University of Chicago Press.

Part II

Nation, Empire, and Beyond

5

Postcolonial Theory in East Asian Studies

The Case of the Qing Empire

Julia C. Schneider

Introduction

Until the late 1990s, China-focused studies of colonialism portrayed the Qing empire exclusively as a victim of colonialism, a semi-colony of the imperialist powers, trapped by unequal treaties. This image, based on undeniable historical facts, continues to be a crucial part of mainland Chinese self-conception and the official narrative of the People's Republic of China (PRC) which emerged from and brought to an end the 'century of humiliation'. However, in recent decades, historians have begun to interpret the Qing empire as itself a colonising power which took possession of and ruled over vast regions in Inner Asia and the southern regions in ways comparable to or even equal to colonialism. Similar to Spain, Portugal, France, and Britain, the Qing empire is believed to have developed its own colonial enterprise, the main difference being that the Qing colonial project was supposed to be continental and not overseas.

Which theories of colonialism are used to conceptualise the Qing as a colonial empire? Does this conceptualisation withstand detailed critical examination and comparison with commonly accepted colonialisms? And how is this conceptualisation related to present-day issues of territorial integrity and ethnopolitics in the two Chinas, the PRC on the mainland and the Republic of China (ROC), since 1949 on the island of Taiwan? This essay answers these questions by analysing the most influential works on Qing rule and Qing colonialism of recent decades on the basis of postcolonial theory and contrasting them with critical voices. It explains how the Qing empire is part of a transregional Eurasian space and that, consequently, its rule by conquest follows ruling strategies stemming from Central Asian governing tradition.

Transnationalism—or, rather, its derivate transculturalism—serves as a useful concept to examine the question of Qing colonialism and can be applied in at least two ways. First, transculturalism (and other related concepts with the prefix 'trans-' that are more suitable for pre-nationalist times) are basic concepts to understand Qing governance. This will come to the fore below when I discuss the Qing Dynasty's ruling strategies, which they learned from their Central Asian predecessors and applied in their trans- and multi-ethnic (-cultural, -religious, -lingual) empire. These characteristics were indeed paramount for Qing understanding of identity and rulership. Some of these ideas are also touched on by Sparvoli in Chapter 3 of this book.

Second, transnationalism can be used as a lens to bring present-day implications of the question of Qing colonialism to the fore. This is related to the fact that the application of the concept is deeply complicated when one translates the term 'nation' into Chinese, usually as *minzu* (民族). However, *minzu* also means 'ethnicity' or 'ethnic group' (and 'nationality'). The basic difference between nation and ethnicity is that, according to theories of nationalism, only a nation is supposed to have its own nation-state, whereas ethnicities are usually supposed to be integrated into larger nations, to be merged with them, and possibly to be dissolved in them. I will explain below how transnationalism becomes a thorny issue in the current debates on Qing colonialism and its effects on present-day issues. It must be mentioned, however, that the Chinese translation of 'transnationalism', *kuaguozhuyi* (跨國主義) does not include *minzu*, but refers to an understanding of the nation not as a people (民, C. *min*) but as a state (國, C. *guo*).

When the Qing empire declined and its last emperor abdicated in 1912, the new ROC understood itself as its successor state with an automatic claim to power over the vast territory the Qing emperors had conquered over the course of the seventeenth and eighteenth centuries in East and Inner Asia. Although many regions were *de facto* not under Republican control, Republican maps inevitably show the ROC as including all Qing territories. This was despite the fact that Mongolia, that is, the territory known as Outer Mongolia in Qing times, had broken away in 1911. Although its declaration of independence was not acknowledged by the ROC, Mongolia has remained beyond Chinese political control ever since and was internationally acknowledged as an independent state. Tibet, East Turkestan, Dzungaria, and Manchuria were not or not continuously controlled by the Republican government after 1912. However, all of these regions came under communist rule after the founding of the PRC in 1949.

The Chinese communists' wish to unite these diverse regions with the Chinese heartland derived from their understanding of the Qing territory as that of 'China' (中國, C. *Zhongguo*, 中華, C. *Zhonghua*). In their view, the Qing empire *was* China. Therefore, both the republican and the socialist successor states strove to 'reunite' this historically, but also quasi-naturally, defined China. The Republican government did not acknowledge Mongolia as an independent state until 2002 but continued to claim sovereignty over it. The PRC on the mainland, on the other hand, acknowledged Mongolian independence immediately in 1949—after all Mongolia was a socialist sister state under the patronage of the Soviet Union.

The perception of China's territory as identical with the Qing empire was powerfully put forward by Republican and socialist governments. Their official historiography has forbidden any understanding of or research into Manchu rule as colonial among Chinese historians. During the last decades of the Qing empire, early Chinese nationalists had indeed accused the Manchu emperors as colonisers of the Chinese, and, together with anti-Manchuism, anti-colonialism was an important driving force of the anti-imperial Chinese revolutions in the first decade of the twentieth century. However, after the Xinhai Revolution in 1911 and its bloody reverberation in 1912, when thousands of Manchus were slaughtered and began to disguise themselves as Chinese, anti-Manchuism quickly dwindled and with it the discussion of Manchus having colonised the Chinese (Rhoads, 2000, 187–205).

Only in the late 1990s did scholars, mainly based in the USA, begin to discuss whether Manchu rule had been colonial after all. In contrast to the early Chinese nationalist discourse, however, they did not describe the conquest of China proper, but rather the Qing conquests in Inner Asia (Tibet, East Turkestan, Mongolia, Dzungaria) and at the fringes of the southern provinces of China proper (the mountainous regions of Yunnan, Sichuan, Guizhou, Shaanxi, Fujian, Taiwan) as colonial. The term 'China proper' refers to the regions inhabited by Chinese people and by extension to all regions under provincial rule in Qing times, also called the 'Eighteen Provinces' and 'Inner China' as opposed to 'Outer China', that is, Tibet, East Turkestan, Mongolia, Dzungaria, and Manchuria. Only in the late nineteenth century, Xinjiang (formerly East Turkestan and Dzungaria) and Manchuria were established as provinces, too. Here, I present recent scholarly concepts and understandings of colonialism in the Qing context, comparing them to findings of postcolonial theory, contrasting them with critical voices, and finally putting them in relation to analyses of Qing rule by New Qing History scholars. Before explaining the theories of Qing colonialism, however, a more detailed explanation of the Qing conquests is in order.

History of Qing Conquests and Cultural-Religious-Lingual Diversity

In 1616, the powerful Jurchen chieftain Nurgaci united the Jurchen, Khorchin (Southern) Mongol, and Northern Chinese (Manchu, hereafter Ma., *nikan*) peoples under his rule and proclaimed himself khan (Ma. *han*) of the Golden Dynasty (Ma. *aisin gurun*). He ruled in the region today known as Manchuria. In Chinese historiography, the Golden Dynasty is known as the Later Jin Dynasty (金, C. *jin* [gold]) to differentiate it from another Golden or Jin Dynasty (1115–1234), founded 500 years previously by the Jurchen. Together with his Jurchen, Mongol, and Nikan allies, Nurgaci expanded his khanate further towards the west and south (Inner Mongolia and the Liaodong Peninsula). After Nurgaci's death in 1626, his son and successor Hungtaiji continued the advance towards the northern regions of the Chinese Ming empire. At the same time, more and more Mongols were won over as allies of the Jurchen Golden Dynasty. In order to create a larger group of loyal people, Hungtaiji renamed his Jurchen, Mongol, and Nikan allies 'Manchu' (Ma. *manju*). He also renamed his dynasty the Great Qing (Ma. *Daicing*, 大清, C. *Daqing*) in 1636. In 1644, the Qing conquered Beijing, the capital of the Ming Dynasty. It becomes obvious that the Jurchen rule had been transcultural and multi-ethnic from the time when Nurhaci founded the Golden Dynasty in 1616. His successors broadened and increased this transcultural approach to identity, rulership, and loyalty over time.

For more than 100 years, the Qing emperors continued their wars of conquest, first in the south to end attempts to restore the Ming Dynasty, then in the west to crush their main rival, the Dzungar Khanate. Over time, the Qing emperors emerged not only as khans of Manchuria and emperors of China proper, but also Khagans of Mongolia and Dzungaria, patrons of Tibet, and protectors of East Turkestan (Perdue, 2005, 209–299). In order to rule their multicultural, -religious, and -lingual populations or "constituencies", the Qing emperors applied a strategy of "simultaneous rulership" (Ma. *kamcime*, 合璧, C. *hebi*) (Crossley, 1999, 11). Since the reign of Timur (Tamerlane), this ruling strategy had been widely used in the Central Asian khanates of multi-ethnic (-cultural, -lingual, -religious) populations and is thus also called post-Timurid or "Altaic" due to the origin of many Central Asian nomadic rulers in the Altai Mountains (Perdue, 2005, 518–546; Darwin, 2008, 4–45). To integrate and address their diverse populations, Central Asian rulers presented themselves in alignment with the respective ruling traditions of those of their populations they considered important due to their political influence, military might, economic wealth, or religious advocacy. The Qing emperors consequently presented themselves as emperors (黃帝, C. *huangdi*) who followed Neo-Confucianism and Chinese imperial ceremonial traditions, as powerful Khagans (*Khaan*, in Mongolian) who were able horsemen and archers according to Mongolian and other post-Timurid traditions, and as bodhisattva-kings and wheel-turning world rulers (*cakravartirāja*, in Sanskrit, *'khor los bsgyur ba'i rgyal po*, in Tibetan) according to Tibetan Buddhist traditions (Crossley, 1999, 224–246). In playing these different roles, the Qing emperors became transcultural, universalist rulers who incorporated, united, but moreover transcended their subjects' different cultures, religions, and languages.

Apart from presenting themselves as rulers in diverse traditions, the Qing emperors moreover strove to become fluent in the languages of their most important populations, namely Manchu, Mongolian, and Chinese, the Qianlong Emperor even mastering Tibetan (Kim, 2007, 84–85). These languages, in particular Manchu, Mongolian, and Chinese, were all used in official communication, depending on the intended audience (Perdue, 2005, 429–442). The Qing empire was thus multilingual in the truest sense. Nevertheless, Qing historians used to rely almost entirely on Chinese sources, despite the large body of official documents in Manchu and Mongolian that was stored in the First Historical Archives in Beijing and elsewhere. Qing historians long claimed that Manchu and Mongolian sources were mere translations of Chinese sources and that they were not worthy of study. Only in the 1980s were the large corpora of Manchu and Mongolian sources rediscovered as important sources for Qing history, particularly for Inner Asian history, as it became clear that the Qing court used Manchu and Mongolian as secret as well as diplomatic languages for Inner Asian affairs (Crossley and Rawski, 1993).

Theories of Qing Colonialism

In 1998, Perdue edited a special issue of *The International History Review* titled "Manchu Colonialism" wherein he and six other scholars published articles on their understanding of Manchu Qing conquest rule. Some concentrated on specific regions, for example, Inner Asia or parts of it, or Taiwan; others compared the Qing conquests with those of the Ottomans and Russia, two other continental conquest empires of early modernity (Perdue, 1998a; Adas, 1998). "Manchu Colonialism" established a discourse that was continued by other historians and developed in different directions. Elsewhere, I have used an approach based on regional focus to differentiate scholars who are advocates of Qing colonialism (Schneider, 2020). Here, I further refine my earlier findings and employ a conceptual division of five groups. At the same time, I problematise each conceptual approach and show why I think them ultimately unsuitable for an analysis of the Qing conquest regime.

First, the Qing as Just Another Colonial Empire

Peter Perdue (1998a) and Laura Hostetler (2001) claim that by defining the Qing empire as a colonising or colonial empire, historians would be able to follow a truly comparative approach when analysing the Qing and European colonial empires. Their definitions of colonialism are rather unspecific, and it remains unclear why it is important to lay the foundation for a comparison between the Qing empire and *European* colonial empires. It seems to be mainly due to the notable Eurocentrism within Euro-American historiography and sinology that certain European empires are considered unavoidable for such a comparative analysis. Interestingly, however, Austria-Hungary which could offer a meaningful model for comparison, being a large continental and multi-ethnic empire, is not mentioned in comparison with the Qing. On the other hand, John Darwin (2008) presented a convincing comparative analysis of the five post-Timurid empires, the Qing empire, the Russian empire, and the three gunpowder empires of the Ottomans, Safavids, and Mughals (see also Struve ed., 2004). These post-Timurid or Altaic empires represent more logical counterparts than the European colonial empires.

Second, Qing Conquests as Settler Colonialism

John Herman (2007; 2018), Perdue (1997), and Hostetler (2001) apply a supposedly neutral definition of settler colonialism to interpret the Qing as a colonial empire. Neutrally understood, settler colonialism is defined as the settlement in and usually cultivation of land that previously has not been used for agriculture. However, postcolonial scholars argue that settler colonialism has never been neutral, at least not in early modern times, as it was not possible for any group of settlers to 'cultivate' (*colere*, in Latin, the root of the noun *colonia* and all related terms) empty, previously uninhabited land. No habitable land was actually 'empty', and colonial settlement thus inevitably caused displacement of and supply shortfalls for other people. Even if land was not visibly cultivated or settled by sedentary people, it was used by hunter-gatherers, or nomads who used the land for grazing and herding (Wolfe, 1999, 2). Moreover, early modern colonial empires often relied on planter slavery as part of settler colonialism. Indigenous societies, particularly in the Caribbean, Central and South America, the Maluku Islands, etc., were wiped out by force or died of diseases that the colonisers brought with them. Slaves were imported from Africa to work in newly established plantations that cultivated goods that brought high prices on European markets, particularly staple crops (sugarcane, cotton, rice, tobacco), but also cash crops (indigo, coffee, cacao) that were shipped to Europe to be processed (Walsh, 2011, 102). Therefore, settler colonies were founded in territories merely defined as "empty" according to the colonial "myth of emptiness" (Blaut, 1993, 15).

Consequently, far from being neutral in a postcolonial sense, settler colonialism is part and parcel of the exploitation colonialism associated with early modernity and modernity.

Third, Classifying the Colonial World

Teng (2004), Perdue (1998a), and Hostetler (2001) use further characteristics of European colonial empires to argue for their suitability for comparison with the Qing: the shared urge to categorise and classify the world, be it the inanimate world of topography and geography, or the animate world of plants, animals, and humans. Ethnography and map-making in particular seem to provide areas for comparison. Similar to their European counterparts, Qing scholars began to produce ethnographic studies of the people in the Qing empire and beyond in the course of the eighteenth century, often on imperial order. At the same time, the Qing emperors supported specialist map-making, wanting to determine and formalise the borders of their empire. Map-making in particular has been interpreted as a means to control and fix state borders, making them increasingly impermeable (Perdue, 1998b). Ethnography served similar ends to control and fix which people belonged to the empire and who was governed by it.

Projects of categorisation and classification of territories and peoples are used as typical characteristics of colonial empires. However, colonialism is certainly more than a stimulus for ethnographic studies or map-making. At the same time, rulers who have no desire for colonies have supported map-making, for example the Dzungar Khans, as Perdue (2005, 307) points out. Though both map-making and ethnography can certainly accompany colonial projects, they are not explicit indicators for colonialism.

Fourth, Internal Colonialism

Harrell (2003 [1995]), Herman (2007), and Teng (2004) base their conceptualisation on analysis of the sociopolitical effects of Qing rule on indigenous societies. Herman uses Michael Hechter's concept of "internal colonialism" to explain the "cultural division of labour" in Guizhou (Hechter, 1975, 9; Herman, 2007, 13). Herman shows that even if non-Chinese people received a classical Neo-Confucian education, they had no access to careers as scholar-officials but remained on the marginalised fringes of China proper. Hechter developed the concept of internal colonialism to explain the sociopolitical effects of cultural discrimination in the twentieth-century United Kingdom, an industrialised and capitalist country. Herman does not explain how Hechter's concepts are to be adapted to be useful in an analysis of Ming and Qing empires. What for example is "labour" supposed to mean in their rural societies based on agriculture?

Closely related to the impermeability of Chinese officialdom is the notion of a *mission civilisatrice* that the Ming and Qing used for legitimising their approaches towards the southern non-Chinese regions (Herman, 2007, 13; Harrell, 2003 [1995]). Herman argues that the strategy of a 'Confucian civilizing mission' that was supposedly implemented by scholar-officials to achieve full inclusion of non-Chinese people into Chinese society and the state apparatus, was a mere myth. He shows that 'civilizing' could only have been truly successful if Chinese society and its state institutions had been open to indigenous people. However, the Ming conquest of the southern regions "was not a 'civilizing mission'"; the civilizing narrative merely concealed the fact that the Ming conquest was a "uninterrupted campaign of state-sponsored violence" (Herman, 2007, 13). Rather than serving as tools of integration and homogenisation, civilising projects tend to "sharpen, or heighten the consciousness of the peripheral people as an ethnic group" (Harrell, 2003 [1995], 6). Do Qing narratives of civilising barbarians therefore indicate that their conquest is equal to European colonial and imperial *missions civilisatrices*, understood as the 'white man's burden'?

Fifth, a New Postcolonial Society

Finally, Teng (1998; 2004) and Shu-mei Shih (2011) are interested in the effects that the label 'colonial' could have on current issues. Teng (1998, 354) uses Edward Said's and Mary Louise Pratt's postcolonial concepts of a sexualised colonial discourse. Teng and Shih assert that by denying that the Qing conquest rule was colonial, scholars perpetuate an official Chinese reading of history that implies that all territories under Chinese Republican and communist rule have been integral parts of China since (at least) Qing times. The perception of non-Chinese regions as colonies of the Chinese nation-state is based on the acceptance of Qing rule as colonial and not only conquest rule. Consequently, never having been colonised in the first place, these territories cannot decolonise and claim independence and sovereignty.

Teng and Shih hereby interpret the term 'conquest rule' as supporting the legitimacy of present-day Chinese claims of Tibet, Mongolia, East Turkestan, Dzungaria, southern regions, and Taiwan. They assume that only the term 'colonialism' acknowledges that the Qing conquests of these regions and the continued claims by the ROC and PRC governments to Tibet, Mongolia, East Turkestan, Dzungaria, and Taiwan have been illegitimate from the start.

It becomes clear that all scholars who categorise the Qing empire as colonial compare it directly with or put it into relation to European empires, putting it to the test based on concepts developed for European cases and histories. They either test whether certain concepts of colonialism like internal colonialism or settler colonialism can be applied to the Qing case or analyse whether certain aspects or characteristics of European colonialism can also be found in the Qing empire. These aspects include colonial discourses using exoticising, eroticising, and racist strategies to other the colonised, political-administrative settings, like extraterritoriality and dual law, and last not least, sociopolitical aspects like forced acculturation and missionising. Necessarily, all analyses that find that the Qing empire was colonial evaluate it in comparison to European empires.

More Problematic Issues

Further questions arise. First, is it sensible to pick only specific aspects of the concept of colonialism, a concept that has been normativised by Euro-American cases, to establish if an empire is colonial? Second, and more importantly, why does Europe figure as the normative model in all the aforementioned conceptual approaches?

Euro-American and Japanese colonial projects and rules provide the patterns and models for modern theories of colonialism: first Portuguese, Spanish, British, French, and Dutch colonialisms from the sixteenth century, plus German, Belgian, Italian, and other European as well as Japanese, US-American, and Russian colonialisms from the nineteenth century onwards. The characteristics and structures of these diverse colonising empires or states not only differ from each other, but each government also had its own approach to the colonies that moreover often changed over time. Sometimes one empire or state employed different approaches in different world regions. A difference in character and degree is sometimes seen between the earlier colonial rules of Portugal, Spain, France, Britain, and the Netherlands in the Americas and the Caribbean, and the later colonialisms of the imperialist powers first in Asia and then also in Africa and Australia.

In their theoretical study of colonialism, historians Jürgen Osterhammel and Jan C. Jansen (2017) see three particular characteristics that bind the 'usual suspects' of colonialism together despite their differences and finally define their conquests specifically as colonial: first, the colonised society is *controlled externally* and "deprived of its self-development" in order to serve "the needs and interests of the colonial masters"; second, the "*foreignness* between colonizers and colonized" is of great importance, particularly in view of the fact that the colonisers are unwilling to adapt to the cultures of the colonised, but expect them to acculturate to "European values and customs"; third, colonialism has been *interpreted* as being the fulfilling of "a divine plan of salvation", a mandate for the West to "civilize the 'barbarians'", the "white man's burden" (Osterhammel and Jansen, 2017, 19–20). These three characteristics of complete external control, foreignness, and interpretation make up colonialism.

The fact that European experiences figure as normative models in approaches to Qing colonialism is related to a wish not thoroughly scrutinised to make the Qing comparable to early modern European empires. These approaches assume somewhat automatically that the logical opposite for a comparative approach to the Qing empire are European empires, reflecting a deeply Eurocentric approach to history and a "fetishization of Western empires over other empires" (Shih, 2011, 709). The scholars mentioned above who align the Qing with European colonial empires finally fail to explain why a comparison with Britain, France, Spain, Portugal, and sometimes Russia is more meaningful than a comparison with other continental conquest empires, particularly Central Asian ones. John Darwin (2008) has convincingly shown how sensible it is to compare the Qing to other post-Timurid empires, such as the Ottomans, Safavids, Mughals, and Russia. A comparison with those empires moreover does not depend on the Qing being labelled colonial and produces equally valid or probably even better results for historians interested in comparative empire studies and global history.

Conclusion: Issues of Territorial Integrity and Ethnopolitics

The question as to whether the Qing empire was colonial or not has implications for present-day issues of territorial integrity and ethnopolitics in the two Chinas that should not be underestimated. As mentioned above, some scholars opt to describe the Qing empire as a colonial empire in order to question the legitimacy of ROC and PRC sovereignty over former Qing territories. They call Tibet, Mongolia, East Turkestan, Dzungaria, and the southern regions including Taiwan (but not China proper) colonies of the Qing empire in order to legitimate decolonising processes today. They aim to increase awareness that many problems non-Chinese people living in and/or from these regions face in Chinese-dominated societies are equal to those of colonised people. Because ROC and PRC governments have generally considered colonial rules elsewhere as illegitimate (Yang, 2011), their claim and rule of Tibet, (Inner) Mongolia, East Turkestan, Dzungaria, and the southern regions should be seen as equally illegitimate. A broad decolonising process in the two Chinas would be the logical consequence.

By no means do I deny the legitimacy of the social and political demands put forward by non-Chinese people, both 'minority nationalities' (少数民族, C. *shaoshu minzu*) in the PRC and 'aboriginal people' (原住民, C. *yuanzhumin*) in the ROC, such as not to be discriminated against on the basis of racism, to be fully accepted as equally 'civilised' and not inferior people, as well as claims for separation, independence, and autonomy. As a historian, however, I ask if it is inevitable that efforts against discrimination and racism, and for equality, acceptance, freedom, liberty, and autonomy today can only be legitimised by the assumption that the Qing empire was colonial. Striving for equality, acceptance, freedom, liberty, and autonomy is a legitimate aim in itself and is not dependent on further legitimation from pre-1912 history. What matters is whether the current situation is tolerable—it deserves to stand for itself without need of further justification and its argument is not strengthened or weakened by conceptualising the Qing as colonial.

By arguing against the notion of Qing colonialism, I explicitly do not argue against the necessity of anti-colonialism and anti-racism as well as processes of decolonisation in the PRC and ROC today. The question remains as to *when* Tibet, (Inner) Mongolia, East Turkestan, Dzungaria, and the southern regions became colonies. At what point in time did a colonial element become part of the relation between the respective central governments and these regions? Was it when they were conquered by the (Ming and) Qing or rather when they came under ROC and PRC rule (and under Japanese rule in the case of Taiwan)? It is beyond the scope of this essay to discuss if and how far ROC and PRC rule resembles colonial rule (Shih, 2011). However, I would like to remind the reader that postcolonial theory sees colonialism closely related to the Industrial Revolution, capitalism, and imperialism, and to then ponder on how that relates to Qing conquests.

What I did intend to answer here is whether the Qing empire was colonial. Therefore, let me return to the double concept of "simultaneous rulership" (Crossley, 1999, 11) and "Altaic" rule (Perdue, 2005, 542–546). The understanding of Qing rule as "simultaneous" and "Altaic" in fact contradicts notions of Qing colonialism. Historians of the so-called New Qing History school especially made the powerful argument that the ROC and then the PRC have been the territorial but not political successors of the Qing empire (Crossley, 1999, 337–361; Esherick, 2006). Both are Chinese nation-states with a clear Chinese nationalist agenda, whereas the Qing empire was a truly multi-ethnic empire, pluralistically (simultaneously) ruled by Manchu emperors and Manchu-Mongol-Nikan ruling elites. When the Qing empire declined and the first Chinese nation-state was founded in 1911/1912, the Republican government claimed to be the Qing's successor and claimed its territory and populations. The Republican government made continuous references to its multi-ethnic population, but this was mere lip service, mainly trying to rein in the separatist Tibetans and Mongols as well as the Xinjiang warlords and prevent the separation of Manchuria. This becomes obvious from the fact that instead of continuing the Qing emperors' strategy of simultaneous rulership, the Chinese national government introduced a Sino-centric strategy of rule which it coupled with an ethno-nationalist understanding of the Chinese nation and its nation-state that left little or no room for non-Chinese identities, particularly among the top-level ruling elites. The Qing emperors had presented themselves as rulers in many different traditions, but the Republican presidents did no such thing. They were supposed to be, first of all, leaders of a Chinese national government.

Similarly, instead of acknowledging the continuing diversity of its population, all people living within the (claimed) territory of the ROC were claimed to be 'Chinese' (中華, C. *Zhonghua*) (Schneider, 2017a, 120, 156–157). Non-Chinese people were said to have become Chinese by acculturation, when the Qing conquered them at the latest. This was based on the 'Sinicisation theory', a Chinese nationalist narrative which states that all non-Chinese rulers who conquered Chinese-inhabited regions (China proper) inevitably assimilated to the Chinese (i.e. Sinicised) after their conquests (Schneider, 2017a). The Sinicisation theory postulates that Sinicisation happens automatically and inevitably due to the power, attraction, and charisma of Chinese culture (Crossley, 1990). Thus, when the Qing conquered China proper, the Manchus became Sinicised, that is, they became Chinese. As a consequence, the Qing empire was a Chinese empire, or rather, was China, and the territories the Qing conquered belonged to this Chinese empire or China—they were Chinese.

Since the 1990s, the Sinicisation theory has been refuted by New Qing History scholars like Crossley and Rawski, who have shown convincingly that the Qing empire was after all a Manchu empire, ruled simultaneously, following an Altaic ruling tradition. At the same time, however, scholars began to develop the idea of Qing colonialism, although theories of simultaneous rulership and Altaic traditions of rule are in conflict with this idea. By affiliating these two conceptualisations of the Qing empire and showing how they contradict each other, I conclude that the Qing empire cannot be convincingly conceptualised as colonial. It requires more comparative studies, more theorising of terms related to the 'colonial', and finally a broad evaluation of the Qing within global history and not just its comparison with European history to ponder if the adjective 'colonial' can be used meaningfully for Qing rule.

One final aspect of transnationalism needs to be addressed, which is not only related to the question of Qing colonialism, but to the question of whether PRC rule today in Tibet, East Turkestan, Dzungaria, Inner Mongolia, and other non-Chinese regions can be conceptualised as colonial. It becomes clear in a comparison of the relation between the PRC and Mongolia on the one hand, and of the PRC and Tibet on the other. From an international relations perspective, the former relation clearly is transnational, that is, a relation between two sovereign nation-states. In the Chinese translation of the term transnationalism, *kuaguozhuyi*, this is even more obvious, as *guo* today clearly refers to states. The latter relation, however, is not transnational, because Tibet today is part of the PRC and therefore not a sovereign state.

This brings us back to the crucial question of nationalism: which people form nations and are thus supposed to build their own nation-states? In the case of the Mongols, no one would deny them their status as a nation and thus the right to their own state today, and indeed this nation-state exists. In the case of the Tibetans, since its founding in 1949 the Chinese Communist Party, the most important actor in this matter due to its political and military power, has denied them the status of a nation. We have to ask what differentiates Mongols and Tibetans? In 1911/1912, their political situations were very similar: both peoples considered themselves nations, both declared their independence, from the Qing empire and the ROC respectively, and both became theocracies. In the 1920s, however, their paths diverged. Whereas Mongolia became socialist under Soviet patronage, Tibet's status as a sovereign state was never internationally acknowledged. Despite the fact that Tibet was ruled independently by the thirteenth and fourteenth Dalai Lamas between 1912 and 1950, the ROC and its successor state, the PRC, never accepted this independence any more than other states.

It becomes clear that the question of whether a people is a nation and can thus build a nation-state is not determined objectively or neutrally (and by whom anyway, one might ask), but is based on power politics, historical circumstances, military might, and other subjective, individual, disputable factors. Therefore, the term transnationalism *ipso facto* implies the nation-state as the smallest unit of comparison and thus denies certain actors like the Tibetans, the Turkic Muslims, etc. the opportunity to be part of meaningful analysis. For my essay, therefore, transculturalism seems to be a more suitable, inclusive concept that corroborates the importance of not losing sight of smaller units of comparison in order to understand histories and societies.

References and Further Reading

Adas, Michael. 1998. "Imperialism and Colonialism in Comparative Perspective". *The International History Review* 20 (2): 371–388.

Blaut, James M. 1993. *The Colonizer's Model of the World: Geographical Diffusionism and Eurocentric History*. New York: Guilford Press.

Crossley, Pamela. 1990. "Thinking about Ethnicity in Early Modern China". *Late Imperial China* 11 (1): 1–34.

——. 1999. *A Translucent Mirror: History and Identity in Qing Imperial Ideology*. Berkeley: University of California Press.

Crossley, Pamela, and Evelyn Rawski. 1993. "A Profile of the Manchu Language in Ch'ing History". *Harvard Journal of Asiatic Studies* 53 (1): 63–102.

Darwin, John. 2008. *After Tamerlane: The Global History of Empire since 1405*. New York: Bloomsbury.

Esherick, Joseph W. 2006. "How the Qing Became China". In *Empire to Nation: Historical Perspectives on the Making of the Modern World*, edited by Joseph W. Esherick, Hasan Kayalı, and Eric Van Young, 229–259. Lanham: Rowman & Littlefield.

Harrell, Stevan. 2003 [1995]. "Introduction: Civilizing Projects and the Reaction to Them". In *Cultural Encounters on China's Ethnic Frontiers*, edited by Stevan Harrell, 3–36. Seattle: University of Washington Press.

Hechter, Michael. 1975. *Internal Colonialism: The Celtic Fringe in British National Development, 1536–1966*. Berkeley: University of California Press.

Herman, John E. 2007. *Amid the Clouds and Mist: China's Colonization of Guizhou, 1200–1700*. Cambridge, MA: Harvard University Press.

——. 2018. "From Land Reclamation to Land Grab: Settler Colonialism in Southwest China, 1680–1735". *Harvard Journal of Asiatic Studies* 78 (1): 91–123.

Hostetler, Laura. 2001. *Qing Colonial Enterprise: Ethnography and Cartography in Early Modern China*. Chicago: University of Chicago Press.

Kim, Loretta. 2007. "Illumination and Reverence: Language, Identity, and Power in the Prefaces of the Manchu Mirrors". In *Proceedings of the First North American Conference on Manchu Studies, Vol. 2: Studies in Manchu Linguistics*, edited by Stephen Wadley and Carsten Naeher, 67–112. Wiesbaden: Harrassowitz.

Osterhammel, Jürgen. 1997. *Colonialism: A Theoretical Overview*. Princeton: Wiener.

Osterhammel, Jürgen, and Jan C. Jansen. 2012. *Kolonialismus: Geschichte, Formen, Folgen*. Rev. ed. Munich: Beck.

Perdue, Peter C. 1998a. "Comparing Empires: Manchu Colonialism". *The International History Review* 20 (2): 255–262.

——. 1998b. "Boundaries, Maps, and Movement: Chinese, Russian, and Mongolian Empires in Early Modern Central Eurasia". *The International History Review* 20 (2): 263–286.

——. 2005. *China Marches West: The Qing Conquest of Central Eurasia*. Cambridge, MA: Belknap Press.

Rhoads, Edward J. M. 2000. *Manchus and Han: Ethnic Relations and Political Power in Late Qing and Early Republican China, 1861–1928*. Seattle: University of Washington Press.

Schneider, Julia C. 2017a. *Nation and Ethnicity: Chinese Discourses on History, Historiography, and Nationalism (1900s–1920s)*. Leiden: Brill.

——. 2017b. "Missionizing, Civilizing, and Nationizing: Linked Concepts of Compelled Change". In *New Religious Nationalism in Chinese Societies*, edited by Cheng-tian Kuo, 89–115. Amsterdam: Amsterdam University Press.

——. 2020. "Were the Qing Colonial? The Qing Empire in Postcolonial Discourse". *Journal of Asian History* 54 (2): 311–340.

Shih, Shu-mei. 2011. "The Concept of the Sinophone". *Publications of the Modern Language Association* 126 (2): 709–718.

Struve, Lynn A. (ed.). 2004. *The Qing Formation in World-Historical Time.* Cambridge, MA: Harvard University Asia Center.

Teng, Emma Jinhua. 1998. "An Island of Women: The Discourse of Gender in Qing Travel Writing about Taiwan". *The International History Review* 20 (2): 353–370.

——. 2004. *Taiwan's Imagined Geography: Chinese Colonial Travel Writing and Pictures, 1683–1895.* Cambridge, MA: Harvard University Asia Center.

Walsh, Lorena. 2011. "Work and the Slave Economy." In *The Routledge History of Slavery,* edited by Gad Heuman and Trevor Burnard, 101–118. London and New York: Routledge.

Wolfe, Patrick. 1999. *Settler Colonialism and the Transformation of Anthropology: The Politics and Poetics of an Ethnographic Event.* London: Cassell.

Yang, Mayfair Mei-hui. 2011. "Post-Coloniality and Religiosity in Modern China: The Disenchantments of Sovereignty." *Theory, Culture and Society* 28 (2): 3–45.

6

Multilingualism as a Tool of Resistance against Homogenising National Narratives

South Korean Female Subjectivities and Colonial Memory in Pak Sunnyŏ's *Ai rŏbŭ yu* ("I Love You", 1962)

Nadeschda Bachem

Introduction

It is a truism by now that the nation state as an analytical category falls short of capturing the multitudes of complex entanglements brought about by the dynamics of imperialism and globalisation. A case in point is Japan's colonisation of its neighbour Korea (1910–1945) and its conflicted imperial legacy that stretches into the twenty-first century. One defining feature of Japanese imperialism was its aggressive assimilation strategy, enshrined in the infamous *naisen ittai* (内鮮一体, "Japan and Korea as One [Body]") doctrine that saw the Korean Peninsula as part of the Japanese empire and its inhabitants as—albeit inferior—Japanese citizens. In a way, then, following Japan's 1945 defeat, both Koreas and Japan had to reinvent themselves as modern nation states. This proved especially hard for those South Koreans who were raised with Japanese propaganda and were faced with a radically different outlook on their collective identity after 1945.

This chapter will introduce South Korean writer Pak Sunnyŏ (박순녀, b. 1928) and her 1962 story "I Love You" (아이러브유, K. *Ai rŏbŭ yu*; Korean original text (Pak, 1962), English translation (Pak, 1986)). Casting a critical gaze back at the colonial period, this piece of short fiction complicates postcolonial South Korean national narratives as defined by male standards that attempt to eradicate all things Japanese and maintain a strict binary view of Japanese perpetrators and Korean victims, of collaborators and heroes of resistance. This is achieved in two ways: firstly, "I Love You" attests to the fact that women are frequently marginalised from conceptions of nationhood. As Korean women's experiences were often excluded from memorial narratives of the colonial period, the text gives voice to a female perspective and thereby reclaims collective memory for women. At the same time, the piece rejects colonial-period Japanese patriarchal discourse and outlines how Korean women were disadvantaged *vis-à-vis* Korean men. Secondly, "I Love You", which is written in Korean, reveals through a careful selective use of both the Japanese and English language the fragility of a concept of national identity that is built upon the doctrine of Korean monolingualism by eschewing all things Japanese. Instead, the text constructs a neutral space in which Japanese-Korean encounters can take place and the mutual relationship is renegotiated.

While not denying the reality of the nation as a structuring principle for the South Korean community, "I Love You" throws a spotlight on who is excluded in the imagining of the South Korean nation, rendering its supposed homogeneity and naturalness fragile. Its impetus to "challenge the naturalness of national narratives as self-contained sites of meaning" (Frassinelli et al., 2011, 4) makes "I Love You" a prime example with which to explore how postcolonial realities in East Asia might be better grasped through a transnational lens.

Background: Japanese Imperialism, Colonial Memory, and Postcolonial Nation Building in South Korea

The Korean Peninsula was made a protectorate in 1905, then formally annexed and integrated into the Japanese empire in 1910, and would remain a colony until Japan's surrender in August 1945. The Japanese case, of course, differs from its European counterparts in that Japan only narrowly avoided colonisation itself. Apart from a social Darwinist approach inherited from European colonial discourse, Japanese colonial doctrine was driven by a politics of assimilation (同化, J. *dōka*) that sought to integrate the colonies into the homeland, both politically and culturally. In Korea, "turning [Koreans] into imperial subjects" (公民科, J. *kōminka*) was exemplified by the *naisen ittai* doctrine that was enforced increasingly aggressively as the 1930s progressed and Japan entered the war. *Naisen ittai* was aimed at making Korea an inseparable part of Japan and eliminating Korean cultural identity (Eckert, 2014, 236). However, at the same time, it should not be forgotten that the colonies were never really regarded as equal to *naichi* (内地, "the inner territories"), the Japanese homeland (Eckert, 2014, 236–241; Peattie, 1997, 230–244; Saaler and Szpilman, 2011, 17–18).

With Japan's defeat in the Second World War and the consequent end of the Japanese empire, which caused the liberation of the Korean Peninsula in 1945 and the subsequent American occupation of Japan and what is now South Korea, the *naisen ittai* doctrine prevalent in colonial-period propagandistic discourse came to an end. Henceforward, both nations had to imagine themselves anew, as separate and part of a newly forming Cold War world order. The Korean case was, needless to say, infinitely complicated by the emergence of two rival brother states and the devastating civil war of 1950–1953. The struggle surrounding issues of ethnonational belonging, of what should be included in the collective memory and what constitutes the boundaries of one's own ethnonation, is a process that to a degree can be said to be still ongoing today.

In South Korea and Japan, the imperial experience came to be subject to national storylines that were marked by disavowals and embellishment. Almost ironically, former coloniser and colonised have in common the fact that narratives of victimhood prevailed, while memories of collaboration, of atrocities committed, of the enthusiastic embrace of the imperial project by ordinary citizens in both Japan and Korea came to be wiped out (Igarashi, 2000; Orr, 2005; Hughes, 2014).

During the administration of Rhee Syngman (Yi Sŭngman), who ruled South Korea autocratically from 1948 to 1960, public discourse was marked by an unforgiving attitude towards Japan (despite the fact that the Rhee regime relied heavily on pro-Japanese colonial collaborators). Rhee Syngman was forced to resign and flee into exile in 1961 following a massive popular movement calling for democracy, the so-called 19 April Revolution. The democratic system, however, was short-lived and came to an end a mere year later with Park Chung-hee's (Pak Chŏnghŭi) coup d'état on 16 May 1961. Both the democratic and the Park Chung-hee administrations pursued a more pragmatic and pro-Japanese course, not least to strengthen economic ties with Korea's neighbour. Indeed, a significant increase in trade volume between the two countries was one of the results of the Japan-Republic of Korea normalisation treaty that came into effect in 1965. While political relations between Japan and South Korea were normalised in the 1960s, colonial memory remains contested to this very day.

The ideological foundation of the South Korean state took root in a perceived ethnonational unity that worked only on the basis of eradicating the North Korean brother state and aspects of the colonial experience. As Theodore Hughes aptly puts it:

> The shifting boundaries of the South Korean cultural field were organized through the late 1980s around three central disavowals: The ban (until 1988) on colonial-period proletarian works, the institutionalized forgetting of the late-colonial-period mass culture of

> mobilization and imperialization, and the effacement of contemporary North Korean cultural production. These disavowals are structured by an acknowledgment, often appearing at the border or on the margins of texts, of what is not to be spoken or seen. (2014, 1–2)

Certainly, the trauma of the partition of the Korean Peninsula and the subsequent birth of two rival Korean states as well as the fact that literature by proletarian writers of the colonial period was banned shaped Korean literature of the 1960s in a profound way. However, the disavowal that I will highlight for the purposes of this chapter is "the institutionalized forgetting of the late colonial mass culture of mobilization and imperialization", a contentious issue for most Korean writers dealing with the colonial period. Relatedly, Nayoung Aimee Kwon highlights that in late colonial Japanese discourse, Korean participation in the war effort was encouraged and justified by emphasis of voluntary engagement, thereby erasing the history of violence by compelling Koreans to participate in labour and the military. In postcolonial South Korea, she explains, a similar erasure took place in retrospective calls for unilateral resistance against the colonial system, leading to Koreans having "to violently suppress a whole range of their experiences from their pasts as if they had never existed" (Kwon, 2015, 199–200).

This is especially true for the South Korean generation of authors born in the 1920s and early 1930s, who lived their childhood and youth under the colonial regime. This group, the so-called post-war generation (전후세대, K. *chŏnhu sedae*), the war being the Korean War (1950–1953), for the most part commenced their literary activities in the mid- to late 1950s or early 1960s. Most South Korean writers of this generation challenge the simplistic binary of collaborators versus patriotic heroes and emphasise the involvement of ordinary Korean citizens in the imperial project as well as their enthusiasm for it. This stance also stems from the fact that for them, participation in the "institutionalized forgetting" required the disavowal of a considerable portion of their childhood and youth.

Having been brought up during the colonial period, the post-war generation had to come to grips with the issue of Korean monolingualism. As Serk-bae Suh explains, in South Korean society Korean monolingualism became the symbol of the ethnonation by eliminating all things Japanese in order to overcome the colonial legacy: "The suppression of postcolonial bilingualism was an essential part of modern nation state-building in Korea" (2013, 138). This passed a dilemma especially for the post-war generation of Koreans who were educated under the colonial system and often acquired knowledge of the native writing system, Hangŭl, only after 1945. Following the liberation, intellectuals defined the national language (국어, K. *kugŏ*) as intrinsically connected to and an expression of the South Korean state: "As Koreans aspired to build a modern nation state, it was not only inevitable but also imperative for them to have one unifying and unified national language" (Suh, 2013, 138). The national language became inextricably linked to the South Korean nation state, which was founded on the assumption of a unity of state, national language, and ethnonation (민족, K. *minjok*—a concept that presupposes a relatively homogeneous people defined by a common language and culture that coincides with the boundaries of the nation-state). This ideology, which postulated a return to a unified Korean language untainted by colonial pollution, is rife with contradictions, as such the fact that no such homogeneous original language before the influences of Sinicisation or colonisation had ever existed to begin with (Suh, 2013, 148–149). The Korean language, much like any other language, was and remains never purely "national" but has at its core an element of hybridity, of translation and transition, because it contains traces of all the communities that shape Korea, making it fundamentally transnational.

While the negotiation of colonial-period remnants in the form of the Japanese language is a pressing concern for South Korean authors of the post-war generation, the postcolonial geopolitical situation and the rise of American hegemony are highlighted by frequent reference to the English language in literature. In "I Love You" the English language becomes a space of freedom, a neutral space where Japanese and Korean characters can meet and a postcolonial relationship between Korea and Japan can be renegotiated.

Analysis: Pak Sunnyŏ's "I Love You"

Pak Sunnyŏ was born in 1928 in South Hamgyŏng Province in what is now North Korea and came to Seoul shortly after the liberation in 1945. In 1950 she graduated from Seoul University's English Literature Department and made her debut with *Case Worker* (케이스 워카, K. *K'eisŭ wŏk'a*) in the newspaper *Chosun Ilbo* (조선일보) in 1960. "I Love You" was published in 1962 in the prestigious intellectual journal *Sasanggye* (사상계). While her active period spanned over 30 years through to the 1990s, in later years she received less critical acclaim than during the initial period of her literary activity (Kim Yunsŏn, 2010, 236–237).

"I Love You", next to "Entrance to the Foreigners' Village" (외인촌입구, K. *Oeinch'on ipku*, 1964), is generally considered Pak Sunnyŏ's most representative work and was runner-up for the *Sasanggye shinin munhaksang* (사상계 신인 문학상), Sasanggye's prize for literary newcomers (Kim Yunsŏn, 2010, 240). The piece is set in a small town in Korea in 1945 spanning the time shortly before and after the liberation. Protagonist Myŏnghwa (명화) is a student at a high school for girls, run by the strict Japanese headmaster

Nero (네로). The girls are proud to attend their school, which they know will guide them on their way to become good citizens of the Japanese empire. The story makes a point of contrasting two of the girls' teachers—the Korean Min (민) and the young and sympathetic Japanese teacher Yamaki (야마키). The girls fondly refer to Yamaki as "Mr. Brown" due to his resemblance to an American comedian, but when a rumour surfaces that he has a sixth toe, they start calling him "Yukpal Sŏnsaeng" (육발선생, "Teacher Six-toe").

At a school outing, Myŏnghwa and her best friend Pongsuk (봉숙) have a lively conversation about students from a boys' school who are destined to become cheap wage labourers and wonder whether they should shout "I love you" (in English) at them. Nero overhears their conversation, and they are punished. Later the girls attend a gala for boys who are being sent off as soldiers and attend the farewell ceremony for a girl who has been drafted as a nurse for the Red Cross. The girls are enraptured and vow to become nurses themselves. However, the atmosphere shifts when they observe the nurse crying and clinging to her young child before she is dragged off to the ferry that will take her to the front line. The next day, Nero presses for the girls to sign up for the Red Cross. Myŏnghwa refuses to comply and starts a small riot among the girls. In the end Myŏnghwa and Pongsuk are expelled from school. About a month later, Korea is liberated and it is now the repatriating Japanese who constitute a pathetic sight in their ragged clothes. Myŏnghwa and Pongsuk are travelling to Seoul when, near the thirty-eighth parallel, they meet Yamaki. In an awkward short conversation in which the two girls are at a loss for words, he insists that he is no longer their teacher and when they part, he shouts "I love you" after them.

"I Love You" doubly complicates monolithic notions of nationhood. Firstly, by addressing how within the imperial system Korean women were disadvantaged to an even greater degree than Korean men, the text challenges the masculine foundations upon which both the Japanese empire and the postcolonial South Korean nation were built, which in the latter case are closely entangled with imperial memory. The nation in East Asia (and elsewhere) being a narrative construct that excludes women's experiences, highlighting those very experiences casts doubt on streamlined national discourse and thus opens a space in which transnational identities can be negotiated, as will be shown in the second part of my analysis. Namely, we will see how "I Love You" implicitly criticises the way a purportedly unified South Korean nation was imagined by excluding all things Japanese and unilaterally marking Japan as aggressor to a victimised Korean Peninsula. The piece arrives at a nuanced outlook on Japan and the way it shaped Korea as it follows protagonist Myŏnghwa's trajectory from ardent supporter of the Japanese empire to anti-colonial activist (significantly, related to her femininity in the text), until, at the close of the story, a space for renegotiating Japanese-Korean encounters is introduced (issues also touched on by Weingärtner in Chapter 9 of this book).

"I Love You" gives us insight into Korean female subjectivities shaped by the colonial experience and complicates a narrative of Korean victimisation as inscribed on women's bodies. Twentieth-century national narratives in Korea have been profoundly gendered, both during the colonial period and after liberation. While female characters were often employed as mere props to exemplify the victimisation of the Korean nation during the colonial period (Jager, 2003), Kelly Y. Jeong argues that the "modern Korean masculine subject [...] is identified with the nation itself" (2011, 9), a conception that has a long genealogy in Korea's Confucian tradition, which is examined by Cawley in Chapter 1. The various historical crises of national unity and modernity from the 1930s to the 1960s are experienced and described as a threat to and a crisis of masculinity: "The postwar South Korean state responded to the threats on its nationhood, both imagined and otherwise, by overmilitarizing the nation, and by constructing a masculine national subject in monolithic, exclusive, and specific ways" (Jeong, 2011, 77). Chungmoo Choi, meanwhile, explains how the nationalistic masculinist rhetoric of the postcolonial South Korean state left little room for women to negotiate their colonial experience: "Nationalism represses ambivalence about and contradictions in women's subjectivity and therefore leaves no room to negotiate. Women of a postcolonial nation are denied an opportunity to decolonize their split (or multiple or hybrid) subjectivity, which is shaped under the colonial oppression" (1998, 28). "I Love You" thus reclaims colonial memory and, perhaps unsurprisingly, arrives at a different outlook on nationalism by including a strong transnational perspective.

Against this social background, Kim Yunsŏn shows how "I Love You" points to the double bind in which Korean women were trapped between patriarchy and imperialism. She explains that the text shows how Korean girls and boys were equally educated to become subjects of the Japanese empire. However, colonial women experienced their second-class position both as members of the colonised nation and in being treated as inferior to men (Kim Yunsŏn, 2010, 241). This double standard becomes apparent at the gala when the girls have this enthusiastic conversation:

> "I wish I had been a boy!"
> "Me too. I wish I could go where they are going!" [...]
> "What if I went as a volunteer nurse?"
> "As a volunteer nurse?"
> "It's the only way a girl can go to the battlefield, isn't it?" (Pak, 1986, 60; Pak, 1962, 368)

Even as supporters of the empire, girls are disadvantaged. Sending them out as nurses instead of soldiers, we see how the empire makes use of a type of femininity classified as caring and nurturing, excluding them from what in a militarised imperial society constitutes the core of the national community. Maybe not coincidentally, Myŏnghwa's subsequent realisation of these very power mechanisms and her criticism of Japanese imperialism results from a specifically female position (Kim Yunsŏn, 2010, 240–241). Her sentiments after her awakening to the violence of the colonial system are described as follows: "Now that I look back on it, I was for the first time experiencing the impurity of my fate as a girl in a colonial country. It was a feeling similar to the shocked, outraged sadness I had felt for my being 'a girl' on the first day of menstruation" (Pak, 1986, 62; Pak, 1962, 370). Here, her experience as a colonial subject is explicitly set in relation to her femininity and it is revealed how in both the colonial and the patriarchal system, Korean women take a subordinate role.

The piece, then, shows the intersectionality between gender and ethnonational belonging and emphasises that the lines do not just run between Japan and Korea but also internally within both societies, since Korean men and women are affected in different ways by Japanese imperialism. "I Love You" thus refutes a dominant South Korean narrative in which resistance is often painted as a heroic struggle to reclaim the ethnonation. At the same time, it points out that women are victimised in overlapping ways but admits to female agency by describing one girl's fight to save her very life from a patriarchal, imperial system (Pak, 1962).

"I Love You" is narrated from a first-person perspective by protagonist Myŏnghwa. The text thus allows the reader to slip into a colonised schoolgirl's place and see the events from her perspective, adding plasticity and nuance to an imagery that reduces Korean femininity to an empty cipher for the nation's victimisation during the colonial period. The piece installs an active and multifaceted female subject to complement the hegemonic male Korean perspective on the colonial experience. Moreover, the symbolic choice of a first-person narrator gives back their own voice to Korean women, who are often marginalised in the discussion of the colonial experience or become stylised symbols of ethnonational suffering rather than humans with complex motivations and horizons of experience. This female perspective reclaims colonial memory, which was to become an important facet of postcolonial South Korean national identity by inserting women into the story, rejecting patriarchal narratives in both colonial Japanese and postcolonial national South Korean discourse. This perspective can also be thought to have informed the work's strong transnational undertone, as women's relatively marginalised position within the national narrative afforded them the freedom to negotiate their colonial experiences in a way that Korean men, with their connection to the Korean nation, might not have been able to.

"I Love You" challenges not only the gendered foundations of both empire and postcolonial nation by zooming in on its protagonist's female perspective, it also complicates an often simplistic nationalistic South Korean view on Japan. The text defies both South Korean postcolonial narratives that see a unified Korean community as the victim of a monolithic Japanese aggressor and a Japanese postcolonial narrative that sees fault for colonial aggression fall fully with the military whilst absolving civil society from responsibility (Orr, 2005; Igarashi, 2000). At the same time, it rejects the colonial-period *naisen ittai* doctrine but gives a positive outlook for a future Japanese-Korean relationship that transgresses strict ethnonational divisions.

One important demarcation line in the text runs between the contrasting characters of the teachers Min and Yamaki. While Min strictly adheres to Nero's rule and Myŏnghwa is even convinced that he would hand them over to the military police if asked to do so by Nero (Pak, 1962, 374), Yamaki is portrayed as a gentle and youthful character who is always willing to champion his students' rights (Pak, 1962, 374–375). When Myŏnghwa confronts him after the gala, the following conversation unfolds between the two characters:

> Suddenly Yukpal Sŏnsaeng spoke in a voice in which I could feel a change of tone.
>
> "You know I never can count on you girls. How should I put it … You are all pure-hearted in a sense, but you are, also, ignorant. You are all so naive and ignorant and that is why you are so pitiable. You seem to all of a sudden find the object of your distrust and anger in what is known as the Japanese people. But if you took a more penetrating view of things in general, you would soon find out that both Japanese and Koreans, in fact, all humanity are divided into two common camps: the camp of victims and the camp of victimizers. I mean not all Japanese are victimizers just as not all Koreans are victims. You may not know it, but I, too, am a sort of victim."
>
> Inwardly I said with all the force I had: "No, no, you are not," but I continued to listen to his voice […] I wanted to say words of retort and words of protest to this Japanese teacher. It was not that I could not comprehend the concept of what he called victims and victimizers but I wanted to ask him this question above anything else, "Are you not a Japanese, then?" (Pak, 1986, 62–63; Pak, 1962, 371–372)

Here the text vocalises its central point of boundaries not running strictly between the ethnonations of Japan and Korea but instead proves that ethnonational identity as defined by national narratives is blurry at best. Thereby, the piece challenges postcolonial constructions of the South Korean ethnonation that rely on the notion of a unified Korean community that has been victimised by a unilaterally malevolent Japanese aggressor. Instead, through the character of Yamaki, it puts forward a perspective in which the entire human race is divided not by national affiliation but by participation in power. As mentioned above, the post-1945 cultural field in South Korea was, amongst others, structured around "the institutionalized forgetting of the late-colonial-period mass culture of mobilization and imperialization" (Hughes, 2014, 1–2). Through the character of Min, "I Love You" recalls that members of Korean society benefited from and actively participated in the imperial project.

However, while in the wake of the 1965 normalisation treaty the Park Chung-hee administration would later be accused of glossing over colonial-period injustice in order to achieve its aim of normalisation for economic ends, the text cannot be said to be apologetic of Japanese imperialism. "I Love You" hints at structural inequalities that affect Koreans and Japanese to differing degrees, as can be seen in the last part of the excerpt above, when Myŏnghwa tries to voice her conviction that Japanese victims are qualitatively different from Korean victims. Furthermore, Yamaki is able to transgress certain boundaries that are binding for Min: "Suppose it was not Yukpal Sŏnsaeng but Min Sŏnsaeng (민선생) who was standing face to face with Nero, would Nero have the patience to hear him through like this?" (Pak, 1986, 66; Pak, 1962, 375). By highlighting the fact that Min would not have been able to confront Nero in the way Yamaki does, the text also highlights the limited influence and scope of action enjoyed even by collaborators, thus drawing attention to imperialism as a power structure that binds all its members rather than an individual choice.

Another aspect of ethnonational belonging that the text discusses is the shift in power with the liberation. As Chung Hye Kyung (Chŏng Hyekyŏng) points out, the meeting between Yamaki, Myŏnghwa, and Pongsuk at the crossing allows the transgression (and thus renegotiation) of national boundaries (Chung, 2011, 601–602). The description of the ragged returning Japanese at the end of the story points to a reversal in the power hierarchy and is reflected also in many other South Korean texts describing the liberation. Yamaki's insistence that he is not their teacher any more proves that with the liberation, the relationship between Koreans and Japanese needs to be renegotiated. The mutually displayed warmth as well as their parting with the words "I love you" show an optimistic outlook on future relationships between the two neighbours. Only in the parting scene, with the new power hierarchy, can Myŏnghwa let go of her grudge against all Japanese and a renegotiation of Self and Other as individuals rather than teacher and students, coloniser and colonised, becomes possible. In this way, "I Love You" also seems to be written against a monolithic notion of the South Korean ethnonation in the 1960s and champions the idea that communities should be rebuilt on a civil society level, detached from the ideologies of nationalism, patriarchy, and imperialism. Rather than relying on Japan as a demonised Other that serves as a backdrop to the national narrative, the piece champions a more hybrid and forgiving ideal of identity, one in which women are not utilised and Japanese not unilaterally demonised.

In "I Love You", this renegotiation symbolically takes place in a neutral, transnational space, exemplified by the English language, where Japanese-Korean encounters can take place beyond the national boundaries constructed in political discourse. Yi Sŏnmi points to the situation for female intellectual writers such as Pak Sunnyŏ in the wake of the 19 April Revolution of 1960. The democratic movement had brought about the promise of individual freedom. However, in the subsequent dominant discourse of modernisation under Park Chung-hee an ideology of personal sacrifice for the greater good became prevalent, in the course of which women in particular were pressed once more into a traditional pattern of "good wife, wise mother". Accordingly, Yi Sŏnmi (Lee, 2006, 417–423) demonstrates how female writers of this period make use of differing discourses on America but ultimately identify the American lifestyle as a symbol of personal freedom, particularly in relation to questions of marriage, love, and sexuality since those questions were strongly connected to the limiting of women's personal freedom. While she does not discuss "I Love You", her article is illuminating in that it offers an overall insight on the role of American culture and language in Pak Sunnyŏ's work, and against this background the role of the English language in the piece becomes more evident.

It is telling that the female writers analysed by Yi Sŏnmi took a radically different position on America from many of their male contemporaries in highlighting the promise of freedom in American values whilst overlooking the political implications of US involvement on the Korean Peninsula. In other literary works of the period, America's position as a neo-imperial power and a threat to South Korean nationhood is foregrounded—canonical works such as Yi Pŏmsŏn's *A Stray Bullet* (오발탄, K. *Obalt'an*, 1959) Ch'oe Inhun's *The Square* (광장, K. *Kwangjang*, 1960) spring to mind. However, in "I Love You", the English language is stripped of these political implications and comes to signify a liberated space detached from colonial and patriarchal oppression. I argue that the text is less concerned with American geopolitics in East Asia (a space from which women were excluded to begin with) but instead uses English as a rhetorical means to create a space of freedom in which women can negotiate their colonial experience. What is at stake are not South Korean-American relations but a personal freedom that allows for encountering Japan at an individual, grassroots level, which is open to women.

The first example of the significance of English in the text is a mission school, a rival to the strict imperial school that Myŏnghwa attends:

> The contrast between S Girls' High School and our school was manifest even in sports meets. When there was a volleyball match between the two schools, for instance, the melodious and pleasant voices of the S Girls' High School champions rose: "One! Two! Three!" [English in Hangŭl in the original] in a carefree, resilient rhythm. But against this, our champions as they met the ball sent by the S chool [*sic*] champions in their typically graceful form shouted soldierlike: "Ichi! Ni! San!" [one, two, three in Japanese] with gusto, to be sure, but without any grace whatsoever. (Pak, 1986, 54–55; Pak, 1962, 363)

The English language here is set in direct opposition to the strict militaristic imperial system as exemplified by the Japanese language and towards the end of the story the liberal ideology of S school is described as superior to that of the strict government school. In this way, the American lifestyle, signified by the English language, is portrayed as a way for Korean women to free themselves from the restrictions of both the imperial and the South Korean postcolonial collective narratives. Meanwhile, the Japanese language serves as a stand-in for the colonial military apparatus. In this respect, then, Pak Sunnyŏ's piece lacks the nostalgia for the Japanese language that is prevalent in some of her peers' fiction. At the same time, her strong reliance on the English language rejects the ideology of Korean monolingualism.

The second example is the politics of nicknames for Yamaki. As mentioned above, he is referred to as "Mr. Brown" in the beginning, when he is introduced as a character contrasting to Min. For most of the text, the girls call him Yukpal Sŏnsaeng because of the rumour that he has six toes. Only in the very last sentence of the piece is the character rehabilitated: "The toes on the barefoot [*sic*!] of Mr. Brown who had made a present with the 'I love you' to us were definitely five, not six" (Pak, 1986, 67; Pak, 1962, 376). We see that the humiliating rumours about his physique were unfounded and in the newly liberated space where Japanese-Korean relationships are renegotiated he is referred to by his English nickname, not his actual Japanese name, indicating that this character is exemplary of a non-delineated idea of national identity that the text advocates. His English nickname indicates that Yamaki is part of the liberated realm signified by the English language, detached from Japanese colonial and South Korean national patriarchal oppression. Within this realm characters are not confined by the limiting notion of belonging to either of the strictly defined Japanese and South Korean ethnonations but seem able to meet simply as people amicably in a transnational space provided by the English language.

The third and final example is the title phrase "I love you" (said in English in the original) which frames the story. In the first instance, it shows the girls proactively taking their sexuality into their own hands by shouting the sentence at a couple of boys, which, within the Japanese imperial power framework, leads to punishment. Only with the liberation is the English phrase shown to be far removed from Korean patriarchal and Japanese colonial oppression, a space where sympathetic Korean and Japanese characters can meet. All these examples show how the English language, which can be assumed to stand metonymically for a liberal spirit envisaged as connected to American culture, thus becomes a counterpoint to both the Japanese imperial brand of patriarchy and the South Korean postcolonial one.

Conclusion

Throughout this discussion, it has become evident that "I Love You" seeks a kind of colonial memory and postcolonial reconciliation that differs from the discursive strands of the Syngman Rhee regime, the democratic interlude, and the Park Chung-hee years.

While the piece does not deny the reality of the nation as structuring the South Korean and Japanese communities, it highlights blind spots in the postcolonial South Korean national narrative, which excludes women and their colonial memory. At the same time, the text seeks ways of overcoming the limitations of nationalism (especially anti-Japanese nationalism), which is ultimately achieved within the neutral transnational space of the English language. Like many writers of the post-war generation, Pak Sunnyŏ thus challenges the post-liberation doctrine of Korean monolingualism by rendering visible Japanese and English influences on the Korean language. She thereby manages to cast a spotlight on the transnational nature of what in nationalist South Korean discourse was assumed to be the cornerstone of a supposedly pure, homogeneous South Korean national identity. What sets Pak apart from many of her male peers, however, is that America is not seen as a political threat to Korean masculinity but is presented, on a cultural level, as a promise of connection on an individual level and personal freedom.

"I Love You" offers a view on the colonial period that is neither unilaterally condemnatory nor apologetic, that through a specific use of language opens up hybrid spaces for encounter beyond the strict lines of ethnonational unity, and that takes into account the experiences of women to rearticulate colonial memory. In this way, even almost 60 years on, it remains a forward-looking work in the South Korean postcolonial literary canon.

References and Further Reading

Choi, Chungmoo. 1998. "Nationalism and Construction of Gender in Korea". In *Korean Women and Nationalism: Gender and Korean Nationalism*, edited by Elaine H. Kim and Chungmoo Choi, 9–32. London: Routledge.

Chung Hye Kyung (Chŏng Hyekyŏng). 2011. "Sasanggye tŭngdan shin'in yŏsŏng chakka sosŏle nat'anan ch'ŏngnyŏn p'yosang" (『사상계』 등단 신인여성작가 소설에 나타난 청년 표상) [Representations of Youth in the Work of Female Writers Debuting in Sasanggye]. *Uri ŏmun yŏn'gu* 39: 579–609.

Eckert, Carter J. 2014. *Offspring of Empire: The Koch'ang Kims and the Colonial Origins of Korean Capitalism, 1876–1945*. Seattle: University of Washington Press.

Frassinelli, Pier Paolo, Ronit Frenkel, and David Watson. 2011. "Traversing Transnationalism". In *Traversing Transnationalism: The Horizons of Literary and Cultural Studies*, edited by Pier Paolo Frassinelli, Ronit Frenkel and David Watson, 1–14. Amsterdam: Rodopi.

Hughes, Theodore H. 2014. *Literature and Film in Cold War South Korea: Freedom's Frontier*. New York: Columbia University Press.

Igarashi, Yoshikuni. 2000. *Bodies of Memory: Narratives of War in Postwar Japanese Culture, 1945–1970*. Princeton: Princeton University Press.

Jager, Sheila Miyoshi. 2003. *Narratives of Nation Building in Korea: A Genealogy of Patriotism*. London: Routledge.

Jeong, Kelly Y. 2011. *Crisis of Gender and the Nation in Korean Literature and Cinema: Modernity Arrives Again*. Lanham: Lexington.

Kim Yunsŏn. 2010. "Wŏlnam yŏsŏng chakka Pak Sunnyŏŭi 'ch'ehŏm' kwa munhak. 'Ai rŏbŭ yu', 'Oeinch'on ipku', 'Ŏttŏn p'ali' rŭl chungsimŭro" (월남 여성 작가 박순녀의 '체험'과 문학. 「아이 러브 유」, 「외인촌 입구」, 「어떤 파리」를 중심으로) [The "Experiences" and Literature of Pak Sunnyŏ, a Female Writer Who Left North Korea: On "Ai rŏbŭ yu", "Oeinch'on ipku", "Ŏttŏn p'ali"]. *Han'guk'ak yŏn'gu* 33: 235–262.

Kwon, Nayoung Aimee. 2015. *Intimate Empire: Collaboration and Colonial Modernity in Korea and Japan*. Durham, NC: Duke University Press.

Lee Sun Mi (Yi Sŏnmi). 2006. "1960 nyŏndae yŏsŏng chisikinŭi 'chayu' tamnongwa miguk—Pak Sunnyŏ, Son Changsun, Pak Sichŏng sosŏlŭl chungsimŭro" (1960 년대 여성지식인의 '자유'담론과 미국 - 박순녀, 손장순, 박시정 소설을 중심으로) [America and the Discourse on "Freedom" by Female Intellectuals in the 1960s: On Novels by Pak Sunnyŏ, Son Changsun, and Pak Sichŏng], *Hyŏndae munhak ŭi yŏn'gu* 29: 417–452.

Orr, James J. 2005. *The Victim as Hero: Ideologies of Peace and National Identity in Postwar Japan*. Honolulu: University of Hawai'i Press.

Pak Sunnyŏ. 1962. "Ai rŏbŭ yu" (아이 러브 유) [I love you]. *Sasanggye* 114: 362–376.

——. 1986. "I Love You". *Korea Journal* 26 (7): 54–67.

Peattie, Mark R. 1997. "The Japanese Colonial Empire, 1985–1945". In *Cambridge History of Japan, Vol. 6: The Twentieth Century*, edited by Peter Duus and John Whitney Hall, 217–270. Cambridge: Cambridge University Press.

Saaler, Sven, and Christopher W. A. Szpilman. 2011. "Introduction". In *1920–Present, Pan-Asianism: A Documentary History*, edited Sven Saaler and Christopher W. A. Szpilman, 10–42. London: Rowman & Littlefield.

Suh, Serk-Bae. 2013. *Treacherous Translation: Culture, Nationalism, and Colonialism in Korea and Japan from the 1910s to the 1960s*. Berkeley: University of California Press.

7

Conjuring a Battling China

Willi Münzenberg and His International Popular Front

Lei Qin

Introduction

The chapter investigates and delineates the rarely studied China-centred internationalist left-wing popular front campaign initiated by the Münzenberg circle. As China of the 1920s and '30s has been primarily defined by dichotomous narratives of the two giant political parties, the Chinese Communist Party (CCP) and the Nationalist Party, or Guomindang (GMD), this popular front cultural political movement—intervention through non-military cultural empowerment—was doomed to be neglected. This chapter is an attempt to highlight the forgotten transnational internationalist movement by tracking the flow of its key personnel as well as that of texts and images across national borders. The fluidity across space and culture opens up alternative possibilities for looking at history through international political articulation.

The chapter hence adopts a bipartite structure with the first part introducing the "top design" of the China-centred internationalist movement (its top facilitators, organisations, major publications, and its agenda), and the second part introducing the texts across media in their collective imagining of a China-centred internationalist collective. Though the texts had a primary audience in the European (primarily German) working class, the campaigns left a lasting imprint on the newly minted image of China (an awakened nation filled with high revolutionary energy and fighting spirits), which became a major theme of left-wing Weimar literature that was introduced to and reciprocated by the Chinese. Responses from Chinese intellectuals were first visible through those who worked closely with or endorsed the Comintern (the Communist International, founded by Lenin in 1919 to advance communist revolution in the world)—Xiao San (萧三, 1896–1983),

poet, the Chinese representative in the Moscow-based International Union of Revolutionary Writers; Qu Qiubai (瞿秋白, 1899–1935), CCP leader in the 1920s; Lu Xun (鲁迅, 1881–1936), known as "father of modern Chinese literature"; and Mao Dun (茅盾, 1896–1981), a leading left-wing writer especially in the 1930s—before this internationalist China image came to be more widely reciprocated by the Chinese left-wing literary circle.

The Shaping of an Internationalist Momentum

Besides the known institutional cooperation of politics and military between Republican China and Weimar Germany, there was also a widely forgotten transnational campaign between Western and Chinese left-wing writers and artists. The campaign adopted an internationalist scope aiming to transcend party politics and armed revolution by constructing an international community to empower ordinary Chinese and European workers unified in their common combat against colonialism and capitalism. Here, internationalism is not taken at its general level as against nationalism, or as some deep cooperation among states that supports the rise of global capitalism or international institutions like the United Nations. On the contrary, it is the Marxist and Leninist term that closely relates to the socialist concept of international solidarity—a call to the global proletariat to break down national boundaries in their shared struggle against global capitalism. The seeds of the internationalist vision were sown by Chinese oversea activists/students in light of Weimar left-wing revolts before it was institutionalised in 1927 by Willi Münzenberg and the Chinese nationalist left-wing leaders Soong Ching-ling (宋庆龄), the widow of Sun Yat-sen, the "father of the Chinese revolution", and Deng Yan-da (邓演达), the GMD's top leader.

The 1920s and '30s saw hundreds of Chinese students matriculated in universities in Germany. Berlin in the late '20s was depicted as a gathering point for the young nationalists and communists, who established the Main Association of Chinese Students (*Hauptverband der chinesischen Studenten*) (Yü-Dembski, 2007, 123). These left-leaning students particularly enjoyed the open climate and large network of internationalists and their anti-colonial and anti-imperialist activities.

Indeed, since the early 1920s, Berlin had been the centre of the Communist International's intelligence work. In the declassified archives of the Communist International, a document issued by the Bureau of the Central Executive Committee on 5 January 1923 passed the proposal that the information centre established in Berlin would no longer be affiliated with the Central Executive Committee and would become an independent institution (Communist Party of Great Britain, 1924, 104–106). Each member state was to assign one person to collect information and data, and to carry out propagandistic work to launch communist revolution in a specific country (Firsov et al., 2014, 51). The activist Chinese community there was naturally absorbed as a crucial part into the circle, with Liao Huanxing (廖焕星, 1895–1964) (more below) as the liaison. The person in charge of the information centre in Berlin was Willi Münzenberg (1889–1940), who, during exile in Switzerland in his early years, met Lenin, who was also in exile in Switzerland, and became a loyal adherent of communism.

This German-born expatriate in Switzerland attracted countless young people to the Communist Youth League that he managed. Besides Münzenberg's hard skills as a superb propagandist (i.e. his ability to deliver inspiring speeches and excellent organisation skills), his biographers have often pointed to his "mysterious" personal charm and appeal as qualities key to his huge success in attracting a powerful network of artists and writers (McMeekin, 2003, 1–3). At the peak of his career in the 1920s and 1930s, he remotely controlled a huge network of communist frontline organisations across Europe, South America, and Asia from his Berlin headquarters. These organisations include charities, publishing houses, newspapers, magazines, theatres, and cinemas. Almost all well-known interwar left-wing intellectuals, writers, and artists in Europe were part of his huge cultural network. In less than a decade, he had organised dozens of international popular fronts and transnational alliances, with themes ranging from defence of Soviet Russia to famine relief, political prisoners rescue, to anti-war, national independence, and anti-fascism. He founded nearly 20 newspapers, magazines, and pictorials, held international workers' cultural events, facilitated exchanges between European intellectuals and artists and their counterparts in the Third World, particularly China (McMeekin, 2003, 86–91; Brasken, 2015, 1–4).

At the core of his network was the International Workers' Relief (Internationale Arbeiter-Hilfe, hereafter IAH), established in 1921 with a core goal to "expose the 'evil essence of capitalist society'" through propagandistic campaigns with wide public participation" (Münzenberg, 1931, 363). Its initial Soviet famine relief fundraising campaign showcased the organisation's luxury line-up of participants—these included German Communist Party (KPD) leader Clara Zetkin, painter Käthe Kollwitz, Albert Einstein, writers Georg Grosz, Anatole France, Henri Barbusse, George Bernard Shaw, and others. These left-wing intellectuals, artists, and writers were to remain the centre pillars of Münzenberg's red propaganda empire for the decade to come.

IAH's China-targeting activities began in 1925. Right after the anti-imperial labour protest, the so-called May Thirtieth Movement broke out in Shanghai in 1925, the IAH's China subcommittee was empowered to launch fundraising activities in Europe for oppressed Chinese workers, and to report extensively on Chinese workers' brave anti-imperial protests. With the help of *Workers' Illustrated Newspaper* (*Arbeiter-Illustrierte Zeitung*, hereafter *AIZ*), published by Münzenberg's New German Press (*Neuer Deutscher Verlag*) and aimed at a general readership, the IAH was able to quickly respond and widely report its large-scale international anti-imperialist movement around the world to support Chinese workers within days of the outbreak of the May Thirtieth Movement (*AIZ*, June 1925). The illustrated newspaper closely reported the massive parades in Moscow and Prague on 5 June with 500,000 and 200,000 participants, respectively, to encourage workers in Shanghai. On the day of the parades, the IAH issued a declaration entitled "To China's Heroic Struggling People", signed by George Bernard Shaw, Henry Barbusse, Upton Sinclair, Clara Zetkin, and others. The British Federation of Trade Unions also telegraphed the China Federation of Trade Unions on 19 June, declaring solidarity with the striking workers (Petersson, 2007, 15). In December that year, *AIZ* reported anti-imperialist demonstrations across Europe organised by the IAH (Fig. 1). Under the headline "International Workers' Relief Activities", photos show rallies in Prague and Württemberg, and the Chinese workers' protest, with a caption reading "a large-scale workers' demonstration launched by the Workers' Relief Society in Beijing against joining the Washington Treaty".

Aus der Bewegung der Internationalen Arbeiterhilfe

Fig. 1. *AIZ*, December issue, 1925.

As solidarity parades gained momentum, the IAH established the "Hands Off China" committee, dedicated specifically to facilitating China's anti-imperialist movement and to garnering international support for the decade to come. With the fading climax of the Soviet communist revolution and the sluggish German labour movement following the humiliation of the Versailles Treaty, China's booming anti-imperialist movement was perhaps the most cheering spirit for international revolutionaries in the 1920s. China hence became the focal point of Münzenberg's international anti-imperialist united front. The IAH's China-related political and cultural activities reportedly attracted wide attention in Germany. Münzenberg reported that the 5,036 events the organisation initiated in 1930, such as rallies, parades, speeches, film screenings, and political satires, attracted more than 1 million attendants. The IAH's great success in ideological and financial operations was also acknowledged by the Comintern (Münzenberg, 1931).

Münzenberg's China campaigns attest to the level of attention the KPD and the Comintern paid to the development of the Chinese revolution since the early 1920s. The up-to-date China coverage and well-targeted mass campaigns would not have been possible without the involvement of Chinese activist students in Germany. Among them were many future Chinese leaders in the arenas of politics, military, and culture, such as Zhou Enlai (周恩来, 1898–1976), Zhu De (朱德, 1886–1976), and Cheng Fangwu (成仿吾, 1897–1984) (Kampen, 2010, 10–15). In his interview with Agnes Smedley (1892–1950) in Yan'an, Zhu De, the highest ranking military leader and founder of the Chinese Red Army, later reflected on his participation in these activities organised by the IAH under slogans like "China for the Chinese" (*China den Chinesen*) and "solidarity with the fighting China" (*Solidarität mit dem kämpfenden China*). Zhu De reflected on how Zhou Enlai introduced him to the group of Chinese communists in Berlin at their weekly discussions on "the basis of Chinese revolution along the Marxist-Leninist line" (Yü-Dembski, 1987, 125–126).

Scholars have identified the student Liao Huanxing (廖焕星, 1895–1964) as the leader of the left-wing Chinese association. Between 1925 and 1927, Liao was the one who drafted all 75 reports on China provided by the Berlin intelligence agency (Krüger, 2002, 177–180). Liao's excellent command of German, his rich past experiences in the Guangzhou Nationalist Government as well as his experiences as translator and consultant on Chinese issues for the Comintern all made him invaluable to the Berlin centre. Münzenberg's widow Babette Gross also recollected how her husband worked frequently with a "young aspiring Chinese Communist named Liao" in Berlin (Gross, 1984).

Liao was often mentioned in the memoirs of other Chinese students, such as Hu Lanqi (胡兰畦, 1901–1994), and was a central figure in the Chinese sector of the German Communist Party (Hu, 1985, 228). The student group grew quickly in its political significance and visibility due to attracting top left-wing GMD leaders in exile after Chiang Kai-shek's crackdown on communists in 1927. These later members included He Xiangning (何香凝, 1878–1972), wife of the assassinated GMD leader Liao Zhongkai (廖仲恺, 1877–1925), their son Liao Chengzhi (廖承志, 1908–1983) and daughter Liao Mengxing (廖梦醒, 1904–1988), the German Communist Party member Xie Weijin (谢唯进, 1899–1978), Soong Ching-Ling, and Deng Yan-da (Krüger, 2002, 177–183). The latter two left the country furious with Chiang, declaring him a traitor to the GMD, and became Münzenberg's long-term collaborators on the internationalist China campaign once in Berlin. Soong adopted Münzenberg's strategy of relying on left-leaning writers' and artists' works to reach the political end of mass empowerment and devoted the rest of her life to calling for international support for China's anti-imperialist struggle.

Hu Lanqi's memoir reveals episodes of Soong's life in Berlin. She escorted Soong back to China for the latter's mother's funeral in 1931, and Soong allegedly stopped over in Moscow and held a closed-door talk with Soviet leaders (Hu, 1985, 228). Given Hu's active association with the Chinese communist group, Soong was likely quickly introduced to her friends Liao Huanxing and Xie Weijin, and through them to Willi Münzenberg and the KPD. Münzenberg must have been eager to have the influential "Madame Sun" on board, especially in a time of desperate need of "new blood" to advance the internationalist anti-imperialist alliance. Soong Ching-ling made a perfect candidate: she was fluent in English, educated in the West, from a prominent family, had devoted her whole life to promoting Sun Yat-sen's principles, was well connected to political resources, left-leaning, and firm in her sympathy for the proletariat. Soong's high-profile debut in Münzenberg's central organ *AIZ* attests not only to their acquaintance but their collaboration on the Comintern's China campaigns.

With Soong's support, Münzenberg was determined to expand the China campaign to an international united front. In February 1927, he organised the "Conference against Colonial Oppression and Imperialism" in Brussels. More than 170 delegates from over 20 countries (half of them outside Europe) attended. A copy of conference minutes entitled *Flammenzeichen vom Palais Egmont* [Torches of the Egmont Palace] indicates that China was a major theme discussed. The first speaker after the opening ceremony was Liao Huanxing, as the GMD representative and the successor of Sun Yat-sen's GMD united front. He was reported to have shouted out to the audience:

> as the true leaders of the Chinese revolution, Chinese workers will never allow any force to distort or change Sun Yat-sen thoughts. On

the contrary, they stand firm with Chinese peasants to unremittingly realize Sunyatsenism. Chinese workers, together with their true ally—the world proletariat—are determined to resist against imperialism that threatens workers in China and other countries. They will triumph. (Krüger, 2002, 177–186)

Liao's speech was followed by a representative of the Chinese Labour Union and a general of the National Revolutionary Army (Buber-Neumann, 1967, 152). The Brussels Conference announced the formal establishment of the "International Anti-imperialist and National Independence League". Four "honorary presidents" were elected: Henri Barbusse, Albert Einstein, Soong Ching-ling, and a GMD general. The chairman of the league was the president of the British Trade Union; Münzenberg and Liao served as members of the executive committee. The headquarters of the League was in Berlin. In the lead-up to the Brussels Conference, *AIZ* devoted a full-page cover (February issue, 1927) to introducing "Mrs. Sun Yat-sen". The cover image (Fig. 2) depicts Soong sitting upright against a background of Sun Yat-sen's manuscript—a clear message that she was the true heir to Sun Yat-sen's thought.

Fig. 2. *AIZ*,
February issue, 1927.

AIZ's introduction of Soong Ching-ling must also be seen as Münzenberg's declaration of continuous faith in the Chinese revolution and Sun Yat-sen's legacy after Chiang's betrayal of the revolution. Münzenberg's earlier glorification of the GMD and the Northern Expedition as the world's revolutionary hope drew backfire from the Comintern after Chiang's massacre of communists in April 1927. The expatriate Soong's representation here, as an outspoken and faithful leader pursuing the unfinished goals of the father of the Chinese revolution, was meant to inspire new faith in the Chinese revolution and its ability to conquer obstacles and reversals on the nation's progressive path. This message was clear in an August issue of *AIZ*, where Chiang's 12 April massacre was referred to as "Verrat in China [treason in China]. A group photo of the revolutionary government's leaders in early 1926 taken by an *AIZ* reporter in front of its headquarters in Guangzhou was placed below the report, and a snapshot of Sun Yat-sen's manuscript in the middle (Fig. 3, the two women in the photo from left on are He Xiangning and Soong).

VERRAT IN CHINA
von Tang Shin-She

Fig. 3. *AIZ*, August issue, 1926.

A few months later, the December 1927 issue of *AIZ* devoted a whole page to the Brussels Conference held at the beginning of the year. Soong Ching-ling's photo is placed in the centre, surrounded by the silhouettes of Liao Huanxing and leaders of the independence movement in Sri Lanka and India (Fig. 4). The text again criticised Chiang Kai-shek's betrayal of Sun Yat-senism and the revolution, and his collusion with imperialism, while lauding "Mrs Sun Yat-sen" as the torch-bearer of the Chinese revolutionary spirit rekindling the light of the anti-imperialist campaign.

II. Brüsseler Kongress

Fig. 4. *AIZ*, December issue, 1927.

As the Soong-Münzenberg alliance was established, the rest is known to history. Upon her return to China, Soong actively connected the resources of both sides, and hence the Chinese revolution with the world. Under her auspices, a large number of international left-wing sympathisers were put in contact with their Chinese counterparts. These included Edgar Snow, Agnes Smedley, American left-wing poet Langston Hughes, Irish playwright George Bernard Shaw, and Harold Isaacs. Song's mansion in Shanghai regularly served as a meeting point for the "international friends".

The approach of intervening in politics through political campaigns led by influential intellectuals and writers is a replica of the Münzenberg strategy—Münzenberg had founded the International Committee for the Defence of Revolutionaries in Berlin in 1930 with a central committee consisting of Clara Zetkin, Bertolt Brecht, Anna Seghers, and Käthe Kollwitz. The organisation telegrammed Soong in August 1931 to request the rescue of the Comintern Far East Bureau fund manager and spy Hilaire Noulens in Shanghai. Soong immediately initiated the International Committee for the Rescue of Noulens, endorsed by Maxim Gorky, Einstein, Smedley, and others. The committee later evolved into the China Civil Rights Protection Alliance (中国民权保障同盟, C. *Zhongguo minquan baozhang tongmeng*) in

Shanghai, in which Cai Yuanpei and Yang Xingfo were leading figures, and served the double purpose of demanding the release of revolutionaries and propagating public criticism of the authorities. The rescue activities of Ding Ling (丁玲, 1904–1986), Liao Chengzhi, and Hu Lanqi were all launched by the Alliance (Shang, 2009, 238–251).

As China became more deeply mired in the Japanese invasion, Münzenberg established the Internationales China Hilfs-Komitee [International China Help Committee] in 1931. Soon afterwards, in March 1932, he launched the Internationale Kampfwoche gegen den imperialistischen Krieg [International Week for the Fight against the Imperialist War]. In August 1932, Münzenberg organised an international conference that led to the founding of World Committee against Imperialist War to which Romain Rolland was elected as president and Soong Ching-ling as honorary president (Gross, 1967).

Three declassified telegrams included in the 1932 volume of *The Soviet Communist Party, the Communist International and the Chinese Soviet Movement* reveal the close cooperation between Münzenberg and Soong Ching-ling: on 15 April 1932, the Comintern ordered Münzenberg to carry out a wide range of fundraising operations through the IAH in support of the Chinese labour movement; at a closed meeting of the Comintern's executive committee on 10 November of the same year, it was decided to adopt the opinion of "Comrade Münzenberg in dispatching a special committee to Manchuria and convening an anti-imperialist meeting in Shanghai"; at another closed meeting of the Executive Committee five days later, specific instructions were given to conduct the "Far East Anti-War Committee's operations in the form of an international conference in Shanghai in about mid-March 1933", and it was announced that the conference "will be supported by the Shanghai Preparatory Committee under the leadership of Soong Ching-ling". On 30 September 1933, the Far East Anti-War Conference was held in Shanghai as planned, coordinated by the China Civil Rights Protection Alliance, with Soong Ching-ling presiding. Due to objections from the German authorities, only 65 people of the originally planned 800 Chinese and foreign representatives attended the conference. Mao Zedong, Zhu De, Lu Xun, Gorky, and Barbusse were elected as honorary presidents (*Liangong (bu), Gongchan Guoji yu Zhongguo Suwei'ai yundong*, Vol. 13, 1997, 136–137, 227–228, 512–520).

The top collaboration, with Münzenberg as the chief strategist for international anti-imperialist and anti-war propaganda and Soong Ching-ling as chieftain in executing the anti-imperialist and anti-war movements in China, has laid strong foundation for the imagination of a transnational proletarian collective in texts and images.

Imagining a Battling China for the United Front

Münzenberg's publishing resources grew rapidly under the political and cultural propaganda campaigns in the 1920s. The main task of the core of Münzenberg's Berlin empire, the IAH, was less funding workers than advocating for a transnational united front in its initial campaign for the Soviet Union during the great famine in 1921. On 2 August, Lenin published an article entitled "Appeal to the International Proletariat" where he stated:

> We need help. The Soviet workers and peasants' republic hopes to receive assistance from workers and small farmers from all over the world. These people who suffered from long-term exploitation of capitalism will understand the misery of soviet workers and peasants. They will deeply feel the needs of the Soviet Republic out of intuition as the exploited working people. (1965, 502)

Despite the lack of terms like "solidarity" or "united front", the appeal points to an imagined international proletariat, a group with a strong class consciousness that can feel for their fellows in suffering. What Lenin called for was an international union of proletarians and not mere international humanitarian relief. Münzenberg knew exactly Lenin's intentions—the establishment of the IAH shortly afterwards was political imagination put into practice.

The IAH had been supporting China's anti-imperialist movement since 1924. A mere browse through the 1926 article catalogue of *AIZ*, *Berlin am Morgen* [Berlin in the Morning], and *Welt am Abend* [The World in the Evening] yields a large number of reports on China: such as "Die kapitalistische Hölle in China" [The capitalist hell in China] and "Das kämpfende China" [The fighting China]. In October 1924, the IAH joined the Hands Off China committee and founded the Hilfskomitee zur Unterstützung der von der Überschwemmung wirtschaftlich schwer geschädigten Massen [Relief Committee to Support People in Financial Difficulties Affected by Floods] (Brasken, 2015, 117–124). On 1 December 1924, the Executive Committee of the Communist International (ECCI) instructed the IAH to immediately launch an international anti-imperialist propaganda campaign in East Asia, especially China, to further mobilise the proletariat of the local national liberation movement against European and American imperialism. The document finally asserted that "[i]t is necessary for the people of these colonized countries with backward economic and ideological development to see that the European and American colonists and the European and American working class are not united. Rather, the proletariat of the oppressed countries in the world are natural allies" (Hering and Schilde, 2003, 57–72). The Comintern was in full agreement with Münzenberg's vision of an internationalist solidarity. At the time, such an international community transcending national boundaries had never been conceived of by the European proletariat before.

Münzenberg's report to the Comintern in mid-June 1925 provided specific descriptions of the Chinese propaganda campaign. The report stated that the IAH had immediately launched international propaganda in major European cities to support China's anti-imperialist demonstrations after learning about the Shanghai protest against foreign business owners. Moreover, a media centre had been established to support the anti-imperialist movement (Hering and Schilde, 2003, 57–72). Since 1925, Münzenberg's publications had been full of enthusiastic reports on China's Northern Expedition and anti-imperialist labour movements, and condemnations on the capitalist oppression of Chinese workers.

On 23 June 1925, the IAH published a flyer calling on the oppressed of the world to unite in support of exploited Chinese workers (Brasken, 2015, 152). The poster presents white workers and Chinese workers united to help each other against their common enemy, caricatured with a classic portrayal of capitalists in left-wing media: evil white males wearing tall hats and suits, usually of European and American descent, choking the Chinese workers with a rope. European and American workers are portrayed as strong, independent, and brave, while Chinese workers are weak victims with a long braid. The message is clear: through the unity of the international proletariat, German and Chinese workers declare to the world that capitalists should take their "hands off China" ("Hände weg von China"). The IAH was also conveying the message that it was a politically neutral organisation of the working class, and not the mouthpiece of the Soviet Union—as some had criticised—and that it was its sole task to advance the interests of the international proletarian alliance against capitalist oppression.

On 1 October 1925, the central organ of the IAH, *Not und Brot* [Distress and Bread], devoted an entire page to reporting the developments of IAH China's rescue operations (Fig. 5). The report reminded German workers that China was still mired in floods, that imperialist oppression continued, and that tens of thousands of Chinese people were being displaced. It requested the German proletariat to lend a helping hand to their Chinese brothers. The text reads, "[t]he only hope for the Chinese proletariat in distress and despair is help from the international proletariat, and the help of European and American workers". To the left of the report was an illustration based on the May Thirtieth Movement (a major workers' anti-imperialist movement in 1925): a man in kimono with a tall hat and leather shoes, representing the Japanese capitalist, gives a cold order to his man to kill a Chinese worker, or protestor. The bottom of the page reports on the rally and parade the IAH organised in Hamburg, Germany, in support of Chinese workers. The big slogan on the side of a truck reads, "Can the imperialist exploiters defeat the Chinese people? Never! Because the International Workers' Relief is in China!"

Die China-Aktion geht weiter!

Anti-Kriegskundgebungen

IAH

Fig. 5. *Not und Brot* [*Distress and Bread*], October issue, 1925.

Besides the IAH's central organ's promotion of its China campaigns, a large number of reports about China were published on the IAH's most popular newspaper, *AIZ*, which circulated at about 500,000 copies. The paper's chief designer, John Heartfield, left a lasting legacy on this highly successful propagandistic newspaper, featuring large eye-catching photos and sketches with lively language to present workers' lives in different parts of the world. Images and texts worked together to construct a solid international proletarian collective with embedded critique of capitalism.

After 1925, reports about China filled *AIZ*. The image of China and Chinese proletarians gradually changed from the weak victims of imperialist oppression in need of help from European workers into awakened and brave fighters for the interests of the proletarian class compatriots, and for an independent new China. The cover of the May 1926 issue bears a photo of a mass gathering of the National Revolutionary Army *en route* to the Northern Expedition. Above the photo reads: "China's war of freedom charges forward!" while the caption below reads: "Chinese students, workers, farmers, and other groups demand that the struggle for freedom of Chinese society and nation continue to the end".

Fig. 6. *AIZ*, May issue, 1926.

The same issue devoted two full pages to introduce the GMD's Northern Expedition. A photo of Shanghai's panorama bears the words "the GMD flag flying over Shanghai" (Fig. 7) and a caption below the photo reads: "The sky above Shanghai is a strong blow to imperialism". The bottom half of the page lines up photos of GMD leaders: Chiang Kai-shek (then the Commander-in-Chief of the Army), Sun Yat-sen, and the Party's Foreign Minister Chen Youren, surrounded by battle photos of the Northern Expedition.

Another issue in 1926 introduced the Chinese revolution with a full page entitled: "Revolution—China's Road to Rebirth. Excerpts from Sun Yat-sen's Diary". The photos included in the page convey a sharp contrast: the top two show poor Chinese peasants waiting to be rescued, while three others depict the revolutionary army as a group of awakened youths fighting for their own fate and that of their country.

As increasing numbers of China operations were rolled out by the IAH in 1926, almost every issue of *AIZ* included in-depth reports on China, covering topics from the Northern Expedition Army and its leaders to the Whampoa Military Academy and its leaders Deng Yanda and Chiang Kai-shek, and Sun Ke, son of Sun Yat-sen (Figs. 9–11).

Die Kuomintang-Flagge weht über Shanghai

Die Eroberung Schanghais ist der stärkste Schlag gegen den Imperialism

Fig. 7. *AIZ*, May issue, 1926.

Die Revolution — der Weg zu Chinas Wiedergeburt

Aus Sun-Yat-Sen's Tagebuch.

Fig. 8. *AIZ*, June issue, 1926.

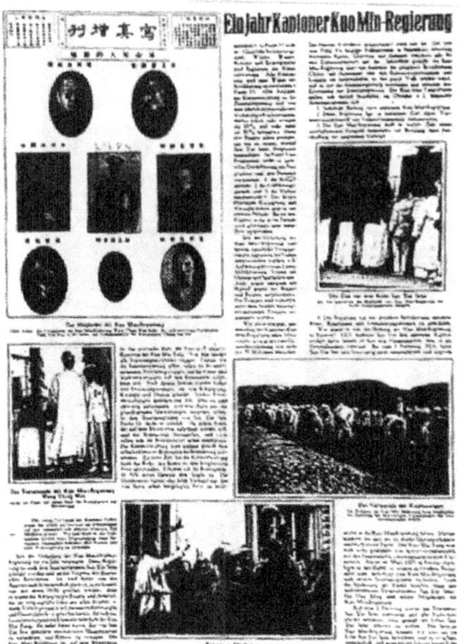

Ein Jahr Kantoner Kuo Min-Regierung

Die Wampoo-Kriegsschule, der Kern der revolutionären Truppen Chinas

BILDER VOM TAGE

Figs. 9–11. *AIZ*, December issue, 1926.

Below are three *AIZ* covers of issues from 1926 and 1927 (Figs. 12–14). On the left, in front of a background of the marching revolutionary army, several soldiers raise up a Chinese peasant from kneeling on the ground, with the words "No more colonial ravages!" The middle cover illustrates "China's liberation struggle", while the cover on the right presents a Chinese farmer with dark skin and strong body, in sharp contrast with the previous image of the weak and hungry, with a highly symbolic title: "Awakened Asia".

Figs. 12–14. *AIZ*, February issue, 1927; April issue, 1926; January issue, 1927.

In *AIZ*'s presentation, the "feudal forces" of the old powers of local warlords, which the CCP named as one of the "two mountains" oppressing the Chinese proletariat along with imperialism, were considered the accomplices of the latter. The warlords were seen as complicit in foreign capitalists' exploitation of Chinese workers and as suppressing their resistance. Therefore, the double task of anti-imperialist and anti-feudal struggle in the Chinese revolutionary discourse was combined in smooth alignment with Münzenberg's international propaganda narrative.

On many occasions, the IAH's imagining of the international anti-imperialist proletarian community was based on China's anti-imperialist resistance. This is clearly conveyed in the 1925 special issue of *Not und Brot* devoted to China:

> German workers are falling step by step into slavery to world imperialism. They see their own future in Chinese coolies. They will be very interested in uniting colonies in China, Egypt, Morocco, and India to launch a revolution. The extent of the exploitation of slaves in these colonies is the upcoming fate of German workers. The living conditions of Shanghai workers will undoubtedly become the common situation of German and the world proletariat. (front page)

In addition to reports, Münzenberg also organised rallies for workers and sympathisers, and a number of "China Night" activities. *AIZ* reports revealed the various forms taken by these activities: the theatre play *The Struggle for Liberation of the Chinese Proletariat* put on by Chinese students, lectures on Chinese cultural history and Chinese revolutionary tasks, etc., all of which usually ended with a performance of traditional Chinese music. The political goal of strengthening the transnational proletarian alliance was often integrated with Chinese cultural elements. Münzenberg proudly reported to Grigory Zinoviev (Chairman of the Comintern) in August 1925 that the IAH had achieved satisfactory results with over 1,000 meetings held in Germany, other European countries, and the United States. A reported 5 million people in Europe participated in the IAH conferences and parades (Gross, 1984). The flyer below was probably posted in the streets of Berlin and Halle (the host city of the event), announcing IAH's rally on July 1, featuring a speech by a GMD party member from Shanghai. The slogan of the "Hands off China" committee was printed in bold: "China den Chinesen, Deutschland dem deutschen werktätigen Volk!" [China for the Chinese, Germany for the German labouring people!].

The German Communist Party organ *The Red Flag* provided more in-depth reports on the Chinese revolution. Beginning in 1927, terms like "Soviet China" and "communist revolution" began to appear frequently in the newspaper—"Von Sowjet-Kanton zu Sowjet-China" [From Soviet Guangdong to Soviet China], "Der Kommunismus in China unüberwindlich" [Communism is invincible in China], "Die erste Sowjet-Banknote in China"

Fig. 15. "Give China back to the Chinese, Germany back to the German working people." Guo Min Dang's Gao-Yuhan from Shanghai will address this topic at 8pm on Wednesday July 1st, in the large hall of the "People's Park". Published 1 July 1925. David M. Rubenstein Rare Book & Manuscript Library at Duke University, https://repository.duke.edu/dc/broadsides/bdsge20014.

[China's first Soviet banknote]—as did the Chinese Soviet's letter of greeting sent to the Soviet Union at their first meeting. Most of these reports are based on German translations of memoirs or correspondence of participants in the Chinese revolution. Yet despite insufficient sources from China, these translations indicated the KPD's high level of interest in the developments of the CCP.

These somewhat romantic reports became materials for further romanticisation and dramatisation into literary works. The most well-known works include firstly several short stories of the 1930s by Anna Seghers, leader of the German Left-wing Writers League and a student of Sinology. Having not been to China at the time, Seghers' stories such as "1. Mai Yanschuhpou" [1 May in Yangpu] and "Die Stoppuhr" [Stopwatch] were most likely based on reports about China in *AIZ* and other newspapers. Brecht also wrote a number of plays with Chinese themes, such as *Der gute Mensch von Sezuan* [The Good Person of Szechwan] and his *Lehrstück* or political education drama *Die Maßnahme* [Measures Taken], the latter adapted from real events reported in the news about a passionate Chinese communist railway worker single-handedly inciting an uprising that risked exposing the Soviet Union intelligence network. Another typical work on China was the collection of literary reportage *China geheim* [Secret China] by the Czech-born German-speaking journalist Egon

Erwin Kisch. Münzenberg and Soong Ching-Ling arranged for Kisch to go to China in 1931 (Segel, 1997), where he met Lu Xun (Lu Xun, 1936) and was held up as a model for Chinese literary reportage writers (Zhou Libo, 1935, 4). Along the same line are *Tai Yang erwacht* [Tai Yang Awakens] (1930) by the popular Weimar playwright Friedrich Wolf and *Autobiography of Tan Shihua* (1932) by the Soviet writer Sergei Tretiakov. Tretiakov's *Roar China!* was also the earliest play on Chinese anti-imperialist topic, written in 1926 and premiered soon afterwards in Weimar Germany (Meserve et al., 2010, 1–13).

From newspaper reports to the major Weimar left-wing plays and stories, the theme of the Chinese revolution and labour movements was consolidated as a mainstream trope for the world revolution in the 1920s and 1930s. Scholars of German literature have seen it as a major turning point in the representation of China—having been synonymous with Taoist metaphysics and Confucianism, the country was now an "awakened", revolutionary, modern country full of fighting spirit and strength (Li, 2010, 18–19).

In building a proletarian cultural solidarity across national boundaries in a literal embodiment of the pen being mightier than sword, 1930s China was not all about local political party rivalry but a shining star on the internationalist cultural stage. Though it had no power to alter the course of history under the shadow of the two mighty political forces in 1920s and '30s China, this internationalist cultural-political movement under the auspices of Münzenberg and Soong Ching-ling opened a window to a possible alternative and invited further problematising of a Chinese history written from a monolithic political perspective. This alternative revolution through radical cultural empowerment, with intellectuals, writers, and artists as major players, presents perhaps the broadest attempts at constructing a new transnational identity and an international community of solidarity on the levels of practice and expression between Berlin, Moscow, and Republican China.

References and Further Reading

Belogurova, Anna. 2017. "Networks, Parties, and the 'Oppressed Nations': The Comintern and Chinese Communists Overseas, 1926–1935". *Cross Currents* 24: 5–24.

Brasken, Kasper. 2015. *The International Workers' Relief, Communism, and Transnational Solidarity: Willi Münzenberg in Weimar Germany*. New York: Palgrave Macmillan.

Brecht, Berthold. 1998. *Die Maßnahme* [Measures Taken]. Frankfurt am Main: Suhrkamp.

Buber-Neumann, Margarete. 1967. *Kriegsschauplätze der Weltrevolution* [Theatres of War of the World Revolution]. Stuttgart: Seewald Verlag.

Communist Party of Great Britain. 1924. *From the Fourth to the Fifth World Congress.* Report of the Executive Committee of the Communist International. 16 King Street, Covent Garden, London.

Dai Jitao (戴季陶). 1927. *Sunwenzhuyi zhi zhexue de jichu* (孙文主义之哲学的基础) [Philosophical Foundation of Sun Yatsenism]. Shanghai: Minzhi shuju.

Fairbank, John K., and Albert Feuerwerker. 2008. *The Cambridge History of China, Vol. 13: Republican China 1912–1949, Part 2.* Cambridge: Cambridge University Press.

Firsov, Fridrikh, Harvey Klehr, and John Earl Haynes. 2014. *Secret Cables of the Comintern, 1933–1943.* New Haven: Yale University Press.

Gross, Babette. 1967. *Willi Münzenberg. Eine politische Biographie* [Willi Münzenberg: A Political Biography]. Stuttgart: Deutsche Verlags-Anstalt.

Hering, Sabine, and Kurt Schilde (eds.). 2003. *Die Rote Hilfe. Die Geschichte der internationalen kommunistischen "Wohlfahrtsorganisation" und ihrer sozialen Aktivitäten in Deutschland* [The Red Help: History of the International Communist "Charity" and Its Social Activities in Germany]. Wiesbaden: Springer VS.

Hu Lanqi (胡兰畦). 1985. *Hu Lanqi huiyi lu 1901–1936 nian* (胡兰畦回忆录 1901–1936年) [Memoir of Hu Lanqi, 1901–1936]. Chengdu: Sichuan renmin chubanshe.

Kampen, Thomas. 2001. "Liao Huanxing oder Tang Xingqi. Für KP und Kuomintang in Berlin" [Liao Huanxing or Tang Xingqi: For KP and GMD in Berlin]. In *Das neue China* [The New China] 28 (2): 29–31.

——. 2004. "Solidarität und Propaganda: Willi Münzenberg, die Internationale Arbeiterhilfe und China" [Solidarity and Propaganda: Willi Münzenberg, the International Workers Relief and China]. *Zeitschrift für Weltgeschichte* [Journal of World History] 5 (2): 99–105.

——. 2010. *Chinesen in Europa: Europäer in China: Journalisten, Spione, Studenten.* Gössenberg: OstAsien-Verlag.

Kisch, Egon Erwin. 1933. *China geheim* [Secret China]. Berlin: Erich Reiss Verlag.

Krüger, Joachim. 2002. "A Regular Chinese Voice from Berlin to Moscow". In *The Chinese Revolution in the 1920s: Between Triumph and Disaster,* edited by Mechthild Leutner, Roland Felber, Mikhail L. Titarenko, and Alexander M. Grigoriev, 177–183. London: Routledge Curzon.

Lenin. 1965. *Lenin, V. I. Collected Works, Vol. 32.* Moscow: Progress Publishers.

Li Weijia. 2010. *China und China-Erfahrung in Leben und Werk von Anna Seghers* [China and China-Experiences in the Life and Work of Anna Seghers]. London: Peter Lang.

Liangong (bu), gong chan guoji yu zhong guo su wei ai yun dong (联共 (布) 、共产国际与中国苏维埃运动) [Soviet Communist Party, the Communist International and the Chinese Soviet Movement]. 1997. Vol. 3 & 13. Beijing: Zhonggong dangshi chubanshe.

Liu Jiaquan (刘家泉). 1994. *Song Qingling liuwang haiwai suiyua* (宋庆龄流亡海外岁月) [Soong Ching-ling's Exile Abroad]. Beijing: Zhongyang wenxian chubanshe.

Lu Xun (鲁迅). 2005 [1936]. "Kaisui·Kelehuizhi banhua xuanji: xumu" (凯绥·珂勒惠支版画选集·序目) [Preface to Selected Woodblock Prints of Käthe Kollwitz]. In *Qiejieting zawen mobian* (且介亭杂文末编) [Zawen Written in Qiejie Studio]. In *Lu Xun quanji* (鲁迅全集) [Collected Works of Lu Xun], Vol. 6, 470–472. Beijing: Renmin wenxue chubanshe.

——. 1980. "Literature of a Revolutionary Period". In *Selected Works of Lu Xun,* translated by Yang Xianyi and Gladys Yang, Vol. 2, 334–341. Beijing: Foreign Languages Press.

MacKinnon, Janice, and Stephen MacKinnon. 1987. *Agnes Smedley: The Life and Times of an American Radical.* Berkeley and Los Angeles: University of California Press.

——. 2019. "Agnes Smedley: A Working Introduction". *Bulletin of Concerned Asian Scholars* 7 (1): 6–11.

McMeekin, Sean. 2003. *The Red Millionaire: A Political Biography of Willi Münzenberg, Moscow's Secret Propaganda Tsar in the West, 1917–1940.* New Haven: Yale University Press.

Meserve, Walter J., and Ruth I. Meserve. 2010. *The Stage History of Roar China! Documentary Drama as Propaganda.* Cambridge: Cambridge University Press.

Münzenberg, Willi. 1931. *Solidarität. Zehn Jahre Arbeiterhilfe* [Solidarity: Ten Years of Workers' Help]. Berlin: Neuer Deutscher Verlag.

Olenik, John Kenneth. 1973. "Left Wing Radicalism in the Kuomintang: Teng Yen-ta and the Genesis of the Third Party Movement in China, 1924–1931". PhD dissertation, Cornell University.

Petersson, Fredrik. 2007. "In Control of Solidarity? Willi Münzenberg, the Workers' International Relief and League against Imperialism, 1921–1935". *Comintern Working Papers* 8: 1–21.

Schlenstedt, Dieter. 1985. *Egon Erwin Kisch. Leben und Werk* [Egon Erwin Kisch: Life and Work]. Berlin: Volk und Wissen.

Segel, Harold B. 1997. *Egon Erwin Kisch: The Raging Reporter—A Bio-Anthology.* West Lafayette: Purdue University Press.

Shang Mingxuan (尚明轩). 2009. *Song Qingling nianpu changbian* (宋庆龄年谱长编) [Long Chronicle of Soong Ching-Ling]. Beijing: Zhongguo shehui kexue chubanshe.

Smedley, Agnes. 1956. *The Great Road: The Life and Times of Chu Teh.* New York: Monthly Review Press.

Spence, Jonathan. 1991. *The Search for Modern China.* New York: W. W. Norton.

Tretiakov, Sergei. 1934. *A Chinese Testament: The Autobiography of Tan Shih-Hua.* New York: Simon & Schuster.

Wagner, Rudolf. 1992. *Inside a Service Trade: Studies in Contemporary Chinese Prose.* Massachusetts: Harvard University Press.

Wolf, Friedrich, and Henning Müller. 1988. *Wer war Wolf? Friedrich Wolf (1888–1953)* [Who was Wolf? Friedrich Wolf (1888–1953)]. In *Selbstzeugnissen, Bilddokumenten und Erinnerungen* [Testimonials, Photo Documents, and Memoirs]. Cologne: Röderberg-Verlag.

Yü-Dembski, Dagmar. 1987. "China in Berlin. 1918–1933. Von chinesischem Alltag und deutscher Chinabegeisterung" [China in Berlin, 1918–1933: About Everyday Chinese Life and German Enthusiasm for China]. In *Berlin und China. Dreihundert Jahre wechselvolle Beziehungen* [Berlin and China: Three Hundred Years of Exchange], edited by Kuo Heng-yü, 117–130. Berlin: Colloquium Verlag.

——. 2007. *Chinesen in Berlin* [Chinese in Berlin]. Berlin: be.bra verlag.

Zhou Libo (周立波). 1981. *Mimi de Zhongguo* (秘密的中国) [Secret China]. Beijing: Qunzhong chubanshe.

8

Fanxiang Toupiao 返鄉投票

Migrating Political Cleavages and Transnational Electoral Mobilisation in Vienna's Taiwanese Community

Julia Marinaccio

Introduction

The rise of transnational lifestyles and diverging migrant patterns in an increasingly globalised world notwithstanding, many emigrants still face procedural and institutional obstacles in exercising their right to vote from abroad. This includes the roughly 2.05 million Taiwanese scattered across different continents. Election laws stipulate that on election day, voters must cast their ballots in the designated polling stations of their registered domiciles in Taiwan, thus imposing considerable costs upon Taiwanese emigrants who want to exercise their right to vote. Despite the institutional absence of an external voting system, politicians continue to solicit the support of emigrant voters, appealing them to return home to vote, and many Taiwanese continue to levy substantial financial and time resources to participate in homeland elections.

While the extant literature has unpacked the impact of Taiwan's changing political landscape on overseas policies and the relationships with overseas communities (Damm, 2012; To, 2014; Gong, 2017; Han, 2019), empirical insights into contemporary Taiwanese overseas' political participation remain scarce (Lin, 2006; Cheng, 2017). What is more, there is a yawning gap in the study of the Taiwanese emigrant electorate. Not only are emigrant voters ignored by polling institutes in Taiwan, a literature research in the databases Web of Sciences and Airiti Library (Taiwanese publications) identifies no articles that specifically deal with the question of emigrant voters and external voting.

My study draws attention to this unfortunate lacuna and aims to contribute with first findings that elucidate how Taiwanese migrants in their countries of residence and political actors in Taiwan deal with the absence of an external voting system. Building on the rubric of political transnationalism,

Fig. 1. Taiwanese associations rallying in front of the UN building in Vienna, courtesy of the Taipei Economic and Cultural Office, https://www.taiwanembassy.org/at_de/album/13/gallery.html.

I analyse actors, processes, and practices of transnational voter mobilisation within Vienna's Taiwanese migrant community during the 2020 presidential elections. While voting and electoral mobilisation of emigrant electorates in migrant communities are both forms of direct and indirect cross-border political participation, they are not essentially transnational. In the Taiwanese case, so I argue, these practices are transnational due to the critical impact of China on the organisation of political movements and choices of voters in and outside Taiwan.

The remainder of the chapter introduces the study's theoretical framework, unpicks the specific sociopolitical space of the Taiwanese migrant community in Vienna in which transnational electoral mobilisation occurs, and analyses the voter process mobilisation and its effects. The chapter concludes with a short discussion of the results and possible trajectories for future research.

Transnational Political Participation and Electoral Mobilisation

Recently, sociologists and political scientists have started to draw more attention to migrants' political practices, analysing their integration into the polity of their destination countries (Day and Shaw, 2002; Goerres et al., 2018; Mügge et al., 2019) and their ties and engagements in the politics of their countries of origin (Adamson, 2005; Janoschka, 2008; Gabrielli and Zapata-Barrero, 2015; Peltoniemi, 2018). On a more general level, the scholarship demonstrates that people migrate with both their bodies and their political ideas and attachments (Mügge et al., 2019). By creating "zones of inter-societal convergence" (Waldinger, 2015, 6), transnational migrants link the "here" and the "there" in the domain of political participation. Specifically, political participation, understood as "actions of private citizens by which they seek to influence or support government and politics" (Milbrath and Madan, 1977, 2), can take different forms among migrants. Gabrielli and Zapata-Barrero (2015, 9) distinguish between "conventional" (e.g. voting) and "unconventional" (e.g. protests) forms of political participation and three possible political arenas to which migrants direct their political actions: the sending country, the receiving country, or the international level.

Voting is the most quintessential "conventional" form of migrants' political participation in their countries of origin. However, emigrant voting does not occur in a vacuum. Similar to their peers at home, voters residing abroad are mobilised by campaigns of political parties (direct) or by interactions within social networks (indirect) (Green and Shachar, 2000; Karp, 2012; Rosenstone and Hansen, 1993). Research focusing on migrant communities proposes that a high degree of the migrant community's geographical concentration and organisational density can facilitate both forms of electoral mobilisation (Leal et al., 2012; Ahmadov and Sasse, 2016), and therefore motivate more migrants to participate in elections in their countries of origin. However, Kostelka (2017, 1064–1065) cautions that mobilisation's effects on mobile individuals are substantially lower than on their sessile peers at home, as the former can easily escape mobilisation. Also, due to the high costs associated with direct mobilisation abroad and the comparatively low impact on election outcomes, parties integrate direct transnational mobilisation into their campaigns only if diasporas are sufficiently large to bring electoral advantage. Therefore, both direct and indirect mobilisation reach only those emigrants who are well integrated into, or well connected to, the emigrant community in their host country.

Both cross-border voting and electoral mobilisation are forms of direct and indirect cross-border political participation that establish social fields between different actors that cross geographic and political borders (Glick-Schiller et al., 1992, ix; Goebel and Pries, 2006, 36). However, they are not *per definitionem* transnational. A central argument of political transnationalism is that migrants' transnational political practices are affected by the polities of more than one country (Bauböck, 2003; Fell et al., 2019; Mügge et al., 2019; Østergaard-Nielsen, 2003). What makes them transnational is "the way that political participation in one country, such as voting pattern or lobbying, is informed by political events in another" (Østergaard-Nielsen, 2003, 762).

In *The Taiwan Voter*, Achen and Wang (2017, 1) argue that Taiwan is unique due to its relationship with China. "No other topic or relationship plays so central a role in Taiwan's politics", as it structures foreign policy, the political party system, and how ordinary citizens orient themselves to politics (Achen and Wang, 2017, 2). Taiwanese society is divided over the question of national identity and senses of belonging (i.e. Chinese or Taiwanese) and how to fashion relations with China. As people do not only migrate with their bodies but also with their minds (Waldinger, 2015), this observation squarely applies to the emigrant electorate and the organisation of political movements abroad.

The 2020 elections provide an excellent lens to study a highly relevant—yet often neglected—aspect of political transnationalism in contemporary Taiwan. Against the backdrop of mounting pressures applied by China and the months-long protests in Hong Kong, "the China factor" (Achen and Wang, 2017, 2) had gained significantly more weight. It generated strong homeland nationalism, which translated into extensive voter mobilisation at home and abroad. Transcending the static territorial boundaries, mobilisation efforts connected Taiwanese politicians, activists, and voters residing in different countries and societies.

Migrating with Bodies and Minds: The Sociopolitical Space of the Taiwanese Community in Austria

Taiwanese migrants represent a very small immigrant community and constitute only a fraction of what the literature refers to as "the large Chinese diaspora", whose size is estimated at 49.21 million (Poston and Wong, 2016, 350). Although they organise community life largely separately from mainland Chinese migrants, they seldom draw public and scholarly attention in their countries of residence. This observation certainly applies to Austria, where the ethnic Chinese community is comparatively well-researched (Springer, 2004; Steiger, 2008; Kwok and Parzer, 2008; Gebesmair, 2009; Pessl and Springer, 2011; Kwok, 2012; Marinaccio, 2016; Schäfer, 2017a, 2017b) but Taiwanese migrants have been left woefully unexplored. The high geographic concentration and dense community organisation of Taiwanese migrants in Austria's capital make the local migrant community a perfect fit to explore this issue in-depth.

According to the Overseas Community Affairs Council (中華民國僑務委員會, C. *zhonghua minguo qiaowu weiyuanhui*) (OCAC), a cabinet-level agency that addresses issues related to overseas Taiwanese, there are currently 2.05 million "overseas Taiwanese" (海外臺灣僑民, C. *haiwai Taiwan qiaomin*) residing abroad (OCAC, 2019, 11). The term refers to emigrants from the current *de facto* sovereign territory of the Republic of China (ROC), Taiwan, and their descendants who possess a permanent household registration in Taiwan and are therefore entitled to the right to vote in home elections. As this number also includes citizens under the eligible voting age of 20, the effective share of the global Taiwanese emigrant electorate amounts to approximately 10 per cent of the total voting population.

In 2021, official Austrian statistics registered 1,579 residents who declared the ROC as their birth country, most of them living in the capital, Vienna (966) (Statistik Austria, 2020). Estimates from the local Taipei Economic and Cultural Office (駐奧地利臺北經濟文化代表處, C. *zhu Aodili Taiwan jingji wenhua daibiaochu*) (TECO), however, put the number higher, at 3,000 (private conversations, May and October 2020). Both the Austrian statistics and the TECO's estimates are problematic for various reasons that cannot be discussed in detail here (see Christiansen, 2005; Damm, 2012; Low, 2013; Han, 2019). More importantly, as neither distinguish between citizenship and voter registration status, the actual size of the Taiwanese emigrant electorate residing in Austria remains unknown but ranges between 1,000 and 1,400 voters. In terms of demographic characteristics, my survey shows that Taiwanese migrants in Austria have a high level of education on average. Almost half of the respondents declared education as their primary migration motivation and 45 per cent have lived in Austria less than five years. Thus, students or recent graduates constitute a large portion of the local community.

Austria's Taiwanese community is organised through several formalised associations, which are mostly located in Vienna. They can be distinguished into three main types: overseas compatriot associations, service-oriented focus group associations, and schools. Furthermore, there are several groups without formal statutes whose members are only loosely connected (see Fig. 2 below).

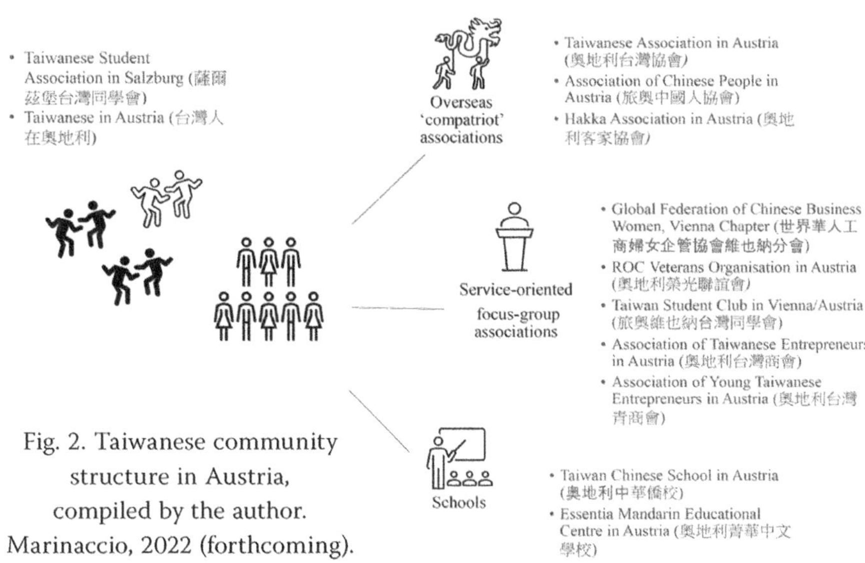

Fig. 2. Taiwanese community structure in Austria, compiled by the author. Marinaccio, 2022 (forthcoming).

Taiwanese in Vienna/Austria are well-connected within their community, and some also participate in organisations with members who come from across the ethnically Chinese community, such as choirs, churches, and professional associations. Membership of Taiwanese associations tends to overlap, particularly between compatriot and service-oriented focus group associations. Many Taiwanese participate in events arranged by different associations to make friends and exchange with other community members (interview, Yu Guan-ru). However, involvement in community life differs considerably across age groups. Older cohorts tend to be much more connected through the (compatriot) associations and regularly partake in community life, whereas younger cohorts, especially students, prefer to stay in loose networks (interview, student Yang). As will be demonstrated later, this divide affected mobilisation strategies.

Although the island of Taiwan acts as a strong, unifying identity-forming element for all Taiwanese in Austria—either in terms of citizenship or place of origin or descent—the local community is divided over the question of whether they belong to one or two "imagined communities" (Anderson, 1983). While some sympathise with the indigenisation movement advocating a Taiwan-centric identity that sees Taiwan as a political and cultural unit in its own right, others stress their belonging to the ROC as part of a greater Chinese sociocultural space, including the mainland. In other words, Taiwanese who migrate to Austria (and elsewhere) take with them the main cleavage that has shaped politics and society in Taiwan for decades: Taiwan's relationship with China.

By implication, identity politics has also shaped local community organisations. General political attitudes have translated into opposing partisan preferences of members within different overseas organisations, particularly in the two main compatriot organisations, the Taiwanese Association in Austria (奧地利台灣協會, C. *Aodili Taiwan xiehui*) (TAA) and the Association of Chinese People in Austria (旅奧中國人協會, C. *lü aozhongren xieshui*) (ACPA). The former advocates a Taiwan-centric identity, and in elections its members generally support parties from the Green camp, including the Democratic Progressive Party (民進黨, C. *minjindang*) (DPP) and so-called "third political force" (第三勢力, C. *disan shili*), whereas the latter promotes a Chinese ethnicity-based identity, and its members typically support political parties that belong to the Blue camp, primarily the Guomindang (國民黨, C. *guomindang*) (KMT). These two associations took the lead in voter mobilisation during the 2020 elections. As the next section will show, the transcendence of the main political cleavage of Taiwan's society into the migrant community and its organisational landscape created opportunities to target the electorates of both camps through direct and indirect electoral mobilisation.

Mobilising Votes in the Online and Offline Spaces

Historically, the overseas communities have always been instrumental for the legitimacy of Taiwanese governments (Damm, 2012, 220). However, democratisation and related constitutional reforms, the growing momentum of identity politics, and the absence of an extraterritorial voting system have considerably reduced overseas Taiwanese's influence on homeland politics. Representing about 10 per cent of the electorate, the impact of their votes is debatable, especially regarding the question of whether these confirm or change election results. Unfortunately, data with which to gauge their effect does not exist.

Mostly due to these historical reasons but probably also because of the uncertainty of electoral advantage, Taiwanese politicians habitually solicit support from overseas Taiwanese, asking them to return to Taiwan and take their share in civic participation. This act is labelled *fanxiang toupiao* (返鄉投票), literally meaning to "return to one's hometown to vote". The term *fanxiang* originally refers to a traditional practice of children (in former times, women) returning to their parents' home for New Year's celebrations. Therefore, when politicians or other individuals solicit the emigrant electorate's support, they appeal to a deeply ingrained social value of loyalty, evoking a sense of obligation and caring.

Taiwan's relationship with China has been described as the main political cleavage in Taiwanese society, structuring its political party system and citizens' political orientation (Achen and Wang, 2017, 2). In the context of mounting pressures from China and the months-long protests in Hong Kong, this relationship gained significant weight during the run-up for the Fifteenth Presidential and Legislative Elections in 2020. After the DPP candidate Tsai Ing-wen (蔡英文) took a clear position at the beginning of August, condemning China's interference in Hong Kong, opinion polls went into reverse, in her favour. After a short hesitation, the KMT's candidate Han Kuo-yu (韓國瑜) followed suit, expressing disapproval of China's threats to intervene with force. However, the damage had already been done. The gap in public opinion grew into an inexorable disadvantage for Han Kuo-yu (*News Lens*, 2019).

The events in Hong Kong clearly amplified the deep political cleavage regarding the question about Taiwan's future and its relationship with China. Tropes like "historic turning point" (十字路口, C. *shizi lukou*) (Li, 2019) and "battle of life or death" (生死戰, C. *shengsizhan*) dominated the public discourse, stimulating strong homeland nationalism across all political camps and informing electoral mobilisation. Like their predecessors, both presidential candidates appealed to the democratic sentiments and loyalty of the overseas electorate. Assisted by a range of activists inside and outside the country and information and communication technologies (ICT), voter mobilisation transcended the static territorial borders.

As analysts expected young voters to help Tsai win the presidential race (Ho et al., 2017, 97), this electorate became a critical target of the DPP's election campaign, also abroad. One campaign output was the video *Return Home to Vote in 2020* (2020回家投票, C. *2020 huijia toupiao*), a collection of audiovisual statements from young Taiwanese on their motivations to return to Taiwan to vote. At the end of December, six regional editions (Taiwan, Europe, Japan, US, Europe, Canada, and the Asia Pacific) were posted on YouTube and social media. Each video lasted between one and three minutes, and its participants were students and professionals who either used Mandarin (國語, C. *guoyu*) or Taiwanese (臺語, C. *taiyu*)—the use of Taiwan's local dialect is a trademark of the indigenisation movement. Each contributor concluded with an appeal to the audience to follow their example: "In 2020, I will return home to vote, what about you?" (2020 我會回家投票, 你呢?, C. *2020 wo huijia toupiao, ni ne?*). The European edition contained statements from two Taiwanese women who lived in Vienna, one was Lin Fang-yu (林芳瑜), the wife of the acting president of the TAA, Yu Guan-ru (余冠儒).

The video campaign was an initiative of the DPP youth organisation (民進黨青年黨部, C. *minjindang qingnian dangbu*). To collect individual statements from Taiwanese emigrants from across the world, the organisation reached out to proponents of DPP-affiliated or sympathetic overseas associations. One of them was the current head of the World Federation of Taiwanese Associations (世界台灣同鄉協會, C. *shijie Taiwan tongxiang xiehui*) (WFTA) and former head of the European Federation of Taiwanese Associations (歐洲台灣協會, C. *Ouzhou Taiwan xiehui*) (EFTA), Fuh Pey-Fen (傅佩芬). Fuh Pey-fen then contacted the leaders of local Taiwanese associations in Europe, whom she knew from EFTA's annual meetings. In late November, the call for contributions (全球台灣青年挺英計畫, C. *quanqiu taiwan qingnian ting Cai jihua*) was published on the Facebook pages of Taiwanese in Austria and the TAA by Lin Fang-yu. When asked about her involvement, Lin Fang-yu tried not to overstate her role in the mobilisation process, pointing out that she was only filling in for her husband, who had been too busy. She emphasised that she did not consider herself to be a "very political person". Still, she cared very much about Taiwan and wanted to support her husband in his function as president of the association (private conversation, Lin Fan-yu). Her statement in the video reflects this political consciousness and care for Taiwan's political future:

> I was born after the martial law was abolished and grew up in a free and democratic Taiwan. The value of freedom should not be forgotten.

> In 2020, I will return home to vote, what about you? (Tsai Ing-wen Support Group, 2019)

The TAA is one of the two principal compatriot associations that was established in 1970 as a local subsidiary of the WFTA. The association has always endorsed a Taiwan-centric identity but aligned with the indigenisation movement in recent history and now advocates a self-assertive Taiwanese identity and Taiwan's independence. For this reason, the association also changed its name, abandoning Taiwan Compatriot Association in Austria (台灣同鄉會, C. *Taiwan tongxianghui*). While the political attitudes of its members regarding Taiwan's place in the international system are unanimous, partisan affiliations differ. They range from the currently governing DPP to smaller parties, such as the State Building Party (基進黨, C. *jijindang*) and the Social Democratic Party (社會民主黨, C. *shehui minzhudang*) (interview, Yu Guan-ru). Contrary to the other compatriot associations, the TAA had recently attracted younger members and functionaries to join its ranks. According to Yu Guan-ru, one-third of members are now between 20 and 35 years old (interview, Yu Guan-ru). The association is very active on social media and has high online visibility, thus reaching young Taiwanese migrants who identify with its political attitudes. Although the TAA promotes the idea of a Taiwan-centric identity, like the DPP, it did not officially support Tsai Ing-wen's election campaign but decided to back the DPP youth organisation's efforts to motivate people to exercise their civic rights.

To avoid internal conflicts and remain politically independent, the association distances itself from partisan politics and prefers not to be directly associated with any specific political party or candidate (interview, Yu Gua-ru; interview, Fuh Pey-fen). This appears to be a common policy, shared by other associations under the umbrella organisation of the WFTA. Nevertheless, the federation and its regional and national chapters offer parties from the pan-Green movement an important political platform for direct electoral mobilisation. It is not uncommon for politicians to deliver "guest lectures" at annual meetings of the WFTA and EFTA. While some politicians personally approach the federation or local associations in countries with high numbers of Taiwanese migrants and pay for their own travel and accommodation costs, others are invited and their expenses are covered by the association. According to Yu Guan-ru, the federation and local associations generally support smaller parties with small budgets. Given its small migrant population and high travel expenses, the cost-benefit ratio does not make Austria an attractive place for political parties to deploy traditional direct electoral mobilisation; however, as shown here, ICT opens new opportunities to reach and involve the overseas electorate in mobilisation.

Although the TAA acted as a critical point of access for the DPP and its support groups to rally electoral support, it would be misleading to reduce mobilisation to the co-optation of overseas associations and their leaders. Electoral mobilisation also originated from individuals who used online and offline spaces to urge their peers to fulfil their civic duty to vote. In Germany, for example, a group of students rallied other students on Facebook and other social media for the purchase of a group flight ticket (團購, C. *tuangou*) (private conversations). Through one of their subscribers, the announcement also found its way onto the Facebook pages of the TAA and Taiwanese Student Associations in Vienna/Austria, as well as Taiwanese in Austria.

Conversely, compatriot associations advocating a more ethnicity-based identity entice politicians from the Blue camp to use the associations' networks for direct electoral mobilisation. The most recent and likewise prominent example is Li Chia-fen (李佳芬)—the wife of the KMT's presidential candidate Han Kuo-yu—who toured both in Southeast Asia and the United States, visiting local overseas communities and soliciting their support for her husband and the KMT (*Express*, 2019; Dongwang, 2020). To my knowledge, she did not do the same in Austria; nevertheless, the ACPA took the lead in indirectly mobilising support for the KMT and its candidate.

The organisation advocates an ethnicity-centred identity that emphasises Chinese people's common cultural roots from an imagined "Greater China". Although not all members necessarily espouse the idea of reunification with the mainland, many back the more China-friendly KMT or support other parties from the Blue camp, such as the People First Party (親民黨, C. *qinmindang*) and the New Party (新黨, C. *xindang*) (private conversations; interview, Yu Guan-ru; interview, Katharina Foung). This political orientation critically affects membership structures. As more and more young people find it hard to identify with China, the association remains a catch basin for Taiwanese immigrants' older cohorts, especially first-generation immigrants. Some of them possess not only considerable authority within the local community but also hold influential functions in transnational associations, such as the European Council of the Taiwanese Chamber of Commerce (歐洲台灣商會聯合綜合, C. *Ouzhou Taiwan shanghui lianhe zonghe*), and direct relations with Taiwanese authorities, including the local representative office.

In contrast to the TAA, which focused on the mobilisation of younger voters and therefore made extensive use of the internet and social media, individuals from the older cohorts drew on more traditional—and more costly—practices to gather their networks. Some well-known and influential members of the ACPA established a Han Kuo-yu Support Group (韓國瑜後援會, C. *Han Guoyu houyuanhui*), organising a one-day excursion with a tour bus for about 50 people in late autumn 2019. Rumour had it that individual prominent Taiwanese community members collected donations for Han Kuo-yu or donated no small amount of money to his election campaign, but this could not be confirmed during in the research process. Others showed their support in the form of signature lists that were then sent to Taiwanese media or the OCAC (interview, Ya-ping Jung).

The practices of electoral mobilisation in Austria's Taiwanese migrant communities beg the question of the effectiveness of direct and indirect mobilisation. Official statistics registered a rebound of voter turnout to 74.9 per cent, after a sharp decline to 66.27 per cent in the 2016 elections and a notable increase of emigrant voters without registered domiciles from 2,420 in 2016 to 5,328 in 2020 (Central Election Commission, 2019). Both figures indicate an increased political interest and higher participation rates than in the 2016 elections. According to my survey conducted in Austria, 37 per cent of respondents cast a ballot in the 2020 elections; 67 per cent of those who did not return declared the reasons to be study or job-related. Only 9 per cent did not show interest in the elections, and 26 per cent indicated other reasons, such as family obligations, prohibitive costs, or merely the fact that they did not want to go back specifically for the elections. Still, 60 per cent considered it very important and 22 per cent important to exercise their right to vote, and 84 per cent favoured the introduction of some form of external voting that would make voting from abroad more convenient and less costly. However, due to the low response rate, the survey's findings are not statistically relevant and are, if anything, indicative.

Conclusions

This chapter has explored Taiwanese migrants' electoral participation in homeland elections in the context of the institutional absence of an external voting system. Departing from the assumption that electoral mobilisation is a critical driver of migrants' participation in national elections in their countries of origin—yet with substantially lower effects than among their sessile peers (Kostelka, 2017)—the chapter has tackled the actors, processes, and practices of transnational electoral mobilisation in the Taiwanese community of Vienna during the 2020 presidential elections in Taiwan. I have argued that while political practices of cross-border voting and electoral mobilisation in migrant communities are not essentially transnational, the Taiwanese case presents an exception due to the profound impact of Taiwan's relationship with China on the organisation of political movements and voter choices. As the Fifteenth Presidential Elections in 2020 were profoundly shaped by political events in Hong Kong, "the China factor" gained even more momentum, critically informing direct and indirect mobilisation at home and abroad.

My findings show that Taiwan's main political cleavage not only structures Taiwan's political party system at home but also overseas community organisation abroad. Thus, besides geographical concentration and dense community organisation (Leal et al., 2012; Ahmadov and Sasse, 2016; Kostelka, 2017), it is the organisational landscape, shaped by Taiwan's main political cleavage, that facilitated direct and indirect electoral mobilisation of the Taiwanese emigrant electorate in Vienna. During the run-up of the 2020 elections, political parties activated transnational networks using overseas associations as gate openers to the overseas electorate. Rather than just an act of co-optation of formal leaders of the overseas associations and their close networks, electoral mobilisation was also initiated by individuals who used associations to rally for their preferred candidates and parties or motivate political participation.

While the small size of the community and the huge geographical distance from Taiwan do not encourage the use of traditional means in direct mobilisation, ICT offers new opportunities to reach and involve the internet-active overseas electorate. While all political organisations and social actors involved in direct and indirect voter mobilisation drew on ICT to rally support, the DPP made savvy use of social media to involve and connect Taiwanese residing abroad and Taiwanese overseas associations at all campaign stages (i.e. dissemination of call, collection of contributions, and redissemination of video). Advocates of the Blue camp, on the other hand, primarily mobilised through traditional tactics in which smartphones and social media were used as mere tools to rally people in the offline space. In his recent book *The Game* (2018), the Italian novelist and intellectual Alessandro Baricco posits that the "world" (offline) and the "otherworld" (online) are two generators of one reality but perceived distinctly by generations. While pre-millennials predominantly sit in one world to navigate the other, digital natives conceive the otherworld as an extension of their reality. The differences in mobilisation approaches might thus be explained by different perceptions of reality endorsed by the principal actors responsible for campaigning.

Although this chapter cannot provide any conclusive answers as to how mobilisation's effects translated into emigrant voter turnout and electoral advantages, the findings show that despite the absence of institutional provisions and the steep travel costs, several Taiwanese migrants decided to arrange an international return journey to Taiwan to accommodate their desire to exercise their civic rights. The motivations of these people and the strategies they use to lower the cost of voting should stimulate further research. Also, against the backdrop of recent migratory trends of young and educated Taiwanese, Taiwan's current transformation from a two-party system into a possible multiparty democracy, and the perceived success of transnational electoral mobilisation, it is likely that political parties will continue to address emigrant voters in future election campaigns. Overseas associations will likely remain critical points of access to overseas communities where political parties compete for their influence at home. Future research needs to be more sensitive to political parties' mobilisation strategies among emigrant voters, their reach and effectiveness, the role of ICT in political representation and electoral mobilisation, and whether overseas electorates use this as an opportunity to put pressure on the Taiwanese authorities to liberalise legislation on external voting.

References and Further Reading

Achen, Christopher H., and T. Y. Wang. 2017. "The Taiwan Voter: An Introduction". In *The Taiwan Voter*, edited by Christopher H. Achen and T. Y. Wang, 1–25. Ann Arbor: University of Michigan Press.

Adamson, Fiona B. 2005. "Globalisation, Transnational Political Mobilisation, and Networks of Violence". *Cambridge Review of International Affairs* 18 (1): 31–49.

Ahmadov, Anar K., and Gwendolyn Sasse. 2016. "A Voice Despite Exit: The Role of Assimilation, Emigrant Networks, and Destination in Emigrants' Transnational Political Engagement". *Comparative Political Studies* 49 (1): 78–114.

Anderson, Benedict. 1983. *Imagined Communities: Reflections on the Origin and Spread of Nationalism*. London: Verso.

Baricco, Alessandro. 2018. *The Game*. Milan: Einaudi.

Bauböck, Rainer. 2003. "Towards a Political Theory of Migrant Transnationalism: IMR". *The International Migration Review* 37 (3): 700–723.

Central Election Commission. 2019. "Di 15 ren zongtong fuzongtong xuanju shenqing fanguo xuanjuquan renshu zongjibiao (第15任總統副總統選舉申請返國選舉權人數統計表) [Number of Applications for Eligibility of Return Voters for the 15th Presidential and Vice-Presidential Elections]". https://2020.cec.gov.tw/articleList.html?cate=C07#gsc.tab=0 [accessed 23 March 2021].

Cheng, Wendy. 2017. "'This Contradictory but Fantastic Thing': Student Networks and Political Activism in Cold War Taiwanese/America". *Journal of Asian American Studies* 20 (2): 161–191.

Christiansen, Flemming. 2005. *Chinatown, Europe: An Exploration of Overseas Chinese Identity in the 1990s*. Chinese Worlds. Richmond: Taylor and Francis.

Damm, Jens. 2012. "From 'Overseas Chinese' to 'Overseas Taiwanese': Questions of Identity and Belonging". In *Taiwanese Identity in the Twenty-First Century: Domestic, Regional and Global Perspectives*, edited by Gunter Schubert and Jens Damm, 218–236. London & New York: Routledge.

Day, Stephen, and Jo Shaw. 2002. "European Union Electoral Rights and the Political Participation of Migrants in Host Polities". *International Journal of Population Geography* 8 (2): 183–199.

Dongwang. 2020. "Han Guoyu qifu dongnanya duo guojia weifu lapiao zhengqu qiaomin zhichi (韓國瑜妻赴東南亞多國家，為夫拉票爭取僑民支持) [Han Kuo-yu's Wife Tours in Southeast Asia to Rally Support from Overseas Taiwanese]". https://hk.on.cc/hk/bkn/cnt/cnnews/20191125/bkn-20191125100519445-1125_00952_001.html [accessed 23 March 2021].

Express, US News. 2019. "Liang qian qiaomin huanying Li Jiafen zhanxian Han Guoyu de gaoren renqi (两千侨民欢迎李佳芬展现韩国瑜的高人气) [Overseas Taiwanese Welcome Li Chia-fen Demonstrating Han Kuo-yu's High Popularity]". https://www.usnewsexpress.com/archives/100189 [accessed 23 March 2021].

Fell, Dafydd, Isabelle Cheng, and Lara Momesso. 2019. "Asset or Liability: Transnational Links and Political Participation of Foreignborn Citizens in Taiwan." *International Migration* 57 (4): 202–217.

Gabrielli, Lorenzo, and Ricard Zapata-Barrero. 2015. "A Reappraisal of the Hirschman 'Exit, Voice and Loyalty' Scheme to Interpret Immigrants' Political Participation in Their Origin Countries". Technical Report, Migration Policy Centre, INTERACT Research Report, Conceptual Paper, 2015/11. https://cadmus.eui.eu/handle/1814/36056 [accessed 6 March 2021].

Gebesmair, Andreas. 2009. *Randzonen der Kreativwirtschaft: türkische, chinesische und südasiatische Kulturunternehmungen in Wien*. Vienna: Lit-Verlag.

Glick-Schiller, Nina, Linda Basch, and Cristina Blanc-Szanton. 1992. "Towards a Definition of Transnationalism: Introductory Remarks and Research Questions". *Annals of the New York Academy of Sciences* 645 (1): ix–xiv.

Goebel, Dorothea, and Ludger Pries. 2006. "Transnationalismus oder ethnische Mobilitätsfalle? Das Beispiel des 'ethnischen Unternehmertums'". In *Transnationale Karrieren*, edited by Florian Kreutzer and Silke Roth, 260–282. Wiesbaden: VS Verlag für Sozialwissenschaften.

Goerres, Achim, Dennis C. Spies, and Sabrina J. Mayer. 2018. "How Did Immigrant Voters Vote at the 2017 Bundestag Election? First Results from the Immigrant German Election Study (IMGES)". Universität Duisburg Essen, Open-Minded. https://ssrn.com/abstract=3133559 or http://dx.doi.org/10.2139/ssrn.3133559 [accessed 23 March 2021].

Gong Youqian (龔尤倩). 2017. "Huaqiao yu gongmin shenfen: yi 1990 niandai Taiwan feilübin huaqiao weili (華僑與公民身分：以1990年代台灣菲律賓華僑為例) [Overseas Taiwanese and Citizenship: Taking the 1990 Generation of the Philippines' Overseas Taiwanese as an Example]". *Shehui fenxi* (社會分析) [Social Analysis] 14: 39–74.

Green, Donald P., and Ron Shachar. 2000. "Habit Formation and Political Behaviour: Evidence of Consuetude in Voter Turnout". *British Journal of Political Science* 30 (4): 561–573.

Han, Enze. 2019. "Bifurcated Homeland and Diaspora Politics in China and Taiwan towards the Overseas Chinese in Southeast Asia." *Journal of Ethnic and Migration Studies* 45 (4): 577–594.

Ho, Karl, Cal Clark, and Alexander C. Tan. 2017. "Politicized to Mobilize? A Longitudinal Study of First-Time Voters' Voting Intentions in Taiwan, 2004–2016". *Election Studies* 24 (2): 97–115.

Janoschka, Michael. 2008. "Identity Politics as an Expression of European Citizenship Practice: Participation of Transnational Migrants in Local Political Conflicts". In *The Making of World Society*, edited by Remus Gabriel Anghel, Eva Gerharz, Gilberto Rescher, and Monika Salzbrunn, 133–152. Bielefeld: transcript Verlag.

Karp, Jeffrey A. 2012. "Electoral Systems, Party Mobilisation and Political Engagement". *Australian Journal of Political Science* 47 (1): 71–89.

Kostelka, Filip 2017. "Distant Souls: Post-Communist Emigration and Voter Turnout". *Journal of Ethnic and Migration Studies* 43 (7): 1061–1083.

Kwok, Kim. 2012. "Chinese Immigrant Economy in Vienna in Transnational Era". PhD thesis, Department of East Asian Studies/Sinology, University of Vienna.

Kwok, Kim, and Michael Parzer. 2008. "Wo es Platz für uns gibt, da gehen wir hin! MigrantInnen chinesischer Herkunft im Industrieviertel". In *Vom selben Schlag ... Migration und Integration im niederösterreichischen Industrieviertel*, edited by Thomas Schmidinger, 361–364. Wiener Neustadt: Verein Alltag Verlag.

Leal, David L., Byung-Jae Lee, and James A. McCann. 2012. "Transnational Absentee Voting in the 2006 Mexican Presidential Election: The Roots of Participation". *Electoral Studies* 31 (3): 540–549.

Li Hsin-fang (李欣芳). 2019. "'Wei you jianding qianxing, Taiwan cai hui geng hao' haiwai qingnian fasheng ting Cai Yingwen (「唯有堅定前行, 台灣才會更好」海外青年發聲明挺蔡英文) ['Only if We Persistently Keep Striding, Taiwan Can Become a Better Place' Young Overseas Taiwanese Send a Declaration of Support to Tsai Ing-wen]". *Liberty Times*. https://news.ltn.com.tw/news/politics/breakingnews/2661972 [accessed 23 March 2021].

Lin, Catherine Kai-Ping. 2006. "Taiwan's Overseas Opposition Movement and Grassroots Diplomacy in the United States: The Case of the Formosan Association for Public Affairs". *Journal of Contemporary China* 46: 133–159.

Low, Choo Chin. 2013. "Taiwanese and German Citizenship Reforms: Integration of Immigrants without Challenging the Status Quo, 1990–2000". *European Journal of East Asian Studies* 12 (2): 269–294.

Marinaccio, Julia [= Julia Ritirc]. 2016. *Chinas Olympische Spiele und chinesische Identität in Österreich: Eine qualitative Inhaltsanalyse einer chinesisch-sprachigen Zeitung in Österreich*. Saarbrücken: AV Akademikerverlag.

Marinaccio, Julia. 2022 (forthcoming). "Dealing With the Absence of Absentee Voting: Transnational Electoral Mobilisation in Taiwan's 2020 Presidential Elections". *China Perspectives*.

Milbrath, Lester W., and Lal Goel Madan. 1977. *Political Participation: How and Why People Get Involved in Politics*. Chicago: RandMcNally.

Mügge, Liza, Maria Kranendonk, Floris Vermeulen, and Nermin Aydemir. 2019. "Migrant Votes 'Here' and 'There': Transnational Electoral Behavior of Turks in the Netherlands". *Migration Studies* 9 (3): 400–422. https://academic.oup.com/migration/article/9/3/400/5543475 [accessed 23 March 2021].

News Lens. 2019. Taiwan 2020 Election Polls. https://international.thenewslens.com/interactive/125385 [accessed 8 November 2021].

OCAC. 2019. *Zhongguo minguo 107 nian qiaowu tongji nianbao* (中國民國107年僑務統計年報) [2018 Statistical Yearbook of Overseas Community Affairs Council, Republic of China (Taiwan)]. Taipei: Overseas Community Affairs Council, Republic of China (Taiwan).

Østergaard-Nielsen, Eva. 2003. "The Politics of Migrants' Transnational Political Practices: IMR". *The International Migration Review* 37 (3): 760–786.

Paarlberg, Michael A. 2019. "Competing for the Diaspora's Influence at Home: Party Structure and Transnational Campaign Activity in El Salvador". *Journal of Ethnic and Migration Studies* 45 (4): 539–560.

Peltoniemi, Johanna. 2018. "Transnational Political Engagement and Emigrant Voting". *Journal of Contemporary European Studies* 26 (4): 392–410.

Pessl, Katja, and Lena Springer. 2011. "MigrantInnen aus China im Wiener Hochschul- und Gesundheitswesen: Dynamische Zwischenzonen und Einzelinitiativen". In *Migration und Integration: Wissenschaftliche Perspektiven aus Österreich*, edited by Julia Dahlvik, Christoph Reinprecht, and Wiebke Sievers, 69–86. Vienna: Vienna University Press.

Poston, Dudley L., and Juyin H. Wong. 2016. "The Chinese Diaspora: The Current Distribution of the Overseas Chinese Population". *Chinese Journal of Sociology* 2 (3): 348–373.

Rosenstone, Steven J., and John M. Hansen. 1993. *Mobilization, Participation, and Democracy in America*. New York: Macmillan.

Schäfer, Carsten. 2017a. "Chinese Language Press in Austria: Discussing the 2008 Tibetan Unrest in Transnational Spaces". *Vienna Journal of East Asian Studies* 8: 163–191.

——. 2017b. "'Nachfahren des Drachen' und 'echte Wiener'? Identitäten und Inkorporationsmuster chinesischer Migranten in Österreich am Beispiel des Webforums www.outuo.net". PhD thesis, Department of East Asian Studies/Sinology, University of Vienna.

Springer, Lena. 2004. "Professionelle und kulturelle Positionierungen von Ärzten für chinesische Medizin aus der VR China in Wien". MA dissertation, Department of East Asian Studies/Sinology, University of Vienna.

Statistik Austria. 2020. *Bevölkerung zu Jahresbeginn 2002–2020 nach detailliertem Geburtsland*. https://www.statistik.at/web_de/statistiken/menschen_und_gesellschaft/bevoelkerung/bevoelkerungsstruktur/bevoelkerung_nach_staatsangehoerigkeit_geburtsland/index.html [accessed 23 March 2021].

Steiger, Katharina. 2008. "Migration und Identität: Chinesische Künstler in Wien". MA dissertation, Department of East Asian Studies/Sinology, University of Vienna.

To, James J. 2014. *Qiaowu: Extra-Territorial Policies for the Overseas Chinese*. Leiden: Brill.

Tsai, Chi-lin. 2015. "Too Far to Vote? A Preliminary Analysis of Residential Absentees' Electoral Behaviour in Taiwan". *Journal of Electoral Studies* 22 (1): 35–69.

Tsai Ing-wen Support Group. 2019. "2020 wo hui jia toupiao, na ni ne? (2020我回家投票，那你呢？) [2020, I Will Return Home to Vote, What about You?]". https://www.youtube.com/watch?v=gjoxavaAuBs [accessed 23 March 2021].

Waldinger, Roger. 2015. *The Cross-Border Connection: Immigrants, Emigrants, and Their Homelands*. Cambridge, MA: Harvard University.

List of Interviewees

Katharina Foung (馮孝慈), principal of the Essentia Mandarin Centre in Austria (奧地利菁華中文學校), Vienna, 23 July 2020.

Pey-fen Fuh (傅佩芬), President of the World Federation of Taiwanese Associations (世界台灣人協會), Bergen-Frankfurt (digital), 31 January 2021.

Ian Hung (洪毅), head of Taiwanese Student Associations in Austria and Vienna (旅奧維也納臺灣同學會), Vienna, 21 July 2020.

Ya-ping Jung (戎亞屏), head of the Association of Taiwanese Entrepreneurs in Austria (奧地利台灣商會), Vienna, 11 August 2021.

Cindy Lai (賴鏡仙) and Kevin Cheng (鄭光佑), principals of the Taiwan Chinese School in Austria (奧地利中華僑校), Vienna, 22 July 2020.

Fang-yu Lin (林芳瑜), wife of Yu Guan-ru, Bergen-Vienna (private conversation online), 2 December 2020.

Yang (楊學生) (anonymised), music student at Mozarteum in Salzburg, Bergen-Salzburg (digital), 11 November 2020.

Yu Guan-ru (余冠儒), head of the Taiwanese Association in Austria (奧地利台灣協會), Vienna, 21 July 2020.

Part III

Transnationalism in Popular Cultures

9

Return Ticket to Pyongyang

Transnational Aspects in the Work of Film-Maker Yang Yong-hi

Till Weingärtner

The protagonist of film-maker Yang Yong-hi's debut novel *Chōsen daigakkō monogatari* (朝鮮大学校物語, A Tale from Korea University) (2018) is Mi-yeon, a young Osaka-born woman belonging to Japan's Korean minority of "*Zainichi* Koreans", known in Japanese as *Zainichi Kankokujin* (在日韓国人) for those holding South Korean nationality or *Zainichi Chōsenjin* (在日朝鮮人) for those holding North Korean nationality, like the character Mi-yeon. The terms "Korean minority" and "*Zainichi* Korean" do not refer to any Korean living in Japan, but only to those who took residence in Japan before the end of Japan's colonial reign over Korea in 1945 and their descendants, who were granted special residence status in Japan without receiving Japanese citizenship. Official figures of the Japanese Ministry of Justice number them at nearly 372,000; more than 90 per cent hold a South Korean passport and the remainder North Korean (Sugimoto, 2021, 208).

The term *Zainichi* can be thought of as a marker of a complex status: literally indicating only the state of being located in Japan, it emphasises this location as a marker of otherness and thus a status as an outsider within Japanese society. As the case of Yang Yong-hi discussed here will demonstrate, it is not simply a case of a group of nationals from one country living in another due to historic circumstances. The *Zainichi*'s relationship to either or both of the two Korean nations is often troubled and reflects the political tension on the Korean Peninsula. Indeed, the *Zainichi* Korean have been referred to as a "Diaspora without Homeland" (Ryang and Lie, 2009).

Yang's novel traces Mi-yeon's path through her four years of study at Korea University (*Chōsen daigakkō* 朝鮮大学校), a real-life institution in Tokyo following a North Korean curriculum and attended by students of the Korean minority. Mi-yeon struggles with the rigid rules, such as the prohibition on using Japanese and the strict curfew, but she enjoys "the outside world"—most importantly, the opportunity to visit many theatre shows in Tokyo and follow her dream of pursuing theatre professionally. In her second year, Mi-yeon starts a brief love affair with Yu, a Japanese student at the art school that is visible from the windows of Mi-yeon's classrooms. While their love initially blossoms under Yu's curiosity about Mi-yeon's experiences of discrimination as a *Zainichi* Korean, Mi-yeon is ultimately hurt by Yu's lack of awareness of, and unwillingness to accept, her fractured identity. After they first have sexual intercourse in Yu's student apartment, Mi-yeon is upset when he says that he is "not bothered" about her minority background (Yang, 2018a, 135–138). Mi-yeon's response is reminiscent of rejections of "the colour-blind" claims of liberals in Europe or the United States—she asserts that she *wants* him to be bothered. Her anger reflects the hurtful impact of Yu's statement though he meant only to assure Mi-yeon of his affection for her. Mi-yeon's recognition of Yu's position of privilege and his inability to give it up ultimately sows doubt in her mind about whether they are on an equal footing in their relationship, and they stop seeing each other after this fight. She herself has no choice but to accept her multilayered identity, no matter how often she might look out of the window at the Japanese students on the neighbouring campus.

Mi-yeon has much in common with the author of her story: like Mi-yeon, Yang Yong-hi was born in 1964 in Osaka into a family belonging to the Korean minority. Both character and author have parents engaged in political activism, supporting the cause of North Korea, and siblings who left Japan to live in North Korea. Both attend schools mirroring the North Korean education system, and while Mi-yeon is set for a career in the theatre scene of Tokyo, Yang gained a master's degree in media studies from the New School University in New York and became a professional film-maker. At the time of writing, Yang has directed and released two documentaries and one feature film, and has announced that her fourth film is complete and ready for release in 2021. All of her films are autobiographical and focus on her relationship with her family, with relatives living in both Japan and in North Korea.

Mi-yeon's reaction to Yu's dismissal of the significance of her *Zainichi* Korean identity reflects Yang Yong-hi's own attitude towards the Japanese majority, which tends to ignore the issues faced by the *Zainichi* Koreans and display ignorance (albeit often cloaked in misguided kindness) about the complexities of a transnational identity with links to both Japan and Korea: as often expressed in interviews and her journalistic writing, Yang is motivated to tell Japanese audiences about her family history because such a personal story may increase their understanding of the *Zainichi* Koreans (Yang, 2018b). Studying Yang's films can help us not only to learn about her specific work and the *Zainichi* Koreans but also to explore the "transnationality" of Asian cinema in a broader sense.

Teaching, studying, and writing about the cinema of Japan and South Korea often occurs within the framework of national cinema. This may seem self-evident, but the concept of "national cinema" as an approach to Japanese cinema is in many ways historically contingent upon and intertwined with the emergence of academic interest in film (Yoshimoto, 2000). The drive to identify and label films as "Japanese" has increasingly been recognised as complex and potentially problematic, not least the ways in which it has led to essentialist readings of Japanese film history and art.

Japanese film historian Yomota Inuhiko (2019), for example, uses the question, "What is Japanese cinema?" as a lens to examine both canonical film directors active in Japan and the role of film as a tool of nationalism. His analysis encompasses Japan's colonial era, the interaction between Japanese and other Asian film industries after the Second World War, and the role of the *Zainichi* Korean minority in Japanese film. Researchers in both film studies and Japanese studies are increasingly interested in the "transnationalism" of Japanese film-makers (Centeno-Martín and Morita, 2020a). The Japanese film industry itself is striving for a stronger position in Asian markets, arguably hoping to piggyback on the success of the Korean film industry. We see this interest in the Japanese film industry's support for initiatives such as the Osaka Asian Film Festival (Weingärtner, 2022 (forthcoming)). In this context, there is a recognition of the potential for *Zainichi* Korean film-makers to "internationalise" the Japanese film industry, as part of a "discourse in Japan that expects non-Japanese minorities to be the vanguards who usher Japanese cinema into the age of globalization and post-national filmmaking" (Ogawa, 2017, 44; cf. Ogawa, 2014, 152–153). Thus, the work of Yang—as a *Zainichi* Korean film-maker who engages with transnational questions—represents an opportunity to build an understanding of Asian film-making which clearly resists the narrow framing of "national cinema".

Andrew Higson argues that the concept of national cinema tends to be used "prescriptively rather than descriptively, citing what *ought* to be the national cinema, rather than describing the actual cinematic experience of popular audiences" (1989, 37). He distinguishes four definitions of national cinema: (1) the economic approach focuses on the financial structure of film production and the industry; (2) the text-based approach considers films' topics, styles, and the extent to which they are "engaged in 'exploring, questioning and constructing a notion of nationhood in the films themselves and in the consciousness of the viewer'" (Higson, 1989, 36); (3) the exhibition-led or audience-focused approach considers which films are watched by audiences; (4) finally, the criticism-led approach examines academic and journalistic writing that evaluates the artistic value of films in the context of the culture of specific nation-states.

In a similar vein, scholars of film studies are developing the concept of transnational film studies. Dina Iordanova uses categories that are similar to those identified by Higson in the context of national cinema:

> Transnational film studies approaches the cycle of film production, dissemination and reception as a dynamic process that transcends national borders and reflects the mobility of human existence in the global age; it explores the narrative and stylistic features of films that come about as a result of this supernational cycle of film-making and reception. (2007, 508)

These categories represent a starting point for engaging with works that we might want to characterise as "transnational". In her 2005 debut documentary, *Dear Pyongyang* (ディア・ピョンヤン, J. *Dia Pyonyan*), Yang Yong-hi explored her family history and relationship with her family, including her parents, who are activists for the pro-North Korean Chongryon (총련, General Association of Korean Residents in Japan). As a second-generation *Zainichi* Korean, the act of crossing from one country to the other is engraved in Yang's family history. Her father left his home on the island of Cheju, in what is today South Korea, during the colonial period to live on what was then the Japanese mainland, where he got married and had children in Osaka after the end of the Second World War. Because of his experiences of colonialism and discrimination, Yang's father identified with the ideas propagated by North Korea. His activism for the Chongryon organisation represents the split in the Japan-based Korean community, mirroring the division of the Korean Peninsula into two opposing political entities. Yang and her brother therefore grew up in what could be described as a transnational state: physically located in Japan, socially immersed in both Japanese and Korean cultures, and ideologically rooted in North Korea as their true homeland.

Yang delves into the impact of her family's history and experiences on her own identity and work. *Dear Pyongyang* focuses on Yang's father and addresses the question of why her older brothers were sent away to live in North Korea in 1971 as young men. They were prevented from ever returning, in line with the "repatriation" project which saw, with the support of both the Japanese and North Korean authorities, 93,340 people relocated from Japan to North Korea between 1959 and 1984. They were promised a better life in the so-called fatherland, despite many of them sharing the situation of Yang's brothers, who were born in Japan and had never called North Korea their home (Ogawa, 2017, 30). Yang follows her father around the family home in

Osaka with a video camera and accompanies him on a trip to Pyongyang to document his interactions with relatives there. Ultimately, she examines regret, guilt, and the political transformation that the elder Yang experienced after sending his sons to North Korea—an experience that ultimately eroded his political convictions about and loyalty towards the communist state he perceives as his fatherland.

Family video shot during Yang's family visits to Pyongyang also forms the backbone of her second documentary, *Sona, the Other Myself* (愛しきソナ, J. *Itoshiki Sona*; 2009). *Sona* focuses on Yang's relationship with her niece, who lives in North Korea, but—as the title implies—also engages with the question of how Yang's own identity is shaped by her childhood experiences and relationships with relatives in Japan and North Korea. After the release of *Dear Pyongyang*, Yang was banned from travelling to North Korea, so she set her next feature film in Tokyo and used professional actors from both Japan and South Korea. The fictional *Zainichi* Korean family at the centre of the film is clearly modelled on her own—an older brother who was sent away to North Korea as a young man makes a short visit home to Japan, which we experience primarily from the perspective of the family's daughter, Rie.

At the time of writing (mid-2022), Yang's latest documentary is about to be released across cinemas in Japan. Called *Soup and Ideology* (スープとイデオロギー, J. *Sūpu to ideologī*), it puts the focus on her mother and was shown at the Yamagata International Documentary Film Festival 2021. In addition to her work in film, Yang is an active writer and has published three books related to her films (Yang, 2006; 2009; 2013) and the aforementioned autobiographical novel set in the world of *Zainichi* Korean university students (Yang, 2018a). All of these works depict the lived experiences of Yang and her family, travelling back and forth between Japan and North Korea, crossing the border between the two countries that comprise Yang's transnational identity.

The transnationality of Yang's films can be identified according to the same principles that appear in Higson's definition of national cinema and Iordanova's description of transnational cinema—that is, their production, content, consumption, and stylistic features. As a documentary film-maker who works independently from big studios, Yang falls outside the category of a national film-maker as defined by industry standards. Recently, she sought funding from both South Korean and Japanese sources, most notably by starting campaigns in both countries to crowdfund the production of the aforementioned documentary film about her mother (Yang, 2018b, 88). While Yang has frequently stated that she is motivated to educate and inform Japanese audiences about *Zainichi* Koreans, she also interacts with South Korean audiences (Yang, 2018b, 88). Furthermore, Yang's style of filming in the private sphere of interactions with members of her family arguably situates her documentary films outside any national context. Indeed, Ogawa recounts that Yang herself described her materials as "nothing more than home videos" when interrogated by the North Korean authorities on her return journey to Japan (Ogawa, 2017, 40). In other words, Yang herself conceptualises her first film project as private rather than as a product of a national film industry.

The remainder of this chapter will analyse the transnationality of Yang's three earliest films, the two aforementioned documentaries and her feature film *Our Homeland* (かぞくのくに J. *Kazoku no kuni*) in terms of their content. Style and content are of course often intimately connected, especially in the work of an autobiographical film-maker such as Yang, which foregrounds her personal story and identity as a transnational film-maker.

Home and "Fatherland"

North Korea is repeatedly referred to as the "homeland" or "fatherland" in Yang's films, *sokoku* (祖国) in Japanese and *choguk* (조국) in Korean. Yang's father is the most prominent voice and spokesperson for the idea that North Korea should be regarded as the family's home, and he refers to the move of his Japan-born sons as a "return to one's country" or *kikoku* (帰国). The intense focus on North Korea manifests in accounts of Yang's parents' activism in Osaka and the regular acts of patriotism that occur in North Korea-sponsored schools in Japan.

In her voice-over to *Dear Pyongyang*, Yang describes her own evolving relationship with the concept of North Korea as the fatherland. As a child, she says, she engaged with it uncritically. As she grew older, however, she started to develop a split identity—she engaged in "patriotic" learning in a North Korean school while also enjoying the cultural possibilities of Japan, such as seeing films or plays and listening to Beatles records. She compares the experience of this cultural divide to the physical separation of East and West Berlin, which made the ideological gap highly visible as people on the other side of the Wall could be seen every day. The connection to Germany is historically interesting because it symbolises the hope that a divided country ultimately can be reunited. At the same time, many individuals in Germany made similar choices to leave their country behind and risk their own lives to search for better prospects in the West, thereby rejecting their own "fatherland". In an interview, Yang reflected on the choice between two irreconcilable sides as a "cruel" reality and an intrinsic part of the lives of second- and third-generation *Zainichi* Koreans (Yang, 2014, 9).

The Berlin Wall also reminds Yang of her emotional separation from her parents in their own home (Nakamura, 2012, 44). During a visit to

Pyongyang, she realised that travelling to North Korea did not feel like the promised homecoming. Instead, she felt alienated and started to perceive North Korea as the home of her family, rather than her own. She expresses this thought in the voice-over to *Dear Pyongyang*, during a passage shot on a ferry ride between Japan and North Korea: "I come not to visit 'the great fatherland'", she says, but "to see people I love".

Yang's struggle to define what North Korea means to her as a country is also reflected in the title of her fictional feature film, *Kazoku no kuni*, whose title literally means "The Family's Country" though the official English title is *Our Homeland*. Harshly contrasting Japan with North Korea, the film interrogates the true nature of the homeland for Yang's alter ego and family. The state is omnipresent; a North Korean "minder" constantly watches the brother during his home visit. Rie is clearly disgusted by the minder and later actively expresses her hatred for North Korea when her frustration at the impossibility to talk freely and connect with her visiting brother reaches a flashpoint.

Family

In *Dear Pyongyang*, there is no minder *per se* who could be verbally attacked. Personal expression and the family's integrity are undermined primarily by the pressure to accept North Korea as one's homeland. One of the most striking aspects of the film is the father's kindness and affection. He flirts with his wife and jokes with his daughter, often in the private setting of their flat, lying on the futon in his underwear. This creates a harsh contrast with both the geographic and experienced distance from relatives, who not only live far away but also lead a life less free under an oppressive regime. Yang recalls that her visits to North Korea and interactions with her brothers were supervised and timed, leaving her brothers no opportunities to speak freely in front of their sister. More extensive family visits are seen in *Sona, the Other Myself*. Here, Yang interacts with her niece and the father interacts with his daughters-in-law while the "repatriated" brothers sit silently in a corner, seemingly unable to interact with their Japan-based relatives. The father's longing is illustrated at one point when he expresses that his greatest wish is to be buried near his sons in Pyongyang. Yang's mother is seen as the driving force in alleviating the conflict between family and country. She attempts to make the situation as positive as possible for everyone. In *Dear Pyongyang*, for example, Yang's mother prepares care packages for the family in North Korea, and the audience learns that this practice began after the first photo sent home from the "repatriated" brothers in North Korea showed them looking miserable and thin—a stark contrast to the good life that is promised to follow relocation. The mother tears the photo into little pieces, hiding the reality from the father. The realities of life in North Korea become the big family taboo, rendering the brothers speechless victims of repatriation. A similar brother character, unable to open up or show affection while under constant surveillance, appears in *Our Homeland*.

The fictional setting of *Our Homeland* allows Yang to not only hint at discontent but have family members actually voice it. An uncle is the voice of reason, advocating for familial love to be prioritised over political ideology and even handing out little envelopes of pocket money to his niece Rie. The split between Yang's alter ego and her parents manifests in their reactions to her brother's visit: the parents' anticipation focuses on the North Korea-sanctioned medical treatment the brother is allowed to receive in Japan, while Rie talks more openly about looking forward to seeing and spending time with her brother. The film demonstrates how private family relationships are profoundly affected by the constant presence of North Korea—both physically (through the minder) and psychologically (through the parents' ideology).

Loyalty

The main potential for conflict lies in the issue of loyalty, as shown in the condensed drama of *Our Homeland*. The conflict between Rie and her brother emerges when he, under pressure from the North Korean secret service, tries to persuade his sister to become an informant. In one of the most emotional scenes of the film, the brother rips his party badge off his shirt after fighting with his sister. When he later meets his mother, he is emotionally conflicted and unable to embrace her.

The constant demand for loyalty to North Korea and the family's attempts to gloss over the contradictions between patriotism and family loyalty are present in all of Yang's films. In the first scene of *Dear Pyongyang*, Yang and her father discuss her marriage prospects, and her father immediately rejects the idea that his daughter could marry a Japanese or American man. Yang's father's activism means that loyalty to the North Korean leader consumes his life. He continues to demand loyalty to the cause from his children, for example in his speech at a family celebration of his birthday in Pyongyang.

In private interviews with her father, Yang ultimately succeeds in identifying an internal conflict—he admits that sending his sons to North Korea may have been the wrong decision, and he might have decided otherwise if he had known then what he knows now. The film ends with what could be called an act of atonement: the father accepts Yang's decision to follow a career as a film-maker and allows her to become a South Korean citizen, making it easier for her to pursue her career by, for example, participating in film festivals all around the world. When asked if she (like his other children) would be expected to remain loyal, he replies no. All that he expects of her is to find a partner and get married, thus fulfilling what could be described as a pure filial duty within the Confucian family framework, something discussed in Cawley's chapter in this book.

Language

Ogawa has pointed out the relevance of Yang's choice to render the Japanese title of *Our Homeland, Kazoku no kuni*, as かぞくのくに, using the hiragana syllabary instead of the commonly used *kanji* for *kazoku* (家族, family) and *kuni* (国, country): for him, the design on the film's title card looks "as if it is written by a Japanese learner or an exile who has forgotten the language" (2017, 44). Right from the beginning, language choice hints at the dislocation experienced by Yang's family and the struggle to find the right words to address the experience of Yang and her relatives, even between themselves.

Yang's role as a film-maker who asks painful questions about her family history puts Yang in the position of the family "rebel". This position is also filled by her alter ego in *Our Homeland*. The family's daughter not only uses a Japanese name, Rie, but also teaches Japanese to foreigners. All of Yang's films show family members interacting in private settings in standard Japanese or—in the documentaries—the Osaka dialect of Japanese; Rie's choice to go one step further and dedicate her professional life to the Japanese language can be seen as a decision to establish yet another barrier between herself and what she perceives as the North Korean propaganda that has destroyed her family.

In fact, all of Yang's works refer to her own identity through several languages and dialects. Yang uses standard Japanese not only to interact with the Japanese audience and tell her story in voice-overs but also as the language of the Tokyo-based family in *Our Homeland*. However, Yang and her parents use the Osaka dialect, creating a private space in which her father ultimately can voice his concerns about his past choices. At the same time, all topics related to loyalty and her father's political convictions are expressed in Korean. Interestingly, Yang addresses her parents with Korean terms such as *abŏji* (아버지) for her father and *omoni* (어머니), even when otherwise communicating with them in Osaka-dialect Japanese. The Korean word for elder brother, *oppa* (오빠), is used in reference to her absent brothers, for example in her journalistic writing where in Japanese texts the word *oppa* appears alongside, and as the intended reading of, the Japanese word *ani* (兄) (Yang, 2019). This nuance reflects her inability to fully reject or suppress the loyalty associated with North Korea and the Korean element of her identity, and it shapes her family relations.

A close observation of the father in *Dear Pyongyang* reveals that he code-switches between Korean and Osaka dialect, often within the same shot or even the same sentence. Korean enables him to express his political beliefs, while Osaka dialect is the language of his private and quasi-unpolitical interactions. Importantly, it is different from standard Japanese, the language of the former coloniser of the Korean Peninsula and one of the main antagonistic states from the official North Korean point of view. On his visit to Pyongyang and during the celebration of his seventieth birthday, the father speaks in Korean when making all official announcements, including his reflections on loyalty, his expectations of his sons and grandchildren, and his determination to urge them to maintain their loyalty to the leaders of North Korea.

In the second half of the film, when Yang asks her father whether she (as a daughter) is exempt from the expectations placed on sons, Yang quotes her father's speech in Korean. Critically, her father uses Osaka dialect to release her from the obligation of nationalist loyalty and then switches to Korean to emphasise the traditional Confucian obligation to find a partner and get married, linking these demands to his conviction and somehow denying his daughter special treatment. When later granting her the more significant privilege of switching from North to South Korean nationality and even that he might visit her one day if she lived in Seoul, he again relies on the private code of Osaka dialect. At the end of the film, the father's own identity appears more complex and fractured than at the beginning. Osaka dialect allows him to carefully address and voice aspects of his identity that contradict his official dedication to North Korea while upholding his political beliefs and expectations for the future of that country.

During scenes in Pyongyang, another language seems to offer the potential for a new form of communication with Yang's niece and connections that transcend ideological borders. The search for another language to fill the silence and possibly speak the unspeakable becomes tangible in scenes that Yang captures during the family visit in Pyongyang. In one shot, her brother leans silently against a wall. The sons and their parents do not appear to be able to go deeper than small talk, exchanging familiar phrases and general observations. A long piano recital by Yang's nephew continues deep into the night, even though the electricity cut-off at night makes it difficult to read the scores. The music and shared pride over the boy's musical talents fills painful silences. When Yang asks her brother how he feels, his English reply—"I am happy!"—might reflect his inability to find the right words in Korean or Osaka dialect, as both languages are tinted with political and personal connotations. As Yang's niece Sona learns English, phrases such as "I love you" become part of their day-to-day interactions. This potential for the family to connect by finding additional forms of expression, music and English, to communicate the otherwise inexpressible was never fulfilled, however; after the release of *Dear Pyongyang,* the North Korean state banned Yang.

Conclusion: A Transnational Cinema of Personal Reconciliation?

Yang Yong-hi's novel *A Tale from Korea University* ends on a positive note: Mi-yeon successfully resists the university's teachers' efforts to steer her towards a teaching career at a Chongryun-run Korean school in Japan. She pointedly leaves the graduation ceremony early, rejecting the university's decision to send her on a "patriotic" path that reflects loyalty to the North Korean leadership. Instead, Mi-yeon successfully enters the theatre scene in Tokyo and makes it her personal form of expression. The last scene depicts her reunion with her former lover Yu, who came to see the premiere of a play directed by Mi-yeon. The language of theatre enables Yu to grasp Mi-yeon's identity, making reconciliation seem possible.

More broadly, Yang's works seem to suggest that reconciliation is possible, but reconciliation can occur only after an initial separation. In both *Dear Pyongyang* and *Sona,* the family is broken as the result of the parents' insistence that their children follow the "patriotic" side of their upbringing, resulting in the brothers living in isolation and Yang limiting her contact with her parents for several years. In *Our Homeland,* Rie leaves her family behind and travels away at the end of the film. Mi-yeon's official announcement that she is breaking with the North Korean education system at the graduation ceremony is the result of living her own life away from her parents for four years in Tokyo. Yang portrays Mi-yeon's choice as painful but ultimately unavoidable.

However, Yang has not run away to leave her *Zainichi* identity behind. And, indeed, reconciliation appears possible again when others are ready to accept her stance on her identity. *Dear Pyongyang* demonstrates this by following her steps of reconciliation with her father. She first scrutinises his past decisions but ultimately witnesses his change in attitude. By allowing his daughter to switch her citizenship from North to South Korean, thereby freeing her from what he perceives as a patriotic duty of loyalty, he gives her licence to continue exploring her family history and her own identity as an internationally active film-maker. That this reconciliation occurs in Osaka dialect hints that despite his self-image, Yang's father too possesses a complex and transnationally shaped identity.

In sum, Yang's films have many features that mark them out as "transnational cinema". They focus on transnational themes—namely, Yang's own transnational identity in the context of the situation of the Korean minority in Japan—and their production and consumption involve Japan, South Korea, and now the world at large (Ogawa, 2017, 30–33). The films offer us a deeper understanding of the transnational state of the *Zainichi* Korean minority: not only showing how tensions arise in trying to balance personal, familial, and public lives across two cultures, but also highlighting the strategies which this duality makes available. Yang shows us the pervasive imposition of the North Korean state on her family and uses her film-making to challenge the promise of a better life in North Korea. Questions of nationality and loyalty invade the family life she depicts, and distinguishing between private and official life is near impossible. The parents must find their own strategies to deal with contradictions, conflicts, and, ultimately, their feelings of guilt. The clearest rejection of North Korean ideology is voiced by Yang's fictional characters in Japanese or Osaka dialect—namely, her alter ego Rie and the heroine Mi-yeon in her debut novel. Some reconciliation with Yang's parents seems possible within the borders of Japan, but Yang's public engagement with her own transnational identity has prevented her from reconnecting with her family across the sea in North Korea. For us, as the audience, her work is a tool not only to understand the specific challenges faced by Yang but also to identify, analyse, and understand the characteristics of "transnational" cinema.

References and Further Reading

Centeno-Martín, Marcos P., and Nori Morita. 2020a. "Editorial: Japan and the 'Transnational Cinema'". *Arts* 9 (50): 1–5.

Centeno-Martín, Marcos P., and Nori Morita (eds.). 2020b. *Japanese Transnational Cinema*. Special Edition of *Arts*. https://www.mdpi.com/journal/arts/special_issues/Japanese_Transnational_Cinema [accessed 18 March 2021].

Dew, Oliver. 2016. *Zainichi Cinema: Korean-in-Japan Film Culture*. Cham: Palgrave Macmillan.

Higson, Andrew Douglas. 1989. "The Concept of National Cinema". *Screen* 30 (4): 36–46.

Iordanova, Dina. 2007. "Transnational Film Studies". In *The Cinema Book*, edited by Cook Pam, 508–509. London: British Film Institute.

Kim-Wachutka, Jackie J. 2020. *Zainichi Korean Women in Japan: Voices*. Abingdon and New York: Routledge.

Nakamura, Fumiko. 2012. "Kin'yōbunka: Naze, ani wa 'kita' ni kaeranakereba naranakatta no ka" (金曜文化—なぜ、兄は「北」に帰らなければならなかったのか) [Friday Culture: Why My Big Brother Had to Return to the "North"]. *Kin'yōbi* 20 (33): 44.

Ogawa, Shota Tsai. 2014. "Revisiting Through the Night (*Yoru o kakete*): A Paradigm or Anomaly in Japanese-Korean Co-Production and Cross-Media Adaptation". *Journal of Japanese and Korean Cinema* 6 (2): 152–166.

——. 2017. "A Long Way Home: The Rhetoric of Family and Familiarity in Yang Yong-hi's Pyongyang Trilogy". *Journal of Japanese and Korean Cinema* 9 (1): 30–46.

Ryang, Sonia, and John Lie (eds.). 2009. *Diaspora without Homeland: Being Korean in Japan*. Berkeley: University of California Press.

Sugimoto, Yoshio. 2021. *An Introduction to Japanese Society*. 5th ed. Cambridge: Cambridge University Press.

Weiner, Michael (ed.). 2009. *Japan's Minorities: The Illusion of Homogeneity*. 2nd ed. Abingdon and New York: Routledge.

Weingärtner, Till. 2022 (forthcoming). "Celebrating the Rival: Korean Films and the Osaka Asian Film Festival". In *Korean Film and Festivals: Global Transcultural Flows*, edited by Hyunseon Lee. Abingdon and New York: Routledge.

Yang Yong-hi. 2006. *Dia Pyonyan: Kazoku wa hanaretara akan no ya* (ディア・ピョンヤン—家族は離れたらアカンのや) [Dear Pyongyang: Families Mustn't Be Separated!]. Tokyo: Arton.

——. 2009. *Kita-chōsen de oppa wa shinda* (北朝鮮で兄 (オッパ) は死んだ) [My Big Brother (*Oppa*) Died in North Korea]. Tokyo: Nanatsumori shokan.

——. 2013. *Ani: Kazoku no kuni* (兄～かぞくのくに) [Big Brother: The Family's Country]. Tokyo: Shōgakukan.

——. 2014. "'Kazoku no kuni': Kita-chōsen, Kankoku, Nihon. Nihon-jin mo sunde iru kuni" (『家族の国』北朝鮮・韓国・日本—日本人も住んでいる国) ["'The Family's Country' North Korea, South Korea, Japan: The Country Where the Family Lives"]. *At Purasu: Shisō to seikatsu* 22: 4–17.

——. 2018a. *Chōsen Daigakkō Monogatari* (朝鮮大学校物語) [A Tale from Korea University]. Tokyo: Kadokawa.

——. 2018b. "Chikakute tōsugiru rinjin. Zainichi chōsenjin to nihonjin (近くて遠すぎる隣人—在日朝鮮人と日本人) [Neighbours, So Near Yet So Far: Zainichi Koreans and the Japanese]". *Daisan bunmei* 701: 86–88.

Yomota, Inuhiko. 2019. *What Is Japanese Cinema? A History*. New York: Columbia University Press.

Yoshimoto, Mitsuhiro. 2000. *Kurosawa: Film Studies and Japanese Cinema*. Durham, NC: Duke University Press.

10

Re-Presenting Sino-Japanese Relations through *Flavors of Youth*

Jamie Coates and Jennifer Coates

Introduction: Transnational Sino-Japanese Relations

The relationship between China and Japan is often typified by conflict, tension, and difference. From differences of opinion about how Japan's wartime aggression should be memorialised (Gustafsson, 2014) to territorial disputes emerging from these historic conflicts (Hara et al., 2015), political disputes abound in the Sino-Japanese context. These issues are mostly disputed and propagated at a formal governmental level for strategic reasons (Pugliese and Insisa, 2016). Yet they also relate to how everyday citizens feel about their neighbours. The Pew Research Center's global attitudes surveys have shown that Chinese and Japanese citizens have some of the lowest opinions of each other (Stokes, 2015), although Chinese attitudes towards Japan appear to be improving according to other surveys (Genron, 2017). While these data suggest the heated nature of *inter-national* relations within the Sino-Japanese context, the lens through which they understand Sino-Japanese relations tends to focus on formal relations, and treats each country as a natural unit of analysis: an approach often referred to as "methodological nationalism" (Wimmer and Glick Schiller, 2002).

Formal governmental initiatives, such as the patriotic education campaign in China (Wang, 2012) and history textbooks in Japan (Takayama, 2009) demonstrate how the presentation of one country in relation to another is a common means of fostering identification with the nation-state as a bounded imagined community (Anderson, 1991). They also seem to be effective on a certain level, contributing to a sense of animosity between the two countries. Despite the importance of formal efforts to shape national culture and memory in China and Japan, Sino-Japanese relations are as much constituted by informal relations as formal relations (Morris-Suzuki and Soh, 2017), resulting in *transnational* relations as much as intergovernmental ones. These transnational relations, in turn, create fields of interaction and publics of consumption, exemplified in Sino-Japanese film productions such as *Flavors of Youth* (詩季織々, J. *Shiki ori ori*, 肆式青春, C. *Si shi qing chun*) by Li Haoling, Jiaoshou Yi Xiaoxing, and Takeuchi Yoshitaka (2018).

What do we mean by "transnational"? The term can refer to any phenomenon that crosses national borders. However, within recent sociocultural studies, the transnational is more specifically defined as not only the transgression of national boundaries, but also the structural connection of two or more spaces (Adey et al., 2014). Transnational Sino-Japanese relations constitute a field of governmental, commercial, and interpersonal ties that often transgress national boundaries. In particular, the technologies and content that mediate these relations often move in ways that blur the distinctions between national territories. One important historical example of how technologies and content blur distinctions between territories and cultures is the shared linguistic heritage of China and Japan. From the adoption of Chinese characters throughout the region to the adaptation of specific characters to create localised scripts in Japan, written language demonstrates the long transnational connections between different places in East Asia. Yet the increase in popular media technologies over the past 100 years also shows an acceleration of these transnational linguistic ties. As media circulates, it crosses national spaces and creates new meaning, generating transnational fields of communication with their own shared semiotics and feelings. In this chapter we focus on how media shapes the Sino-Japanese context, understood here as both a *transnational field* and an *affective public*. We take inspiration from recent scholarship on "trans-Asia as method" (Kloet et al., 2019) that treats "Asia as a dialogic communicative space in which people across borders collaborate to connect diverse voices, concerns, and problems in various, unevenly intersecting public sites in which the national is still a major site but does not exclusively take over public interests" (Iwabuchi, 2019, 28).

We envision these processes as producing transnational *fields* (Bourdieu, 2011; Fligstein and McAdam, 2012) where strategic actions over time produce a sense that certain kinds of activity occupy distinct spaces. For example, in Asia the creative industries can be understood as multiple overlapping transnational fields of competition and collaboration (Keane, 2016). As Iwabuchi notes, these fields also relate to how *publics* emerge. A public can be understood as a form of imagined community (Anderson, 1991) that develops in relation to the discourses that surround specific media texts (Warner, 2005). The most obvious examples of a public are fan communities, but publics can take on many forms depending on the distribution and circulation of media.

People's relationships with media texts, however, are not only discursive or linguistic but can often be deeply emotional. And so, we recognise that publics are as much affective as discursive. In this chapter we focus on how Sino-Japanese media collaborations have produced a transnational field of creativity that emphasises shared emotional states and commonalities to produce affective publics that connect everyday Chinese and Japanese language, imagery, and feeling.

While at first glance China and Japan may appear to be adversaries, Sino-Japanese transnational fields are constituted by creative collaboration, co-production, and consumption of shared vernacular and media texts. Indeed, the rise of mass media in twentieth-century China and Japan was a transnational process, where new technologies and ideas circulated between major cities such as Tokyo and Shanghai (Fu, 2003, 2). Historical Sino-Japanese co-productions were a cornerstone in the early development of media industries in China and Japan. They also created symbolic imagery and popular vernacular that are now shared between Chinese and Japanese cultural milieux. We start this chapter with a brief overview of the history of media collaborations between China and Japan in order to avoid the assumption that transnational processes are inherently new in Asia. After this overview we explore how more recent genres and digital formats have accelerated old continuities to produce specific kinds of contemporary transnational publics. Taking *Flavors of Youth* as a key text that exemplifies recent developments in Sino-Japanese creative collaboration, we identify a renewed emphasis on shared emotional states and affective commonalities between China and Japan.

Flavors of Youth was developed by Japanese production studio CoMix Wave Films and the Chinese animation company Haoliners Animation League as a co-production for Netflix and StudioCanal. At the industry level, it draws attention to the transnational production of animation styles that were once imagined as distinctly Japanese, and represents the rise of a shared language of feeling produced through collaborations within the Northeast Asian media industry. At the same time, the content of *Flavors of Youth* represents the Sino-Japanese context as a transnational field closely bound together through common cultural scripts, terminology, and sensory experiences. Through three shorts about the role of food, fashion, and sound in personal stories based in China, the text shows the centrality of language, taste, and place to how relationships are constructed. Yet, from Japanese audio for the international release to established tropes from Japanese animation, these three Chinese stories tell us something about the transnational Sino-Japanese context. They suggest how animation increasingly serves as a shared aesthetic language that produces transnational publics in Northeast Asia through appeals to emotion, relationships, and nostalgia.

Early Sino-Japanese Film Co-Production

In the early twentieth century, international attention and competition over export markets framed Chinese and Japanese cinema as two separate national cinemas. Chinese cinema scored early international recognition when Cai Chusheng's (1906–1968) *Song of the Fishermen* (渔光曲, C. *Yu guang qu*, 1934) won an honorary award at the Moscow Film festival of 1935. However, with the rise of Japan's economic and military power, Japanese cinema later dominated the international film festival scene into the early postwar era (Coates, 2018). From the late 1930s, Japan's imperial expansion across Northeast Asia not only saw the spread of military endeavours, but also film productions intended to bolster the ideological projects of the time. In particular, in alliance with the last members of the former Manchu Qing imperial family, Japan posited the establishment of Manchukuo in Northern China's Manchurian region as an independent nation under "Japanese protection". The expansionist narrative used to justify the establishment of Manchukuo was accompanied by a vast media industry that was often used to support Japan's imperial vision (Taylor-Jones, 2017; Young, 1999). In this context, the Manchurian Film Cooperative (満洲映画協会, J. *Manshu Eiga Kyōkai*, or 満映, J. *Man'ei*), was the home of a very particular kind of Sino-Japanese co-production. Initially funded by the Manchukuo government and the South Manchuria Railway Company, yet largely operated and overseen by Japanese personnel, Man'ei produced films starring Japanese actors set in China, for distribution in Japan and in Japanese-controlled areas of China. Many of these productions are now considered historically significant, including Ueno Shinji's *Honeymoon Express* (蜜月快車, J. *Mitsugetsu kaisha*; 蜜月快車, C. *Mi yue kuai che*, 1938), Otani Toshio's *Tōyūki* (東遊記, 1940), and the Man'ei-Tōhō co-production series known as the "Continental Trilogy" (大陸三部作, J. *Tairiku sanbusaku*); *Song of the White Orchid* (白蘭の歌, J. *Byakuran no uta*, 1939), *China Nights* (シナの夜, J. *Shina no yoru*, 1940), and *Vow in the Desert* (熱砂の誓い, J. *Nessa no chikai*, 1940).

The legacy of imperial Japanese co-production arrangements influenced the export of Japanese film to areas that had been occupied by the imperial Japanese army. In such areas, audiences had been attuned to Japanese cinema since the 1930s. However, memories of imperial expansion and Japan's wartime conduct could also present obstacles to establishing a Japanese film fan base in East Asia. Yau Shuk-ting argues that while the Japanese wartime concept of *Daitōa eiga* [films of Greater East Asia] "should be regarded as the blueprint of present East Asian film networks" (2010, 10), restrictions on the screenings of Japanese films in post-war Taiwan and South Korea resulted in a greatly reduced viewership for Japanese cinema in these countries, as opposed to its enthusiastic reception in Hong Kong and Southeast Asia. At the same time, leftist Japanese cinema found a market in China, which imported 53 Japanese films between 1949 and 1959.

Chinese director Xie Jin's *Woman Basketball Player No. 5* (女籃五號, C. *Nülan wu hao*, 1957) won the silver prize at the 1957 World Youth Festival, while Japanese cinema dominated the European film festivals and the US awards ceremonies of the 1950s. During mainland China's gradual retreat from international film exports during the 1960s and the cessation of formal Sino-Japanese diplomacy in the same period, Chinese-language productions nonetheless circulated widely. For example, several films produced by Shaw and Sons in Hong Kong brought back the actors of the Man'ei-Tōhō collaborations for Japanese- and Chinese-speaking audiences in such films as Wang Yin's *The Plum in the Golden Vase* (金瓶梅, C. *Jinpingmei*, 1955), Bu Wancang's *The Unforgettable Night* (一夜風流, C. *Yi ye fengliu*, 1958), and Toyoda Shiro's *The Legend of the White Serpent* (白夫人の妖恋, J. *Byaku fujin no yōren*; 白蛇傳, C. *Baishe zhuan*, 1956).

As relations between China and Japan began to "normalise" from 1972 onwards, film import, export, and collaboration began to change between the two nations. Wesley Jacks dates a peak era of collaboration in film-making from "the re-launch of China's nationwide import distribution in 1978 to the start of a revenue-sharing import system in 1994" (2019, 202). Early collaborative activities included annual film weeks, in which Japanese films were shown to Chinese audiences from 1977 (Jacks, 2019, 207). A number of Japanese film-makers visited China in this period and were granted import releases. For example, Yamada Yoji had nine Chinese import releases between 1979 and 1990, which represented more than 10 per cent of Japanese imports at the time (Jacks, 2019, 207). Such collaborative activities eventually led to further collaboration and co-production. For example, Satō Jun'ya was invited to lead two Sino-Japanese co-production projects after his *Manhunt* (君よ憤怒の河を渉れ, J. *Kimi yo Fundo no Kawa o Watare*, 1976) proved popular with Chinese audiences (Jacks, 2019, 208).

This period of tentative collaboration led to a boom in Sino-Japanese co-production over the following decades, as film-makers such as Satō and Xie Jin, actors such as Takakura Ken and Komaki Kurihara, import groups such as the Tokuma group led by Tokuma Yasuyoshi, and theatres such as Tokyo's Iwanami cinema and Bungeiza boosted Chinese awareness of Japanese cinema, and vice versa (Jacks, 2019, 209). Stephanie DeBoer argues that the narratives produced during this period of collaboration recalled earlier periods of economic and political conflict between Japan and China, but would work to "overcome" old animosities through plot resolutions within the films themselves (DeBoer, 2014, 6), echoing the earlier "collaboration films" of the 1940s.

This boom era of collaboration ended in the late 1980s. Jacks argues that "the connection dwindled as changes in politics, technology and new regional media industry connections presented challenges" (2019, 210). The mass saturation of television across China and Japan exacerbated a move away from cinema, which impacted the popularity of imported films. Yet, "[a]lthough Japanese films faded from cinema screens in the nineties, the legacy of the Sino-Japanese connection endured" (Jacks, 2019, 211). The film market at the 2017 Beijing International Film Festival was represented by Shochiku Studio (Jacks, 2019, 202), The Shanghai Film Distribution and Exhibition Association hosted a film festival in Tokyo in May 2018 to showcase Chinese films (Momchilova, 2019, 65), and a China-Japan film co-production treaty was signed in May 2018 (*Xinhua*, 2018). In addition to these more formal film collaborations, Japanese studios and producers were important to the development of Chinese independent cinema. For example, the director Jia Zhangke has been supported by Office Kitano in many of his productions over the past 20 years, and collaborated with Japanese producers and sound designers throughout his film work (Mello, 2019).

Of particular note, however, is China's increasing importance in Japan's animation industries (Fung and Ho, 2017). In its production, anime not only connects major cities and studios in China and Japan, but also in Vietnam, South Korea, and beyond. Moreover, its rapid popularisation over the past 30 years has seen an increase in the repetition and recombination of stylistic conventions and tropes (Suan, 2019), alongside the rise of a new shared vernacular through the adoption of Japanese terms in other languages. Today, specific studios specialise in aspects of the animation process, and jobs are often outsourced across multiple sites. Hunan, Beijing, and Shanghai have become hubs for outsourced animation production tasks, from the development of backgrounds for cell animation to digital animation. Chinese studios are now an important part of the transnational production of anime in Northeast Asia (Suan, 2019).

Flavors of Youth as Transnational Production

Although widely recognised as "Japanese" in much anglophone literature, anime now operates as a media form that transgresses national boundaries (Suan, 2019). However, while the labour of animation often involves transnational collaboration, the creative development of content and characters is often dominated by Japanese writers and producers. *Flavors of Youth* is a promising exception that suggests increasing levels of collaboration in the creative direction of transnational anime in the Sino-Japanese context. Literally translated as "From Season to Season" in Japanese, and "Wanton

Youth" in Chinese, *Flavors of Youth* emphasises presumed shared experiences of growing up among Japanese and Chinese audiences. This animated anthology film is comprised of three short films addressing taste, sound, and aesthetics, all contextualised by a strong sense of nostalgia.

The film was made by Japanese producer Noritaka Kawaguchi and Chinese directors Li Haoling and Jiaoshou Yi Xiaoxing with Japanese director Toshitaka Takeuchi. At the industry level, this is a true collaboration, involving the Japanese studio CoMix Wave Films, known for the work of director Shinkai Makoto, and Haoliners Animation League, a Shanghai-based company that owns the Emon Studio in Tokyo. *Flavors of Youth* was released in Japan via Netflix and in Chinese cinemas simultaneously on 4 August 2018. At the same time, it was made available to a global audience through Netflix and the European Studio Canal. The film took CN¥2.8 million at the Chinese box office (Endata, 2018). At the *Anime News Network*, Kim Morrissy noted the "polished background art" but complained of "weak character animation", awarding the film a B grade (2018, n. pag.). Yet Morrissy did draw attention to the co-production element and its implications, arguing that "*Flavors of Youth* may be far from a masterpiece, but I'm glad that it brought the talented artists at CoMix Wave Films together to portray this sentimental image of China's beautiful cities".

Suan notes that all three short films evoke the "characteristic style of CoMix Wave", which he associates with Shinkai's bestselling works (2019, 149). The style includes "detailed, painterly backgrounds and nostalgic, often bittersweet undertones" (Suan, 2019, 149), which render the towns, cities, and streets of various areas of China in a manner associated with Japanese animation traditions. The first segment, titled "The Rice Noodles" (陽だまりの朝食, J. *Hidamari no choshoku*), is set between the rural areas of Hunan and big city scenes of Beijing. Protagonist Xiao Ming recalls the care and love of his grandmother when he was a child, evoked through the scent and taste of *san xian* (三线) noodles. Food—quality and care of preparation—and ideas of home and family are interlinked in subplots involving a local family who make handmade noodles near the young Xiao Ming's home. After a family disturbance involving the half-understood shadow of violence which blurs in Xiao Ming's childish recollections, the family moves away and is replaced by another, less diligent and happy family, who sell ready-made noodles, but with more toppings. While the child Xiao Ming is ambivalent, enjoying the new toppings but mourning the fresh noodles, the adult Xiao Ming expresses disappointment in a portion of *san xian* noodles served in a fast food restaurant in Beijing, before hearing the news of his beloved grandmother's death. In this way, food, love, care, and family ties are brought together around the sense memory of *san xian* noodles. While the dish itself is explicitly local, the association of family and rural hometown recalls the Japanese imaginary of the *furusato* (故郷), which connotes nostalgia (Robertson, 1998).

The second segment, "A Little Fashion Show" (小さなファションショー, J. *Chiisana fashon shō*) carries this emphasis on food and family to Guangzhou, where fashion model Yi Lin lives with her shy younger sister Lulu. While Yi Lin struggles with ageing in a youth-obsessed profession, Lulu quietly creates beautiful Chinese feasts and European-style birthday cakes for her sister, who forgets to eat or even come home by dinner time. After a mental and physical breakdown, Lulu rehabilitates her sister's career by staging a fashion show for her featuring Lulu's own designs. Like "The Rice Noodles", "A Little Fashion Show" plays with the CoMix style of background design to infer the city as a threat to family unity, and a distraction from the loving care symbolised by food. Yi Lin's period of anorexia during her breakdown maps her changing relationship to family onto her changing body, as she pulls away from Lulu both literally, by running all day, and figuratively, by refusing Lulu's food. A different mode of caring for the body, by dressing Yi Lin in Lulu's modest and childlike fashion designs, brings this character back to herself and her family, with a happier ending than that of the first short film.

Set entirely in a major city, the final segment, "Love in Shanghai" (上海恋, J. *Shanghai koi*) veers away from the rural-to-urban trajectory of the previous two narratives. However, the young protagonists of this third film are shown growing up in a traditional style of housing complex called a *shikumen* (石庫門) or *lilong* (里弄) architecture. These low houses of two or three storeys arranged in rows allow for a nostalgic sense of neighbourliness, as each home reaches up to the edge of the next. As Li Jie notes, this style of architecture also acts as a palimpsest of Shanghai's history, the traces of the city's colonial sectors and revolutionary history etched into the design of this now archetypal style of housing (Li, 2014). The main characters of "Love in Shanghai", Li Mo and Xiao Yu, live here with their families, tentatively developing a special bond through the sharing of voice recordings on cassette tapes. A misunderstanding over university applications sees the two would-be lovers separated in a "just-missed" romantic motif that recalls the *surechigai* genre of Japanese romance film in which lovers repeatedly come close to declaring themselves, but miss the opportunity (see also Shinkai's *Your Name*, 君の名は, J. *Kimi no na wa*, 2016). Oranges are used as a food motif to draw the characters back to memories of their grandparents living with their children in a three-generation household, until the demands of education and careers separate the families.

After the credits, we see the protagonists of each short film meeting again in a series of airport scenes that celebrate reunification. The airport setting is used to connect the protagonists to one another, and also implicitly to connect the viewers to the protagonists, and to one another, by emphasising the experiences of travel, parting, and meeting again that are common to viewers in China, Japan, and beyond. However, it is the opening sequence, which shows an adult Xiao Ming travelling through an airport to what we will later learn is his grandmother's funeral, that sets the terms of reference to shared feeling throughout the three short films.

In narration over images of a rainy Beijing, Xiao Ming says, "[h]unger is eating at my soul". This first line of dialogue draws attention to a core theme of *Flavors of Youth*—the use of food-related idioms and metaphors to communicate feelings and sentiments shared across cultures. Common experiences of city life are described through food: "As if slurping a cold soup, the subway systematically gulps the people down". Xiao Ming laments the sterility of modern city life, concluding that, "[n]umbed, we lose the taste of home [故郷, J. *furusato*]". Nostalgia is communicated as a flavour: "That taste [感覚, J. *kankaku*, lit. "sense"], which I had forgotten, now comes back to me". The "expressionless" (無表情, J. *muhyōjō*) faces of the people moving through the city are contrasted with the things cherished in life (好きだった物、大事にした物, J. *sukidatta mono, daiji ni shita mono*), associated with the feeling of home (故郷の感覚, J. *furusato no kankaku*).

Both the Japanese voice-over and the English subtitles in this opening scene connect the complex emotions of nostalgia, ennui, and longing for the past with the senses, specifically smell and taste, by using food-related idioms to communicate amorphous experiences. These feelings—nostalgia and out-of-placeness—and the food-related sensory reference points that communicate them, are experiences that we can presume a number of people to share, and are not defined or confined by national boundaries. In this way, the senses and the presumed shared feelings of ambivalence towards modern life are bound up in the focus on "taste" (as in flavour, or as in aesthetic preference) that links all three short films. This motif of presumed shared experience in taste creates a sense of commonality or shared feeling between China and Japan, through the Japanese narration, Chinese settings and characters, and common food products featured.

Sino-Japanese Sentiments: Co-Feeling within a Transnational Affective Public

As Jacks and Zhen have argued, "[w]hen Japanese import success is mentioned in media histories, it is often attributed to the nation either being 'first' among importers or to a shared 'cultural proximity'" (Jacks, 2019, 202; Zhen, 2003). Yet Jacks notes that, "although these factors were assets, the relationship required multifaceted sustenance" (2019, 206). While Jacks is interested in the use of personal relationships and national-level relations in the founding of the Sino-Japanese collaborative connection (2019, 206), we argue that the use of presumed shared sensations and feelings within the metaphors, narrative, character design, and settings of *Flavors of Youth* is key to the successful creation of a transnational production with meanings sensible to both Chinese and Japanese viewers.

As Stevie Suan notes, what defines anime today has less to do with its "Japanese-ness" than its adherence with "anime-esque" conventions (2019, 146). These include a tendency towards characters with slender bodies and large eyes, and the use of specific facial expressions and symbols to connote emotional states like embarrassment. It also includes the use of shared idioms, metaphors, and popular cultural vernacular. The implications of understanding anime as a transnational media form rather than a Japanese product are multiple. Suan builds on his observations about anime-esque conventions to reflect on how trans-Asian cultural forms challenge our assumptions about creative industries and creativity today, echoing Thomas Lamarre's point that media allows us to trace how regions are constantly "something coming into common" (2019, 142). We further suggest that the emergence of anime as a global media form means that anime-consuming publics across Asia can be understood as transgressing national boundaries through an appreciation of anime-esque conventions. Much of the potential for co-feeling found within these three short animations rests on both a familiarity with anime as a media form and with subject matter that invokes quotidian experiences of language, food, care, and sensing.

The themes revealed in *Flavours of Youth* speak to wider questions of the relationship between language, feeling, and cultural affinity. Today, culture is understood to be more than linguistic signs, symbols, and practices (Kalekin-Fishman, 2016; Laplantine, 2020). It is experienced and mediated through embodied sensory experiences, such as taste, smell, touch, and sight (Turner, 1994). These processes in turn create the grounds on which we communicate, affecting and being affected through various sensory encounters (Gregg and Seigworth, 2010). Yet there is disagreement as to whether sensory experiences are universal or contingent on the cultural contexts within which they emerge. In particular, there is disagreement as to whether a gap exists between how the sensory, as a form of *affect*, is experienced, and how affects such as these are represented in language and symbols (Massumi, 2016). These philosophical debates are beyond the remit of this chapter, but they highlight the importance of feeling in how we understand language and social life. Further, they suggest that the representation of taste and sympathy are likely to signify something beyond the immediate cultures within which they are produced. In the context of anime-esque representations of taste and feeling, we argue that shared tropes for portraying everyday affects are emerging. Further, they foster transnational anime-consuming publics that emphasise co-feeling and empathy through a focus on affective themes. Our use of the terms "affect" and "co-feeling" is not an imposition of non-Asian theory within the Sino-Japanese context. Rather, it draws inspiration from Chinese and Japanese discourses of sentiment to consider how co-feeling is represented in transnational Asia.

Empathy, sympathy, and shared feeling have a number of equivalences in Japanese, from *omoiyari* (思いやり), defined as "understanding of the unexpressed feelings, desires, and thoughts of others, and doing something for them on the basis of this understanding" (Travis, 1998, 55), to *kyōkan* (共感), which literally translates as "shared feeling". Similarly, discourses of human sentiment (人情, C. *renqing*) and the importance of shared practices of consumption are central to wider discussions of how social relations and sympathy are produced in Chinese contexts (Farquhar, 2002; Kipnis, 1997; Yang, 1994). It is this second term that we have explored here, as the use of food (taste, smell) and aesthetics (taste, in the sense of taste in music or taste in clothes) is a theme that connects both the three short films, and the imagined Chinese, Japanese, and Anglo-European viewer.

As the analysis of the opening scene above demonstrates, taste as a presumed shared experience is used throughout all three short films to create a sense of the quotidian urban experience in China and Japan as sensorially similar. This can be understood as a means of building empathy between the Japanese or Japan-aligned viewer, listening to the Japanese voice track, and the animated Chinese characters of the film. There was initially no formal Chinese voice track, though there is an English dub available on Netflix, and subsequent Chinese audio releases have been made available in China. Having Chinese protagonists voiced by Japanese actors makes sense from a transnational production perspective, as the Japanese-associated aesthetics of anime are present both in the typical vocal stylings and in the character design, attracting viewers who have come to expect these anime-esque tropes and codes. At the same time, however, the narratives, background settings, and character names offer regular reminders that the short films are all set in China. This has the effect of making stories about Chinese characters take on the "flavour" or, as Koichi Iwabuchi (2002) may argue, the "odorlessness" (*mukokuseki*) associated with anime that obscures, and yet today is associated with, its origins in Japan.

In this way, we can think of *Flavors of Youth* as a transnational text in both production terms and its content to build co-feeling, or even empathy, between viewers and characters of various nationalities. In closing this short chapter, however, we must note the critiques of empathy offered by Lauren Berlant and Amy Shuman, which add much-needed nuance to our understanding of the political operations of empathy. Berlant (2002) argues that claims to empathy pose political dangers by constructing a fiction or fantasy of knowing another without full understanding of the histories of oppression and structural violence that may underpin that subject's suffering. Shuman similarly notes that "empathy is almost always open to critique as serving the interests of the empathizer rather than the empathized" (2010, 18). An easy claim to empathy between viewers and characters across Sino-Japanese political, historical, and social divides based on the presumed shared experiences that engender *kyōkan*, or co-feeling, risks obscuring the difficult histories and contested future imaginaries that drive persisting difficulties in Sino-Japanese relations.

We cannot assume transnational communities of shared political feeling based on shared sentiments referenced in and conjured by transnational media productions. Indeed, political attitudes research suggests that a preference for anime in China does not correlate with pro-Japan attitudes (Ishii, 2013), and it follows logically that presenting Chinese characters to Japanese audiences within the Japan-informed conventions of the anime-esque is similarly unlikely to inspire the deep empathy of *omoiyari*, which requires not only "understanding of the unexpressed feelings, desires, and thoughts of others", but also "doing something for them on the basis of this understanding" (Travis, 1998, 55). Instead, the co-feeling of *Flavors of Youth* may simply be *kyōkan*, which notes shared sensory experiences without the concomitant requirement to "do something" for those empathised with, or felt for. Whether this transnational co-production inspires *omoiyari* or *kyōkan* in its viewers, however, the novelty of the hierarchies within its production model, and the success of the endeavour, suggests that Sino-Japanese relations as practised by co-production (if not as represented within media productions themselves) are continually taking on new forms and meanings.

References and Further Reading

Adey, Peter, David Bissell, Kevin Hannam, Peter Merriman, and Mimi Sheller (eds.). 2014. *The Routledge Handbook of Mobilities*. London: Routledge.

Anderson, Benedict. 1991. *Imagined Communities: Reflections on the Origin and Spread of Nationalism*. New York: Verso.

Berlant, Lauren. 2002. "The Subject of True Feeling". In *Left Legalism/Left Critique*, edited by Wendy Brown and Janet Halley, 105–133. Durham, NC: Duke University Press.

Bourdieu, Pierre. 2011. "The Forms of Capital (1986)". In *Cultural Theory: An Anthology,* edited by Imre Szeman and Timothy Kaposy, 81–93. Oxford: Wiley and Blackwell.

Coates, Jennifer. 2018. "Alternative Viewership Practices in Kyoto, Japan". In *The Palgrave Handbook of Asian Cinema*, edited by Aaron Magnan-Park, Gina Marchetti, and Tan See-Kam, 221–241. London: Palgrave Macmillan.

Deboer, Stephanie. 2014. *Coproducing Asia*. Minneapolis: University of Minnesota Press.

Endata Box Office. 2021. https://www.endata.com.cn/BoxOffice/ [accessed 21 February 2021].

Farquhar, Judith. 2002. *Appetites: Food and Sex in Post-Socialist China*. Durham, NC: Duke University Press.

Fligstein, Neil, and Doug McAdam. 2012. *A Theory of Fields*. Oxford: Oxford University Press.

Fu, Poshek. 2003. *Between Shanghai and Hong Kong: The Politics of Chinese Cinemas*. Stanford: Stanford University Press.

Fung, Anthony Y. H., and Vicky Ho. 2017. "Animation Industry in China: Managed Creativity or State Discourse?" In *Handbook of Cultural and Creative Industries in China*, edited by Michael Keane, 276–292. Cheltenham: Edward Elgar.

Genron. 2017. "The 10th Japan-China Public Opinion Poll Analysis Report on the Comparative Data". www.genron-npo.net/en/pp/archives/5153.html [accessed 22 February 2018].

Gregg, Melissa, and Gregory J. Seigworth. 2010. *The Affect Theory Reader*. Durham, NC: Duke University Press.

Gustafsson, Karl. 2014. "Memory Politics and Ontological Security in Sino-Japanese Relations". *Asian Studies Review* 38 (1): 71–86.

Hara, Kimie, Tim F. Liao, and Krista Wiegand. 2015. *The China-Japan Border Dispute: Islands of Contention in Multidisciplinary Perspective*. London: Ashgate.

Ishii, K. 2013. "Nationalism and Preferences for Domestic and Foreign Animation Programmes in China". *International Communication Gazette* 75 (2): 225–245.

Iwabuchi, Koichi. 2002. *Recentering Globalization: Popular Culture and Japanese Transnationalism*. Durham, NC and London: Duke University Press.

——. 2019. "Trans-Asia as Method: A Collaborative and Dialogic Project in a Globalized World". In *Trans-Asia as Method: Theory and Practices*, edited by Jeroen de Kloet, Yiu Fai Chow, and Gladys Pak Lei Chong, 25–42. London: Rowman & Littlefield International.

Jacks, Wesley. 2019. "The Personal, the Political and the Popular: Sino-Japanese Film Collaboration in the Early Reform Era". *Journal of Chinese Cinemas* 13 (3): 202–214.

Kalekin-Fishman, Devorah. 2016. *Everyday Life in Asia: Social Perspectives on the Senses*. London: Routledge.

Keane, Michael. 2016. *Handbook of Cultural and Creative Industries in China*. Cheltenham: Edward Elgar.

Kipnis, Andrew. 1997. *Producing Guanxi: Sentiment, Subculture and Self in a Northern China Village*. Durham, NC: Duke University Press.

Kloet, Jeroen de, Yiu Fai Chow, and Gladys Pak Lei Chong. 2019. *Trans-Asia as Method: Theory and Practices*. London: Pickering & Chatto.

Laplantine, François. 2020. *The Life of the Senses: Introduction to a Modal Anthropology*. London: Routledge.

Lebra, Takie Sugiyama. 1976. *Japanese Patterns of Behavior*. Honolulu: University of Hawai'I Press.

Li, Jie. 2014. *Shanghai Homes: Palimpsests of Private Life*. New York: Columbia University Press.

McVeigh, Brian. 1996. "Commodifying Affection, Authority and Gender in the Everyday Objects of Japan". *Journal of Material Culture* 1 (3): 291–312.

Massumi, Brian. 2016. "Such as it Is: A Short Essay in Extreme Realism". *Body & Society* 22 (1): 115–127.

Mello, Cecília. 2019. *The Cinema of Jia Zhangke: Realism and Memory in Chinese Film*. New York: Bloomsbury.

Momchilova, Maria. 2019. "Cultural Differences in Chinese Animation and Japanese Anime". *Intercultural Communication, Media, Arts*, 57–70.

Morris-Suzuki, Tessa, and Eun Jeong Soh. 2017. *New Worlds from Below: Informal Life Politics and Grassroots Action in Twenty-First-Century Northeast Asia, Vol. 9*. Canberra: ANU Press.

Morrissy, Kim. 2018. "Flavors of Youth". https://www.animenewsnetwork.com/review/flavors-of-youth/.133278 [accessed 18 February 2021].

Pugliese, Giulio, and Aurelio Insisa. 2016. *Sino-Japanese Power Politics: Might, Money and Minds*. London: Springer.

Robertson, Jennifer. 1998. "It Takes a Village: Internationalization and Nostalgia in Postwar Japan". In *Mirror of Modernity: Invented Traditions of Modern Japan*, edited by Stephen Vlastos, 110–132. Berkeley: University of California Press.

Shuman, Amy. 2010. *Other People's Stories: Entitlement Claims and the Critique of Empathy*. Urbana: University of Illinois Press.

Stokes, Brian. 2015. "How Asia-Pacific Publics See Each Other and Their National Leaders". *Pew Research Centre Global Attitudes and Trends*. https://www.pewresearch.org/global/2015/09/02/how-asia-pacific-publics-see-each-other-and-their-national-leaders/ [accessed 8 January 2021].

Suan, Stevie. 2019. "Repeating Anime's Creativity across Asia". In *Trans-Asia as Method: Theory and Practices*, edited by Jeroen de Kloet, Yiu Fai Chow, and Gladys Pak Lei Chong, 141–160. London: Rowman & Littlefield International.

——. 2020. "Anime's Spatiality: Media-form, Dislocation, and Globalization". *Mechademia: Second Arc*, 12 (2): 24–44.

Takayama, Keita. 2009. "Globalizing Critical Studies of 'Official' Knowledge: Lessons from the Japanese History Textbook Controversy over 'Comfort Women'". *British Journal of Sociology of Education* 30 (5): 577–589.

Taylor-Jones, Kate. 2017. *Divine Work, Japanese Colonial Cinema and Its Legacy*. New York: Bloomsbury Academic.

Travis, Catherine. 1998. "*Omoiyari* as a Core Japanese Value: Japanese-Style Empathy." *Speaking of Emotions: Conceptualisation and Expression*, edited by Angeliki Athanasiadou and Elżbieta Tabakowska, 55–83. Berlin: De Gruyter.

Turner, Terrence. 1994. "Bodies and Anti-Bodies: Flesh and Fetish in Contemporary Social Theory". In *Embodiment and Experience: The Existential Ground of Culture and Self*, edited by Thomas Csordas, 27–47. Cambridge: Cambridge University Press.

Wang, Zheng. 2012. *Never Forget National Humiliation: Historical Memory in Chinese Politics and Foreign Relations*. New York: Columbia University Press.

Warner, Michael. 2005. *Publics and Counterpublics*. London: Zone Books.

Wimmer, Andreas, and Nina Glick Schiller. 2002. "Methodological Nationalism and beyond: Nation–State Building, Migration and the Social Sciences". *Global Networks* 2 (4): 301–334.

Xinhua. 2018. "Film Experts Have High Hopes for Sino-Japan Co-Production". *ChinaDaily*. http://www.chinadaily.com.cn/a/201811/06/WS5be0dcf5a310eff303286b49.html [accessed 18 February 2021].

Yang, Mayfair. 1994. *Gifts, Favors and Banquets: The Art of Social Relationships in China*. New York: Cornell University Press.

Yau Shuk-ting, Kinnia. 2010. *Japanese and Hong Kong Film Industries: Understanding the Origins of East Asian Film Networks*. London: Routledge.

Young, Louise. 1999. *Japan's Total Empire: Manchuria and the Culture of Wartime Imperialism*. Berkeley: University of California Press.

Zhen, Ni. 2003. *Memoirs from the Beijing Film Academy: The Genesis of China's Fifth Generation*. Durham, NC: Duke University Press.

11

Translation/Transplantation of Queer in South Korea

Allan C. Simpson

Within the universe of transnationalism, there are different uses of and purposes for which queer-identified language is used, within and beyond the Anglosphere. This chapter seeks to explore the extent to which South Korean translations and transplantations make use of Anglosphere linguistic and acronymic identities. Within this universe of transnationalism, translations seek to repurpose while transplantations are sought to serve a purpose. Such terms as "queer" and "LGBT" have been adopted in South Korean activist and artistic (literary) contexts. This essay seeks to explore some South Korean translations and transplantations of queerness, with reference to the contemporary novels of the South Korean author Kim Hyena. Kim is perhaps most known for her 2012 novel *Chŏngk'ŭ* (정크, Junk), a work that offers glimpses into South Korea's queer-identified worlds and their reception and use of transnational language.

In the South Korean queer-identified worlds which Kim Hyena's *Chŏngk'ŭ* reflects, do we also find similar homonormative tendencies as we do in North American, European, and other contexts? I aim to explore the different uses of non-heteronormative language, and especially the question as to whether or not Asian contexts should adopt English-originated queer language at all.

Distinctions between LGBT and Queer

I make a distinction between the Anglosphere terms "LGBT" and "queer". While certain acronyms advocate an LGBT combination with Q for "queer" included—with numerous other potential combinations as well—the Q still seems to linger on the end of some acronymic formulations, as if it were an afterthought of an otherwise clear-cut identity-based categorisation. In a 2009 seminar-based survey submitted to the *Journal of Bisexuality*, it was concluded that "there was no consensus about what 'queer' meant" (Barker et al., 2009, 6–7). A certain trend has long prevailed which is characterised by "the 'umbrella' nature of the term 'queer' and how many people use the word as shorthand" (Barker et al., 2009, 7). Singular labels are more commonly used in legal and other contexts dealing with anti-discrimination rights for non-heterosexuals and trans people. On the other hand, "queer" is rarely used in these same formal contexts. This tells us that, at least in some contexts, LGBT terminology prevails in discourses of legality, whereas the term "queer" prevails in discourses of subjectivity. Although this umbrella term is often utilised for its convenience, there is "the possibility of the erasure of some of the identities encompassed within it" (Barker et al., 2009, 8). This problem of utilising queer as an all-encompassing, umbrella term or as a synonym for LGBT politics has been iterated in South Korean discourse (Chŏng, 2012, 57).

Still, it can be argued that not everyone is fluent in the variety of identities covered by this umbrella, and so, confusingly or otherwise, some people "may well assume that 'queer', in such a context, simply means 'lesbian and gay'" (Barker et al., 2009, 8). According to a 2016 study of over 2,000 non-heterosexuals in the *Journal of Sex Research*, it would appear that the LGBT acronym is somewhat outdated in the Anglosphere, in that "queer and pansexual identities appear most" (Morandini et al., 2016, 1).

If it is true that, as linguist Roman Jakobson asserts, "it is possible to understand what is signified by a word even if we have never seen or experienced the concept or thing in real life" (qtd. in Munday, 2008, 37), then the transplantation of Anglosphere queer and LGBT terminology might be somewhat productive outside of the Anglosphere. The term "queer", for example, might productively act as "a flexible identity that's constantly in motion, constantly becoming, constantly transgressing" (Gunther, 2005, 23). The term *seksŭ* (섹스, sex) is also a commonly used English-originated and transplanted word in Korean, and features in the works of Kim Hyena, one of its Korean translations being *sŏng kwangye* (성관계, sex relations). Specifically relating to non-heteronormative South Korean language, the terms from the Anglosphere LGBT acronym are sometimes used pragmatically, most commonly to identify with such western sociopolitical practices as *kei p'ŏreidŭ* (게이 퍼레이드, gay parade), or to launch legal challenges for such rights as same-sex marriage. *Kei* is also one of the terms used by Kim Hyena in *Chŏngk'ŭ*, for example in the context of gay clubbing, although Kim also uses the phrase *tongsŏngaeja k'ŭllŏp* (동성애자 클럽, same-sex lovers' club) instead of *kei k'ŭllŏp* (게이클럽, gay club). In *Cheri*, in an instance when a friend who has had transgender surgery is discussed, *iban ch'ingu* (이반친구, *iban* queer and *ch'ingu* friend) is used.

It may be useful at this juncture to talk about "Konglish", that is English-appearing words used in Korean and in contexts other than those of their origin. Similar to other linguistic phenomena such as Chinglish and Japlish, Konglish words are not meant to be exact translations of English words but exist more because "the use of these terms is for ease [...] irrespective of the correct representation of these words in the corresponding native language" (Kent, 1999, 198). In David Kent's paper, Konglish's incorporation of other languages is split into five different means: "direct loanwords; hybrid terms; truncated terminology; through substitution; and, by the creation of pseudo loanwords" (1999, 201). I would rather state that "direct loanwords" are not Konglish but Hangŭlisations (Hangŭl being the name for the Korean alphabet) of loanwords. I would argue also that "hybrid terms" are not Konglish but are "hybrid" or compound terms; and that "truncated terms", too, are separate from Konglish. The truncating of Hangŭlised loanwords is more an extension of the Korean people's tendency to prefer the truncation of words in writing and especially in speech. This is similar to the Korean tendency to omit grammatical particles or markers when speaking. "Pseudo-loanwords" is probably the category I would equate to my own understanding of Konglish. Kent defines this category as "ideologically restructured terms, possessing semantically modified meanings" (1999, 202). As he states, "[t]he placing of a loan item, with the same pronunciation and semantic conceptualisation as an English word, within a simple sentence then creates an environment from which the learning of grammar can be inferred and the function and forms of linguistic competence can be focussed upon" (1999, 205). Another commonly used example of Konglish is *sŭk'insip* (스킨십, skinship), which can be defined as "the affectionate touching that often occurs between members of the same sex without necessarily being construed as sexual" (Cho, 2020, 270).

What "can be inferred" through Konglish is important in Kim's novels and other non-heteronormative Korean contexts, as Konglish acts as this non-heteronormative code that is a translation but also a literal transplantation. Yet the latter exists only as a disguise for the former, on the surface meaning nothing to either the native English speaker or the listeners who are otherwise unaware of what is "meant". So it is not needed as a transplantation, yet it is also commonly used by Koreans, and so this transplant apparent must be an attempt to translate something *else*.

In the activist realm, terms are also regularly transplanted from English, and utilised so that solidarity with both South Koreans and foreigners in the physical and virtual environments may quickly be gained regardless of the foreigners' Korean language ability. Consider, for example, the Facebook group "LGBTQIA and Allies in Korea" (한국 퀴어와 그 친구들, K. *hanguk k'wiŏ wa kŭ ch'ingu tŭl*) founded by Heezy Yang. Much of Yang's work is produced using English translations alongside the original Korean, or only English, which is also the language the Facebook group primarily communicates in. This allows for a common, globalised queer language to be readily used and understood via which various groups and agendas may intersect. I view globalised queer language as that which linguistically mirrors a globalising, generally homonormative LGBT rights movement, influenced in part by Anglosphere terminology and the mass consumption of western LGBT cultural products. Scholars such as Dennis Altman, Natalie Oswin, Joseph Massad, among others, have written not only of this queer globalisation but also on the importance of decentring this form of globalisation.

There are several Korean terms that are more local, e.g. *iban* (이반, queer), *tongsŏngaeja* (동성애자, same-sex lover), as well as Korean translations of English-originated terms which sound similar to English, such as *kei* (게이) and *k'wiŏ* (퀴어). In grassroots activism specifically, globalised queer terms are deployed instead of local terms. On academic, legal, and activist fronts, there seems to be more of a mixture of both globalised and locally translated terms. The theorists Sŏ Tongjin and Chŏng Minu both use the transplanted term *k'wiŏ* in academic papers on queer family and queer theory, respectively, and John (Song Pae) Cho advocates that we focus on "unmooring these categories from their static and sedentary locations in the 'West' and transplanting them into Asia" (2020, 264). There is an abundance of more different terms to be considered, even including combinations of terms to equate other terms—according to one source, *taik'ŭ* (다이크, dyke) and *p'aegŭ* (패그, fag) together equate to *k'wiŏ*: "다이크 dyke + 패그 fag = 퀴어 queer". Chŏng Chini's dictionary of literary terms (2005, 512) includes a host of relevant terms, including the hybrid term *kei pip'yŏng* (게이 비평, gay criticism, 143) and *k'wiŏ iron* (퀴어 이론, queer theory); *homo erotisijŭm* (호모에로티시즘, homoeroticism), *namsŏng kan ŭi ujŏng* (남성간의 우정, male bonding; the *ujŏng* (우정) here can also mean "friendship"), *pokjang toch'akja* (복장도착자, transvestite), *sŏng toch'akja* (성도착자, transexual), *isŏng aeja* (이성애자, heterosexual), *tongsŏng sahoe* (동성사회, homosocial), *namsaek* (남색, pederasty), *taendi* (댄디, dandy), *yangsŏng aeja* (양성애자, bisexual), and *t'omboi* (톰보이, tomboy).

Kim Hyena uses the term *namsaek* in the main text of *Chŏngk'ŭ*, in relation to a sociolectal term *okkama* (오까마) for which some etymology and definition is provided:

> '오까마'란 여장 남자를 뜻하는 우리들만의 은어였다. 남색 (男色) 을 뜻하는 일본어 '오카마(おかま)'에서 유래한 말이었지만, 우리들 사이에서는 남성에서 여성으로 성전환 수술을 한 사람을 비롯해 여장만 좋아하는 드래그 퀸이나 크로스드레서까지 다 '오까마'라고 불렀다. (2012, 95)

[*Okkama* was a slang word that we just used between us. It was a phrase of Japanese descent, coming from the Japanese おかま (*okkama*) to mean *namsaek*, but among us we started to use it for people who had undergone male-to-female gender reassignment surgery, to drag queens or cross-dressers who only liked women's clothing, all of them were called *okkama*]

In English-language articles and essays on Korean queer studies, the term "queer" is almost always used, although sometimes italicised. We can consider for example the use of *queer* in "Globalizing Korean *Queers*?" (Koh, 2013). Some western academics engaging with Korean studies in English simply maintain the English "queer" without involving any translation. The South Korean journal *Ppira* also described itself as a *k'wiŏ inmun chapji* (퀴어 인문 잡지, queer humanities magazine) and in one issue included the transplanted term *t'ŭraensŭ chendŏ* (트랜스젠더, transgender). Publications like *Ppira* provide a platform for Korean academic and cultural activism, but these same strands of activism can be found in individual academic papers which are categorised as queer theoretical readings of texts. These queer theoretical readings tend also to use the transplanted term *k'wiŏ*. The term *sosuja* (소수자, minority person) does not exclusively denote those marginalised due to non-normative sex, sexuality, and/or gender identity. Specifically pertaining to sex, gender, and sexuality would usually be *sŏngsosuja* (성소수자, literally "sex/gender minority person"). Sometimes the transplantation *chendŏ* (젠더, gender) is also used, for example in Yŏng et al. (2011), *Namsŏng sŏng kwa chendŏ* (남성성과 젠더, Masculinity and Gender). *Sŏngsosuja* is a term important for both academic forms of activism and grassroots activism, for which it is often a keyword to identify activists, activist groups, and the various media they produce. *Sŏngsosuja* therefore embodies a term more than simply signalling a marginalised community, becoming both an identity and a cultural marker.

In some *kei* male Korean circles, English-derived terms such as *pat'om* (바톰, bottom) and *t'ap* (탑, top) are frequently used in common parlance to discern sexual position preferences, as well as the term *ol* (올, all)—that is, versatile; *pŏsŏt'ail* (버서타일, versatile) is also found (Im, 2004). In Kim Hyena's *Chŏngkŭ*, these two terms are also used and even defined in footnotes within the novel:

*남성 동성애자 사이에서 여성성을 지향하는 사람.
**남성 동성애자 사이에서 남성성을 지향하는 사람

[*The male same-sex lover who is oriented toward the female.
**The male same-sex lover who is oriented toward the male] (Kim, 2012, 53)

Furthermore, terms such as *ttaejja* (때짜, the one who does the hitting) and *majja* (마짜, the one who takes the hitting) are also used. In terms of derogatory terminology found in common parlance, the transplanted *kei* is sometimes used by heterosexuals to disparage gay males in particular. This could be caused by an observation of a male's femininity, gender nonconformity, or choice of accessory. In more disparaging instances, where homosexuality specifically is being negated, the term *homo* (호모, homo) or *homo saekki* (호모 새끼, literally "homo pup" or "homo bastard") is quite common. For example, the openly gay male celebrity Hong Sŏkch'ŏn was quoted by *Chosun News* as saying that he no longer wanted to hear the term *homo saekki* being used (Lee, 2008). In *Chŏngk'ŭ*, we find the examples of *mich'in kyejibae* (미친 계집애, crazy sissy or crazy bitch) and *pyŏngsin* (병신, dickhead or idiot), *homo saekki* being used to attack the protagonist Sŏngjae's femininity:

> 책가방 속에 온갖 화장 용품과 패션 잡지를 넣어 가지고 다니는 나를 보며 아이들은 미친 계집애에 병신 호모 새끼라고 욕했다
>
> [They would look at me, going around with my book bag full of all kinds of makeup products and fashion magazines, and called me names from crazy sissy to dickhead homo] (Kim, 2012, 33)

Hong Sŏkch'ŏn's comments on these verbal abuses are in a similar vein to western discourse about the ongoing disparaging uses of "gay" and such phrases as "that's gay!" The term *pyŏnt'ae* (변태, pervert) is also used in common parlance, although it is seemingly both used in derogative and self-identifying ways. In some magazines and grassroots literature, *pyŏnt'ae* seems to be used as part of a taking-it-back strategy which disarms the phobia and trauma associated with language by (re)claiming and optimising it for a simultaneously personal and radical politics, for example in the 2015 zines *Halmal* (할말, Things To Be Said) and the third issue of *Wan Byun Pyun #P'yŏn*. The producers of such zines are very important members of the queer-identified community as they intersect on fundraising grassroots *sŏngsosuja* activism as well as cultural production. They are producers of a queer subjectivity that is unrepresented in other dimensions. Layoung Shin has described contemporary South Korea as exhibiting an "imbalance between an increase in homophobia, on the one hand, and a lack of legal, physical, and psychological protections for queer youth, on the other" (2020, 306). This imbalance perhaps therefore necessitates the transplantability of queer-identified terms, as a way of addressing more urgent social issues, over translatability which tends to place more emphasis on semantics, theory, and cultural neologisms.

There are a number of *rejŭbiŏn* (레즈비언, lesbian)-related terms also. Contemporary examples include *t'ibu* (티부)—an abbreviation of *t'I nanŭn buc"i* (티나는 부치, obvious butch, or an obviously butch person)—and *kŏlk'ŏ* (걸커)—an abbreviation of *kŏrŏ taninŭn k'ŏming aut* (걸어 다니는 커밍아웃, walking around, coming out), that is, someone who has come out and walks around openly as such. Both of these are terms for noticeably *rejŭbiŏn* people and/or those known to have come out. Although some claim that the Korean terms *paji ssi* (바지씨, Mx. Pants) and *ch'ima ssi* (치마씨, Mx. Skirt) are purely queer terms specifically attributed to the lesbian community, Han (2006, 209) points out that from the 1960s onwards these words came to simply represent synonyms for, in the case of the former, *namja* or *namja aein* (남자, 남자애인, man, boyfriend), while *ch'ima ssi* has likewise come to mean merely the opposite, heteronormalising the terms somewhat. While some still attribute these words to a pure Korean non-heteronormative code of sorts, Han suggests that the terms are rather archaic now and that, perhaps less desirably, more current non-heteronormative terms either combine Korean with non-Korean or transplant whole English-originated queer terms (especially "top" and "bottom") for everyday spoken deployment. *Namsŏng tongsŏngaeja* (남성동성애자, gay men) is distinguished from *rejŭbiŏn*, the latter sometimes in combination with Korean words, for example *rejŭbiŏn moim* (레즈비언 모임, lesbian meeting/gathering) or *rejŭbiŏn chojik* (레즈비언조직, lesbian group/organisation) or *rejŭbiŏn chapji* (레즈비언 잡지, lesbian magazine), the latter being used in Kim Hyena's *Chŏngk'ŭ* (Han, 2006, 205, 207).

Queer Theory, Translation Theory

Previously I used the terms "transplantation" and "translation". The linguist Eugene Nida proposed two theories of equivalence which might be useful here: "formal equivalence" and "dynamic equivalence". Jeremy Munday's discussion of Nida describes the former as "focus[ing] all attention on the message itself, in both form and content [...] concerned that the message in the receptor language should match as closely as possible the different elements in the source language" (2008, 42). The latter, by contrast, "is based on what Nida calls 'the principle of equivalent effect' where 'the relationship between receptor and message should be substantially the same as that which existed between the original receptors and the message" (Munday, 2008, 43). It should be noted that Nida's equivalence theories have since been criticised, by linguist Qian Hu in the 1990s and Edwin Gentzler in 2001. The former attributed to Nida's work subjective biases and cultural shortcomings, while the latter specifically claimed that "dynamic equivalence serves the purpose of converting the receptors, no matter what their culture, to the dominant discourse and ideas of Protestant Christianity" (Munday, 2008, 43). By transplantation and translation, then, I refer to these "formal" and "dynamic" equivalences linguistically speaking, but I also extend this to mean queer/*k'wiŏ*/*iban* theoretically speaking. I mean more specifically a concept or understanding that western queer theory is both borrowed from an Anglosphere context and resisted, and that it is adapted or unadapted to local South Korean theoretical contexts. Transplantation may also be described as direct borrowing, as in the sense of a loanword. In this vein, I would argue that western queer theory, too, can be borrowed in the same way.

In the context of French queer-identified theorists who make use of Anglosphere, western queer theory, there is the argument that "even if the ideas originated in the U.S., the concepts themselves are essentially anti-American" (Gunther, 2005, 25) due to the understanding that American theoretical discourse more generally is already imperialistic. Cultural theorist and translator Tejaswini Niranjana has written on the "power relations" implicated in the act of translation and translation studies. Jeremy Munday echoes Niranjana's warning about "the colonial power to construct a rewritten image of the 'East'" and that "the colonial context builds a conceptual image of colonial domination into the discourse of western philosophy" (2008, 132–133). This is a warning that also speaks not only to the potentially colonial ideology of assuming that a South Korean non-heteronormative language can or must be translated into a western language, but also to the colonial potentiality of any attempt to translate western queer theory into and/or onto a South Korean theoretical language—a potentiality stemming from an impression that South Korea or elsewhere will serve as a "mirror of Western sexualities" (Jackson, 1998, 86). On this point, both Niranjana (qtd. in Munday, 2008, 132) and the scholar Peter A. Jackson have warned of the Western conceptions of theoretical "truth" whereby the West "has at times been perceived as claiming, often implicitly, that the non-West needs to learn a Western theoretical idiom to be able to speak its own truth" (2007, 337). Todd A. Henry argues that this west-originated theory derives from a specific sexual politics that "must be cautiously extended to Korea" (2018, 13). In light of globalisation and developments in translation studies, it is doubtful that western theory could account for any universal truth pertaining to linguistic and theoretical translation.

Especially thanks to the globalisation of predominantly United States-originated LGBT identity via the internet, contemporary South Korean *sŏngsosuja* communities experience at least partly—especially in terms of language—a certain *ŏnŏjŏk honhapch'e* (언어적 혼합체, mixture of languages), *kŭllobŏl kei ŏnŏ* (글로벌 게이 언, global gay language), *kei yŏngŏ* (게이 영어, gay English), rendering Korean a *kibanhan yuyŏnhan ŏnŏ* (기반한 유연한 언어, flexible language) (Sŏ, 2011, 101). In the field of translation studies, similar to western queer theory, translation has recently been defined as "similarly imbricated with issues of gender and sexuality, playfulness and power" (Epstein and Gillett, 2017, 1). The most obvious transplantation that has been associated with theory, then, is the aforementioned transliteration of the English word "queer" into the Korean *k'wiŏ*. However, beyond this there is the transplantation of western understandings of "queer", for the most part unchanged, into South Korean contexts that are then able to disseminate and reperform the ideas of identity that are implicated in these understandings. Of course, transplantation of the Western term "queer" also occurs in contexts where western literary and queer theory are studied objectively from South Korean perspectives and in South Korean spaces. A most interesting example of this can be observed in certain South Korean university seminars or more informal gatherings, where western queer theory and queer theorists are discussed (usually in Korean translation), though this is more a subject of interest that focuses less on local comparisons. In some cases, this kind of transplantation entails an outside-looking-in approach, and what some might describe as Occidentalism or exoticism. Crucially though, through the transplantation of queer or queer theory from the West, the transaction often goes only in one direction, excluding the transplanted subjects (primarily *kei*) from equal dialogue with local contexts.

While on occasion non-western equivalents may enter the Anglosphere and find western audiences, predominantly it is a globalised western queer that prevails. In short, the Western term "queer" is not translated, but brought over to the local context without necessarily carrying local significance. There is a degree of slippage therefore with certain terms, for example "trans" being not only transliterated or Hangŭlised as *t'ŭraensŭ* (트랜스) but also locally confused or conflated with the identities associated with *tongsŏngae* (동성애, same-sex love). This is also sometimes true for such words as "gay", transliterated or Hangŭlised as *kei* (게이) and taken to encompass more than an indication simply of homosexuality. Indeed, the work of Nida would "point the road away from strict word-for-word equivalence" (Munday, 2008, 43), while some pose the question surrounding western queer theory and the Western term "queer": "how do we go about fixing the meaning of a term that challenges the fixity of meaning itself?" (Gunther, 2005, 23). Some contemporary researchers would also argue that the Western term "queer" is not a word that even has a correspondence in Korean, that it is untranslatable:

> 우리에게 퀴어의 역어가 존재하는가? 당신은 '퀴어' 라는 단어에 상응하는 한국어로 된 어휘를 묻고 있지 않다. (Chŏng, 2012, 66)
>
> [Does a queer tongue exist for us? You are not asking if there is a Korean equivalent of the word "queer".]

In Scott Gunther's *Alors, Are We "Queer" Yet?*, the problems with transplanting and translating western, Anglosphere queer theory are also highlighted. In the francophone academic context, the English term "queer" was rejected on at least two levels: (1) based on the feeling that the pronunciation was "ugly"; and (2) due to the importing of American-identified theory being deemed as inappropriate (Gunther, 2005, 23). Even within the Anglosphere there are different significations of and reactions to both the "transnational" and "intralingual transplantation of" queerness (Peeren, 2006, 59). In an analysis of the transatlantic television series *Queer as Folk*, Esther Peeren proposes an idea of the "linguistic resignification" of western queerness, which essentially involves taking, for example, a term that is positive in one context and importing it to a context where it is negative, but through its original signified positivity it in turn makes the latter context positive or "queered". In turn we might also apply this to the resignification of western queer theory, wherein a kind of theoretical currency exchange "challenges the dominant politics of representation in their respective national contexts" (Peeren, 2006, 59). Peeren's work thus might also imagine a proverbalisation of western queer theory which, while perhaps partly translated, can still be located within South Korean theoretical discourses.

For western queer theory to be translated, therefore, I do not merely mean that an equivalent term in one language (in this case, Korean) must be found to appropriately account for the original. I mean also that an attempt to locate, to consider the closest and most effective rendering of the original in the local context has been made. This is difficult because, while The Western term "queer" is frequently transplanted as well as other terms such as "gay", even so there has been the necessary answer to Niranjana's "calls for an 'interventionist' approach from the translator" (Munday, 2008, 133) where some South Koreans argue that "*k'wiŏ* is not a term but exists as a foreign language" (Chŏng, 2012, 67). Depending on the language, dialect, sociolect, etc. of the context in question, there are differences in how the Western term "queer" is translated; and if no such question is asked of the incoming subject, then that subject has merely been transplanted, and if a translation is absolutely necessary then we might even ask: "Can it mean the same thing if it only exists as a translation?" (Gunther, 2005, 24). Even though Roman Jakobson argued that "the problem of meaning and equivalence thus focuses on differences in the structure and terminology of languages rather than on any inability of one language to render a message" (qtd. in Munday, 2008, 37–38), there are in reality those who advocate for transplantation and those who advocate for translation. In fact, Nida in comparison represented a "move away from the old idea that an orthographic word has a fixed meaning and towards a functional definition of meaning in which a word 'acquires' meaning through its context and can produce varying responses according to culture" (Munday, 2008, 39).

For translations of "queer" specifically, then, the local context may ultimately appear to do at least one of three things: (1) it may surmise that to some extent an equivalent subject in the local context is locatable, and so the incoming term is transliterated so as to orthographically resemble (or at least sound) as similar as possible to the original; (2) it may agree that some local idea or phenomenon is connoted by the original, but that a local alternative word or language already exists or can be readily located, thus lessening the power the incoming word or language has to impact the local context; (3) it may for some reason reject the incoming subject, perhaps due to a denial of any local existence of what the incoming subject purports to represent, or perhaps because the original is in fact deemed inadequate to represent what is nevertheless acknowledged to be a local counterpart. On this third possibility, we should now compare the significances of such terms as *tongsŏngaeja*, *k'wiŏ*, and *iban* in South Korean theoretical contexts, and how they are translated or transplanted. Instead of giving preference to transplanted terms, some propose *iban* as an appropriate translation of "queer" into the Korean language. Importantly, this may be on the condition that the term "queer theory" also be translated to *iban* theory, decentring white, Anglosphere authority and proposing a decolonised, South Korean queer theory that is concerned with *uri* (우리) or "us" and is not determined by "them" (white, Anglosphere queer theorists).

For some, it is imperative that South Korean non-heteronormative researchers and theorists begin with an effective articulation of *tongsŏngae* and *tongsŏngaeja*, as an attempt to verbalise the negative emotional experiences associated with the terms. Sŏ Tongjin advocates for an accommodation of western theory seemingly, at least in part, as a response to these negative emotional experiences, echoing the potentiality of Peeren's perspective on queerness being "reaccented as a positive term" (2006, 60). Although this is an advocacy which involves a resonance with negativity, there is a certain amount of delay or estrangement felt from translating a foreign history of negativity into a present history.

In the West, theories about queers have for decades intersected with the academy, in both negative and positive ways that did not operate together but were more consecutive foci. The word "queer" was first used to mean "homosexual" in the late nineteenth century, the word "homosexual" itself also being a highly negated topic in western European academia well into the twentieth century. When used by heterosexual laypeople, too, "queer" was originally a mild observation of something deemed non-normative, evolving into an aggressively derogatory term that historically and linguistically was born out of the term "homosexual" (and not "homosexual" being born out of "queer"). That is, "homosexual" was a product of European religious and psycho-medical persecutions, spanning generations and present in both private and public discourses. The specificity of South Korean (or Korean) history does not necessarily mean that "queer" cannot or will not be adopted in South Korean non-heteronormative theories and South Korean academic spaces more generally. It does mean, however, that perhaps due to what political theorist and feminist Iris Marion Young termed "asymmetrical reciprocity" (qtd. in Anderson, 2019, 3), such an adoption will still remain in part different from the original historical contexts from which the terms are derived. According to Anderson, it is within this understanding that Simone de Beauvoir also "acknowledges an inability to grasp the other's freedom" (2019, 3). The South Korean theorist adopter of "queer" will be rendered unable to authentically embody the now freedom-inducing effects that the word connotes in many contemporary European and North American academic spaces. As such, queer theory cannot be authentically transplanted into a South Korean theoretical, indigenous discourse. However, it may also be a term that South Korean theorists reserve as pertaining only to the West, to queer theory-invested academics, or something simply unheard of. While western queer studies, queer theory, and queer culture tend to be associated with non-normative sex, sexuality, and gender identity, some have highlighted that because normativity itself is a fluctuating construct over space and time, it is possible for that perceived normativity to undergo its own reframing, critique, or challenge.

Even so, it is crucial to keep in mind that "queer" is not merely an abstract linguistic identifier to be theorised or pontificated over but a mark on the bodies, behaviours, and relationships of those actively representing non-heteronormative sex, sexuality, and gender identity. This markedness carries a real risk of different violences being enacted against queer-identified individuals. While not a fixed, unchanging force, heteronormativity is still most powerful for its continued assigning of privilege to heterosexual citizens.

References and Further Reading

Anderson, Ellie. 2019. "From Existential Alterity to Ethical Reciprocity: Beauvoir's Alternative to Levinas". *Continental Philosophy Review* 52 (2): 171–189.

Barker, Meg, Christina Richards, and Helen Bowes-Catton. 2009: "'All the World Is Queer Save Thee and Me ...': Defining Queer and Bi at a Critical Sexology Seminar". *Journal of Bisexuality* 9 (3–4): 363–379.

Cho, John (Song Pae). 2020. "The Three Faces of South Korea's Male Homosexuality: Pogal, Iban and Neoliberal Gay". In *Queer Korea*, edited by Todd Henry, 263–294. Durham, NC: Duke University Press.

Chŏng, Chini. 2005. *Munhwa pip'yŏng yongŏ saejŏn* (문화 비평 연고새전) [Yŏngo Saejŏn Cultural Criticism]. Seoul: Kukhag Charyowŏn.

Chŏng, Minu. 2012. *K'wiŏ iron, sŭlp'ŭn mogugŏ* (퀴어 이론, 슬픈 모국어) [Queer Theory, Sad Mother Tongue]. *Munhwa wa sahŭi* [Culture and Society] 13: 53–100.

Epstein, B. J., and Robert Gillett (eds.). 2017. *Queer in Translation*. London: Routledge.

Gunther, Scott 2005: "Alors, Are We 'Queer' Yet?" *The Gay and Lesbian Review Worldwide* 12 (3): 23–25.

Han, Ch'aeyun 2006: "Pyŏgjang piugi—rejŭbiŏn segsyuŏllit'i wa isŏngaejuŭi" (벽장 비우기—레즈비언 섹슈얼리티와 이성애주의) [Emptying the Closet—Lesbian Sexuality and Heterosexuality]. In *Segsyuŏllit'i kangui, tubŏn jjae* [Sexuality, Second Edition], edited by Pyŏn Hyejŏng, 249–270. Map'ogu: Tongnyŏg.

Henry, Todd A. 2018. "Queer/Korean Studies as Critique: A Provocation". *Korea Journal* 58 (2): 5–26.

——. (ed.). 2020. *Queer Korea*. Durham, NC: Duke University Press.

Im, Jaeu. 2018. "Tongsŏng kunin hab ŭi sŏnggwangye mujwoi p'angyŏl … '70nyŏn man e ch'ŏum'" (동성 군인 합의 성관계 무죄 판결 … '70년만에 처움') [Judgement Rules Consensual Same-Sex Soldier Relations Are Not Guilty … "A First in 70 Years"]. http://www.hani.co.kr/arti/society/society_general/833340.html [accessed 2 February 2022].

Jackson, Peter A. 1998. "Male Homosexuality and Transgenderism in the Thai Buddhist Tradition". In *Queer Dharma: Voices of Gay Buddhists*, edited by Winston Leyland, 55–90. San Francisco: Gay Sunshine Press.

——. 2007. "Autonomy and Subordination in Thai History: The Case for Semicolonial Analysis". *Inter-Asia Cultural Studies* 8 (3): 329–348.

Kent, David Bradley. 1999. "Speaking in Tongues: Chinglish, Japlish and Konglish." Paper presented The Second Pan Asian Conference in Seoul.

Kim, Hyena. 2012. *Chŏngk'ŭ* (정크) [Junk]. Seoul: Minŭmsa.

Koh, Dong-Yŏn. 2013. "Globalising Korean *Queers*? *Project L(esbian)*, the First Exhibition of Lesbian Arts in South Korea". *Inter-Asia Cultural Studies* 14 (3): 378–400.

Lee, Hŭijin. 2008. "Hong Sŏgch'ŏn, '"homo saeggi" ranŭn mal tŭdgo shipji anha ogi ro pŏt'yŏttda'" (홍석천, " '호모 새끼' 라는 말 듣고 싶지 않아 오기로 벗였다") [Hong Sŏgch'ŏn, "I Didn't Want to Hear the Word 'Gay' so I Endured"]. *Chosŏn Nyusŭ* [Chosun News]. http://news.chosun.com/site/data/html_dir/2008/12/11/2008121101250.html [accessed 2 February 2022].

Morandini, James S., Alexander Blaszczynski, and Ilan Dar-Nimrod. 2016. "Who Adopts Queer and Pansexual Sexual Identities?" *The Journal of Sex Research* 54 (7): 911–922.

Munday, Jeremy. 2008. *Introducing Translation Studies: Theories and Applications*. 2nd ed London: Routledge.

Peeren, Esther. 2006. "Queering the Straight World: The Politics of Resignification in Queer as Folk". In *The New Queer Aesthetic on Television: Essays on Programming*, edited by James R. Keller and Leslie Stratyner, 59–74. Jefferson: McFarland.

Shin, Layoung. 2020. "Avoiding T'ibu (Obvious Butchness): Invisibility as a Survival Strategy among Young Queer Women in South Korea". In *Queer Korea*, edited by Todd Henry, 295–322. Durham, NC: Duke University Press.

Sŏ, Tongjin. 2011. "K'wiŏ kajok? Kajok, sahoe, kugga sai ŭi kŏri rŭl ŏddŏhge ch'ŭkhŏng hal kŏsinga?" (퀴어 가족? 가족, 사회, 국가 사이의 거리를 어떻게 측형할 것인다?) [Queer Family? Between Family, Society, and State—How Will They Side?]. *Chinbo p'yŏngron* [The Radical Review] 48: 88–119.

Yŏng, Kwŏnggimhyŏn, et al. 2011. *Namsŏngsŏng kwa chendŏ* (남성성과 젠더) [Masculinity and Gender]. Kyŏnggi: Chaŭm kwa maŭm.

12

A Transnational Approach to Understanding Japanese Colonial Influence in Taiwan

Manifestations in Taiwan's Cinema and Popular Music

Yu-Wen Chen

Introduction

Japan colonised Taiwan from 1895 to 1945. Although colonial influences can still be observed in modern-day Taiwan, their manifestations are varied. This chapter examines the Japanese colonial influence on the development of Taiwan's cinema and popular music, mainly from 1895 to today. As Taiwan's musical and cinematic productions were able to fuse languages, cultures, and techniques from various localities affiliated with Taiwan, such as China, Japan, and the vaguely conceived West, the Japanese colonial influence on these industries' development has not always been clear and important, even if it does play a crucial role. In addition, this chapter will show that Taiwan's musical and cinematic productions have been able to cross-fertilise beyond geographical and national boundaries. A transnational approach to language and cultural studies is thus useful to understand the scope of the colonial influence. Each industry is examined in its own section, and a comparison is provided in the conclusion.

It is first important to mention the language system used throughout this article. Mandarin-English terms are mainly used to describe pop music and cinema in Taiwan. These terms are commonly known not just in popular culture but also in English academic writing. For instance, "Taiyupop" refers to Taiwanese-language pop and "Taiyupian" refers to Taiwanese-language films. The Taiwanese language is also known as Hokkien, Holo, Minnan, or Southern Min. Ideally, it would have been better if Taiyupop and Taiyupian were known by their Taiwanese or Minnan pronunciations, as the Minnan language is the main language in which these pop music and cinematic presentations are performed. Thus, Taiyupop should be referred to as *Tâi-gí koa* (台語歌), and Taiyupian should be referred to as *Tâi-gí phì*^{n} (台語片).

The challenge of using terms such as *Tâi-gí koa* and *Tâi-gí phì*^{n} is that most non-native speakers will not have heard of them. Interestingly, many native speakers of Taiwanese (Tai.) have also adopted Mandarin (Man.) pronunciations when they speak about pop music or films performed in Taiwanese, as Mandarin is the dominant power in the Sinitic-language sphere. Whereas the Taiwanese people used to speak the local Taiwanese language, the pro-Mandarin governmental policies of the former Chinese Nationalist Party (Kuomintang, or KMT), and the spread of Mandarin via radio, film, and television, have given that language the power and convenience of a lingua franca. As a result, most Taiwanese people now use Mandarin pronunciations, such as Taiyupop and Taiyupian, when talking about Taiwanese-language pop music and films.

In the following section, I will give an overview of Japanese rule in Taiwan and subsequent historical developments on the island. The aim here is not to provide an exhaustive historical account; rather, I seek to comprehend the historical background and general context for the development of cinema and pop music in Taiwan. After the overview, I will examine the Japanese influence on these two industries, and then compare the two at the end of the chapter. The main conclusion of this chapter is that even though Japan has played a role in the development of Taiwanese cinema and pop music, its influence should not be overstated, nor should these industries be characterised as colonial productions. Echoing the central premise of this book as a whole, a transnational approach is more useful and accurate for understanding the growth of these two different industries and for teasing out the true extent of Japanese influence.

General Background

The Japanese ruled Taiwan for 50 years, beginning with the Treaty of Shimonoseki in 1895, in which the Qing empire ceded Taiwan to Japan, and concluding with the Japanese defeat in the Second World War in 1945. For half a century, all aspects of life in Taiwan—from industrialisation to media output, from education to transport—were controlled by the Japanese. In the film and music industries specifically, Japan also controlled the systems of production, distribution, performance, and exhibition. It was also common in this period for Taiwanese people who wished to further their careers in these industries to pursue their education and training in Japan.

The Japanese were more tolerant of the local population's usage of local languages in their daily life and in consuming music and films in the early years, and then became more repressive in the 1930s in the context of the invasion of Manchuria. In the late 1930s, Japan had initiated the Japanisation or *kōminka* movement (皇民化運動), literally meaning forcing people under its rule become loyal subjects of the Japanese emperor, such as by using Japanese names and speaking Japanese. In this context, Japan's policies towards its Taiwanese colony became assimilative: Japan expected Taiwan's loyalty as well as support for its stance on China. In music and film, repressive measures were enforced, banning productions made in the Chinese and Taiwanese languages. In their place, Japanese-language productions were promoted in conjunction with the expansionist ambitions of the Japanese military.

After Japan's defeat in the Second World War, Taiwan was subsequently ruled by the Chinese Nationalist Party from mainland China until the year 2000. The early KMT regime was authoritarian and it implemented a long period of martial law from 1949 to 1987. The regime only started to take major steps to implement democratic reforms in the late 1980s, and was eventually elected as ruling party rather than just remaining in power with the help of martial law.

The prevailing cultural policy during the KMT's early authoritarian rule was to encourage more productions to be made in Mandarin in line with the party's ideology and ultimate objective to use Taiwan as a base from which to regain the Chinese motherland. Neither Japanese- nor Taiwanese-language productions were permitted. The KMT government maintained a strict control over mass media, censoring productions that were not in line with or were critical of the government's propagandistic narratives and ideology. At the same time, it offered subsidies to help cultural productions in line with its aims. For instance, film studios were taken over by the government to generate anti-communist propagandistic films.

As Taiwan gradually moved towards democratisation in the 1980s and 1990s, the societal context became more liberal, which affected the music and cinema industries positively, and the climate of fear around creative products that would usually invite governmental censorship and repression began to subside. During the democratic transition, the Taiwanese identity also became more and more salient: increasing civilian and governmental efforts were made to support new Taiwanese-language productions or to recover old Taiwanese-language productions lost in the long martial law period.

In sum, local efforts to create Taiwan's own cultural products were curtailed during the Japanese colonial period. The martial law period under the KMT's rule did not offer local artists opportunities to create their work either, due to its repressive cultural policy. In turn, this gives us impetus to ask whether Taiwan's local artists were able to create Taiwan's own traditions of cinematic and musical development given the difficult political and historical contexts they operated in, and how the past affects the contemporary transformation. The focus of this chapter is on determining the possible existence and nature of the Japanese colonial legacy and exploring what Japan has meant to Taiwan's popular music and cinema as they developed. This chapter uses the term "influence" to mean the existence of colonial legacy as manifested in both conscious and unconscious adaptation of Japanese culture and technology into Taiwan's mediascape and cultural industry. Colonialism and transnational forces have prompted such "cultural flows", a term coined by anthropologist Appadurai back in 1990. But as the chapter will reveal, the flows are not unidirectional and coherent with Japanese culture directly affecting Taiwan's mediascape. In the next section, we will first look at the example of popular music.

Popular Music

Contemporary Taiwan is seen as one of the development hubs of Mandarin-language pop, or "Mandopop", in East Asia. Mandopop is also popular in mainland China, Hong Kong, Macau, South Korea, Japan, Vietnam, Singapore, and Malaysia. The music industry, consumers, and even scholars have generally recognised Taiwan as the most fertile ground for Mandopop and its musicians since the 1970s. However, the development of Mandopop requires a transnational approach to the exploration of the industry as it developed.

A close relation of Mandopop is Taiyupop, a type of Chinese pop music sung in the Taiwanese language. As noted above, the Japanese colonial rulers were initially tolerant of the presence and use of Mandarin and Taiwanese. In the mid- to late 1920s, a leading Japanese record company, the Nippon Phonography Company (and predecessor of Columbia Music Entertainment), started to operate in Taiwan. The company formed production teams with local performers of traditional opera and released recordings of music such as Taiwanese opera (歌仔戲, Tai. *koa-á-hì*) and popular folk songs. With the growth of the phonographic industry, recordings of Taiyupop took off in the 1930s (Huang, 2019). At that time, it was common to remake Japanese songs into Taiyu songs, giving rise to the term "Taiyu songs with Japanese tunes" (Huang, 2019). Meanwhile, homegrown Taiyupop also became popular, with songs such as "Longing for the Spring Breeze" (望春風, Tai. *Bāng Chhun-hong*) and "A Flower in the Rainy Night" (雨夜花, Tai. *Ú Iā Hoe*). These productions absorbed the strophic forms from Japan that used and repeated multiple short stanzas in song form (Huang, 2019).

In the earlier days of Japanese rule, Taiwan was still able to obtain and create Chinese-language productions given its close historical, cultural, and linguistic ties with mainland China. For instance, it was common for Taiwanese lyrics to be added to melodies from mainland China. However, as Japan's policy towards Taiwan became more assimilative and repressive in the late 1930s, Japan banned Chinese-language songs. Instead, Japanese lyrics were added to Taiwanese and Mandarin pop songs. In addition, propaganda songs with Japanese lyrics were produced to boost morale in the fight against China. For instance, the Japanese turned the aforementioned "Longing for the Spring Breeze" into "The Land Is Calling" (大地は招く, J. *Daichi Wa Maneku*), advocating support for the Manchu state on the Chinese mainland. Likewise, "A Flower in the Rainy Night" was appropriated and converted into "Proud Military Worker" (誉れの軍夫, J. *Meiyore No Gunpu*) to encourage support for the Japanese imperial army (Huang, 2019). People in modern-day Taiwan generally know both songs in their original and adopted forms, but for those who have lived under Japanese rule, the Japanese versions may be more familiar (Huang, 2019).

Taiyupop witnessed a resurgence during the short period between Japan's exit from Taiwan after the Second World War and the Chinese Nationalist Party's rise to power on the island. Yet, as noted earlier, the Chinese Nationalist Party government, which imposed rule by martial law in 1949, was set on promoting the Mandarin language, and Mandopop was seen as one of the primary means to do so. In the 1960s, through state-controlled television and other media, Mandopop was widely disseminated, while Taiyupop continued to be performed in theatres and cinemas. In the 1970s, the government intervened further, passing laws to prohibit the use of the Taiwanese language in lyrics, which stymied the development of Taiyupop. The censorship lasted until the early 1980s, and Taiyupop was only able to re-emerge after the lifting of martial law in 1987.

The clearest evidence of the Japanese colonial influence is the way in which both Mandopop and Taiyupop adopted the Japanese *enka* (演歌) style, which evokes melancholy. Taiyupop and Mandopop audiences will be familiar with the sorrowful tendencies inherent in both genres. However, it cannot be assumed that *enka*'s influence was imposed without finding acceptance among local audiences. Audiences in the Chinese-speaking world are generally known to appreciate (extreme) sadness in music. Since the majority of Mandopop and Taiyupop expresses sadness, this seems to be a trait that is enjoyed by their audiences. More specifically, successful and popular Taiyupop singers whose work has shown a clear *enka* influence include the "king of Taiyupop", Chris Hung (洪隆宏, Tai. *Âng Êng-hông*, Man. *Hung Jung-Hung*, born 19 March 1963). Born in Tokyo in 1963, Hung is the son of a Taiwanese singer and received strict musical training from his father. During his youth, he was also sent to Japan to advance his education in music. Hung is now a well-known Taiwanese *enka* singer.

Another example of the *enka* influence is Jody Chiang (江蕙, Tai. *Kang Hūi*, Man. *Jiang Hui*, born 1 September 1961), often considered the queen or diva of Taiyupop. Below are the lyrics from a popular Taiyupop song called "Sad Hotel" (傷心酒店, Tai. *Siong-sim Chiú-tiàm*, 1993), sung as a duet by Jody Chiang and Michael Shih (施文彬, Tai. *Si Bûn-pin*, Man. *Shi Wenbin*, born 10 December 1964). At the end of this chapter, readers can find a YouTube link to listen to the song.

Cold light	冷淡的光線
Sad song	哀怨的歌聲
All people drink alone with loneliness	飲酒的人無心晟
The prosperity of the world	世間的繁華
is like a dream	親像夢一攤
It is all worthless	也是無較詛
In a dim light hotel	暗淡酒店內
Sorrow is known to no one	悲傷誰人知
Pain swallowed to my stomach	痛苦吞腹內
Give me another drink	一杯擱再來
If you understand	你若有瞭解
Don't ask me where I come from	甭問阮對叼位來
I don't want to tell	不願講出來
I keep depressed feelings inside my heart	鬱卒放心內
Feeling helpless about my loss of love	感情失落的無奈
Bitterly wait	苦苦塊等待
But I still have no one to love	還是等無愛
All of them are just like false displays of affection	虛情的對待
In this passionate world	多情的世界
I cannot find true love	找無真情愛
It makes me sad	引阮心悲哀
Whether I have love	有愛也罷
or without love, I live	無愛嘛快活
Tonight, only loneliness keeps me company	今夜伴阮是孤單

Table 1. Lyrics of "Sad Hotel"

Earlier Taiyupop singers and/or songwriters received training in Japan and maintained their Japanese connections to some extent. However, some scholars have cautioned against casting Taiyupop as merely a colonial product. C. S. Stone Shih (2019), for example, has used the example of Hsu Shih (許石, 1919–1980), the seminal pioneer of Taiyupop in the post–Second World War period, to argue that Hsu in fact tries to present Taiyupop as a kind of decolonial modernity. Hsu received his musical education in Japan in the 1940s, specialising in theoretical composition and vocal *enka*. When he returned to Taiwan in the 1950s, he strove to write original Taiyu songs, at a time when many Taiyu songs were remakes of Japanese songs. Hsu even travelled all over the island, collecting folk songs of various kinds and then adapting them into symphonic compositions to elevate them to a higher status (Shih, 2019).

While Hsu had the ambition to create new Taiwanese pop songs, thereby constructing a clear new Taiwanese identity, he was also faced with the challenging political environment outlined above, which stressed Chinese identity above all else. Hsu eventually opted for a pragmatic strategy of compromise, in an attempt not to agitate the KMT regime. As well as creating new Taiwanese songs (which was more problematic from the government's perspective), he also reworked a large number of foreign songs into Taiyupop. The sources of these songs were generally from countries (e.g. United States, South Korea, Japan) and regions (e.g. Shanghai, Hong Kong) that were somehow related to Taiwan. They came to be known as "medley mixed-blood songs" (大雜燴混血歌, Man. *dazahui hunxue ge*). While critics may denounce these medley mixed-blood songs for their lack of originality, they performed well in the mainstream consumer market. Because Taiyupop was able to infuse languages and cultures from various localities affiliated with Taiwan, a purely (Japanese) colonial perspective is therefore insufficient to examine the growth of Taiyupop. Rather, a transnational approach is more useful, especially one that focuses on how music production can cross-fertilise beyond geographical boundaries.

Market performance was strong during Hsu's time because most of Taiwan's population spoke Taiwanese rather than Mandarin before and well after 1945, into the early years of nationalist Chinese rule. During those years, Taiyupop retained its popularity, and the mournful influence of *enka* was evident. Meanwhile, the nationalist Chinese government prioritised the promotion of Mandarin through Mandopop; in its attempt to capture the hearts and minds of audiences as Taiyupop had, Mandopop perpetuated Taiyupop's melancholic style. Hence, one can assert that Taiyupop absorbed *enka*, which then influenced Mandopop in Taiwan. A concrete example of the KMT government's policy is its support for the so-called campus songs, recruiting university students to sing and promote Mandarin Chinese songs to the public. The songs were not just promoted on campus, they were even widely broadcast on television. Taiyupop, in comparison, was not given such support.

An example of the melancholic style of Mandopop can be seen in the surprise global success of an old made-in-Taiwan song via social media in 2021. Titled "A Spray of Plum Blossoms" (一剪梅, Man. *Yi Jian Mei*, 1983), the song was originally sung by famous Taiwanese singer Fei Yu-Ching (費玉清, born 17 July 1955) in the early 1980s and has been popular in the Chinese-speaking world ever since. In January 2021, when Chinese social media user Zhang Aiqin (張愛欽) posted himself singing part of the song, his unique egg-shaped head and his voice immediately made the video a hit across the globe. In countries as far afield as Finland and New Zealand, the song even ranked top or second on Spotify in 2021. The main part of the song that went viral is the lyric "Xue hua piaopiao bei feng xiaoxiao" (雪花飄飄北風嘯嘯), whose meaning is not comprehensible to many non-Chinese speakers. Written in literary Chinese, it means "snow falls and north wind blows". Although the song is sung in Mandarin and evokes fanciful connotations of the snowy winter in the Chinese far north (i.e. with no connection to Japan), it is generally cited as an exemplar of the sorrowful type of music produced in Taiwan.

Marc Moskowitz (2010) further discerns the different kinds of sadness manifested in Taiyupop and Mandopop. The distinction is that the former emulates the Japanese *enka* by focusing on rural and working-class concerns and arousing nostalgia for an often-romanticised past. Mandopop, on the other hand, is more centred on momentary cheerfulness and downheartedness, appealing to urbanites whose main language is Mandarin. It should also be noted that Taiwan's Mandopop sometimes uses melodies from Hong Kong's Cantonese pop songs as well as Japanese, American, European, and other pop songs, reproducing them with Mandarin lyrics. As with Taiyupop, cross-fertilisation in the local and transnational music industries has contributed to the growth of Taiwan's Mandopop. This makes the transnational approach to studying the topic even more pertinent. In other words, the Japanese colonial influence should be seen as only one of many transnational influences in the emergence of Mandopop and Taiyupop.

Another manifestation of transnational development is that Japan's influence on Taiwan is not limited to Taiwan. Taiwan has acted as a springboard for spreading Japanese pop culture, including music, to Chinese-speaking audiences around the world. The Chinese term *harizu* (哈日族) is commonly used to refer to people who are fond of Japan and its culture. This Japanophile appreciation has several levels. On a very superficial level, certain Japanese words are used sporadically in Mandopop and Taiyupop to give listeners a taste of Japan. For example, *anata* (あなた) in Japanese nowadays means "the other person" or "you" but it is almost a synonym of "darling" (husband), especially among older generations. In Japanese, husbands never call their wives *anata*; it's only wives who call husbands *anata*. In Taiyupop (and less so in Mandopop), however, *anata* is sometimes inserted into Chinese lyrics to address someone in whom an individual has a romantic interest. In Jody Chiang's 2004 song "Red Thread" (紅線, Tai. *Âng Sòa*ⁿ, 2004), the lyrics include the phrase "my beloved *anata*". Furthermore, the song opens with the line: "My little finger tied with a red thread, I am waiting for him to take me to see spring's *sakura*". *Sakura* (桜) is the Japanese term for cherry blossom, a world-renowned symbol of Japanese culture. Significantly, the song's composer is the Japan-based Taiwanese composer Mori Yuji (森祐士). While native Japanese speakers may find this appropriation of Japanese terms in Chinese lyrics awkward, this phenomenon is not uncommon in pop music in Taiwan.

The "sadness paradigm" (a term borrowed from Chris Berry's 2020 analysis of Taiwanese-language films) in Mandopop and Taiyupop is not unique to East Asian music. It is also present in traditional literature, contemporary literature, soap operas, and films. Sorrow is often accompanied by loneliness and alienation. Some scholars have suggested that the sorrowful tone in Japanese literature has even influenced Taiwan's own, which has in turn affected its film and music (Moskowitz, 2010). The next section turns to Taiwanese cinema. It is not intended as a detailed analysis of its development; rather, it opens the discussion about how Taiwan's colonial past has affected its film industry.

Cinema

The term "Taiwanese cinema" is controversial. Indeed, there is no consensus on the existence of Taiwanese cinema or whether it has its own unique tradition. This chapter does not address this debate. The controversy, however, shows that Taiwan's achievements in film are relatively less recognised or esteemed than the successes of Mandopop and Taiyupop. One of the key reasons is that film-making requires more sophisticated skills, which Taiwan lacked until the 1980s. Taiwan's political history has not provided fertile ground for film-making.

The Japanese were the first to bring film to Taiwan. They introduced this new form of entertainment during colonial rule. However, the Japanese had no interest in cultivating local Taiwanese film-making talent; they commanded all aspects of film-making, from production, through distribution, and on to exhibition (Wilson, 2014). Films that were shot in Taiwan during the colonial period were low in quality. While there were collaborations between Japan and Taiwan with Taiwanese sponsorship, local Taiwanese film-makers found few opportunities to gain professional film-making knowledge and skills. Moreover, the local Taiwanese population was not given the opportunity to become consumers and appreciators of films, either. Japanese products dominated the earliest Taiwanese theatres. Foreign films from Europe and the US could be screened in Taiwan, but subtitles were provided in Japanese, which most locals could not understand; the films were essentially screened exclusively for Japanese people living in Taiwan (Wilson, 2014). Until the end of the Second World War, 70 per cent of audiences going to cinema in Taiwan were Japanese (Wilson, 2014). Together, these developments under Japanese rule prevented Taiwan from building the necessary capacity to establish its own cinematic identity, industry, and market.

Before Japanese rule, Taiwan's culture was partly Chinese due to Han farmers who migrated from the Chinese mainland. There were also different indigenous groups with their own cultures. Japanisation during colonial rule attempted to reduce the influence of Chinese culture. Hence, When the Chinese nationalists seized power over Taiwan after the Second World War, their priority was to (re-)Sinicise Taiwanese citizens. In addition to the promotion of Mandarin at the expense of the Taiwanese language, all films created during the Japanese colonisation were discredited and destroyed (Chang, 2019). Censorship and the promotion of certain types of Mandarin films during the early days of National Chinese rule hindered the growth of native Taiwanese cinema. In the 1980s, however, "Taiwan New Cinema" managed to break through, and some directors, such as Hsiao-hsien Ho (侯孝賢) and Edward Yang (楊德昌) gained international acclaim. With Taiwan's democratic development, the government also started to offer support for native productions. Since the late 2000s, the political conditions for producing films in Taiwan have improved significantly (Chang, 2019; Lee, 2013). While some productions may not have achieved commercial success, Taiwanese cinema has garnered attention in an increasing number of academic publications. In recent years, film scholars such as Chris Berry and Ming-yeh Rawnsley have cooperated with many European universities (e.g. the University of Helsinki, University of Naples) to screen Taiyupian cinema; their Taiwan's Lost Commercial Cinema website contains rich information on the artform (https://taiyupian.uk). Students are encouraged to explore the website, and most of the Taiyupian films mentioned in this chapter are further analysed there. It is also here that we begin the discussion of the Japanese influence on film-making.

Taiyupian started in the mid-1950s and died out in the 1970s, by which point Japan had left Taiwan. However, the Japanese influence on Taiwanese cinema is far-reaching: from film-making technology and styles to themes.

Taiwanese elites, who had the financial and artistic capacity to benefit from Japan's formal education and/or apprenticeships in Japan's film studios, adopted the Japanese style. Lin Tuan-Qiu (林摶秋, 1920–1998) is one example of the Taiwanese Taiyupian directors and producers who studied film-making in Japan before applying their skills in Taiwan. Crucially, the Japanese influence can be more clearly seen in Taiyupian than in Mandarin films. Despite the Nationalist Chinese intention to support Mandarin films, the population still spoke mostly Taiwanese and had a clear memory of Japanese occupation. This facilitated the growth of Taiyupian. The adoption of Japanese themes and styles was also made easier because Taiwanese film-makers had progressed their technical knowledge, while local audiences could still relate to Japanese productions; indeed, some critics would even argue that Taiyupian was simply plagiarising Japanese cinema.

Lin Tuan-Qiu's *The Husband's Secret* (丈夫的秘密, Tai. *Tiōng-hu ê Pì-bi't,* 1960) offers an example. Although set in Taiwan, Japanese *tatami* mats can be seen in the Taiwanese houses, and the way the wife greets her husband upon his return home is Japanese. As well as reflecting the Japanese way of life, the sadness paradigm also gained popularity in Taiyupian. Again, however, as with music production, not all cinematic productions followed the tear-jerking sadness paradigm; comedies found success on the screen as well, including the two series *Brother Wang* and *Brother Liu on the Roads in Taiwan* (王哥柳哥遊台灣, Tai. *Ông-ko Liú-ko Iû Tâi-oân*) made in 1958 and 1959, respectively. Another Japanese influence is the focus on women as the narrators of the clash between modernity and tradition. Such narratives include those that contrast the yearning for the opportunities to be found in the city with the fear of corruption and loss of innocence that can ensue. Contradictions between old and new ways of life, city and countryside, purity and corruption, and good and evil were common themes in Japanese films adopted by Taiyupian.

The Japanese influence on Taiwan's film production seemed to be significant during the early days of Nationalist Chinese rule. This does not mean, however, that there was no resistance to this development. As noted earlier, Japanese films were discredited during this period, and postcolonial Taiwan aspired to distance itself from its colonial past. In reality, the Japanese and Taiwanese film industries continued to cooperate, suggesting a complicated love-hate relationship between the ex-coloniser and the ex-colonised. Paradoxically, like the situation in the music industry, the number of films arousing Japanophilia outnumber those arousing Japanophobia. Indeed, there is evidence of the ongoing adoption of cinematic technology from Japan. Ultimately, though, most of this technology came from the West; Japan was just a means for Taiwan to access Western technology. In other words, during the Cold War, Japan was no longer considered a colonial master. Rather, it was seen as an excellent exemplar of the early adoption of new Western technologies from which to learn and develop. The claim that Taiwan's film-making had a colonial legacy is therefore inaccurate; a transnational approach to understanding this topic is more appropriate.

As with the music industry, situating the development of cinema within a transnational framework positions Japan as only one source of influence. This also guards against attributing Taiwan's cinematic development solely to colonial influence. Moreover, some scholars have argued that distinguishing between the Japanese and other influences can be difficult. For example, *Back to Anping Harbour* (回來安平港, Tai. *Tńg-lâi An-pêng-káng*, 1972) is a Madame Butterfly-style romance between a Taiwanese girl and a Dutch doctor. The relevance of the transnational framework can also be seen through the Taiyupian films that depict societies outside Taiwan. For instance, *Dangerous Youth* (危險的青春, Tai. *Gûi-hiám ê Chheng-chhun*, 1969) was filmed in Taiwan. However, probably because its critique of urban corruption and materialism would have challenged martial law and the authoritarian regime in Taiwan, the film's setting was Hong Kong.

Several scholarly publications have explored the portrayal of Japanophilia in the Taiwanese blockbuster *Cape No. 7* (海角七號, Man. *Hǎijiǎo Qī Hào*, 2008). The film's use of Mandarin, Taiwanese, Japanese, and Hakka depicts Taiwan as a multilingual, multicultural, and inclusive society. Several critics have argued that the film romanticised and induced nostalgia for Taiwan's colonial past, striking a chord with some Taiwanese elders who might pine for the symbols of modernisation, progress, and fashion associated with the colonial rulers despite their feelings of bitterness at being treated as second-class citizens. The film also speaks to the younger generation who, like some youth in other parts of the world, had become Japanophile and *harizu*.

Overall, despite some hints of Japanese influence, contemporary Taiwan's popular cinema flourished amid multidirectional transnational cultural flows. In this process, the line between what is national and what is transnational becomes blurred, and Japanese influence is no longer easily detectable (Lin, 2019).

Conclusion

Table 2 presents the Japanese colonial influence on Taiwan's music and cinema. It provides only a partial explanation for the development of both industries. The influence on the music industry is associated with the *enka* performance style, which is still pervasive in Mandopop and Taiyupop. The sadness paradigm is also one of Japanese cinema's influences on Taiyupian.

	Music	Cinema
Skills/styles	*Enka*, sadness paradigm	Technology, styles, themes, sadness paradigm
Use of Japanese words	Sometimes (connected to Japanophilia)	Sometimes (connected to Japanophilia)
Medium to present Taiwan's Japanese-influenced lifestyle	No	Yes
Medium to portray or arouse Japanophilia	Yes (to some extent)	Yes
Medium to portray or arouse Japanophobia	No	Yes
The Japanese influence is only one of the contributing factors in the development of the industry. The transnational approach is more appropriate for analysis.	Yes	Yes

Table 2: Japanese colonial influence on the development of Taiwan's music and cinema

Despite the *enka* influence, not all Taiwan's Mandopop and Taiyupop can be considered a form of colonial reproduction. Some songwriters and performers like Hsu Shih managed to break through and present Taiyupop as a kind of decolonial modernity. Both Mandopop and Taiyupop have a local flavour from production to consumption. Furthermore, their popularity has spread beyond Taiwan and across the Chinese-speaking world. This includes East Asia and the Chinese-speaking diaspora in Southeast Asia and the West; it is not unusual to hear Mandopop or Taiyupop being played as background music in a Chinese restaurant in Berlin.

Compared with Mandopop and Taiyupop, Taiwan's cinematic development lacked an initial fertile ground and has only started to gain more local and international recognition since the late 2000s. Yet film is a suitable medium for us to explore Japanese colonial influence, especially evoking both positive and negative emotions about the ex-coloniser. This is related to Taiwan's search for collective identities and memories in the context of its historical and political relations with mainland China and its former coloniser, Japan. Film's capacity to discuss and induce such sentiments is greater than that of music, given its ability to explore issues more deeply.

This examination of film and music shows that the Japanese colonial influence is neither linear nor identical in either industry. In addition, the Japanese influence could be interrupted during a particular political period, only to re-emerge or be transformed subsequently. The transnational approach is useful for analysis because it interrogates the various routes to being an influence and being influenced. These transnational pathways sometimes create difficulty in attributing every external cultural influence to Japan. This is becoming even more apparent as both industries have adopted various kinds of transnational models, involving expertise from the US, Japan, China, and Europe in their more recent production and distribution models. Transnational expertise helps improve the quality of production while at the same time charting further channels for regional and even global distribution. Transnational cooperation also elevates both the national development of Taiwan's music and film industries while at the same time bringing Taiwanese productions to the attention of international audiences. In these processes, it becomes even more difficult for experts to discern what constitutes colonial influence from Japan and what does not. Perhaps the question itself will become less relevant in contemporary and future productions.

References and Further Reading

Appadurai, Arjun. 1990. "Disjuncture and Difference in the Global Cultural Economy". *Public Culture* 2 (2): 1–24.

Berry, Chris. 2020. "An Alternative Cinema of Poverty: Understanding the Taiwanese-Language Film Industry". *Journal of Chinese Cinema* 14 (2): 140–149.

Chang, Ivy I-Chu. 2019. *Taiwan Cinema, Memory, and Modernity.* Singapore: Palgrave Macmillan.

Huang, Yu-Yuan. 2019. "The Cultural Hybridization of Taiyu Pop Songs". In *Made in Taiwan: Studies in Popular Music*, edited by Eva Tsai, Tung-hung Ho, and Miaoju Jian, 91–104. London: Routledge.

Lee, Daw-Ming. 2013. *Historical Dictionary of Taiwan Cinema.* Lanham: Scarecrow Press.

Lin, Ting-Ying. 2019. "Charting the Transnational Within the National: The Case of Contemporary Taiwan Popular Cinema". In *Positioning Taiwan in a Global Context: Being and Becoming*, edited by Bi-Yu Chang and Pei-Yin Lin, 196–210. London: Routledge.

Moskowitz, Marc L. 2010. *Crises of Joy, Songs of Sorrow: Chinese Pop Music and Its Cultural Connotations.* Honolulu: University of Hawai'i Press.

Shih, C. S. Stone. 2019. "Entangled Identities: The Music and Social Significance of Hsu Shih, a Vanguard Composer of Taiyu Ballads". In *Made in Taiwan: Studies in Popular Music*, edited by Eva Tsai, Tung-hung Ho, and Miaoju Jian, 75–90. London: Routledge.

Taiwan's Lost Commercial Cinema. 2021. https://taiyupian.uk/ [accessed 12 March 2021].

Wilson, Flannery. 2014. *New Taiwanese Cinema in Focus: Moving within and beyond the Frame*. Edinburgh: Edinburgh University Press.

Filmography

Lin Tuan-Qiu (林摶秋). 1960. *Tiōng-hu ê Pì-bi't* (丈夫的秘密) [The Husband's Secret].

Li Xing (李行), Fang Zhen (方震), and Tian Feng (田豐). 1959. *Ông-ko Liú-ko Iû Tâi-oân* (王哥柳哥遊台灣) [Brother Wang and Brother Liu on the Roads in Taiwan].

Wei Te-Sheng (魏德聖). 2008. *Hǎijiǎo Qī Hào* (海角七號) [Cape No. 7].

Wu Fei Jian (吳飛劍). 1972. *Tńg-lâi An-pêng-káng* (回來安平港) [Back to Anping Harbour].

Xin Qi (新奇). 1969. *Gûi-hiám ê Chheng-chhun* (危險的青春) [Dangerous Youth].

Discography

Chiang, Jody (江蕙). 2004. "Âng Sòa^{n}" (紅線) [Red Thread]. Composer Mori Yuji (森祐士), lyrics by Mori Yuji (森祐士). https://www.youtube.com/watch?v=aP__dJPDrJg.

Chiang, Jody, and Michael Shih (施文彬). 1993. "Siong-sim Chiú-tiàm" (傷心酒店) [Sad Hotel]. Composer Ji Ji-San (吉幾三), lyrics by Luo Wen-Cong (羅文聰). https://www.youtube.com/watch?v=VwNZ4en7SmE.

Fei, Yu-Ching (費玉清). 1983. "Yi Jian Mei" (一剪梅) [A Spray of Plum Blossoms]. Composer Chen Yu-Zeng (陳玉貞), lyrics by Chen Shin-Yi (陳信義). https://taichinotebook.com/2015/07/26/yi-jian-mei-lyrics/.

Part IV

Transnationalism in Global East Asia

13

A Gateway to Exciting Opportunities?

The Lives of African Migrants Inside and Outside Taiwan's University Campuses

Sarah Hanisch

Introduction

In recent decades, East Asian countries became key players shaping cultural, economic, and political affairs beyond the confines of their national territories. This has not only changed the way they interact with the West (Berry and Engels, 2018) but has also changed their image in the eyes of transnational migrants. Historically, East Asia was a sending region whose citizens migrated to rich nations in the Global North (Wang, 1993). With growing income levels and rising standard of living, East Asia has also become a popular destination for transnational migrants, especially from the Global South. A good example is African migration (Khan, 2014, 95; Röschenthaler, 2017). Building on their shared experience of colonisation and history of independence struggles, connections between Asia and Africa have experienced a renaissance. While political interactions are mainly bilateral and dominated by national interests and policies, people-to-people interactions are truly transnational (Bodomo, 2010).

African migrants across Asia constitute a heterogenous group with different socio-economic backgrounds and varying durations of stay. Although Africans can be found in almost every country in East Asia, the bulk of existing research has focused on African migrants in the People's Republic of China (PRC) (Bodomo, 2010; Haugen, 2013; Matthews et al., 2017). Most of these studies have focused on African traders in big cities like Guangzhou and Yiwu in the PRC (Li et al., 2012; Bredeloup, 2012; Liu, 2013; Castillo, 2014; Burgess, 2016) and only a few on African students (Haugen, 2013). Clearly traders are an important group among African migrants in the PRC and other Asian countries. However, African migrants have not only established a visible presence in the trading and business sector, but also on university campuses across Asia—making them part of the growing community of international students.

International students are the fastest-growing migrant group globally (Lipura and Collins, 2020). UNESCO statistics on in-bound student mobility show that Europe and North America host the largest numbers of international students. However, East and Southeast Asia have witnessed the fastest growth during the last few decades. While there were only 176,911 international students in 2000, by 2018 Asian countries hosted 693,567 students from abroad. UNESCO estimates that there were 2,339 African students in 2000. By 2018 around 19,853 Africans were studying in Asia (UNESCO, 2018). The rising number of African students in East Asia can be linked to the fundamental changes that have taken place over the last decades. On the one hand, sustained efforts by Asian governments to turn their universities into world-class institutions altered the perception of Asia as a study destination and gateway to career opportunities (Röschenthaler, 2017). On the other hand, it seems that government-sponsored scholarship programmes for foreign students in general, and African students in particular, further increased East Asia's attractiveness as a study destination. In some cases, these scholarship programmes are also linked to wider foreign policy goals. The PRC is perhaps the most outspoken country in this regard. There, the promotion of African student migration, as Haugen (2013) shows, is a means to increase soft power and promote South-South cooperation and solidarity. This chapter proposes that African student migration to East Asia enhances our understanding of transnational East Asia because it allows us to understand how tentative historical links between Asian and African states led to complex transnational links and networks in the twenty-first century that are increasingly shaped on the grassroots level.

Considering the cultural and historical complexity of the different East Asian countries, this chapter will focus on African student migration to Taiwan as an example of transnational links and interactions in the region. Taiwan mirrors the wider student migration trends discussed above. There were only 6,380 foreign students enrolled in the academic year 2001/2. By 2018, 126,997 foreigners were studying in Taiwan (De Aeth, 2019). The majority were from the United States, Europe, or Southeast Asia. Still, the number of African students in Taiwan grew from only 75 students in 2000 to 2,700 in 2018 (MOE, 2018). Despite this rapid growth, we know little about African student migration to Taiwan. Journalistic accounts (Charlier, 2009) indicate that African students experience a cultural shock and face difficulties finding employment after graduation.

However, there are no systematic studies of African student migration to Taiwan. This chapter fills this gap by providing a comprehensive analysis of the historical circumstances that created tentative links between certain African countries and Taiwan. Over time, migration between Taiwan and African became self-sustaining and influenced by factors that were related to neither bilateral cooperation nor migration policies. African students are transnational because they cross borders for educational and professional purposes while maintaining links to their home countries. Coming from very different historical and socio-economic contexts, they have a unique profile among international migrants in Taiwan. This also shapes their individual experiences and motivations to stay or leave Taiwan. Overall, the chapter suggests that African students in Taiwan have limited professional opportunities outside the university campuses.

Methodology

Theoretically and methodologically, this chapter is grounded in the transnational migration perspective (Glick-Schiller et al., 1994). This perspective proposes that migration is not a unidirectional movement from sending to receiving country, and that migrants form multiple ties and identities. More importantly, the perspective argues that migration needs to be understood beyond the container of the nation state because migrants construct and inhabit transnational social spaces. It also urges researchers to look at migrants as complex actors whose motivations cannot be reduced to economic considerations alone. In light of these considerations, we opted for a qualitative research design including research methods such as semi-structured interviews, expert interviews, document analysis, and group discussions.

The data for this chapter was collected during an intensive one-month research field trip to Taiwan in 2017. The initial target group was African students in Taipei. Since I and my research assistant quickly discovered that African students were dispersed across different universities and cities, we enlarged the target group accordingly. The final sample consisted of 38 students from Gambia, Burkina Faso, Ethiopia, South Africa, Uganda, Malawi, and Eswatini. The students were aged between 20 and 28. They included PhD, master's, bachelor's, and language students enrolled in different academic disciplines. In addition, five South African language teachers and two migrants from Burkina Faso and Chad who had lived in Taiwan for over seven years were interviewed. To understand the macro-structures and implementation of educational cooperation, interviews were conducted with representatives of the Ministry of Foreign Affairs and administrators of major Taiwanese universities. This allowed us to approach African migration to Taiwan from different angles and identify its unique characteristics.

Initiating and Sustaining African Student Migration

Transnational migration scholars have stressed the importance of historical links between countries for initiating and sustaining migration flows (Faist, 2010). Recent research by de Haas (2011, 23) also suggests that non-migration related policies may be crucial. As I show below, this applies to Taiwan. African student migration was spurred by two factors, which at first sight appear unrelated: a shift in Taiwan's foreign policy in the mid-2000s and a quest to internationalise Taiwanese universities. Historically, Taiwan's foreign policy has been marked by competition for diplomatic allies with the PRC and reflected an uneven dollar diplomacy (Lee, 1993; Chan, 1997). Taiwan typically provided short-term technical training courses in Taiwan as well as in the home country of their partners (Lee, 1993). The training courses were part of aid projects between the 1960s and '90s. With one partner after the other recognising the PRC, Taiwan cut major aid programmes in Africa. Nevertheless, Taiwan continued to provide technical training in Africa and specialised short-term training in Taiwan to its diplomatic allies. As of 2019, Eswatini was the last diplomatic ally and African beneficiary of these programmes. This development does not render Taiwan-Africa interactions a thing of the past. On the contrary, Taiwan has simply changed its mode of interaction with African countries.

Already towards the end of the 1990s, Taiwan embarked on a new way to engage with African countries in the field of educational cooperation. Back then, 30 countries, mostly in the Global South and many in Africa, still recognised Taiwan (Tubilewicz, 2007, 12). Instead of providing short-term courses for technical experts engaged in Taiwan's aid projects, Taiwan offered long-term study opportunities in Taiwan to aspiring Africans from different parts of society. These changes reflected a broader shift in Taiwan's foreign policy. The absolute count of diplomatic partners was less important than "improving its international reputation, and containing aid spending" (Atkinson, 2014, 409). The first (and yet last) Taiwan-Africa summit organised in 2007 is a good example for the move from quantity to quality cooperation. The summit was attended by the heads of state of Eswatini, Burkina Faso, Sao Tome and Principe, Malawi, and Gambia (MOFA, 2007). The goal was to "set new directions for future cooperation and to demonstrate that Taiwan genuinely hopes to assist its allies achieve progress, health and co-prosperity" (MOFA, 2007).

To maintain these relations, Taiwan introduced an exclusive scholarship programme. The programme was initiated by the International Cooperation Development Fund (ICDF) in 1998 and was open only to citizens of Taiwan's official diplomatic partners and designed for exclusive study programmes at

Taiwanese universities. The scholarship included 31 programmes in English at 21 universities (interview, MOFA representative, Taipei, 4 April 2017). The scholarship covered airfare, housing, tuition fees, textbook costs, and insurance. The monthly allowance ranged from NT$12,000 to NT$17,000 (€355 to €503) per month. Each year the ICDF awarded 175 scholarships exclusively to Taiwan's diplomatic partners. There are no annual statistics on African recipients but our interview with a representative of the MOFA indicated that the programme was effective in attracting African students and maintaining diplomatic relations (interview with MOFA representative, Taipei, 4 April 2017). MOFA and ICDF cooperated closely with African countries and actively promoted the scholarship programme. A representative of the MOFA reported that 88 scholarships were given to students from Eswatini and Burkina Faso between 2013 and 2016, when they both still recognised Taiwan (ICDF, 2019). In the case of Eswatini, the number of applicants surpassed the number of scholarships allocated: more than 100 Swazi students applied for the scholarship in 2013 but only 20 received one (Embassy of the Republic of China (Taiwan) in the Kingdom of Eswatini, 2013). As of 2019, Swazi nationals are the only Africans eligible for the ICDF scholarship. Therefore, the programme is no longer the driving force behind African migration to Taiwan.

Since it became clear that diplomatic relations were difficult to maintain, Taiwan launched a second programme in 2004. The programme involved the MOFA, the Ministry of Education (MOE), the Ministry of Economic Affairs, and the National Science Council in 2004 (ICDF, 2015). The Taiwan Scholarship Programme included fellowships for research, the Huayu Enrichment Scholarship, and scholarships for regular degree programmes. Taiwan awarded 1,200 such scholarships every year (MOFA, 2012), which were not tied to diplomatic recognition of Taiwan. Unlike its predecessor, the new programme aimed to promote Taiwan as a world-class study destination, and presumably to present Taiwan as an alternative to the PRC.

At first sight, the new programme appeared to broaden the opportunities for African students. However, the specificities of the application procedure meant that only a few African countries could benefit. Applications had to go through the Taiwanese embassy or local Taiwan Representative Offices in Africa. With the growing presence of the PRC in Africa, Taiwan reduced its physical presence on the continent significantly. The limited presence in Africa was officially linked to pressure on African governments from Beijing to cut all ties with Taiwan. However, in other parts of the world, Taiwan has maintained a strong presence through liaison and trade offices—despite the Beijing's insistence on the One-China Policy. For instance, Taiwan is represented in 23 out of 28 EU member states in 2019. In comparison, Taiwan has only an embassy in Eswatini, a trade office in Nigeria, and a Taipei Liaison

Office in South Africa. Since information is promoted through the offices and applications have to be send to them, applicants from countries with an official Taiwan representative office have better chances of being awarded a scholarship. As a result, most African countries were effectively excluded from these scholarships after they recognised the PRC.

While the scholarship programmes discussed above helped to place Taiwan on the map of possible migration destinations for African students, a third programme helped boost the number of African students in Taiwan and has become the main driver of African migration to Taiwan. The programme is decentralised, and scholarships are offered directly by Taiwanese universities. The main driver is the MOE, which wanted to internationalise Taiwanese universities. This development was related to changes in the national educational system. Since the late 1980s, the MOE has successfully promoted new private universities to diversify and modernise the higher education landscape (Mok and Chan, 2008, 472). There were only 21 universities in 1991; by 2017, there were already 129, the majority being private (NBS, 2019). This demonstrates that demand for higher education has surged. In the long run, however, demand will decrease due to demographic change in Taiwan. In bringing international students to Taiwan, the MOE hoped to compensate for a shrinking future demand. This approach is reflected in calls to internationalise higher education (Chen and Lo, 2013, 35).

Taiwanese universities took up the call from the MOE in different ways. Some prioritised becoming world-class universities, others set up different scholarship programmes. Key determinants for the scope of these programmes are internal budget constraints and internationalisation strategies. For African students, Taiwanese university scholarships offer an attractive and accessible alternative to the Taiwan Scholarship Programme. In 2019, 94 of 160 universities offered scholarships including prizes, one-year scholarships, tuition waivers, and full degree scholarships. Monthly stipends varied greatly and tended to be lower than government scholarships. The National Dong Hwa University scholarship stipend ranged from NT$4,000 to NT$6,000 (€118 to €177) per month and offered reduced tuition fees. Enrolled students could also apply for tuition waivers and accommodation scholarships (FICHET, 2017). The University of Taipei offered monthly stipends of NT$10,000 (€295) to BA students and NT$15,000 (€445) to MA and PhD students (FICHET, 2017). The variety of scholarships allows African students to carefully select the best option and to apply to several universities simultaneously. Overall, African students benefited from the internationalisation of Taiwanese universities and Taiwan's quest to strengthen its soft power.

Africans in Taiwan

Since the 1990s, Taiwan has transformed from being a sending country to a major recipient country of international migrants (Lipinsky, 2015). Taiwan is especially popular among migrants from Southeast Asia and the PRC (Lipinsky, 2015; Cheng and Momesso, 2017), but it is not perceived as a popular migration destination for Africans. There are arguably fewer Africans in Taiwan than in the PRC, Europe, or the United States. Their minority status among international migrants in Taiwan gives Africans a unique status. In Europe, Africans are often equated with low-skilled and illegal migrants (Carling, 2007; De Haas, 2008; Small, 2018). In the PRC, Africans are often negatively described in public discourse (Bodomo, 2010; Mathews and Yang, 2012; Lan, 2014; Liang and Le Billon, 2018). In Taiwan, these negative roles are mainly ascribed to migrants from mainland China and Southeast Asia (Lan, 2006; Liang, 2011; Everington, 2019), who constitute the biggest immigrant groups and often work in low-paid and labour-intensive jobs.

It is difficult to pin down Africans in Taiwan to selected nationalities or exclusive localities. Data from the Taiwanese Immigration Services includes around 40 African nationalities dispersed across all major Taiwanese cities (Ministry of Interior National Immigration Agency Republic of China Taiwan, 2019). It is worth noting that the numbers of African migrants from former diplomatic allies have remained relatively stable. This suggests that diplomatic relations do not play a major role. In terms of occupation, our interviews suggest that white South African teachers are the biggest group among African professionals. South Africa is the only African country recognised by the MOE as a native English-speaking country—even though many African countries have English as an official language. Public schools in Taiwan only employ foreign teachers from officially recognised English native-speaking countries. Most schools tend to hire white South Africans because the management fears that parents will not accept black South African teachers (interview with English language teacher, Taipei, 16 April 2017). Private schools make exceptions, but they offer less attractive renumeration packages. Migrants from other African countries work primarily in foreign representative offices, IT-related industries, or in international trade companies (interview with Gambian professional, Taipei, 25 April 2017). Among our informants, a woman from Burkina Faso worked for a Taiwanese trading company. She knew of several fellow Africans who found employment in Taiwan, but she added that these were rare instances.

Year	2013	2014	2015	2016	2017	2018	2019	2020
Total	1,444	1,905	1,895	2,085	2,139	2,334	2,615	2,704

Table 1: Number of African nationals in Taiwan 2013–2020
(Source: Taiwan Immigration Data)

Higher pay and bureaucratic hurdles make hiring foreigners an unattractive choice for Taiwanese employers. In 2017, the New Foreign Talent Act was passed to address this problem (Everington, 2017). Labour statistics reveal mixed results. Applications for special talent visas have gone up, from 467,464 in 2016 to 560,232 in 2019. However, the number of effective employment permits has dropped slightly during the same period. In 2016, there were 31,025 permit holders, and only 30,283 in March 2019 (MoL, 2018). The data does not contain information on the number of African beneficiaries. However, it suggests that Japanese and US citizens are the main beneficiaries of the new policy (MoL, 2019). Moreover, permit holders were either specialised workers or full-time foreign language teachers for supplementary schooling—two occupations in which Africans rarely engage.

Students constitute the biggest group among Africans in Taiwan. Our African informants were studying at major universities in Taipei, Kaohsiung, and Hualien. Male students enrolled in BA and MA programmes were predominantly unmarried. A few female students were married or single mothers. They had left their families and children in the care of relatives back home. Regardless of gender, these informants chose degrees related to their first field of study, such as international business, medical sciences, or computer science. Other students had worked in their home countries after graduating, and later pursed a degree in Taiwan. For example, a Swazi student had worked in the IT department at a local bank before coming to Taiwan, while a Gambian student had worked in ecotourism and then chose to further his studies in Taiwan. African postgraduate students were mainly enrolled in natural sciences. Some had completed MA degrees at a Taiwanese university and been invited by their Taiwanese professors to pursue a PhD degree. These postgraduates often left their spouses and children in their home country and returned only after the completion of their degree. Our Ethiopian informants explained that a PhD degree from Taiwan would pave the way for a promising career in Ethiopia.

Our interviews suggest that African students were connected through informal networks rather than official organisations. Embassies and representative offices typically organise events at which their citizens and other Africans can network. However, due to the One-China Policy, few African countries are officially represented in Taipei. According to our informants, when it was still active, the Burkinabe Embassy in Taipei was the only institution hosting events for all African citizens. Every year on Africa Day, the embassy sent formal invitations to Burkinabe students. Information about this event was spread by word of mouth and attendance of non-Burkinabe students was incidental and non-organised. Our informants who were not from Burkina Faso reported that they were surprised when they attended the event. They had assumed they were the only Africans in Taiwan. They said that they had never met so many Africans at a single event. Their surprise is understandable given that our informants came to Taiwan independently. After their arrival, they often had little contact with other Africans. This prevented the formation of social and religious organisations as are found in other countries (Haugen, 2013; Castillo, 2014). At the time of our research, Swazi students in Taipei were the only Africans who organised Sunday church services regularly. These services were held in either Swazi or English. A few African students based in Hualien also organised a network event for all Africans in Taiwan. However, compared to the situation in the PRC, the level of organisation and networking among Africans in Taiwan is rather limited.

Motivations of African Students

Before coming to Taiwan, many African students had never left their home country. Financial concerns and bureaucratic hurdles were the main obstacles. Historically, former colonial centres and North America constituted the main destinations for African students. However, in recent decades, countries in the Global South, like Taiwan, have emerged as popular destinations. Studies on transnational student migration have highlighted the importance of financial incentives, human capital development, and historical connections between sending and receiving countries (Raghuram, 2013, 142–144; Ahmad and Shah, 2018). Our informants confirmed this trend. Those with migration experience had lived in neighbouring African countries. For instance, Swazi students had often studied in South Africa. Geographical proximity, lower bureaucratic barriers, and better universities and job prospects were stated as key criteria.

Our African student informants saw Taiwan as an opportunity to study in a developed country. To them, developed was equated with tangible aspects such as a high standard of living, technological advancement, and good public infrastructure. Their perception matches Taiwan's self-image as a developed and industrialised country with a special position in the Global South. Although the PRC can offer the same material markers of "development", none of our informants had considered the PRC as an alternative. A Ugandan student explained that she would like to visit the PRC but did not consider studying or working there. In fact, it seemed that our informants considered the PRC as only one of many (equally unlikely) future destinations. Other African students had considered studying in the Global North. In the end, they chose Taiwan because it offered excellent educational opportunities. To African students, the quality of Taiwanese education is on a par with high international standards, but has the advantage of comparatively low study fees and cost of living. Taiwanese universities offer full-degree programmes taught in English, and often model their curricula on the US system. The North American character of Taiwanese universities bolsters their image as "international universities". Therefore, their degrees are seen as a ticket to universities in the Global North.

Like earlier generations elsewhere, these African students were motivated to study in a developed country not only for personal reasons. They felt safe in Taiwan and praised the convenience of the electronic pay system, the metro system, and the train system. However, African students appreciated these amenities beyond their immediate value for their personal life. They often discussed how these amenities could contribute to their home countries' development. A student from a rural village in Eswatini argued that her country would benefit from such a transport system (interview with Swazi BA student, Taipei, 20 April 2017)—buses in Eswatini run infrequently and are not safe after certain hours. Another student from Gambia praised the honesty of the Taiwanese and wished Gambians would follow their lead (interview with Gambian student, Taipei, 14 April 2017). She felt that the Taiwanese returned lost items (including cash) and rarely stole unwatched personal belongings. To her, this kind of honesty would be beneficial in Gambia, too. Overall, African students took up local practices and norms with the aim of taking some of them back to their African home countries.

Studying in Taiwan catered to individual aspirations for upward social mobility and broader societal contributions. This applied especially to Swazi students on special scholarship programmes which Taiwan had offered them because Eswatini remained an official diplomatic partner of Taiwan (interview with ten medical students, Kaohsiung, 25 April 2017). The university in Eswatini had neither the technical equipment nor the academic staff to teach medical sciences. I-shou University in Kaohsiung offered this subject, attracting Swazi nurses and medical students. Students completed the theoretical and lab training in Taiwan, the practical training was split between Taiwan and Eswatini, and they did an internship at a local hospital in Taiwan. But they only observed Taiwanese doctors because they were prohibited, legally and socially, from doing examinations themselves. Legally, the training for Swazi students stipulated that they would not have any hands-on training, but simply shadow Taiwanese staff to learn by observing. Socially, many Taiwanese patients refused to be examined by a black doctor or nurse. When we asked the Taiwanese administrator of the programme, we were bluntly told that "Taiwanese patients cannot accept a black person" (interview with Taiwanese administrator, Kaohsiung, 25 April 2017). After the completion of their degree, they were qualified to work as specialists in Eswatini. Some Swazi students told us that they were afraid that they could not use their specialised knowledge because the hospitals in Eswatini lacked basic equipment. Nevertheless, they were certain that they would enjoy a significant rise in status while also improving medical services in Eswatini.

Financial incentives were another motivation for African students. Study costs were considerably lower in Taiwan than in Europe or North America. Many African students came from families of modest backgrounds, some even from single-headed families. University scholarships were the most common source of funding, but there were other alternatives. A few Ugandan students came to Taiwan through the Rotary Club in Uganda, where they had met Taiwanese businessmen. These businessmen actively recommended studying in Taiwan and helped the Ugandan students with their application and logistics. In Taiwan, the Ugandans took part in Rotary Club activities and helped build up a Rotary Youth Club. One of the Ugandan students was a woman in her late twenties. She wanted to open her own private school in Uganda after her studies in Taiwan. She planned on using the teaching methods she had observed in Taiwan and her new connections with fellow Rotarians. Clearly, the number of Africans coming to Taiwan through the Rotary Club is limited. Nevertheless, many of those interviewed who were already in Taiwan eagerly joined the new Rotary Youth Club. They believed that they could benefit from this network in the future.

In rare instances, African students came to Taiwan at the invitation of a Taiwanese parent. Some connections go back to the days when Taiwan had still diplomatic missions in Africa. A Malawian girl was invited by her Taiwanese father to do a bachelor's degree. He had come to Malawi as part of an agricultural team and married her mother in the 1990s. He divorced her mother and returned to Taiwan, and the girl stayed with her Malawian mother but maintained contact with her father. In another case, connections were established through the diplomatic community in Europe. One Kenyan student had a Taiwanese father and a Kenyan mother. His parents were both diplomats and had met in Vienna. They divorced, and the student returned to Kenya with his mother. He had no contact with his father for many years, but on his eighteenth birthday, he received an invitation to Taiwan from his father. After initially declining, he came to Taiwan in 2016. In these cases, tuition and living costs were covered by their Taiwanese relatives.

Everyday Interactions Inside and Outside University

Everyday interactions between African students and their Taiwanese counterparts were, on the surface, harmonious. The African students considered the Taiwanese polite and helpful when it came to getting directions and study-related information. Unlike in the PRC and in European countries, the Taiwanese police neither harassed African students openly nor raided their homes regularly (Sautman, 1994; Li et al., 2012; Liu, 2013). Negative experiences with the Taiwanese authorities stemmed mostly from language barrier–related misunderstandings. On campus, a lack of clear communication regarding the fees and additional costs were a source of discontent. In Hualien, students had believed that their scholarship would include study fees and housing. After their arrival, they were presented with huge bills for fees and housing. Students further complained that they could apply for a fee waiver only one year after their arrival. Waivers were granted based on study results and the university's funding situation. While this is standard procedure in Taiwan, to African students it came as an unpleasant surprise putting their plans in jeopardy. One student from Gambia had to rely on his Malaysian classmate for food because he could no longer afford meals. Another student did not get the fee waiver because the university had secretly raised the performance score for eligibility.

African students in Taiwan were also confronted with stereotypes of Africa being "poor, sick, and backward" (interview with Gambian student, Hualien, 18 April 2017). Such stereotypes are not unique to Taiwan but led to disturbing incidents. In one, a student discovered the following public Facebook comment on his presence in a team photo: "Who is the monkey?" The Taiwanese commentator could not understand why the African student was upset and refused to apologise. A Swazi medical student experienced a similar incident at an official function. As she entered the room, she saw a Taiwanese child pointing at her and asking her mother in Chinese, "Mama, what kind of animal is this?" Our informant was upset not only about the question, but also about the mother's reaction. Assuming our informant could not understand the question, the mother neither reprimanded her child nor showed any embarrassment at her child's ignorance. The incident had a lasting impact and the Swazi girl never attended any public functions again. African students felt that the Taiwanese were unwilling to confront their stereotypes about Africa, let alone consider that they might learn something from their African peers. Instead, they expected African students to praise Taiwan and Taiwanese and learn from them.

Everyday interactions had a clear gendered dimension. Male African students felt that Taiwanese girls were more approachable than their male counterparts. Although many Taiwanese girls "ran away" or did not respond to greetings from our informants, some formed tentative friendships with African students. Our informants felt that girls were interested and more genuine. Still, romantic relationships between African and Taiwanese students were rare. Our male informants told us that Taiwanese boys and sometimes their parents pressured Taiwanese girls who had a relationship with an African student. Only relationships with very brave Taiwanese girls would survive this pressure in the long run (interview with Gambian student, Hualien, 18 April 2017). Our female African informants felt that Taiwanese boys were not interested in them. Taiwanese girls were friendly but often made them feel uncomfortable. They constantly commented on physical differences, treating our African informants as the exotic "other" (interview with South African student, Taipei, 25 April 2017). Still, when compared to their male African peers, African women found it easier to establish relationships with Taiwanese women. All our informants complained that their friendships with Taiwanese were often superficial. Their Taiwanese friends or work colleagues did not return greetings on campus if they were with other Taiwanese. Some of our informants were recruited to university sports teams but never invited to any private social gatherings.

In the view of African students, Taiwanese behaviour towards Africans was a mixture of racial stereotypes and a culturally constructed hierarchy of desirable nationalities. Taiwanese also believe that "the white and yellow races were opposed to darker races" (Sautman, 1994, 428). The incidents described above are extreme examples, but all our informants reported that they were treated differently due to their skin colour. Taiwanese get up and move if an African student sits next to them on the metro. Female African students complained that people touched their hair and skin. A Malawian woman was outraged when a Taiwanese woman tried to scratch her skin white. Our informants argued that such behaviour was displayed towards black people regardless of their nationality. However, they felt that the fact that they were from Africa meant additional disadvantages. Their black American and European classmates had Taiwanese girlfriends. Taiwanese seemed generally more open to learning about American and European culture. A Malawian student always introduced himself as Mike from the US to Taiwanese because he discovered that they were more relaxed and interested in him if they thought he was Afro-American. Most Africans agreed that there was an unspoken hierarchy of "desirable" international students, in which Africans were at the bottom.

A few informants had more positive experiences because they had a "Taiwanese family". It is common for universities in Taiwan to encourage local families to host foreign students during major holidays. The most successful experiences among our informants were described by a girl from Gambia who had completed her BA and MA degrees in Taiwan. She had a Taiwanese family with whom she developed close bonds over the years. They not only invited her for holidays but also for all major family events and frequently to weekend activities. She attributed this success to her own patience, overlooking their initial prejudices and patronising efforts. She persisted in convincing them that Africans were not poor and uneducated. Her Taiwanese sister even accepted an invitation to visit her in Gambia. Still, she felt that she would always be treated differently by Taiwanese no matter how well she spoke Mandarin or how well she adapted to Taiwanese practices. Other African students with Taiwanese families had looser bonds and regarded the infrequent invitations as a welcome distraction but not as a way of fostering mutual understanding and respect.

Overall, African students were in an awkward position. They expected to study and live in a "developed" country. They imagined that they would get access not only to a materially better life, but also to job opportunities. They soon realised that they could not work more than 20 hours per week. Africans in Taiwan were only accepted for low-paid and low-status jobs. They worked mostly as dishwashers in restaurants and as porters and chambermaids in hotels. Unlike in the PRC, where African students have (theoretically at least) the opportunity to secure a language teaching job, our African informants were completely barred from teaching English. Most applicants felt that they were not hired due to their skin colour. Many interviewees told us of enthusiastic phone conversations with prospective employers, only to be turned down once they met in person. Employers justified their change of heart by saying, "oh, but you are black", "oh, you are African", or "the parents and students cannot accept this". Taiwanese labour laws prohibited discrimination based on race (United States Department of State, 2017, 19), but in practice this is rarely enforced because African students have neither the legal knowledge nor the backing of Taiwanese advocacy groups.

The African students developed several strategies to deal with their exclusion from job opportunities and Taiwanese social networks. First, they focused on what they came here to do. They invested all their time in studying and spent their free time either with African/international friends or in their dorms. Similar to Chinese migrants in Africa (Driessen, 2019), they often experienced their stay in Taiwan as a suspension of "normal life". Future rewards, such as better opportunities at home or qualifications to study in North America or Europe, consoled and motivated them. Second, they set out to "change the image of Africa" by educating Taiwanese about it. To achieve this, they disseminated information about their home countries on social media or through conversations with Taiwanese. Arguably, only a few African students were fully committed to this mission. Among them, another dissemination strategy was the preparation of Africa-related topics for study assignments. Such efforts did not reach beyond the immediate class environment due to structural constraints, yet these strategies ameliorated immediate personal challenges while failing to solve underlying tensions.

Conclusion

Over the last three decades, transnationalism has become a dominant paradigm for understanding the complexities of global migration, highlighting the importance of transnational ties, the fluidity of migrants' identities, and their flexibility. While migration policies are often seen as key to explaining the origins of migration, I have shown that African migration was initially spurred by Taiwan's Africa policy, and a quest to internationalise its higher education system. For less than a decade (1998–2005), Taiwan actively recruited and supported African students. However, with more African countries establishing diplomatic relations with the PRC, Taiwan adjusted its policies. While these adjustments attest to the diminishing influence of Taiwan in Africa, they cannot conceal broader contradictions in Taiwan's Africa policies. For decades, Taiwan tried to win African support by paying for the pet projects of African heads of state (Taylor, 2002; Liu, 2009). These efforts were often short-term oriented and executed half-heartedly. Taiwan's educational cooperation with Africa could face a similar fate. Taiwan actively invited African students in the mid-2000s. However, despite needing foreign talent to make up for its demographic changes, Taiwan failed to recruit African students to attractive jobs in Taiwan. The current situation suggests that Taiwan is likely to leave the lion's share of cooperation with Africa to the PRC and to focus on Southeast Asia instead. This policy change has also affected universities' recruitment policies. University administrators told us that they had adjusted their scholarships to the "New Southbound Policy". Instead of recruiting Africans, universities are actively participating in job fairs in Southeast Asia. Scholarships and promises for later employment in Taiwan were the main incentives offered to Southeast Asian students. This might not only be rooted in foreign policy considerations. Rather, it speaks to the failure of Taiwanese leadership to see African students as assets and showcases the continued marginalisation of African talent.

State policies, historical ties, and other incentives play a crucial role in transnational migration. However, once initiated, migration often becomes self-sustaining as individual transnational networks of support and information exchange are established (Faist, 2010). African migration to Taiwan is no exception. Over time, aspiring young Africans themselves became the main driver sustaining migration flows between Africa and Taiwan. In fact, the number of African students increased after 2005 despite the loss of state support. In their everyday life, African students face many challenges. Racial discrimination, which also occurs in many other countries, is the biggest (De Haas, 2008). Taiwan, like the Global North, pays lip service to lofty principles and values while practically denying Africans access to career opportunities. Despite these challenges, all our informants recommended studying in Taiwan. They were well aware of the globalised orders of inequality that tend to place them in a disadvantaged position, regardless of their individual efforts. They did not accept the positions assigned to them. On the contrary, they made cost-benefit analyses to determine the best short-term opportunities. Taiwan provided such opportunities, as well as a ticket to future social mobility. In this sense, they appeared to be just as flexible and opportunity-seeking as other transnational migrants (Haugen, 2013; Burton, 2019).

References and Further Reading

Ahmad, Ahmad Bayiz, and Mahsood Shah. 2018. "International Students' Choice to Study in China: An Exploratory Study". *Tertiary Education and Management* 24 (4): 325–337.

Atkinson, Joel. 2014. "Aid in Taiwan's Foreign Policy: Putting Ma Ying-Jeou's Aid Reforms in Historical Perspective". *Pacific Review* 27 (3): 409–431.

Bakewell, Oliver. 2008. "'Keeping them in their place': The Ambivalent Relationship between Development and Migration in Africa". *Third World Quarterly* 29 (7): 1341–1358.

Berry, M., and B. Engels. 2018. "Global Prospects: The Asian Century?" In *The New Oxford Handbook of Economic Geography*, edited by Gordon L. Clark et al., 19–39. Oxford: Oxford University Press.

Bertoncello, Brigitte, and Sylvie Bredeloup. 2007. "The Emergence of New African Trading Posts in Hong Kong and Guangzhou". *China Perspectives* 1: 94–105.

Bischoff, Paul Henri. 2017. "African Transnationalism in China: At the Interface of Local, Transnational, Bilateral and Multilateral Responses". *Journal of Asian and African Studies* 52 (7): 897–914.

Bodomo, Adams. 2010. "The African Trading Community in Guangzhou: An Emerging Bridge for Africa-China Relations". *The China Quarterly* 203: 693–707.

Bredeloup, Sylvie. 2012. "African Trading Post in Guangzhou: Emergent or Recurrent Commercial Form?" *African Diaspora* 5: 27–50.

Burgess, Lisa Maria. 2016. "Conversations with African Students in China". *Transition* 119: 80–91.

Burton, Eric. 2019. "Navigating Global Socialism: Tanzanian Students in and beyond East Germany". *Cold War History* 19 (1): 63–83.

Carling, Jørgen. 2007. "Migration Control and Migrant Fatalities at the Spanish-African Borders". *International Migration Review* 41 (2): 316–343.

Castillo, Roberto. 2014. "Feeling at Home in the 'Chocolate City': An Exploration of Place-Making Practices and Structures of Belonging amongst Africans in Guangzhou". *Inter-Asia Cultural Studies* 15 (2): 235–257.

Chan, Gerald. 2011. "Taiwan as an Emerging Foreign Aid Donor: Developments, Problems, and Prospects". *Pacific Affairs* 70 (1): 37–56.

Charlier, Phillip. 2009. "Expat Chat: Being Black in Taiwan", 26 December. http://www.thewildeast.net/2009/12/expat-chat-being-black-in-taiwan [accessed 2 August 2019].

Chen, Dorothy I-ru, and William Yat Wai Lo. 2013. "Internationalization or Commodification? A Case Study of Internationalization Practices in Taiwan's Higher Education". *Asia Pacific Education Review* 14 (1): 33–41.

Cheng, Isabella, and Lara Momesso. 2017. "Look, the World Is Watching How We Treat Migrants! The Making of the Anti-Trafficking Legislation during the Ma Administration". *Journal of Current Chinese Affairs* 46 (1): 61–99.

Cissé, Daouda. 2013. "South-South Migration and Sino-African Small Traders: A Comparative Study of Chinese in Senegal and Africans in China". *African Review of Economics and Finance* 5 (1): 17–28.

Collins, Francis Leo, and Sarah Jane Lipura. 2019. "Towards an Integrative Understanding of Contemporary Educational Mobilities: A Critical Agenda for International Student Mobilities Research". *Globalisation, Societies and Education* 18 (3): 343–359.

De Aeth, Duncan. 2019. "Foreign Students in Taiwan 10% of Total University and College Students in 2018", *Taiwan News*, 3 February. https://www.taiwannews.com.tw/en/news/3631340 [accessed 29 July 2019].

De Haas, Hein. 2008. "The Myth of Invasion: The Inconvenient Realities of African Migration to Europe". *Third World Quarterly* 29 (7): 1305–1322.

——. 2011. "The Determinations of International Migration: Conceptualising Policy, Origin and Destination Effects." *IOM Working Papers* 32: 1–35.

Driessen, Miriam. 2019. *Tales of Hope, Tastes of Bitterness: Chinese Road Builders in Ethiopia*. Hong Kong: Hong Kong University Press.

Embassy of the Republic of China (Taiwan) in the Kingdom of Eswatini, 2013. "Swazis Flock Taiwan Embassy for Scholarships", *Embassy News*, 15 March. https://www.taiwanembassy.org/sz_en/post/960.html [accessed 21 July 2022].

Everington, Keoni. 2017. "Top 10 Incentives Included in New Foreign Talent Act", *Taiwan News*, 1 November. https://www.taiwannews.com.tw/en/news/3287461 [accessed 30 July 2019].

——. 2019. "413 Vietnamese, Indonesian Illegal Workers Arrested in Taiwan", *Taiwan News*, 17 June. https://www.taiwannews.com.tw/en/news/3725740 [accessed 2 August 2019].

Faist, Thomas. 2010. "Towards Transnational Studies: World Theories, Transnationalisation and Changing Institutions". *Journal of Ethnic and Migration Studies* 36 (10): 1665–1687.

Foundation for International Cooperation in Higher Education of Taiwan (FICHET). 2017. "Study in Taiwan: Featured Universities 2017–2018". Taipei.

Gargano, Terra. 2009. "(Re)conceptualizing International Student Mobility". *Journal of Studies in International Education* 13 (3): 331–346.

Glick-Schiller, Nina, Linda Basch, and Cristina Szanton Blanc. 1994. "From Immigrant to Transmigrant: Theorizing Transnational Migration". *Anthropological Quarterly* 68 (1): 48–63.

Haugen, Heidi Østbø. 2013. "China's Recruitment of African University Students: Policy Efficacy and Unintended Outcomes". *Globalisation, Societies and Education* 11 (3): 315–334.

Hsiao-Pong, Philip Liu. 2009. "Planting Rice on the Roof of the UN Building: Analysing Taiwan's 'Chinese' Techniques in Africa, 1961–Present". *The China Quarterly* 198: 381–400.

Huang, Shu Min, and Shao Hua Liu. 2016. "Discrimination and Incorporation of Taiwanese Indigenous Austronesian Peoples". *Asian Ethnicity* 17 (2): 294–312.

International Cooperation and Development Fund (ICDF). 2015. "International Training and Education". https://www.icdf.org.tw/ct.asp?xItem=5269&CtNode=30489&mp=2 [accessed 21 July 2019].

——. 2019. "International Higher Education Scholarship Program", https://www.icdf.org.tw/ct.asp?xItem=12505&CtNode=30316&mp=2 [accessed 21 July 2019].

Khan Mohammad, Guive. 2014. "The Chinese Presence in Burkina Faso: A Sino-African Cooperation from Below". *Journal of Current Chinese Affairs* 43 (1): 71–101.

King, Russell, and Parvati Raghuram. 2013. "International Student Migration: Mapping the Field and New Research Agendas". *Population, Space and Place* 19 (2): 127–137.

Lan, Pei-Chia. 2006. *Global Cinderellas: Migrant Domestics and Newly Rich Employers in Taiwan*. Durham, NC: Duke University Press.

Lan, Shanshan. 2014. "State Regulation of Undocumented African Migrants in China: A Multi-Scalar Analysis". *Journal of Asian and African Studies* 50 (3): 1–16.

Lee, Wei-chin. 1993. "Taiwan's Foreign Aid Policy." *Asian Affairs: An American Review* 20 (1): 43–62.

Li, Anshan. 2005. "African Studies in China in the Twentieth Century: A Historiographical Survey". *African Studies Review* 48 (1): 59–87.

Li, Zhigang, Michal Lyons, and Alison Brown. 2012. "China's 'Chocolate City': An Ethnic Enclave in a Changing Landscape". *African Diaspora* 5: 51–72.

Liang, Kelly, and Phillippe Le Billion. 2018. "African Migrants in China: Space, Race and Embodied Encounters in Guangzhou, China". *Social and Cultural Geography* 21 (5): 602–628.

Liang, Li Fang. 2011. "The Making of an 'Ideal' Live-in Migrant Care Worker: Recruiting, Training, Matching and Disciplining". *Ethnic and Racial Studies* 34 (11): 1815–1834.

Lipinsky, Astrid. 2015. *Immigration Societies: Taiwan and Beyond*. Münster: Lit Verlag.

Liu, Jennifer A. 2012. "Aboriginal Fractions: Enumerating Identity in Taiwan". *Medical Anthropology: Cross Cultural Studies in Health and Illness* 31 (4): 329–346.

Liu, Phillip. 2013. "Petty Annoyances? Revisiting John Emmanuel Hevi's *An African Student in China* after 50 Years." *China: An International Journal* 11 (1): 131–145.

Lyons, Michal, Alison Brown, and Zhigang Li. 2012. "In the Dragon's Den: African Traders in Guangzhou". *Journal of Ethnic and Migration Studies* 38 (5): 869–888.

Ma, Enyu. 2012. "Yiwu Mode and Sino-African Relations." *Journal of Cambridge Studies* 7 (3): 93–108.

Mao-Kau, Michael Ying. 2003. "Opportunities and Challenges: Taiwan's Diplomacy in the Globalization Era". *Journal of Third World Studies* 20 (1): 19–25.

Mathews, Gordon, Linessa Dan Lin, and Yang Yang. 2017. *The World in Guangzhou: Africans and other Foreigners in South China's Global Market Place*. Chicago: University of Chicago Press.

Mathews, Gordon, and Yang Yang. 2012. "How Africans Pursue Low-End Globalization in Hong Kong and Mainland China". *Journal of Current Chinese Affairs* 41 (2): 95–120.

Ministry of Education Republic of China Taiwan (MOE). 2006. "Students from Latin America Increase Every Year". Taipei.

——. 2016. "The Way to Be Outstanding: Technical and Vocational Education in Taiwan". Taipei.

——. 2017. "International Comparison of Educational Statistical Indicators". Taipei.

——. 2018. "Statistical Summaries: Non-Citizens in Universities, Colleges and Junior Colleges", 2 November. https://english.moe.gov.tw/cp-26-18880-df66b-1.html [accessed 31 May 2019].

Ministry of Foreign Affairs Republic of China Taiwan (MOFA). 2007. "Taiwan-African Summit Concluded Successfully", News and Events, 9 September. https://www.mofa.gov.tw/en/PrintContent.aspx?n=1EADDCFD4C6EC567&t=FB01D469347C76A7 [accessed 21 July 2019].

——. 2012. "About Taiwan Fellowships and Scholarships". http://tafs.mofa.gov.tw/Contents.aspx?loc=en [accessed 1 July 2019].

——. 2017. Report by Minister of Foreign Affairs of the Republic of China (Taiwan) at the Foreign Affairs and National Defense Committee of the Legislative Yuan. MOFA-6BD73391.

Ministry of Interior National Immigration Agency Republic of China Taiwan. 2019. "Foreign Residents by Nationality", 26 June. https://www.immigration.gov.tw/5475/5478/141478/141380/189027 [accessed 2 August 2019].

Ministry of Labour Republic of China Taiwan (MoL). 2018. "Foreign Workers for Special Professions or Technical Assignments by Sex and Categories of Work". http://statdb.mol.gov.tw/html/mon/c12100.html [accessed 31 July 2019].

——. 2019. "Foreign Workers for Special Professions or Technical Assignments by Permit Authority Agency and Nationality". http://statdb.mol.gov.tw/html/mon/c12120.htm [accessed 31 July 2019].

Mok, Ka Ho, and Ying Chan. 2008. "International Benchmarking with the Best Universities: Policy and Practice in Mainland China and Taiwan". *Higher Education Policy* 21 (4): 469–486.

National Bureau of Statistics Republic of China Taiwan (NBS). 2019. "Education, science and technology, culture and mass communication". https://eng.stat.gov.tw/ct.asp?xItem=41873&ctNode=6343&mp=5 [accessed 1 July 2019].

National Chengchi University. 2013. "Degree Students: Scholarships". http://oic.nccu.edu.tw/files/11-1000-280.php [accessed 21 July 2019].

National Immigration Agency Republic of China Taiwan. 2018. "Dream Land for High-End Talents Four-in-One Employment Gold Card." Taipei.

Pelican, Michaela, and Li Dong. 2017. "Baohan Street: An African Community in Guangzhou". In *Global Africa: Into the Twenty-First Century*, edited by Dorothy Hodgson and Judith Byfield, 193–201. Oakland: University of California Press.

Raghuram, Parvati. 2013. "Theorising the Spaces of Student Migration". *Population, Space and Place* 19 (2): 138–154.

Rawnsley, Gary. 2012. "Approaches to Soft Power and Public Diplomacy in China and Taiwan". *Journal of International Communication* 18 (2): 121–135.

Rich, Timothy S, and Vasabjit Banerjee. 2015. "Running out of Time? The Evolution of Taiwan's Relations in Africa". *Journal of Current Chinese Affairs* 44 (1): 141–161.

Röschenthaler, Ute. 2017. "In Constant Search for Money to Survive: African Youths in Malaysia". In *African-Asian Encounters: New Cooperation and New Dependencies*, edited by Arndt Graf and Azirah Hashim, 17–46. Amsterdam: Amsterdam University Press.

Sautman, Barry. 1994. "Anti-Black Racism in Post-Mao China". *The China Quarterly* 138: 413–437.

Small, Stephen. 2018. "Theorising Visibility and Vulnerability in Black Europe and the African Diaspora". *Ethnic and Racial Studies* 6: 1182–1197.

Taylor, Ian. 2002. "Taiwan's Foreign Policy and Africa: The Limitations of Dollar Diplomacy". *Journal of Contemporary China* 11 (30): 125–140.

Tubilewicz, Czeslaw. 2016. "State Transformation and the Domestic Politics of Foreign Aid in Taiwan". *The Pacific Review* 29 (1): 45–66.

UNESCO. 2018. Number and Rates of International Students (Inbound and Outbound). http://data.uis.unesco.org/Index.aspx?DataSetCode=EDULIT_DS [accessed 21 January 2019].

United States Department of State. 2017. "Country Reports on Human Rights Practices for 2017". https://www.state.gov/reports/2017-country-reports-on-human-rights-practices/taiwan/ [accessed 30 July 2019].

Van Bekhoven, Jeroen. 2016. "Identity Crisis: Taiwan's Laws and Regulations on the Status of Indigenous Peoples". *Asia Pacific Law Review* 24 (2): 202–232.

Wang, Gungwu, 1993. "Greater China and the Chinese Overseas." *The China Quarterly* 136: 926–948.

Wang, Hongying, and Yeh-Chung Lu. 2008. "The Conception of Soft Power and its Policy Implications: A Comparative Study of China and Taiwan". *Journal of Contemporary China* 17 (56): 425–447.

Wang, Li-jung. 2004. "Multiculturalism in Taiwan". *International Journal of Cultural Policy* 10 (3): 301–318.

Wu, Meiyao. 2017. "Moral Education and the Aboriginal Peoples of Taiwan: From Sino-Centrism to the Ethnic of Multiculturalism". *Journal of Moral Education* 46 (1): 69–78.

Zhong, Yang. 2016. "Explaining National Identity Shift in Taiwan". *Journal of Contemporary China* 25 (99): 336–352.

Zhou, Min, Tao Xu, and Shabnam Shenasi. 2016. "Entrepreneurship and Interracial Dynamics: A Case Study of Self-employed Africans and Chinese in Guangzhou, China". *Journal of Ethnic and Racial Studies* 39: 1566–1586.

14

Transnationalism and Medical Cooperation in Family Planning in East Asia (1950s–1970s)

Aya Homei

Introduction

It has become evident in the global response to the Covid-19 pandemic that transnational cooperation and competition are an indispensable aspect of medicine and healthcare today. Medicine had witnessed a "transnational turn" by the early twentieth century, as the institutionalised effort to promote health internationally materialised with the establishment of the League of Nations Health Organisation (LNHO) after the First World War. After the Second World War, the effort was consolidated with the founding of the World Health Organization (WHO) (Packard, 2016).

Family planning constituted an integral part of the endeavour to promote health and welfare worldwide (Connelly, 2008). However, the integration of family planning into global health came only in the 1960s (Packard, 2016, 181–229). Moreover, family planning had a slightly different trajectory from other global health initiatives. One of the most salient features of the promotion of family planning was the centrality of the world area as a unit of assessment and a rhetorical register. In population studies that justified family planning programmes in global health, world regions, such as East or Southeast Asia, which were consolidated in the middle of the twentieth century in the context of Cold War international politics (Szanton, 2004), were presented as a category to show the correlation between population trends and the level of socio-economic attainment, and to determine whether a country/society within the region needed an intervention with family planning to modify the demographic pattern and to stimulate the country's economy and social development (Greenhalgh 1996; Szreter 1993). Through this process, world regions such as Asia, Latin America, and Africa came to constitute a focal point in the transnational movement to spread the practice of family planning. In the middle of the twentieth century, Asia was *the* target of transnational family planning advocacy. Asia's population during this period was one of the fastest growing in the world. Observing this demographic trend in relation to the growing evidence of hunger, poverty, and underdevelopment that they saw prevailed in the region (Cullather, 2010), demographers and family planning activists endorsed birth control. They claimed birth control was an effective means with which to solve the population problems, to trigger socio-economic development, and/or to promote the health and welfare of the people in those Asian countries labelled "underdeveloped" (Sharpless, 1997). In parallel, governmental, non-governmental, and other philanthropic organisations offered support to implement family planning initiatives in the region (Sharpless, 1997). Initially, much of the support originated from outside of Asia, most conspicuously from the US (Sharpless, 1995; Donaldson 1990). However, from the 1970s, initiatives emerged from within the region, fostering inter-Asian medical cooperation.

This chapter examines the Asian Parasite Control Organization (APCO) as an example of the organisations based in East Asia that promoted such inter-Asian medical cooperation. The APCO was a regional non-governmental organisation established in 1974 by the Japanese health activist Kunii Chōjirō with fellow activists, health officials, and doctors from Japan, Taiwan, and South Korea. Despite the organisation's name, the APCO was a portal through which Kunii promoted the family planning initiative he devised called the Integration Project (IP). The IP integrated family planning with parasite control (and nutrition advice in later years). The "target" countries of the APCO were initially South Korea, Taiwan, Indonesia, Thailand, and the Philippines, but over time the list expanded to include South Asian countries such as Sri Lanka and countries in Latin America (Mexico, Colombia, and Brazil). With the case of APCO, the chapter analyses the transnationalism that was manifested in the inter-Asian medical cooperation in the middle of the twentieth century.

Over the past decade or so, historians of science and medicine have been adopting the "transnational" as a lens through which to reappraise the post-war science, technology, and medicine developed through international diplomacy (Krige, 2019; Turchetti et al, 2012; Secord, 2004). They pointed out the significance of the Cold War world order as a factor that shaped the intersection of medico-scientific activities at the national and international levels (Oreskes and Krige, 2014). Drawing from these works, this chapter shows that the Cold War was as a critical background factor also for the transnational medical cooperation in family planning developed under the aegis of the APCO (Homei and Huang, 2016). At the same time, the chapter also elaborates on two additional elements that played a pivotal role in the inter-Asian medical exchange. One such element was the specific understanding of Asia and its recent past involved. The chapter shows that the APCO's membership, mission, and activities were predicated on the specific articulation of the common "Asian" heritage and the legacy of Japanese colonialism, which were formed through the geopolitical reconfiguration of the region after the demise of the Japanese empire in 1945 (Homei and DiMoia, 2020). The other element was the discourse of universalism on which Cold War international health and overseas development assistance were premised (Somsen, 2008). This chapter describes how APCO in the 1980s began to insist on the universal applicability of the IP as a strategy to internationalise the health programme, and this marginalised the emphasis on the Asian identity that characterised APCO at its inception.

The case study examined in this chapter argues that the "transnationalism" that shaped the inter-Asian medical cooperation in East Asia in the middle of the twentieth century had multiple dimensions and its meanings shifted over the period. By unravelling complex ways in which transnationalism was enacted in the characterisation of regional medical cooperation, the chapter argues that transnationalism magnified and reduced the importance of East Asia depending on the historical and political contexts. In arguing this way, the chapter proposes that medicine and healthcare is a useful lens through which to appreciate the influence of transnationalism on relations between individuals and states in East Asia.

Family Planning, Cold War, and Transnational Exchanges in East Asia, 1950s–1960s

Fertility control by artificial means, such as induced abortion, contraception, and sterilisation, became a subject of intense debate across East Asia among activists, doctors, feminists, politicians, intellectuals, and other social commentators from the late 1910s due to its ramifications for highly contested issues such as the problems of life, race, and nationhood (David, 2018; Kim, 2008; Tipton, 1997). In addition, from the late 1940s onwards, "family planning" emerged as a policy item in various East Asian countries as a solution to the interlinked demographic, economic, and social problems. In Japan, the repatriation of civilians and soldiers after the end of the Japanese empire and the "baby boom" in the context of the Allied Occupation (1945–1952) catalysed a discourse of "overpopulation" and "racial crisis" and the subsequent policy proposal in the 1950s to adopt "family planning" (家族計画; Jp. *kazoku keikaku*) as a solution to these population problems (Homei, 2016a; Tama, 2016; 2006; Ogino, 2008b; 2008a; Norgren, 2001; Matsubara, 2000). In the People's

Republic of China (PRC), the Chinese Communist Party (CCP) considered taking up birth control as part of state planning after the first population census conducted in 1953 revealed that China's population had reached 600 million (Kohama, 2020, 54; Greenhalgh, 2008; White, 2006, 61–70; Greenhalgh and Winckler, 2005, 93–116). In July 1954, the Ministry of Health submitted to the State Planning Commission the first outline plan for *jihua shengyu* (计划生育), literally "birth planning", as a policy tightly linked to the country's economic planning that would be implemented in cities in the first instance. Thereafter, with the exception of the periods of the Great Leap Forward and Cultural Revolution, the CCP promoted family planning under the name *jihua shengyu*. Finally, in Taiwan and South Korea, "family planning"—*jiating jihua* (家庭計畫) in Taiwan and *kajok kyehoek* (가족 계획) in South Korea—were implemented in the 1960s as a health policy integral to socio-economic development (Lin, 2020; Huang, 2016; Kuo, 2008; 2002; DiMoia, 2008).

These family planning programmes in East Asia represented a transnational movement aiming to curb the world population growth by fertility control, which, from around the mid-1960s, was integrated into international health and overseas development aids (Packard, 2016, 181–229; Connelly, 2008, 237–326). The transnational population control movement had roots in the early twentieth century, maintaining links to the expanding communities of eugenics, international birth control advocacy, colonial science, and missionary medicine (Merchant, 2017; Connelly, 2008). After the Second World War, activities in these domains became consolidated with the foundation of transnational, non-governmental organisations dedicated to family planning and/or population issues, such as the Population Council (PC) and the International Planned Parenthood Federation (IPPF) (Merchant, 2017, 92–98; Claeys, 2010; Donaldson, 1990) through voluntary family planning, to a comprehensive approach to sexual and reproductive health and rights (SRHR). From the mid-1960s, international organisations, hitherto hesitant to endorse family planning due mainly to ideological and religious reasons, joined forces when the US government under President Lyndon Johnson decided to fund population programmes as part of its overseas development aid (Donaldson, 1990, 43). Following the US decision, in 1969, the United Nations created the United Nations Fund for Population Activities (UNFPA). In tandem, in 1967, the World Bank began to fund population programmes. Along with non-governmental bodies, these international organisations encouraged the integration of family planning into development aids and health projects.

For the family planning programmes developed under the aegis of the transnational population control movement, the Cold War was a critical factor (Sharpless, 1997; 1995; Donaldson, 1990). Amidst the rising tensions between the USA and USSR, the idea of "overpopulation" as a threat to security spread widely in the Western Bloc. Specifically, it was argued that starvation and poverty inflicted by "population pressure" would first lead to social disorders and then create space for communist aggression (Sharpless, 1995, 85). Under the circumstances, family planning came to be seen as not only addressing the issue of global population growth, but also presenting the "free-world" alliance a tool for the containment of communism. As many family planning programmes endorsed by the transnational movement during this period had developed in nonaligned countries, contemporaries, such as noted American demographer Kingsley Davies, interpreted these programmes as the free world's endeavour to win the trust of nonaligned nations (Davis, 1956).

In East Asia, a core target region of the transnational population control movement, the movement fostered transnational exchanges of population researchers, family planning advocates, and bureaucrats between the US and its "free world" allies in the region, especially South Korea and Taiwan. In Taiwan, Colonel Hubert G. Schenck, former Chief of Natural Resources Section of the General Headquarters of the Supreme Commander for the Allied Powers in Japan and Chief of US Economic Cooperation Administration in Taiwan, was among the first who considered tackling Taiwan's overpopulation issues with US aid. In the 1950s, Schenck's plan led to studies of population growth and family systems in Taiwan as a prelude to implementing a family planning programme in the country. These studies were enabled by the financial support of the Rockefeller Foundation, organised by the Sino-US Joint Commission of Rural Reconstruction (JCRR), and executed by Taiwanese technocrats and the demographic team at the Princeton University Office of Population Studies led by Frank W. Notestein (Huang, 2016, 381–383). In the 1960s, the Ford Foundation indirectly helped the US-Taiwan collaboration scheme to continue, by funding the University of Minnesota Population Studies Center (PSC) (Lin, 2020). The founder of the PSC, Ronald Freedman, led the service-cum-survey family planning scheme organised by the JCRR in Taichung, which left a lasting impact on the government-led family planning initiative when it was implemented from 1964 (Lin, 2020, 829–832; Huang, 2016, 384).

Likewise, in South Korea, the state family planning programme of the 1960s under President Park Chung-hee was built on interactions across the Pacific involving American and South Korean researchers. For instance, the Koyang study led by Dr Yang Jae-mo at Yongsei University, which served as the critical foundation for mobilising national family planning campaign like the Taichung programme in Taiwan, involved the consultancy of Ronald Freedman and the PSC team (DiMoia, 2014, 136–140; 2008, 364–365). In addition, the PC facilitated the transnational transfer of contraceptives into

South Korea, most notably, the Lippes Loop and Marguiles intrauterine devices, whose development the PC had been funding (Takeshita, 2011; DiMoia, 2008, 371–373). Similar to Taiwan, these transnational exchanges undergirded the state family planning initiative and directly shaped people's reproductive practices in South Korea in the 1960s (Lin, 2020, 832–837; Kuo, 2008, 339–345; DiMoia, 2008).

In contrast, the PRC, outside of the "free world" network, was largely untouched by the influence of the kind of transnational exchanges witnessed in Taiwan and South Korea. Consequently, in the 1950s and 1960s, the PRC developed its family planning programme on its own, focusing on the role of fertility regulation in the planned economy (Kohama, 2020, 55–56; Mellors, 2019; White, 2006, 32–41; Greenhalgh and Winckler, 2005, 62–74). In the early 1960s, having witnessed the sudden rise in fertility rates from 1962, which was compounded by the food shortage that began during the period of the Great Leap Forward, the CCP strengthened the family planning policy, with the Central Committee issuing the directive entitled "On Enthusiastically Promoting Planned Births" on 28 December 1962 (White, 2006, 48; Greenhalgh and Winckler, 2005, 74–80). The family planning work was compromised during the early years of the Cultural Revolution, with the comeback of the Maoist ideology that prioritised economic production over birth limitation as a population measure. But, from the early 1970s, the birth planning work intensified, as Zhou Enlai stressed the importance of planned birth in preparation for the Fourth Five-Year Plan (1971–1975). Due to Cold War politics, in the PRC the state family planning programme acquired different qualities from those developed in the "free world" countries in East Asia.

In the 1950s and 1960s, governments in East Asian countries adopted family planning as a domestic policy to curb their expanding populations. This move within East Asia coincided with the rising transnational effort to contain the world population growth via fertility control. As Asia's rapidly growing population was *the* focal point of the transnational population control movement, participants in the movement actively engaged with the state family planning programmes organised in the East Asian countries. However, in the context in which the US agenda in the Cold War shaped the transnational movement, the "transnational" that influenced family planning in East Asia chiefly referred to the exchanges between American demographers, family planning activists, and officials and their colleagues in the region's "free world" allies, most prominently Taiwan and South Korea. Family planning in the PRC developed in tandem with, but divergent from, the US-centred Cold War transnational family planning network forming in the region.

In the 1970s, in addition to the US-centric transnational collaboration, a new layer of transnationalism pivoted the family planning in East Asia. As the next section shows, it was based on inter-Asian exchanges predicated on the specific articulation of the legacy of Japanese colonialism and of the shared "Asian" heritage.

The Legacy of Japanese Colonialism and Asia's Shared Heritage: The Asian Parasite Control Organization and the Integration Project

From around the late 1960s, a new discourse emerged in the international debate on health and population (Packard, 2016, 227–248). Participants of the debate in the WHO, for instance, shifted their attention away from the earlier mass disease eradication campaign based on the principle of technological fixes through health interventions and towards building capacities for delivering comprehensive basic health services. In tandem, there was a surge in criticism of the transnational population control movement, that the family planning programme endorsed by the movement was neglecting the welfare of recipients. The criticism ultimately led to increased efforts to integrate family planning into primary healthcare (Packard, 2016, 215–225; Connelly, 2008, 309–339).

Following the trend, in East Asia, too, both non-governmental and governmental organisations made attempts to merge family planning with primary healthcare in an overseas development aid maternal and child health programme. One outcome of this endeavour was the non-governmental Asian Parasite Control Organization (APCO). Founded in 1974, the APCO advocated the Integration Project (IP), a health-cum-development programme that integrated family planning into a parasite control campaign, which was implemented in coordination with the national government and local grassroots activists.

The APCO was a fruit of the campaigns deployed by the Japanese health and family planning activist Kunii Chōjirō (1916–1996). Since the late 1940s, Kunii had been successfully running grassroots parasite eradication programmes, and then family planning campaigns within Japan (Kunii, 1977). However, in the 1960s, he shifted his activism from the domestic to the international sphere, in part due to the declining demand for his campaigns within Japan (Obayashi, 2006, 186–187). With the support of politicians, businesspeople, family planning activists, and medical researchers, in April 1968, Kunii launched the Japanese Organization for International Cooperation in Family Planning (JOICFP), a Japan-based non-governmental organisation dedicated to family planning and maternal and child health in developing countries overseas which worked closely with the Japanese government's overseas development aid organisation, the Japan International Cooperation Agency (Kunii, 1988). After the JOICFP's launch, Kunii conceived the idea of the IP, and embarked on establishing a regional organisation working closely with the JOICFP to promote the IP. Consequently, the APCO was launched in February 1974, at its inaugural meeting held in Tokyo.

The APCO was built on the aforementioned Cold War transnational population/family planning network formed in East Asia in the 1950s and 1960s (Homei, 2016b). For this reason, the founding members comprised activists, medical experts, and health officials from the region's US allies, namely, Japan, South Korea, and Taiwan. Similarly, in its early years, participants in APCO meetings were also experts and health officials from other "free world" or non-aligned countries, namely, Indonesia, Thailand, and the Philippines (Kunii, 1991, 85–106). In addition, Kunii maximised his connections with the UNFPA and IPPF, which, as mentioned above, played a pivotal role in the US-centric transnational population control movement. Finally, Kunii invited L. S. Sohdy to the inaugural meeting as a guest of honour (Nihon Kiseichū Yobōkai APCO Kaigi Jimukyoku, 1974). Sohdy was the Secretary of the Inter-Governmental Coordinating Committee, Southeast Asia Regional Cooperation in Family and Population Planning (IGCC), and collaborated closely with the IPPF and UNFPA ("Tōnan Ajia Kazoku Jinkō Keikaku Seifukan Iin IGCC", 1974). The PRC, which was outside of the US-centric Cold War clique in East Asia, was excluded from the APCO. The region's family planning communities at the domestic, regional, and transnational levels, informed directly by the US exigencies in the Cold War, were the foundation of the APCO.

Significantly, in addition to the Cold War, the inter-Asian transnational network, predicated on a specific portrayal of Asia's shared tradition and past, also shaped the APCO's profile in its early days. First, the connections between Japan, Taiwan, and South Korea that Kunii mobilised for the founding of the APCO drew on the network originally forged during the period of Japanese colonialism (Homei and DiMoia, 2020; Nihon Kiseichū Yobōkai APCO Kaigi Jimukyoku, 1974; 1976). For instance, Kunii used the bilateral medical cooperation in parasite eradication between the Republic of Korea and Japan as a springboard to develop the APCO, and this cooperation involved contact between the South Korean Soh Jin-tak (1921–2016, Yonsei University Professor, and Vice President of the Korean Association of Parasite Eradication) and his Japanese colleagues Hasegawa Shūji (Gunma University) and Sasa Manabu (University of Tokyo), whom Soh knew already during the period of Japanese colonial rule in Korea (Kunii, 2001, 63).

Second, APCO participants stressed Asian identity when characterising the APCO's profile, mission, and programme. For example, the APCO report produced after the inaugural meeting pointed out that "parasite infection" was a "serious public health issue in various Asian countries" and invited "all Asian countries to join in the APCO" (Nihon Kiseichū Yobōkai APCO Kaigi Jimukyoku, 1974, 5). The report also transcribed the speech delivered by the President of the Japan Medical Association Takemi Tarō, who stressed that "it is essential that Asian countries collaborate in studying and combating parasite diseases to promote health" (Nihon Kiseichū Yobōkai APCO Kaigi Jimukyoku, 1974, 8). Finally, the report also recorded Sohdy's speech at the meeting, which described the meeting as "of great significance in that it marked the first step in the fight against human suffering and illness in Asia" (Nihon Kiseichū Yobōkai APCO Kaigi Jimukyoku, 1974, 9).

Furthermore, when assessing the IP pilot project launched in Indonesia in 1976, Kunii suggested the Indonesian custom of mutual aid called *gotong-royong* was a critical factor behind the project's potential for success. Kunii then compared *gotong-royong* to the social organisation in Japan that became the basis for the Japan Agricultural Cooperatives. He also likened *gotong-royong* to the community organisation supporting the South Korean Saemaul Undong, the rural life-improvement programme that the APCO used to deploy the South Korean IP pilot programme. Based on these, Kunii concluded that "these organizations [encouraging] solidarity among the residents are a character of rural community which is very Asian", and "defending, expanding and encouraging such a community organization is key to the success of the Integration Program [*sic*]" (Homei and DiMoia, 2020; Kunii, 1978, 28–29).

As such, in the early years of the APCO's existence, the rhetoric of Asia's shared colonial past, suffering, and customs formed the basis of the inter-Asian medical collaboration it developed. However, as the US agenda in the Cold War still informed the collaboration, the parameter of "Asia" as a register that constituted the APCO largely excluded the PRC and other communist countries in East Asia. However, from the late 1970s, as the region's geopolitics changed and as the APCO expanded its reach beyond Asia, it became increasingly untenable for the APCO to stress Asia's shared heritage. It was at this point that the PRC joined the APCO and the rhetoric of Asia that buttressed the APCO was subsumed by a discourse that emphasised health as a universal value.

"Applicable experiences": Semantics of Universalism

During the 1970s, there were significant changes in the Cold War geopolitics that affected the deployment of the transnational population control movement in East Asia. A significant trigger was the passing of the United Nations General Assembly Resolution 2758 on 25 October 1971, which shifted the Chinese representative to the United Nations from the Republic of China (Taiwan) to the PRC. Thereafter, the PRC and international family planning/population organisations actively forged links (Yang, 2004, 213–216; Peng, 1997, 1123–1126). The PRC began sending representatives to the United Nations Population Commission and had a representative at the World Population Conference organised by the United Nations in Bucharest on 19–30 August 1974 (Yang, 2004, 214; Peng, 1997, 1123–1124). In turn, on 1–26 April 1972, an IPPF delegate made a mission tour in the PRC, which was enabled by the invitation of the Chinese Medical Association (Ma, 1985, 64). In April 1979, a UNFPA delegate visited the PRC to propose a collaboration on population matters. The UNFPA visit led to the signing of a Memorandum of Understanding between the PRC State Council Population Small Group and UNFPA in May, in which they agreed that the UNFPA would grant US$50 million to provide provinces, cities, and autonomous regions with 16 items to be used for family planning promotion (Shi, 1988, 179–181).

This last arrangement with the UNFPA paved the way for the PRC's entry into the APCO, by giving it opportunities to establish links with the JOICPF, the APCO's institutional base in Japan. Shortly after the PRC and UNFPA signed the aforementioned Memorandum of Understanding, in June 1980, Rafael M. Salas, the Executive Director and Undersecretary General of the UNFPA, urged the Japanese government to implement bilateral cooperation in family planning with the PRC (Kokusai kyōryoku jigyōdan, 1982, 1). This led to the signing of the Memorandum on 12 September 1980, in Tokyo, between the JOICFP and the Chinese Family Planning Association (CFPA), for cooperation in family planning ("Nicchū Kazoku Keikaku Kyōryoku Ni Kansuru Kaidan Oboegaki Ni Chōin—Kazoku Keikaku Bunya Niokeru Sōgo Kōryū Fukamaru", 1980). In the early 1980s, the scope of the cooperation expanded to include promotion of the IP. In 1983, the CFPA and JOICFP signed another Memorandum, this time for the implementation of the IP in the PRC, after the Tripartite Seminar on Family Planning involving the two organisations and the IPPF (Kunii, 1994, 5). After that, the PRC joined the APCO.

The shift in the APCO's membership during this period coincided with the changing profile of the recipient countries of APCO's services. As mentioned above, countries in East and Southeast Asia were the main recipients of the IP in the early days. However, from the late 1970s, the APCO's reach of influence expanded outside of Asia, to Latin America, specifically in Colombia, Mexico, and Brazil. In the 1980s, the APCO implemented the IP in the African countries Tanzania and Zambia, and in the Oceanian countries of Vanuatu, Fiji, and Tonga, in addition to Bhutan and Vietnam. By the end of the 1980s, the APCO had developed into a major player in the domains of international health and overseas development assistance worldwide, thriving through collaboration with the crucial inter- and transnational population/family planning organisations of the IPPF and UNFPA.

Through this process of change, the narrative of Asia that was so central to the characterisation of the APCO was gradually displaced by a discourse that stressed the universal applicability of the IP. The APCO meeting held in Tokyo on 4–11 December 1985, which reviewed the organisation's activities in its first decade, characterised the IP implementation processes as "applicable experiences" (The Asian Parasite Control Organization et al., 1985). The meeting stressed the compatibility of the IP with the current trend in global health endorsing "Primary Health Care" (The Asian Parasite Control Organization et al., 1985, 26), and that in socio-economic development, emphasising the necessity of a "more comprehensive conceptualization" that "take[s] into account the various socio-economic and demographic interactions in the formulation of a more comprehensive integrated population-development policies" (The Asian Parasite Control Organization et al., 1985, 3). In this context, the "experiences" with the IP in various Asian countries were documented in parallel, as if to offer participants of the meeting sample materials through which to consider general issues associated with the IP, such as the validity of its modus operandi, the cost of delivering the programme, and the organisation of healthcare professionals on the local level, issues which they believed would crop up if the IP was applied to other parts of the world. Through this process, APCO's activities were transformed from a specifically "Asian" cause informed by a certain understanding of the region's shared past and identity, to an example of global health and socio-economic development from Asia that could be applicable universally.

Conclusion

The transnationalism that shaped the inter-Asian medical cooperation in family planning that took place under the aegis of the APCO in the middle of the twentieth century was multifaceted. First, Cold War politics acted as a critical basis for determining the contours of the APCO. Specifically, US interests in the Cold War informed the ways in which family planning was promoted in East Asia as part of the transnational population control movement, and the specific deployment of family planning in the region determined the APCO's founding members and the nations that implemented its IP. In addition to the Cold War, the region's specific past experience of Japanese colonialism also played a pivotal role in the transnational exchanges among the Asian participants of the APCO. Moreover, in the context of the APCO, Asia was not just a world region, but a discursive register that directly affected the transnational dialogue on the implementation of the IP in the region. However, as time went by, the rhetoric focusing on Asia's regional specificity was subsumed by a discourse of universalism that prevailed in the transnational exchange in global health and socio-economic development. As a result of this process, the APCO no longer served only the health and welfare of Asian people, but of populations around the world. Over this period, the transnationalism manifest in the inter-Asian medical cooperation also changed its quality, at times magnifying and at others reducing the significance of East Asia for cooperation, which resonated with the shifting regional geopolitics.

References and Further Reading

Claeys, Vicky. 2010. "Brave and Angry: The Creation and Development of the International Planned Parenthood Federation (IPPF)". *The European Journal of Contraception & Reproductive Health Care* 15 (s2): S67–76.

Connelly, Matthew James. 2008. *Fatal Misconception: The Struggle to Control World Population*. Cambridge, MA: Belknap Press.

Cullather, Nick. 2010. *The Hungry World: America's Cold War Battle against Poverty in Asia*. Cambridge, MA: Harvard University Press.

David, Mirela. 2018. "Female Gynecologists and Their Birth Control Clinics: Eugenics in Practice in 1920s–1930s China". *Canadian Bulletin of Medical History* 35 (1): 32–62.

Davis, Kingsley. 1956. "Population and Power in the Free World". In *Population Theory and Policy: Selected Readings*, edited by Joseph John Spengler and Otis Dudley Duncan, 342–356. Glencoe: Free Press.

DiMoia, John P. 2008. "'Let's Have the Proper Number of Children and Raise Them Well!': Family Planning and Nation-Building in South Korea, 1961–1968". *East Asian Science, Technology and Society: An International Journal* 2: 361–379.

——. 2014. "Counting People: The Emerging Field of Demography and the Mobilization of the Social Sciences in the Formation of State Policy in South Korea since 1948". In *A World of Populations: Transnational Perspectives on Demography in the Twentieth Century*, edited by Heinrich Hartmann and Corinna R. Unger, 129–146. New York: Berghahn.

Donaldson, Peter J. 1990. *Nature Against Us: The United States and the World Population Crisis, 1965–1980*. Chapel Hill: University of North Carolina Press.

Greenhalgh, Susan. 1996. "The Social Construction of Population Science: An Intellectual, Institutional, and Political History of Twentieth-Century Demography". *Comparative Studies in Society and History* 38 (1): 26–66.

Greenhalgh, Susan, and Edwin A. Winckler. 2005. *Governing China's Population: From Leninist to Neoliberal Biopolitics*. Stanford: Stanford University Press.

Homei, Aya. 2016a. "The Science of Population and Birth Control in Post-War Japan". In *Science, Technology, and Medicine in the Modern Japanese Empire*, edited by David G. Wittner and Philip C. Brown, 227–243. London: Routledge.

——. 2016b. "Between the West and Asia: 'Humanistic' Japanese Family Planning in the Cold War". *East Asian Science, Technology and Society* 10 (4): 445–467.

Homei, Aya, and John P. DiMoia. 2020. "Integrating Parasite Eradication with Family Planning: The Colonial Legacy in Post-War Medical Cooperation in East Asia". *Social History of Medicine*. 23 June. https://doi.org/10.1093/shm/hkaa005.

Homei, Aya, and Yu-Ling Huang. 2016. "Population Control in Cold War Asia: An Introduction". *East Asian Science, Technology and Society* 10 (4): 343–353.

Huang, Yu-Ling. 2016. "Biopolitical Knowledge in the Making: Population Politics and Fertility Studies in Early Cold War Taiwan". *East Asian Science, Technology and Society*, August, 3678460.

Kim, Sonja. 2008. "'Limiting Birth': Birth Control in Colonial Korea (1910–1945)". *East Asian Science, Technology and Society: An International Journal* 2 (3): 335–359.

Kohama, Masako. 2020. *Hitorikko seisaku to chūgoku shakai* (一人っ子政策と中国社会) [One-Child Policy and Chinese Society]. Kyoto: Kyoto daigaku gakujutsu shuppankai.

Kokusai kyōryoku jigyōdan (国際協力事業団). 1982. "Chūgoku kazoku keikaku purojekuto jizen chōsadan hōkokusho" (中国家族計画プロジェクト事前調査団報告書) [A Report by the China Family Planning Project Pre-Investigation Group], https://openjicareport.jica.go.jp/982/982/982_105_10546851.html [accessed 1 July 2019].

Krige, John (ed.). 2019. *How Knowledge Moves: Writing the Transnational History of Science and Technology*. Chicago: University of Chicago Press.

Kunii Chōjirō (国井長次郎). 1977. *Watashi no sengo undōshi: roman to genjitsu no hazama de* (私の戦後運動史ーロマンと現実のはざまで) [A History of My Post-War Activism]. Tokyo: Hoken kaikan.

——. 1978. "Ningenteki kazoku keikaku no yoake" (人間的家族計画の夜明け) [The Dawn of Humane Family Planning]. JOICFP Archives. National Institute of Public Health Library, Wako-shi, Saitama-Prefecture, Japan.

—— (ed.). 1988. *Joisefu no nijūnen* (ジョイセフの二十年) [Twenty Years of JOICFP]. Tokyo: Japanese Organization for International Cooperation in Family Planning.

——. 1991. *Chōjukokoku nihon: sore wa mushi kara hajimatta* (長寿国日本ーそれは虫から始まった) [A Nation with Long-Lived People: It Started with Worms]. Tokyo: Zaidan Hōjin Hoken Kaikan.

——. 1994. "Preface". In *A Grassroots Movement to Improve the Quality of Life: Integrating Family Planning with Health Care and Community Development Activities 10 Year Experience of the Integrated Project in China 1983–1993*, 5–6. Tokyo: Japanese Organization for International Cooperation in Family Planning.

Kunii Wataru (国井渉). 2001. *Hoken kaikan monogatari, gekan* (保健会館ものがたり) [Story of the Hoken Kaikan Hall, Vol. 2]. Tokyo: Hoken Kaikan.

Kuo, Wen-Hua (郭文華). 2002. "When State and Policies Reproduce Each Other: Making Taiwan a Population Control Policy, Making Population Control Policy for Taiwan". In *Historical Perspectives on East Asian Science, Technology, and Medicine*, edited by Alan K. L. Chan, Gregory Clancy, and J.-C. Loy, 121–137. Singapore: Singapore University Press.

——. 2008. "Mei yuan xia de weisheng zhengce-1960 niandai Taiwan jiating jihua de tansuo" (美援下的衛生政策：一九六〇年代台灣家庭計劃的探索) [Public Health Policy under the American Support: An Exploration on Family Planning in Taiwan in the 1960s]. In *Diguo yu xiandai yixue* (帝國與現代醫學), edited by Li Shang-ren (李尚仁), 325–364. Taibei: Lianjing.

Lin, Yi-Tang. 2020. "Local Actions, National Policies and International Knowledge: Family Planning and Statistical Practices in Taiwan (1949–1980s)". *Social History of Medicine* 33 (3): 819–842.

Ma Zhengliang (马正亮). 1985. "Guoji jihua shengyu lianhe hui jianjie" (国际计划生育联合会简介) [A Brief Introduction to the International Planned Parenthood Federation]. *Xibei renkou* (西北人口) 2: 64.

Matsubara Yoko (松原洋子). 2000. "Nihon: Sengo no yūsei hogohō toiu nano danshuhō" (日本－戦後の優生保護法という名の断種法) [Japan: A Post-War Sterilization Law under the Name of the Eugenic Protection Law]. In *Yūseigaku to ningen shakai: seimei kagaku no seiki wa doko e mukaunoka* (優生学と人間社会：生命科学の世紀はどこへ向かうのか), by Shohei Yonemoto (米本昌平) et al., 169–236. Tokyo: Kodansha.

Mellors, Sarah. 2019. "Less Reproduction, More Production: Birth Control in the Early People's Republic of China, 1949–1958". *East Asian Science, Technology and Society* 13 (3): 367–389.

Merchant, Emily Klancher. 2017. "A Digital History of Anglophone Demography and Global Population Control, 1915–1984". *Population and Development Review* 43 (1): 83–117.

"Nicchū kazoku keikaku kyōryoku ni kansuru kaidan oboegaki ni chōin: kazoku keikaku bunya niokeru sōgo kōryū fukamaru" (日中家族計画協力に関する会談覚書に調印－家族計画分野における相互交流深まる) [Memorandum of Understanding on Japan-China Family Planning Cooperation Signed: Deepening Mutual Exchange in the Field of Family Planning]. 1980. *Sekai to Jinkō* (世界と人口) 83: 6–7.

Nihon Kiseichū Yobōkai APCO Kaigi Jimukyoku (日本寄生虫予防会APCO会議事務局). 1974. "Ajia Kiseichū Yobō Kikō (APCO) Dai 1 kai kaigi hōkokusho" (アジア寄生虫予防機構 (APCO) 第1回会議報告書) [The Report on the First APCO Meeting]. Tokyo: Nihon Kiseichū Yobōkai.

——. 1976. "Ajia Kiseichū Yobō Kikō (APCO) Dai 2 kai kaigi hōkokusho" (アジア寄生虫予防機構 (APCO) 第2回会議報告書) [The Report on the Second APCO Meeting]. Tokyo: Nihon Kiseichū Yobōkai.

Norgren, Christiana A. E. 2001. *Abortion before Birth Control: The Politics of Reproduction in Postwar Japan*. Princeton: Princeton University Press.

Obayashi Michiko (大林道子). 2006. "Sengo nihon no kazoku keikaku fukyū katei nikansuru kenkyū" (戦後日本の家族計画普及過程に関する研究) [A Study of the Process to Popularize Family Planning in Post-War Japan]. PhD dissertation, Ochanomizu University, Tokyo.

Ogino Miho (荻野美穂). 2008a. "Jinkō seisaku no sutoratejī 'umeyo fuyaseyo' kara 'kazoku keikaku e'" (人口政策のストラテジー—「産めよ殖やせよ」から「家族計画」へ) [Strategies of Population Policies: From "Give Birth, Multiply" to "Family Planning"]. In *Tekuno/baio poritikkusu: kagaku iryō gijutsu no ima* (テクノ/バイオ・ポリティクス—科 学医療技術の今—), edited by Kaoru Tachi (舘かおる), 145–159. Tokyo: Sakuhinsha.

——. 2008b. *"Kazoku keikaku" eno nichi: kindai nihon no seishoku wo meguru seiji* (「家族計画」への道—近代日本の生殖をめぐる政治) [Paths to "Family Planning": Politics Surrounding Reproduction in Modern Japan]. Tokyo: Iwanami Shoten.

Oreskes, Naomi, and John Krige. 2014. *Science and Technology in the Global Cold War*. Cambridgem MA: MIT Press.

Packard, Randall M. 2016. *A History of Global Health: Interventions into the Lives of Other Peoples*. Baltimore: Johns Hopkins University Press.

Peng Peiyun (彭珮云) (ed.). 1997. *Zhongguo jihua shengyu quanshu* (中国计划生育全书) [An Unabridged Book of Family Planning in China]. Beijing: Zhongguo renkou chuban she.

Secord, James A. 2004. "Knowledge in Transit". *Isis* 95 (4): 654–672.

Sharpless, John. 1995. "World Population Growth, Family Planning, and American Foreign Policy". *Journal of Policy History* 7 (Special Issue 01): 72–102.

——. 1997. "Population Science, Private Foundations and Development Aid: The Transformation of Demographic Knowledge in the United States, 1945–1965". In *International Development and the Social Sciences: Essays on the History and Politics of Knowledge*, edited by Frederick Cooper and Randall M. Packard, 176–202. Berkeley: University of California Press.

Shi Chengli (史成礼). 1988. *Zhongguo Jihua shengyu huodong shi* (中国计划生育活动史) [A History of Family Planning Activities in China]. Wulumuqi: Xinjiang renmin chuban she.

Somsen, G. J. 2008. "A History of Universalism: Conceptions of the Internationality of Science (1750–1950)". *Minerva* 46: 361–379.

Szanton, David L. 2004. "The Origin, Nature, and Challenges of Area Studies in the United States". In *The Politics of Knowledge: Area Studies and the Disciplines*, edited by David Szanton, 1–33. Berkeley: University of California Press.

Szreter, Simon. 1993. "The Idea of Demographic Transition and the Study of Fertility Change: A Critical Intellectual History". *Population and Development Review* 19 (4): 659–701.

Takeshita, Chikako. 2011. *The Global Biopolitics of the IUD: How Science Constructs Contraceptive Users and Women's Bodies*. Cambridge, MA: MIT Press.

Tama Yasuko (田間泰子). 2006. *"Kindai kazoku" to bodī poritikkusu* (「近代家族」とボディ·ポリティクス) ["Modern Family" and Body Politics]. Kyoto: Sekai shisōsha.

——. 2016. "Jutai chōsetsu (bāsu kontorōru) to botai hogohō" (受胎調節(バース·コントロール)と母体保護法) [Birth Control and Eugenic Protection Law]. In *Umi sodate to josan no rekishi: kindaika no 200-nen wo furikaeru* (産み育てと助産の歴史：近代化の200年をふり返る) [History of Birth, Childcare and Midwifery: Looking Back at 200 Years of Modernisation], edited by Chiaki Shirai (白井千晶), 110–135. Tokyo: Igaku shoin.

The Asian Parasite Control Organization, The Japanese Organization for International Cooperation in Family Planning, The International Planned Parenthood Federation, and The United Nations Fund for Population Activities. 1985. "Applicable Experiences: Review of the Integrated Project, 1975–1985 and Its Future Direction. The 7th Workshop on the Management of the Integrated Family Planning, Nutrition and Parasite Control." Proceedings. Tokyo: The Asian Parasite Control Organization, The Japanese Organization for International Cooperation in Family Planning, The International Planned Parenthood Federation, and the United Nations Fund for Population Activities.

Tipton, Elise K. 1997. "Birth Control and the Population Problem". In *Society and the State in Interwar Japan*, edited by Elise K. Tipton, 42–62. London and New York: Routledge.

"Tōnan Ajia Kazoku Jinkō Keikaku Seifukan Iin IGCC" (東南アジア家族人口計画政府間委員IGCC). 1974. *Sekai to Jinkō* 24 (July): 14–15.

Turchetti, Simone, Néstor Herran, and Soraya Boudia. 2012. "Introduction: Have We Ever Been 'Transnational'? Towards a History of Science across and beyond Borders". *The British Journal for the History of Science* 45 (3): 319–36.

White, Tyrene. 2006. *China's Longest Campaign: Birth Planning in the People's Republic, 1949–2005*. Ithaca and London: Cornell University Press.

Yang Faxiang (杨发祥). 2004. "Dangdai zhongguo jihua shengyu shi yanjiu" (当代中国计划生育史研究) [A Study on the History of Family Planning in Contemporary China]. PhD dissertation, Zhejiang University, Hangzhou.

15

From Liberation to the Great Leap Forward

Ethnic Koreans and Assimilation in North-East China, 1945–1962

Adam Cathcart

Introduction

In September 2022, the Chinese Communist Party (CCP) celebrated the seventieth anniversary of its establishment of the Yanbian Korean Autonomous Prefecture. Separated from North Korea by the narrow Tumen River, the six counties of Yanbian prefecture constitute the easternmost edge of the People's Republic of China (PRC) and Jilin province. The Chinese Koreans who live in Yanbian are known as Chosunjok or Chaoxianzu (朝鲜族), and have been characterised as a "model minority" within the PRC (Gao, 2008; Schubert-Zhang, 2016). They are also one of the most transnational of groups, given their ties to ethnic Koreans in Russia, Central Asia, the two rival Koreas on the adjacent peninsula, and Japan. Recent research demonstrates how interlinked their population has become with South Korea and the global economy (Park, 2015), and further considers whether terms like "transnational" or "diaspora" are still applicable given the huge diversity among ethnic Koreans globally (de Valk, 2021). Historians of the Cold War have recognised the significance of transnational movement between China and North Korea, both prior to and after the Korean War (Shen and Xia, 2014; Kraus, 2014). Today, Chinese Koreans in Yanbian and beyond deserve our critical attention, particularly as the CCP continues to deepen and accelerate its assimilationist drive imposed on ethnic minority groups along its securitised peripheries (Ma, 2018; Zhao and Xu, 2017). Particularly with respect to its entanglement with migration studies, the concept of ethnic assimilation in China is an area of active debate, and merits further discussion with respect to interregional migration (Chen and Liu, 2018), *hukou*/residency permit status (Tan et al., 2022), and educational factors (Lin and Jackson,

2021). The construction of Chinese Korean identity, and the inclusion post-1945 of Koreans within a communist Chinese polity, were both difficult processes. In the immediate aftermath of Japanese imperial rule over both Korea and Manchuria/Northeast China, Koreans were faced with an array of confounding and often deadly choices regarding political loyalty, national identity, local allegiance, and cultural orientation. Ultimately, those who did not depart for the Korean Peninsula in the late 1940s were considered among the most politically loyal and strategically significant of China's minority ethnicities, a perception that was consolidated by their important service to the CCP and the socialist bloc during the 1950–1953 Korean War. However, as work by Dong Jo Shin (2016; 2021) has demonstrated, the Maoist mass movements unleased in the late 1950s would shake these bonds to the Party and call into question the CCP's own ability to endow a "minority nationality" with genuine cultural and political autonomy. In the Great Leap Forward and the political turbulence that preceded and birthed it, the CCP began to single out the presence of what they called "local nationalism" (地方民族主义, *difang minzuzhuyi*) among ethnic Korean intellectuals and leaders, seeing it as a threat to Maoist political hegemony. With the cooling off of the Great Leap in 1962 and the arrival of Zhou Enlai in Yanbian that year, some of the worst excesses were rolled back, but hundreds of Korean Chinese targeted for cultural persecution were not "rehabilitated" until 1979, and others did not survive the Cultural Revolution at all. As Kwon (2019, 77) describes it, the latter half of the twentieth century dug traumatic furrows in Yanbian and resulted in a bifurcated sense of identity: "Korean Chinese", she writes, "have struggled with a duality mainly derived from their geopolitical and ethnic condition—as a group of migrant settlers from the Korean Peninsula *and* as a Chinese ethnic minority". This chapter will look back at two distinct episodes—the Chinese civil war and the years around the Great Leap Forward—in order to investigate the assimilation of the Chosunjok across periods of time which have received relatively little attention, doing so by focusing on political struggle and language.

A Chaotic Liberation from Colonial Rule, 1945–1949

When Emperor Hirohito announced Japan's unconditional surrender on 15 August 1945, Koreans in Manchuria (the region known today as Northeast China) were in an ambiguous position. Korea as a nation had been formally annexed by Japan in 1910, and the 1930s had seen a massive acceleration of migration to Manchuria, largely from the peninsula's southern provinces (Kim, 2016, 64). By 1945 there were hundreds of thousands of Koreans who were relatively new migrants into Northeast China, alongside others with roots going back to the nineteenth century and earlier. In February 1932, with the delayed but vigorous backing of the Japanese state, the Japanese Kwantung Army set up the puppet state of Manchukuo. Although the interaction between Korea and the new Japanese puppet state was idealised as smooth and vital, in fact it was not always easy for Koreans to move between the two states, nor was their legal position in doing so particularly clear (Han, 2004; 2005). An organised Japanese push was initiated to move more Koreans into Manchuria, and then accelerated in 1937 along with a drive to more effectively control undocumented or "stateless" Koreans in the region (Kim, 2014, 122; Kim, 2016, 64–65). Some Koreans argued for "embracing radical assimilationist policies [as a] strategy for enhancing Koreans' standing in Manchukuo" (Kim, 2016, 65). In an idealised and propagandised harmony of the races, Koreans were supposed to have been elevated for their service to the Japanese empire. However, the reality was very different. Japanese language education continued for Koreans in Manchukuo, as in Korea itself, although in some villages girls were prevented by their families from attending language classes (Piao and Li, 2013, 185). Some Korean farmers in Manchuria were placed into "strategic hamlets" and isolated from both education and the metropole (Lee, 1967; Han, 1999, 225).

In the summer of 1945, Japanese power collapsed, and Korean individuals and families in Northeast China faced an intimidating and often dangerous battery of choices (Ahn, 2017). These choices—imperatives, really—ranged from surviving and finding food to avoiding Soviet Red Army looting and rape, to mitigating the desires of the newly arriving Chinese Nationalists/Kuomintang to expropriate Korean-owned property. The CCP offered some hope of land ownership and citizenship in an as-yet-unborn communist republic (Dai and Lin, 2017, 66–69, 135–141), but Koreans in Manchuria also faced a core dilemma regarding repatriation (Kim, 2010). One Soviet document indicated that in the weeks following Japan's surrender, some 800,000 Koreans in Manchuria made a swift decision and repatriated to one of the two occupied halves of the Korean Peninsula (Kim, 2014, 122).

There was no shortage of dangers for the Koreans who remained in Shenyang, the largest city in industrial and commercial Manchuria. In one survey by the Shanghai-based Korean Provisional Government, in the year from August 1945 to August 1946, in Shenyang 44 Koreans were murdered, 63 wounded, 15,450 arrested, 215 Korean women raped, and 123,506 Koreans "subjected to indignities" in the city. Shenyang took the brunt of atrocities against Koreans in urban areas, although 58 Korean women were reported raped in Jilin city in the same document (Huang, 2013, 173; Kim, 2004, 94). Food rationing hierarchies connected to ethnic identity in Manchukuo (Kim, 2016, 66) were upended, while discrimination against Koreans as "secondary devils", a reference to collaboration with Japan, continued (Kraus and Cathcart, 2014, 87). Nevertheless, these pressures did not result in wholesale repatriation of Koreans to the peninsula. The logistical hurdles to repatriation were immense, and not only due to the intensification of warfare in Northeast China. As Kim Chun-seon explains, North Korea took a "firm position that [it] would not allow massive disorganised entry of Koreans from China" and the main border crossings were policed by Soviet forces into spring 1946 (2004, 102).

In Yanbian, Koreans took advantage of the Japanese surrender to immediately set up new organisations, and to take up arms. In the immediate aftermath of Japanese rule, impromptu militias and participation in nascent CCP structures in Yanbian tended to be led by Koreans rather than Han Chinese. However, the Soviet Red Army was the pre-eminent military force in the area for several months, and itself was a source of violence against some Koreans. One area where clashes occurred was Nanping, a small river village in Helong county known best today as a contentious border crossing point for North Korean refugees and occasionally hungry Korean People's Army soldiers (Perlez, 2015). Soviet troops arrived in Nanping on 9 September 1945, seeking entry to a gathering in a school where a group of youth were politically organising. Denied entry by a local militia, the Soviets opened fire, immediately killing nine in the small town (Yanbian History Research Office, 1988, 26, 42). Two other locals who had been badly wounded by the Soviet gunfire in Nanping died shortly thereafter (Xu and Wang, 1992, 620). Friendship associations with the USSR nevertheless continued to grow that autumn, and Korean intellectuals used such affiliations to gain access to cultural materials left behind by the Japanese (Yanbian History Research Office, 1988, 55–56), showing how internationalism also had its nationalistic uses. In Hunchun and more rural Wangqing, the Soviets did not prevent representatives of the Nationalist Party/Kuomintang from setting up rival youth organisations like the Three People's Principles Youth League, so the CCP had to set up its own rival "Democratic League (民主同盟, *minzhu tongmeng*)" for the youth (Yanbian History Research Office, 1988, 35–38). While small institutions had to make a choice between Chinese regimes and also navigate the Soviet presence, schools in Yanbian nearly all transitioned away from the Japanese empire immediately, in a process which was, in some cases, accompanied by violence.

In Helong county, the grounds of an elementary school were used as the stage for executions of pro-Japanese landlords. On 2 September 1945, landlord Ri Yong-ch'un was killed; he was a native of Onsŏng-gun, just across the river in northern Korea's Hamgyŏng province, and had been a Chinese citizen for some 30 years prior to his death (Yanbian Committee on Literary and Historical Materials, 1984, 169). The CCP encouraged the production of dramas and local operas to commemorate and guide struggle sessions against class enemies like Ri, focusing on heavily Korean areas on the Chinese side of the border in Tumen and Longjing (Yanbian History Research Office, 1988, 58, 63–64). The stakes for the loyalty encouraged by such productions were high. One writer likened life in Longjing in autumn 1945 to "sitting atop a volcano" amid a "proliferation of traitors, running dogs, police, and secret agents" (Ai, 1990, 39). The arts were an important means of shaping the evolving history of the civil war as it unfolded, as well as emphasising Yanbian's pre-1945 past as a terrain of anti-Japanese resistance. Further studies are needed of how (or if) local currents in fields like opera and theatre in border regions with North Korea might have resulted in transnational exchanges, for example celebrating the process of land reform or struggles of civil war.

Amid the violent uprooting of the colonial past, the CCP was trying to shape emerging new norms for education in Yanbian. By the end of March 1946, 35 middle schools had been opened in the region, enrolling nearly 12,000 students, many of whom were seen by the Party as a pool of logistical support in the civil war. Far more numerous were the elementary schools, numbering 388 across the region with an estimated 106,000 students (Yanbian History Research Committee, 1988, 85, 102). Well before the renewed drive for Marxist education in the region, pushed by the ethnic Korean communist leader Chu Tŏkhae/Zhu Dehai, Korean militias were opening their own schools and pushing for education on the history of the anti-Japanese guerrilla struggle (Yanbian History Research Committee, 1988, 74, 98). Some students demonstrated their fluency in the argot of resistance by testifying at accusation meetings (控诉会, *kongsuhui*) against pro-Japanese members of the community. In a November 1946 public trial focusing on retribution for the killings of the Hailan River Incident of 1931–1933, a 14-year-old boy surnamed Kim testified that, while he himself was still *in utero* at the time, his father's murder in the Hailan River Incident had left him with an agonising childhood (Han and Yao, 1991, 458).

Changes to education were meant to bring personal transformation to the newly conscious youth like Kim, linking individual fates to projects of deep yet imperilled political change. One individual involved in uprooting the Japanese educational norms was Kang Sint'ae. Kang had been in close cooperation with Kim Il-sŏng in the Soviet Far East; he was named First Secretary of the CCP in Yanji on 20 October 1945. After a busy month of fighting "bandits" and Party-building, Kang sent out a wide-ranging directive seeking an intensification of political education in the region and the "elimination of slave education", by which he meant remnants of the old Japanese system (Han and Yao, 1991, 427). Kang would be superseded by the arrival of Zhou Baozhong, an ethnic Bai from south-western China and a firm representative of Mao Zedong and the politics of the CCP Central Committee. Kang left Yanji in June 1946, went to North Korea, joined the North Korean People's Army, and died in the Korean War, having left behind his legacy in the formation of communist power and education in Yanbian (Kraus and Cathcart, 2014, 86).

As the CCP consolidated political power and undertook land reform in Yanbian, Korean language education was improved. In March 1947, Longjing Medical University, which would become Yanbian University, started teaching courses in Korean history, Korean geography, and Korean culture (Han and Yao, 1991, 362). An array of new institutions were set up in 1948 and 1949, including Korean-language newspapers like the *Yonbyŏn Ilbo* or *Yanbian Ribao.* In June 1949, the Party organised five days of debates over Korean language instruction at the elementary and middle school levels (Yanbian Archives, 1990, 136). Yanbian University, the regional centre for research and cultural study of Korean, was formally established in March 1949. Yanbian's ethnic composition at the end of the 1940s was 76 per cent Korean, with an internal estimate from July 1949 showing 563,080 Koreans out of a total population for the region of 744,620 (Chinese Communist Party Yanbian Committee, 1949, 70). At Yanbian University and elsewhere, the atmosphere was suffused with Maoist argot and the curriculum was unquestionably that approved by the CCP, but it also allowed for multiple routes of connection to, and even modelling on, North Korea (Cathcart, 2010, 38–39, 43–44). During the Korean War, Yanbian sent to North Korea 1,773 labourers with the Chinese army, 2,157 interpreters, and 898 nurses, all ethnic Koreans. Of the 6,981 deaths of individuals from the Yanbian region recorded in North Korea during the Korean War, 98 per cent were ethnic Koreans (Li, 2012, 41). However, in spite of the sacrifices made by the region in the Korean War and the legal deepening of its autonomous status in 1954 (Schubert-Zhang, 2016, 24), Korean language usage and development would be threatened in Yanbian. Ultimately, in one bitter assessment, "the period from the late 1950s to the late 1970s [would be] culturally sterile and politically brutal for Korean Chinese" (Kwon, 2019, 79).

Korean Culture in Yanbian amid Socialist Upsurge, 1957–1962

The Chinese state would seek to accelerate the drive towards socialism from the mid-1950s, all the while codifying and reshaping its policy towards ethnic minorities around the country, ultimately settling on a recognition of 56 official ethnic groups (Mullaney, 2010). Those years would also see tensions running high with some border regions of the PRC, as the pressures of collectivisation and national mobilisation for mass campaigns clashed with the norms and expectations of minority nationality groups. The CCP's drive to collectivise and settle Tibetans in Kham/western Sichuan and in Amdo/Qinghai province were two such arenas where tensions over the speed and character of democratic reforms boiled over into revolt and violence (Li, 2016; Weiner, 2012). The late 1950s also saw growing migration of Han Chinese into areas like Inner Mongolia, creating new assimilationist realities in certain counties and accelerated orientation towards Beijing (Schwartz, 1963). In Xinjiang, the Anti-Rightist Campaign of 1957 revealed a wide gulf of trust between Uighurs, Kazakhs, and the Han Chinese bureaucratic class, amid accusations of "local nationalism" (Jacobs, 2016, 192–193), and the subsequent famine stimulated the movement of over 2 million Han Chinese "hunger refugees" to the region (Joniak-Lüthi, 2013, 160).

In this context, the transnational potential of the Chosunjok and their ties to North Korea in particular drew suspicion due to their "double" identity. Following on from the pioneering work by Shin (2016 and 2021), this section looks at impacts of the Anti-Rightist Campaign and the Great Leap Forward through a more transnational lens, shedding light upon the campaigns and how labels such as "revisionist" and "capitalist" were more or less randomly applied to people of non-Chinese identity in order to condemn their incongruity with the Han majority. Accusations of "local nationalism" were vague yet powerful, in that they were difficult to refute but also pointed to ethnic difference and transnational potential as a point of weakness in individual and collective striving towards socialism in Yanbian.

The Great Leap Forward did not summon a wave of overt physical violence in Yanbian, but it did result in significant steps back for Korean language education and intellectual life. Accusations of "local nationalism" abounded, particularly levelled at ethnic Korean intellectuals in Yanbian whose efforts to maintain and expand Korean language education were seen as hindering the advance towards socialism (Shin, 2021, 195–198). While Shin correlates the "anti-local nationalism movement" precisely to the Anti-Rightist Campaign of 1957, Li (2012, 66) shows the campaign's justification as having roots in a 15 October 1957 Central Committee directive rectifying socialist education in ethnic minority regions. A local Party history (Cui, 1993) dates the movement to spring 1958. Top leaders of the prefecture could refute the more outlandish accusations of localism (Park, 2015, 163) but Korean intellectuals in Yanbian had to bear their burden stoically (Shin, 2021, 195–196). Cultural circles were tarred with labels such as "revisionist", "right-wing capitalist", "local nationalists", and "reactionary writers" (Li, 2012, 134). Accordingly, the labelling of rightists as targets for political struggle had a sharp impact upon cultural institutions like the *Yanbian Daily* (Jin, 1988, 50–51). Among the reasons for self-criticisms made within the *Yanbian Daily* and at Yanbian University in spring 1958 were "reluctance to take Chinese nationality, refusal to learn Chinese, discontent over the size and administrative status of self-rule areas, and disapproval of the appointment of Han Chinese officials to administrative positions in self-rule areas". Nevertheless, in the spring of 1958 Yanbian University published a collection of highly critical wall posters, including essays that equated "the act of making Koreans into Chinese" to Japan's colonial assimilation policy (Park, 2015, 156–158).

The Great Leap Forward formally arrived in the region in June 1958, when the prefectural Party committee resolved to unleash the movement across the five counties of Yanbian. In July and August, the push for expansion of communes developed, including growth in communal kitchens (Li, 2012, 68–69). Yanbian cadres looking for a model for massive collectives were pointed towards Henan, Mao's home province and a site that would prove, in Yang Jisheng's sprawling assessment, "the epicenter of the disaster" (2008, 23–86). Mao's personal guidance for communes was haphazard and improvisatory, and advice on how to balance the unique needs of nominally autonomous ethnic areas of the PRC with the new agricultural push was undeveloped and scant. In a significant early collection of Mao Zedong's commentaries on the emerging shape and character of the collectives, entitled *Socialist Upsurge in the Chinese Countryside* (中国农村的社会主义高潮, *Zhongguo nongcun de shehuizhuyi gaochao*), questions about the role that ethnic difference might play in the campaign only elicited the barest of thought (Mao, 1957a; 1957b). While Yanbian did not have the same tensions between ethnographic and political overlap as, say, Tibetan border areas of majority-Han provinces like Sichuan, the push for Han-led assimilation or cultural imperatives still caused problems.

Mao's remarks at Beidaihe hit a high watermark for utopianism, and were loaded with directives and momentum. Over a number of days in late August 1958 at Beidaihe, Mao endorsed deep ploughing ("it creates a big reservoir for water and a big cistern for manure"), mused about controlling the countryside ("combining Marx and Qin Shihuang" and banning "people walking around uncontrolled"), previewed the Cultural Revolution in the academy ("a fierce kind of struggle [that] may take a few years [is needed] to sort out the bourgeois monopoly in science"), and compared the new campaign to military mobilisation ("at least all this kills fewer people than fighting wars") (1989 [1958], 425). Whatever conflicting rhetoric he put forth about combining decentralization and local initiative, Mao was also deadly serious about pushing to hit his new targets (Mao, 1989 [1958], 425). Local energies in Yanbian were quickly thereafter turned towards steel production, flowing out of a 4 September 1958 Party meeting in Yanji. The prefectural party committee pledged 56,000 tonnes of steel and by late October 1958 it was expected to have some 100,000 people engaged in manual mass labour throughout the night (Li, 2012, 90–91). Like the reopening of Japanese-era coal mines to feed low-quality steel furnaces, deep planting methods wasted thousands of days of cumulative labour. The 1959 harvest for all of Yanbian was smaller than the previous year's by about 4.6 tonnes of grain, and livestock numbers were down significantly, 5.3 per cent on the 1952 figure (Cao, 2000, 31, 34; Li, 2012, 91, 95). By summer 1960, hunger was widespread in Yanbian (Li, 2012, 97–98). That year, in rural Wangqing county, residents were forced to generate meat substitutes and the local Party attempted to guide the public in their often-hazardous search for edible herbs in the mountains (Cui and Jin, 2000, 45–50; Wang, 2000).

The velocity of change and the fissile political culture of the Great Leap Forward led Yanbian towards Sinicisation from 1958 to 1961, in both the demographic and the linguistic sense. In his recent study of ethnicity and state alteration of religious architecture, Lloyd Ridgeon notes: "Sinicization is related to the notion of assimilating with the majority Han culture of China (which accounts for some 1.2 billion, predominantly in the south and east of the country), although the designation of a monolithic group and culture has been challenged by many scholars" (2020, 576). Amid the zeal to create ever larger units of labour in the Great Leap, the CCP enlarged Yanbian's territory by incorporating Dunhua as a sixth county in November 1958. Dunhua itself consisted of only slightly above 10 per cent ethnic Koreans, meaning that its inclusion made the overall Yanbian Korean Autonomous Prefecture suddenly and substantially more Han Chinese. Shin (2021, 193) describes the decision as having been made by the Jilin Provincial Government, but Li says the decision was made by the State Council in Beijing. In either case, the motivation for the move was linked to the collectivist fever that autumn of 1958, and in the context of the campaign it resulted in an increase in the number of communes within Yanbian's borders (Li, 2012, 69). Exodus figures for population in the period of the Great Leap Forward are also unclear. Some estimates exist of about 150,000 ethnic Koreans resettling in North Korea during the famine (Schubert-Zhang, 2016, 25–26). Alongside (or perhaps included in) these numbers are estimates of the movement of some 52,000 Chinese citizens for resettlement into North Korea as part of the means of making up for labour shortages in the DPRK after the punishing Korean War (Kim, 2016, 140). Such resettlement would certainly have been in line with North Korea's broader push in the late 1950s to attract skilled Korean migrants from Japan.

The population movements are hard to pin down, but the questions about language learning and education in Yanbian are more solid. As Li (2012, 150) described, there was an increase in hours of Korean language education for youth in Yanbian. However, the number of Chinese language hours also went up, exceeding those of Korean. These numbers certainly transformed daily life in the classrooms of Yanbian, but the effects of the political campaigns were more chilling as the Great Leap Forward took hold over the region. In late October 1958, Yanbian University's most powerful official, the Party Secretary, was singled out by a Jilin-based Party discipline organisation for four days of criticism, after which he was judged guilty of crimes of cultural miseducation, and stripped of his Party membership (Li, 2012, 65). The meeting officially labelled 1,006 rightists across the prefecture. The reasons given were worrying, ranging from jokes made whilst drinking alcohol, for having spoken out in 1957 when the Party had asked for criticism, for having listened to and "worshipping foreign radio broadcasts", a reference to North Korean radio (Li, 2012). Nearly two years later in September 1960, 77 of these people were rehabilitated. The arrival of Zhou Enlai in the prefecture in 1962 brought a moderation of the line, and an explicit endorsement of North Korean broadcasting quality by the Premier (Li, 2012, 147), immediately exonerating some of the alleged rightists. Some 747 of the rightists were rehabilitated shortly thereafter, a trend seen again after the Cultural Revolution, as Tsurushima (1979) noted after a field visit to the region in the late 1970s.

Conclusion

As the CCP recently marked 70 years of formalised autonomy for ethnic Koreans in China, the traumas of the post-liberation and Great Leap Forward eras seem more distant than ever (Denney and Green, 2018). The 1990s and the early 2000s were years of relative prosperity (Morris and Hoare, 2021; Park et al., 2020). Today, the future beckons in Yanbian, with burgeoning economic metrics, enhanced living standards, efficient transport networks, and growing PRC national power. Xi Jinping, in his summer 2015 visit to the region, took in some light ethnic entertainment, eyed the three-dimensional "ethnic unity" in the part of the prefectural history museum meant for leadership photo ops, and sagely noted the need for "more urban infrastructure in rural areas" (Fang, 2015). Whether or not the "Belt and Road" ever connects to the Korean Peninsula, the Yanbian region is better integrated than ever to the urban trunk of the north-east, and to Beijing beyond.

But the ability of ethnic Korean students to study in their native language in Yanbian appears to be eroding further. In January 2021, a decision by the Legislative Affairs Commission of the National People's Congress Standing Committee effectively said that Korean language instruction in Yanbian was in violation of the PRC Constitution (Wei, 2021). Even as Chosunjok transnational linkages to and cultural orientation towards South Korea appear to be strong, linguistic assimilation in Yanbian continues (Zhou, 2012; Chaguan, 2021). And to read the overall emphasis of Liu Hui, the chairwoman of the State Ethnic Affairs Commission, after a trip to the north-east, the years of high Maoism are, stylistically speaking, not that far off: "The most crucial thing is that General Secretary Xi Jinping is supported by the whole Party, loved by the people, and unreservedly accepted as the core of the Party, as the military marshal, and as the people's leader who is the helmsman of the ship" (PRC Ethnic Affairs Commission, 2018).

References and Further Reading

Ahn, Chong Eun. 2017. "Surviving the Second World War in Manchukuo: Memories of Korean experiences of the War in Manchurian Farming Villages". *Journal of Modern Chinese History* 11 (2): 323–340.

Ai Wen (爱文). 1990. "Jiefang chuqi Yanji xian, renmin fanjian qingsuan douzheng" (解放初期延吉县人民反奸清算斗争) [The People's Struggle to Oppose Traitors and Clear Accounts in the Early Period of Liberation in Yanji County]. In *Longjing Wenshi Shiliao* (龙井文史资料), Vol. 3, 39–42. Yanji: Zhengxie Longjingxian wenshi ziliao yanjiu weiyuanhui.

Cao Xianfa (曹宪法). 2000. "Wanren dalian gangtie" (万人大炼钢铁) [Ten Thousand People Smelt Steel]. In *Wangqing Wenshi Ziliao* (汪清文史资料), 6 (February): 30–34.

Cathcart, Adam. 2010. "Nationalism and Ethnic Identity in the Sino-Korean Border Region of Yanbian, 1945–1950". *Korean Studies* 34 (December): 25–53.

Chaguan. 2021. "Becoming More Chinese: Assimilation of Minorities Is Not Just for Uyghurs and Tibetans". *The Economist*, 30 January: 50.

Chen, Zhenxian, and Kayuet Liu. 2018. "Assimilation of China's Rural-to-Urban Migrants: A Multidimensional Process". *Chinese Journal of Sociology* 4 (2): 188–217.

Chinese Communist Party Yanbian Committee (Zhonggong yanbian diwei / 中共延边地委). 17 July 1949. "Yanbian shengchan de qingkuang fangzhen sixiang yu guachu qijian gongzuo" (延边生产的情况方针思想与挂锄期间工作) [Situation, Policy, and Ideology of Production in Yanbian with Respect to Work during the Slack Agricultural Period of Summer]. In *Zhonggong Yanbian Diwei Yanbian Zhuanshu: Zhongyao Wenjian Huibian. Di'erji: 1949.6–1952.8* (中共延边地委延边专署: 重要文件汇编. 第二集: 1949.6–1952.8), 70–84. Yanji: Yanbian Chaoxian zizhizhou dang'anguan bian. 1986 (December).

Cui Jinzhe (崔锦哲) and Jin Zhengkui (金正奎). 2000. "Wangqingxian de 'Dayuejin' he renmin gongshehua yundong" (汪清县的大跃进和人民公社化运动) [The Great Leap Forward in Wangqing County and the People's Communisation Movement]. In *Wangqing Wenshi Ziliao*, edited by Zhengxie Wangqingxian weiyuanhui wenshi ziliao bangongshi, Vol. 6, 40–50. [No publisher listed].

Cui Yinghai (崔英海). 1993. *Zhonggong Yanbian Zhouwei Dangxiao Xiaoshi, 1948–1993* (中共延边州委党校校史, 1948–1993) [History of the Party School of Yanbian Prefecture Committee of the Chinese Communist Party, 1948–1993]. Jilin: Dongbei Chaoxian minzu jiaoyu chubanshe.

Dai Maolin (戴茂林), and Li Bo (李波). 2017. *Zhonggong Zhongyang Dongbeiju, 1945–1954* (中共中央东北局) [The Chinese Communist Party Central Committee Northeastern Bureau, 1945–1954]. Beijing: Zhongyang wenjian chubanshe.

De Valk, Victor. 2021. "A Model(led) Minority: Socioeconomics Transforming Korean Diasporic Identities in China, Japan, and Germany". *Sino-NK*. https://sinonk.com/2021/11/19/a-modelled-minority-socioeconomics-transforming-korean-diasporic-identities-in-china-japan-and-germany/ [accessed 17 December 2021].

Denney, Steven, and Christopher Green. 2018. "History and Identity: Chosunjok in Yanbian". *Sino-NK*. https://sinonk.com/2018/07/02/yanbian-chosunjok-identity/ [accessed 25 May 2021].

Fang, Sha. 2015. "President Xi Visits Ethnic Community in Jilin Province". *China Daily*, 17 July. https://www.chinadaily.com.cn/m/jilin/2015-07/17/content_21313824.htm [accessed 25 May 2021].

Gao, Fang. 2008. "What it Means to Be a 'Model Minority': Voices of Ethnic Koreans in Northeast China". *Asian Ethnicity* 9 (1): 55–67.

Han, Hongkoo. 1999. "Wounded Nationalism: The Minsaengdan Incident and Kim Il Sung in Eastern Manchuria". PhD dissertation, University of Washington.

Han Junguang (韩俊光) and Yao Zuoqi (姚作起). 1991. *Jiefang zhanzheng shiqi de dongman genjudi* (解放战争时期的东满根据地) [The Eastern Manchuria Base Area in the Early Period of the War of Liberation]. Yanji: Yanbian renmin chubanshe.

Han, Suk-Jung. 2004. "The Problem of Sovereignty: Manchukuo, 1932–1937". *Positions: East Asia Culture Critique* 12 (2): 457–478.

——. 2005. "From Pusan to Fengtian: The Borderline between Korea and Manchukuo in the 1930s". *East Asian History* 30 (December): 91–106.

Huang Youfu (黄有福) (ed.). 2013. *Zhongguo Chaoxianzu yanjiu, 2010–2011* (中国朝鲜族研究, 2010–2011) [Research on Ethnic Koreans in China, 2010–2011]. Beijing: Minzu chubanshe.

Jacobs, Justin M. 2016. *Xinjiang and the Modern Chinese State*. Seattle: University of Washington Press.

Jin Chenggui (金成贵). 1988. *Yanbian Xinwenzhi: Yanbian Ribao Xinwenzhi* (延边新闻志: 延边日报新闻志) [Gazeteer of *Yanbian News* and the *Yanbian Daily*]. Yanji: Yanbian Ribao.

Joniak-Lüthi, Agnieszka. 2013. "Han Migration to Xinjiang Uyghur Autonomous Region: Between State Schemes and Migrants' Strategies". *Zeitschrift für Ethnologie* 138 (2): 155–174.

Kim, Chun-seon. 2004. "The Settlement and Repatriation of Koreans in Northeast China after Liberation". *Korea Journal* 44 (4): 85–110.

Kim, Donggil. 2014. "The Chinese Civil War and the Ethno-Genesis of the Korean Minority in Northeast China". *The Chinese Historical Review* 21 (2): 121–142.

Kim, Jaeeun. 2016. *Contested Embrace: Transborder Membership Politics in Twentieth-Century Korea*. Stanford: Stanford University Press.

Kim, Michael. 2010. "The Lost Memories of Empire and the Korean Return from Manchuria, 1945–1950: Conceptualizing Manchuria in Modern Korean History". *Seoul Journal of Korean Studies* 23 (2): 195–223.

Kraus, Charles. 2014. "Bridging East Asia's Revolutions: The Overseas Chinese in North Korea, 1945–1950". *The Journal of Northeast Asian History* 11 (2), 39–70.

Kraus, Charles, and Adam Cathcart. 2014. "Nation, Ethnicity, and the Post-Manchukuo Order in the Sino-Korean Border Region". In *Key Papers on Korea: Papers Celebrating 25 Years of the Centre of Korean Studies, SOAS, University of London*, edited by Andrew D. Jackson, 79–99. Leiden: Brill.

Kwon, June Hee. 2019. "Forbidden Homeland: Divided Belonging on the China-Korea Border". *Critique of Anthropology* 39 (1): 74–94.

Lee, Chong-sik. 1967. *Counter Insurgency in Manchuria: The Japanese Experience 1931–1940*. Santa Monica: Rand.

Li, Jianglin. 2016. *Tibet in Agony: Lhasa 1959*, translated by Susan Wilf. Cambridge, MA: Harvard University Press.

Li Ming'gen (李明根). 2012. *Yanbian Chaoxianzushi* (延边朝鲜族史) [History of Ethnic Koreans in Yanbian, Vol. 2]. Contributions by Jin Zhizhu, Li Fengxi, Li Songrong, Wang Shunkui. Yanji: Yanbian renmin chubanshe.

Lin, Cong, and Liz Jackson. 2021. "Assimilation over Protection: Rethinking Mandarin Language Assimilation in China." *Multicultural Education Review* 13 (4): 338–361.

Ma Zhenchao (马振超). 2018. "Bianjing anquan shijiaoxia Chaoxianzu xiangcun kongxinhua wenti shenzhe: Yi Zhong-Chao bianjing diqu Yanbian duan weilie" (边境安全视角下朝鲜族乡村空心化问题探析——以中朝边境地区延边段为例) [An Analysis of the Hollowing Out of the Ethnic Korean Group in Rural Region from the Perspective of Border Security: Taking Yanbian Border Region as an Example]. *Wujing xueyuan xuebao* (武警学院学报) 34 (9): 20–25.

Mao, Zedong. 1957a. "Editor's Note on 'Township and Village Officials Can Lead the Formation of Co-operatives". In *Socialist Upsurge in China's Countryside*, 178. Peking: Foreign Languages Press.

——. 1957b. "Wage a Relentless Struggle against Counter-Revolutionary Wrecking". In *Socialist Upsurge in China's Countryside*, 336–337. Peking: Foreign Languages Press.

——. 1989 [1958]. "Talks at the Beidaihe Conference (Draft Transcript)". In *The Secret Speeches of Chairman Mao*, edited by Roderick MacFarquar, Timothy Cheek, and Eugene Wu, 397–442. Cambridge, MA: Council on East Asian Studies/Harvard University Press.

Morris, Warrick, and James E. Hoare. 2021. "The Yanbian Korean Autonomous Region 1990: A Journey to the Border in Time of Flux". In *Decoding the Sino-North Korean Borderlands*, edited by Adam Cathcart, Christopher Green, and Steven Denney, 217–34. Amsterdam: Amsterdam University Press.

Mullaney, Thomas. 2010. "Seeing for the State: The Role of Social Scientists in China's Ethnic Classification Project". *Asian Ethnicity* 11 (3): 325–342.

Park, Hyun Ok. 2015. *The Capitalist Unconscious: From Korean Unification to Transnational Korea*. New York: Columbia University Press.

Park, Woo, Robert Easthope, and Kyung-Sup Chang. 2020. "China's Ethnic Minority and Neoliberal Developmental Citizenship: Yanbian Koreans in Perspective". *Citizenship Studies* 24 (7): 918–933.

People's Republic of China (PRC) Ethnic Affairs Commission (国家民委). 2018. "Liu Hui pu Jilin diaoyan minzu gongzuo" (刘慧赴吉林调研民族工作) [Liu Hui Goes to Jilin to Investigate and Research Ethnic Work]." *Sina News*, 18 September. http://news.sina.com.cn/o/2018-09-18/doc-ifxeuwwr5693482.shtml [accessed 25 May 2021].

Perlez, Jane. 2015. "China Wary as Violence Spills from North Korea." *New York Times*, 30 January. https://www.nytimes.com/2015/01/30/world/asia/for-north-koreans-on-chinese-border-welcome-turns-into-wariness.html [accessed 15 June 2021].

Piao Jinhai (朴今海) and Li Yunli (李云丽). 2013. "Koushu lishi shijiaoxia de weiman shiqi Chaoxianzu jiaoyu (口述历史视角下的伪满时期朝鲜族教育) [Oral History Perspectives on Education for Ethnic Koreans in the Manchukuo Period]. In *Zhongguo Chaoxianzu Yanjiu, 2010–2011*, edited by Huang Youfu, 183–197. Beijing: Minzu chubanshe.

Ridgeon, Lloyd. 2020. "The Problem of Sinicizing Beijing's Mosques". *Journal of Muslim Minority Affairs* 40 (4): 576–596.

Schubert-Zhang, Amelia. 2016. "Impacts of Female Out-Migration on Ethnic Korean Communities in China". PhD dissertation, University of Colorado, Boulder.

Schwartz, Henry G. 1963. "Chinese Migration to North-West China and Inner Mongolia, 1949–59". *The China Quarterly* 16 (October–December): 61–67.

Shen, Zhihua, and Yafeng Xia. 2014. "Chinese-North Korean Relations and Chinese Policy toward Korean Cross-Border Migration, 1950–1962." *Journal of Cold War Studies* 16 (4): 133–158.

Shin, Dong Jo. 2016. "Factional Violence and Ethnic Relations in a Korean Borderland: Mao Yuanxin's Cultural Revolution in Yanbian, 1966–1968". *Modern China Studies* 23 (2): 141–162.

——. 2021. "'Utopian Speak': Language Assimilation in China's Yanbian Korean Borderland, 1958–1976". In *Decoding the Sino-North Korean Borderlands*, edited by Adam Cathcart, Christopher Green, and Steven Denney, 191–215. Amsterdam: Amsterdam University Press.

Tan, Yiming, Mei-Po Kwan, and Yanwei Chai. 2022. "How Chinese *Hukou* System Shapes Ethnic Dissimilarity in Daily Activities: A Study of Xining, China". *Cities* 122: 1–10.

Tsurushima, Setsure. 1979. "The Effects of the Cultural Revolution on the Korean Minority in Yanpian". *Korean Studies* 3: 93–124.

Wang Yongming (王永明). 2000. "Huiyi Wangqingxian chidai shipin qingkuang" (回忆汪清县吃代食品情况) [Recalling the Situation of Food Substitutes in Wangqing County]. In *Wangqing Wenshi Ziliao*, edited by Zhengxie Wangqingxian weiyuanhui wenshi ziliao bangongshi, Vol. 6, 51–63.

Wei, Changhao. 2021. "Recording & Review Pt. 7: Constitutionally Mandated Mandarin-Medium Education". *NPC Observer*, January 20. https://npcobserver.com/2021/01/20/recording-review-pt-7-constitutionally-mandated-mandarin-medium-education/ [accessed 25 May 2021].

Weiner, Benno. 2012. "The Chinese Revolution on the Tibetan Frontier: State Building, National Integration and Socialist Transformation, Zeku (Tsékhok) County, 1953–1958". PhD dissertation, Columbia University, New York.

Xu Zhenwu (许正昊) and Wang Guoxiang (王国祥). 1992. *Helong Xianzhi* (和龙县志) [Helong County Gazeteer]. Changchun: Jilin wenshi chubanshe.

Yanbian Archives (延边朝鲜族自治州档案馆编). 1990. *Yanbian dashiji, 1712–1988* (延边大事记，一七一二——九八八) [Large Chronicle of Events in Yanbian, 1712–1988]. Yanji: Yanbian daxue chubanshe.

Yanbian Committee on Literary and Historical Materials (延边文史资料委员会). 1984. *Yanbian wenshi ziliao* (延边文史资料) [Materials on Yanbian Literature and History]. Yanji: Yanbian renmin chubanshe. Vol. 4.

Yanbian History Research Office (延边历史研究编辑部). 1988. *Yanbian lishi yanjiu* (延边历史研究) [Research on Yanbian History]. Yanji: Xinhua. Vol. 5.

Yang, Jisheng. 2008. *Tombstone: The Great Chinese Famine 1958–1962*. New York: Farrar, Straus and Giroux.

Zhao, Lei, and Huiying Xu. 2017. "Ethnic Issues of China's Neighboring Countries and Their Impact on National Security". *Contemporary International Relations* 5 (September–October): 69–97.

Zhou, Minglang. 2012. "Historical Review of the PRC's Minority/Indigenous Language Policy and Practice". In *China's Assimilationist Language Policy: The Impact of Indigenous/Minority Literacy and Social Harmony*, edited by Gulbahar H. Beckett and Gerald A. Postiglione, 18–32. London: Routledge.

16

The New Challenges of Transnational Security in Twenty-First-Century East Asia

The Case of North Korea

Marco Milani

Introduction

Security is an idea that is often associated with the concepts of state, nation, and territorial sovereignty. The importance of protecting the territorial dimension of a political entity, for example a modern state, to ensure the stability and survival of the regime in power, and to protect the nation from external threats, lies at the centre of international relations and foreign policy. All these characteristics are by definition the constituent elements of the traditional idea of security in world politics.

In recent years, however, the concept of security in international relations has been challenged by new emerging trends that have completely overturned these traditional characteristics. While traditional security was based on the idea of protecting state borders from external military threats, the dramatic changes caused by the advent of globalisation and the end of the Cold War in the early 1990s led to the emergence of new security threats that went beyond its traditional national dimension. With the disappearance of one of the two superpowers, and the system of alliances connected to it, the perennial danger of a global nuclear war disappeared as well. While, on the one hand, the chances of interstate military conflicts decreased, on the other, new dangers emerged and started to become increasingly significant. At the start of the twenty-first century, transnational security issues began to dominate the agenda of international relations and led to the reinvention of the concept of security by nation-states that could no longer control and limit these new threats alone. A concept that for decades has been closely associated with the idea of state and pertaining only to the domain of the "national", became part of the broader trend of deterritorialisation and globalisation's challenge to state sovereignty (Hughes, 2001, 408–410). The complexity of transnational interactions started to permeate a set of issues that had been addressed and managed through a state-centric approach and often supported by nationalistic narratives.

This new perspective on security also strongly influenced East Asian countries. Transnational security became a priority for all the regional actors, specifically China, Taiwan, Japan, and the two Koreas, according to their involvement in international affairs and their engagement with the rest of the international community. Nevertheless, not a single country, no matter how isolated from the rest of the region and the world, was able to avoid this sort of revolution in security affairs. Issues such as terrorism, migration, nuclear proliferation, environmental protection and climate change, health security and disease control have emerged as existential threats that can only be effectively addressed through international cooperation. However, this approach has proved to be extremely difficult in a region in which supranational institutions and transnational cooperation are very weak, while strategic mistrust, nationalistic narratives, and historical controversies abound, together with traditional factors relating to the centrality of nation-state and national security. This sort of cognitive dissonance between the new emerging threats and the institutional infrastructure to address them has led to poor management of transnational security in East Asia. In this context, North Korea represents a paradigmatic example of a country that has put the pre-eminence of the nation-state dimension, territorial sovereignty, and very limited international cooperation at the centre of its security policy, but in the last three decades has been forced to start facing growing dangers from transnational security issues and has become itself a source of transnational insecurity in several aspects.

This chapter aims to explore the evolution of the concept of security in East Asia in the post-Cold War world focusing on the case of North Korea as a paradigmatic example of how non-traditional and transnational security has become an unavoidable new factor in contemporary international politics.

What Is Security? A Key Concept for Understanding International Relations

When analysing relations among different actors in the international community—and in particular among states—the concept of security certainly plays a central role. Ensuring the survival of the political entity and the social community in which we live is understandably one of the most important, if not the most important, goal of every actor endowed with political and military power. For this reason, the concept of security has been widely described and analysed in the study of international relations and world politics. It has been also defined in several different ways according to spatial and temporal differences and the theoretical model applied to the analysis.

In the complex and multifaceted landscape that has developed in modern and contemporary history two key components have emerged as defining characteristics for the analysis of security in international relations. The first concerns the question of what can be defined as security or as a security issue. A basic definition of security in the context of international relations is that it is about survival: when the very existence of a specific object is threatened, a set of extraordinary measures can be implemented in order to counter this threat and preserve the existence of that specific object. This definition shares many characteristics with the broader concept of security in everyday language and in the context of domestic politics; however, it does not encompass the social dimension of security, which represents one of its defining characteristics in its most common meaning (Buzan et al., 1998, 21). Hence, the importance of security has led to the possibility of using extraordinary measures and allocating great amounts of resources in order to confront this kind of existential threat. For a very long time, these threats have been understood only as military threats to the sovereignty over a specific territory (Browning, 2013, 17). As a result, for centuries security issues have been equated to war or military conflicts in general.

Once what has been considered as security in international politics is defined, a second key aspect of the traditional view of this concept needs to be pointed out: what is the object that needs to be protected from existential threat? This question leads directly to the idea of the centrality of states in international relations. States are traditionally considered as the most important actors in international politics. The system that has emerged in modern history in Europe—and later spread to almost every other region of the world, including East Asia—was based on the concept of state sovereignty and formal equality between states. This system was called "Westphalian" because it started to emerge and consolidate after a series of treaties signed in 1648 among the main European powers known as the "peace of Westphalia" (Kang, 2010, 2–3). The system became the foundation of international relations in Europe and was refined and institutionalised over the following centuries to consolidate the practices and rituals that came to dominate—and in large part still dominate—foreign policy. Security thus started to be equated with the idea of protecting state borders from external military aggressions.

This perspective remained the dominant approach to security not only in the modern era of international politics but even more after the end of the Second World War and the emergence of the Cold War. In this new context of bipolar rivalry between the United States and the Soviet Union, the two superpowers and their respective allies were constantly under an existential threat represented by a possible military attack from the other side; a situation that was made even more dangerous by the development of nuclear weapons with their potential to completely annihilate the enemy. The Cold War with its precarious situation of constant danger was the *meta-event* that led to the formation of contemporary security studies, that were thus based on the idea of defending states from military threats (Buzan and Hansen, 2009, 34). These characteristics led to the dominance of the concept of "national security" in international politics, according to which the main goal of states was to defend their own national interests, regardless of the security of the other members of the international community. Security thus became "national", pertaining only to national governments, and nationalistic narratives started to be used in order to win support from the population and to justify state decisions in matters of security, including the use of extraordinary measures.

The end of the Cold War, between the late 1980s and early 1990s, inevitably led to a rediscussion and redefinition of the concept of security, a process that had in fact already been underway since the 1970s. For decades after 1945, the identification of what constituted a "security issue" in international politics was relatively straightforward, given the centrality of states (as the object to defend) and military attacks (as the threats to defend against). The relatively peaceful end of the Cold War led to a partial restructuring of the international order with profound consequences for every actor in the system. The bipolar rivalry between the two superpowers disappeared with the collapse of the Soviet Union and its system of alliances. In this new situation the priorities and goals of states in the international community started to change with a redefinition of the meaning and aspects of security. Maintaining the idea that security is ultimately about survival, every threat that may endanger the existence of a specific object can be considered a security threat and in the new post-Cold War world it became obvious that it was not only external military attacks that represented this kind of threat. In fact, several different issues started to be perceived as a danger for the security and stability of a state.

At the same time, the consolidation of the process of globalisation led to a world that was much more economically and technologically interdependent, bringing with it a whole series of issues that appeared to be vital to the stability of international actors. Issues such as economic development, migration, human rights, the protection of the environment, drug trafficking, and national identity became crucial for both international and domestic politics (Tow et al., 2000, 1). This process led to a broadening and deepening of the concept of security, and thus of what states consider as security

(Caballero-Anthony and Emmers, 2006, 1). At the same time, new non-state actors in the international community started to emerge both as providers of security, such as in the case international organisations, non-governmental organisations, and even private entities, and also as important specific objects that needed to be protected from existential threats, such as societies, human communities, non-material aspects (identities, ideologies, traditions, religions, etc.). Even individuals started to be considered legitimate referent objects for international security, to be protected from existential threats, as in the case of human security and the development of the "responsibility to protect" doctrine (Acharya, 2001; Evans, 2004; Kondoch, 2012). This new characterisation of security in international relations started to be defined as non-traditional security, to distinguish it from its so-called traditional version—military threats—while maintaining the urgency and importance of security issues.

The revolution of the concept of security that took place with the end of the Cold War saw the centrality of states remarkably reduced with the emergence of a plurality of relevant actors. In addition to this, another crucial feature of security emerged in these years. If in the previous era the "national" dimension of security had been considered the most important, after the end of the Cold War it became clear that the new existential threats to states and other actors in international politics could not be addressed through a merely national, state-centred approach. The new security issues had an inherently transnational character: very often they did not originate within a single specific country, transcending state borders which were considered fundamental in order to understand and govern traditional security; at the same time, the effects of these issues were not confined to a single state and so represented a threat for a plurality of actors. Issues such as migration, organised crime, terrorism, health security and disease control, natural disasters and environmental problems represent perfect examples of the new forms of security that began to dominate the agenda of international politics. The transnational dimension of security became central for understanding and addressing the new threats and accordingly a new approach to the governance and management of security was also required, with an emphasis on multilateral and transnational cooperation (Hameiri and Jones, 2013). In this new context, international and regional institutions started to play an important role in facilitating cooperation and collaboration among states.

East Asian countries were clearly involved in this process of the redefinition of security, being at the forefront of both the Cold War and the new trends of globalisation. In particular, the shift that took place at the end of the twentieth century forced the governments in these countries to redefine their priorities and strategies for foreign and security policy. In order to fully understand the changes that took place in the region in terms of security it is important to analyse the historical evolution of the concept in this area and in particular the influence of Western-based concepts and of the Cold War balance of power.

The Evolution of Security in East Asia

The Westphalian concept of sovereignty and formal equality among states was new to East Asian countries before the nineteenth century (Moon and Chun, 2003, 115). It was with the arrival of imperialist Western powers that these new ideas regarding the management of international relations started to spread in the area. Up to that moment, the East Asian system of international relations was dominated by the hegemonic position of the Chinese empire, in what was later defined as the Sino-centric tributary system. The order was thus hierarchical with China at the centre and not based on the formal equality of sovereign states as in the case of the Westphalian order (Fairbank, 1968; Kang, 2010). Compared to the situation in Europe, the East Asian system of international relations proved to be much more stable and less prone to interstate war and conflicts (Kang, 2010, 2).

The traumatic arrival of Western powers, which used military force in order to grant themselves privileges and advantages in the region, led to a reconstruction of the mechanisms of international relations based on the Westphalian system of modern territorial states (Park, 2017, 77–78). China, which had been considered at stand the top of the previous order in material and moral terms, began to transform into a modern—and ordinary—sovereign state with formal equality with the other members of the international system (Moon and Chun, 2003, 117). The process of "Westernisation" of international relations in East Asia was not passively accepted by all countries in the same way: it led to different processes of resistance and imitation and also to domestic contestation and turmoil. Nevertheless, the concept of the formal sovereignty of states also became crucial for East Asian countries and led to "the creation of a shared language of sovereign autonomy. Contemporary security concepts, such as sovereignty, autonomy and (state) power, were recreated through translation, transliteration, or recombination following regional encounters with Western powers in the nineteenth century" (Park, 2017, 13). Between the late nineteenth century and 1945, the idea of state sovereignty and regional order were strongly influenced but also undermined by colonial domination and imperialism, both Western powers and the expansionist drive of the Japanese empire. With the advent of the Westphalian system in East Asia, security priorities started to take the form of what we have defined as traditional security: a state-centred approach that put utmost importance on countering military threats and the defence of state borders from external attacks.

The end of the Pacific War in 1945 and the beginning of the Cold War led to a new evolution of the regional order and the security regime in East Asia, but it did not challenge the basic assumptions related to the importance of territorial sovereignty, political autonomy, and thus military threats from external actors. Traditional state-centred security remained the key lens through which security policies were evaluated. The beginning of the nuclear era and the establishment of a nuclear stand-off between the two superpowers, with the potential of destroying not only each other but the entirety of human civilisation, exacerbated these concerns. The Westphalian concepts of sovereignty, equality, and non-interference in domestic affairs became the foundation of foreign and security policy for the countries in the region, together with nascent nationalism (Moon and Chun, 2003, 118). Security became increasingly associated with the concept of the "national" and with an extremely state-centric approach. A further characteristic of this period in East Asia is that the Cold War was, in fact, in many cases a real war, the Korean War between 1950 and 1953 and the three Indochina wars between 1946 and 1979 being the most relevant examples of how military conflicts played a crucial role in the sociopolitical development of the region during those years. For this reason, traditional military security that aimed to defend state borders from external attacks remained the main priority for several countries in the region.

The end of the Cold War brought important changes to the concept of security also in East Asia. The collapse of the Soviet bloc and the growing economic interdependence of globalisation reduced the threat of interstate military conflicts while emphasising the importance of non-traditional and transnational security issues. In this new context, countries in East Asia found themselves poorly equipped to cooperate with each other, compared to other regions of the world—such as Europe—or even Southeast Asia, which could count on the Association of Southeast Asian Nations (ASEAN) and on several other fora for multilateral collaboration connected to ASEAN. As pointed out by Robert Manning in 1993, the region was lacking a multilateral and multidimensional framework to manage regional security, a set of institutions intended to respond in a collective way to the security and economic challenges of the area, while at the same time trade and economic exchanges among the countries in the region were growing exponentially (Manning, 1993). The lack of trust between the regional actors and the persistence of traditional security threats—such as the North Korean nuclear programme, the Taiwan issue and territorial disputes—undermined the development of institutionalised and stable cooperation, which is crucial in order to effectively address transnational security. This situation, that Manning called the "Asian paradox", remained in place after the 1990s and throughout the first two decades of the twenty-first century, in some occasions intensifying even more, as in the case of controversies related to the colonial past between Japan and South Korea, such as the so-called "comfort women", forced labourer issues and the Dokdo/Takeshima territorial dispute (Snyder and Glosserman, 2015). The growing economic interdependence among the countries in the region did not mitigate strategic mistrust and intense security competition. The "Asian paradox" has survived until today, and in some ways it has even intensified. The pattern of "cold politics, hot economics" has remained largely unchanged, thus hindering the possibility of addressing transnational security issues more effectively. In this context, a peculiar case is represented by North Korea. Since the end of the Cold War, the country has been closely associated with traditional military security—because of the development of the nuclear programme—and has been isolated from the international community, both due to political decisions of the regime and by diplomatic isolation. The reality of North Korea is much more nuanced than it is often portrayed: while nuclear security concerns certainly are still relevant, and despite isolation, non-traditional and transnational security has become crucial for the country and for the stability and peace of the entire region.

Transnational Security and North Korea

The revolution of the concept of security and the emergence of the so-called non-traditional security affected also countries that were not integrated into the post-Cold War liberal world order and not as strongly affected by the dynamics of globalisation, as in the case of North Korea. On the one hand, traditional security which focused on defence from possible military aggressions from external actors remained fundamental to ensure the survival of the regime and the sovereign autonomy of the state; at the same time, however, other sectors of security started to play a pivotal role and, despite North Korea's international isolation, the transnational dimension of security also became relevant. One key aspect that has to be highlighted in the North Korean case—and also for several other states that have remained at the margins of the international system—is the fact that the widening and broadening of the concept of security did not lead to the emergence of new specific referent objects that had to be protected. Since the foundation of the North Korean state, the survival of the regime has been considered the most important goal for the country's security. This dynamic reached the point at which the security of the regime in power coincided with the security of the state. Hence every threat not only to the sovereignty of the state but also to the stability of the regime was considered an existential threat and therefore a security issue. The broadening of security was limited to the inclusion of potential sources of domestic instability, related to material aspects (food and energy supplies for example) and non-material ones (threats to ideologies and collective identity), in addition to military threats.

The situation in the post-Cold War world in terms of security looked particularly concerning for the North Korean regime. The collapse of the Soviet Union in the early 1990s deprived Pyongyang of its most important military security guarantee, its alliance with a superpower and the deterrent of its nuclear arsenal. In addition, the only remaining global superpower was the United States, a country against which North Korea had fought during the Korean War and with whom it was still formally at war. As a response to this precarious security situation, the regime started to allocate a massive amount of resources to the development of an autonomous nuclear deterrent. The decisive push towards the development of atomic weapons started in the early 1990s and raised tensions and security concerns in the region, especially from the United States, leading to the eruption of the so-called "first nuclear crisis" in 1993–1994. In this moment, diplomacy intervened in order to defuse the situation, leading to the signing of a bilateral agreement between Washington and Pyongyang in October 1994, the so-called "Agreed Framework", that froze the nuclear programme in exchange for security guarantees and the provision of energy assistance (Pollack, 2011, 99–130). The accord temporarily resolved the situation, but it did not eradicate the root of the security problem in which North Korea was entangled. The lack of mutual trust between the two parties and the inability to move forward on a path for institutionalising and normalising their relations led to the eruption of a second nuclear crisis in 2002–2003, when the US accused North Korea of secretly enriching uranium. In this case, the diplomatic framework put in place to defuse tension was not based on a bilateral negotiation between Pyongyang and Washington, which North Korea considered as its main security threat, but on a multilateral framework that also included South Korea, China, Russia, and Japan. This framework—called the "Six Party Talks"—failed to achieve any substantial agreement, thus leaving North Korea time to continue developing its nuclear and missile programmes.

The two nuclear crises and the continuing efforts by North Korea to develop nuclear weapons and long-range missiles to deliver them can be analysed and understood in the framework of traditional military security. The hostile situation in which the regime found itself after the end of the Cold War left North Korea vulnerable to attacks from external actors, threatening not only the stability of the political system in the country but also the crucial aspect of state sovereignty over the territory. The response to this threat took an equally traditional form with a military countermeasure based on the nuclear deterrent, exactly the same form that was provided by the Soviet Union during the Cold War years. In this perspective, while traditional security lost its prominence for a large part of the international community in the post-Cold War world, for North Korea it remained a key aspect.

But military security was not the only area in which North Korea found itself struggling after the end of the Cold War. The collapse of the Soviet Union, and to a lesser extent also of the communist regimes in its satellite states, deprived North Korea of its main trading partner and provider of aid and assistance. Pyongyang became virtually isolated and its economic problems were exacerbated. North Korea's economic situation was severely worsened by a series of natural disasters between 1994 and 1997 that caused a devastating famine in which millions of North Koreans perished. The inability to provide food and other basic necessities to the population in turn created problems for the legitimacy of the regime, already weakened by the collapse of the communist regimes around the world, by the process of reforming and opening to others, and lastly by the death of the leader and founder of the nation Kim Il-sung, in July 1994 (Milani, 2019, 102–103).

In this transformed situation, economic security and identity security, strongly linked to the ideology and legitimisation of the leadership, became existential threats to the stability of the North Korean regime, bringing non-traditional security issues to the centre of state policy alongside military security. The idea of security that dominated the decisions of the North Korean leadership after the end of the Cold War remained strongly connected to the national, state-centred dimension. The emphasis on transnational security and the reduction of the role of states did not affect the policy-making process of the regime. This did not mean that North Korea remained impenetrable to the revolution of the idea of security that took place in the early 1990s. However, these changes mostly concerned the kind of threat that were considered an existential danger for the regime, and they did not broaden the number of actors to be protected. For example, the idea of human security that emerged as one of the most pressing issues for a large part of the international community starting from the mid-1990s, was not considered a priority by the North Korean regime, which continued to value the survival and stability of the regime as the most important issue. From this perspective, issues such as human rights protection and other aspects of the well-being of the population—supply of food and water, healthcare—remained subordinated to the stability of the regime. This sort of cognitive dissonance between the direction travelled by the international community in terms of security, with its growing emphasis on the protection of individuals instead of political entities, and the behaviour of North Korea's leadership became a further cause of tension (Kondoch, 2012). The continued violations of human rights of which the regime was accused started to play an increasingly important role in the relations between Pyongyang and the international community, in particular European countries and the United States. The publication in February 2014 of the report by the commission of inquiry on human rights in the Democratic People's Republic of Korea, by the United Nations Human Rights Council consolidated these concerns and provided an official platform for the international community to condemn the actions and failures of the regime.

Despite the fact that traditional military security remains a major concern for the North Korean leadership, as we have seen, non-traditional security issues have become important for the stability and survival of the regime. In this context, transnational security started to play a significant role, despite the country's international isolation. The emergence of new threats linked to a supranational dimension has had the effect of undermining the centrality of the regime and of state institutions to control and reduce them. The process of destatalisation of security has thus also affected North Korea, a country that historically has maintained the pre-eminence of the role of state power to address security issues and the "national" dimension of security; the result has been a deterioration of the country's security situation and a new emphasis on vulnerabilities that cannot be addressed only through regime's decisions and policies, but require some degree of cooperation—or at least interaction—with other international actors. This new attention to the transnational dimension of security can be analysed from two different perspectives: threats to North Korea and threats originating in North Korea.

As for the first group, there are several different domains of security from which dangerous threats to the country have emerged in recent years and that are connected to transnational dynamics. One that has become increasingly relevant in recent years is that of natural disasters and their consequences on the country's food, health, and more generally human security. These threats are connected to regional and global dynamics related to the protection of the environment and climate change. While extreme weather events are not new to North Korea—they were one of the causes of the "great famine" in the second half of the 1990s—in the last few years events such as floods, typhoons, and droughts, have strongly affected the Korean Peninsula with grave consequences especially for the North, which has a weaker system to prevent or mitigate the effects. During the summer of 2020, for example, a series of typhoons caused severe damage to the northern provinces of North Korea, compromising agricultural production. These negative effects had serious repercussions on food production and on the country's food security (Song and Habib, 2020). While devising countermeasures for the effects of these security threats and improving the systems to manage and mitigate the effects can be brought back to a national level, addressing the causes certainly requires a high level of international cooperation, which is currently not pursued by the North Korean regime.

The recent COVID-19 pandemic, the most dangerous health security threat of recent decades, can certainly be considered another example of the importance of the transnational dimension of security. While North Korea was able to strongly limit the diffusion of the new coronavirus, this result was achieved thanks to a series of draconian measures of isolation from every other country, including China which is its most important trading partner and provider of resources. The COVID-19 pandemic represents a serious threat to the country's health security and to its healthcare system, which still presents several deficiencies especially in terms of access to treatments and existing disparities between different parts of the population (Lee et al., 2020). From this perspective, transnational cooperation with neighbouring countries and the international community would be extremely helpful for providing aid and assistance and improving the health security situation of the country. While the decision to completely isolate the country at the beginning of the pandemic also included the inflow of humanitarian aid, more recently the North Korean regime have accepted medical supplies and other assistance to control the pandemic from the World Health Organization (Ahn, 2021). The COVID-19 crisis has had inevitable repercussions on other aspects and levels of security of North Korea's regime and population, such as economic security, food security, and human security more generally (Nebehay, 2021).

The porousness of North Korea's border with China represents another transnational security threat to the stability of the regime. Smugglers are able to introduce products into the country that are prohibited, including for example South Korean and Western cultural products that are perceived by the leadership as a possible threat to its grip on power and thus as an existential threat to stability. The border with China represents a sort of paradox for North Korea's security and in particular for its complicated relations with the transnational dimension. On the one hand, as previously mentioned, the influx of prohibited goods across the border represents a real threat for the stability of the regime and its control over the production and dissemination of information within the country; on the other hand, the border is also a fundamental lifeline for the sustainability of the economic situation, both in terms of legal exchanges and illegal but tolerated trade, for a country that is subjected to a very harsh regime of international sanctions. The contradictory situation of the border with China can be seen, at a micro-level, as an example of the contradictions that characterise the North Korean regime caught between isolation to protect itself and the need for greater transnational cooperation to address non-traditional security issues.

In recent years, North Korea has been increasingly seen as a source of security threats for the international community, and not only for the development of nuclear weapons or human rights violations, but also for non-traditional transnational security issues. For many years several countries have accused North Korea of being involved in transnational crime, in particular counterfeiting, money laundering, drug trafficking, and other activities. Obtaining definitive evidence of these illegal operations is very complicated but nonetheless these accusations have been a major transnational security concern for the international community for years (Kang, 2013, 75–99). Another issue of transnational security that has long involved North Korea is represented by its support for terrorist operations abroad. The North Korean regime has been accused of supporting and also directly organising several terrorist operations during the Cold War years motivated by political and ideological reasons (Bechtol, 2010). More recently this role has certainly diminished to the point that the country was removed from the US State Department list of state sponsors of terrorism in 2008 by the Bush administration. In 2017, however, the Trump administration decided to put North Korea back onto the list in a move that has been considered as a further way to put pressure on Pyongyang (Byman, 2017). In recent years other issues of transnational security involving North Korea have emerged. One of the most prominent examples is represented by cybersecurity threats and the role played by North Korean organisations. Cyber operations and attacks by groups directly connected to the regime in Pyongyang have grown exponentially in recent years, and North Korea has become a sophisticated cyber actor. While these activities were initially related to intelligence and covert operations, such as gathering information and/or disrupting systems mostly in South Korea and the United States, more recently the illicit cyber activities have been aimed at generating revenue and evading international sanctions (DuBois, 2020). Several important cyberattacks have been traced back to North Korea's operations, for example, the WannaCry ransomware attack of 2017 or the attack against the Bangladesh central bank in 2016 (Iyengar, 2017). In both cases the main intent of the attackers was to illegally obtain money by direct theft or demanding a ransom. Considering the growth of advanced technologies to manage and move financial resources—in particular with the proliferation of the so-called cryptocurrencies—these activities by the North Korean regime will likely increase in the future as they represent a crucial instrument for countering international sanctions.

In the case of transnational threats both to and from North Korea, the main factor in producing insecurity can be seen in the growing international isolation of the country. The attention of the international community has been overwhelmingly focused on the nuclear programme and the danger it represents for the region. However, looking beyond the level of military security, North Korea's isolation has produced increasing insecurity within the country, especially for the living conditions of its population, and also pushed the regime towards illegal activities that represent transnational security threats for other countries. As we have pointed out, international cooperation and collaboration are of paramount importance in order to effectively address transnational security issues. This is obviously true also in the case of North Korea. A broader effort to socialise the country into the regional and global community would represent an important step towards minimising the repercussions of transnational security threats within North Korea, and also reducing the role of the regime as a source of transnational insecurity.

References and Further Reading

Acharya, Amitav. 2001. "Human Security: East versus West". *International Journal* 56 (3): 442–460.

Ahn, Sung-mi. 2021. "North Korea accepts COVID aid from WHO amid border shutdown". *The Korea Herald*, 8 October. http://www.koreaherald.com/view.php?ud=20211008000645 [accessed 27 January 2022].

Bechtol, Bruce E., Jr. 2010. "North Korea and Support to Terrorism: An Evolving History". *Journal of Strategic Security* 3 (2): 45–54.

Browning, Christopher S. 2013. *International Security: A Very Short Introduction*. Oxford: Oxford University Press.

Buzan, Barry, and Lene Hansen. 2009. *The Evolution of International Security Studies*. Cambridge: Cambridge University Press.

Buzan, Barry, Ole Waever, and Jaap de Wilde. 1998. *Security: A New Framework for Analysis*. London: Lynne Rienner.

Byman, Daniel L. 2017. "Putting the North Korea Terrorism Designation in Context". *Brookings*, 21 November. https://www.brookings.edu/blog/order-from-chaos/2017/11/21/putting-the-north-korea-terrorism-designation-in-context/ [accessed 27 January 2022].

Caballero-Anthony, Mely, and Ralf Emmers. 2006. "Understanding the Dynamics of Securitizing Non-Traditional Security". In *Non-Traditional Security in Asia: Dilemmas in Securitisation*, edited by Mely Caballero-Anthony, Ralf Emmers, and Amitav Acharya, 1–12. Burlington: Ashgate.

DuBois, Eun. 2020. "Building Resilience to the North Korean Cyber Threat: Experts Discuss". *Brookings*. 23 December. https://www.brookings.edu/blog/order-from-chaos/2020/12/23/building-resilience-to-the-north-korean-cyber-threat-experts-discuss/ [accessed 27 January 2022].

Evans, Paul M. 2004. "Human Security and East Asia: In the Beginning". *Journal of East Asian Studies* 4 (2): 263–284.

Fairbank, John K (ed.). 1968. *The Chinese World Order.* Cambridge: Harvard University Press.

Hameiri, Shahar, and Lee Jones. 2013. "The Politics and Governance of Non-Traditional Security". *International Studies Quarterly* 57: 462–473.

Hughes, Cristopher W. 2001. "Conceptualizing the Globalization-Security Nexus in the Asia-Pacific". *Security Dialogue* 32 (4): 407–421.

Iyengar, Rishi. 2017. "How North Korea is Hacking Companies and Governments". *CNN Business*, 15 November. https://money.cnn.com/2017/11/15/technology/north-korea-hacking-fallchill-volgmer-fbi-dhs/index.html [accessed 27 January 2022].

Kang, David C. 2010. *East Asia before the West: Five Centuries of Trade and Tributes.* New York: Columbia University Press.

—. 2013. "Securitizing Transnational Organized Crime and North Korea's Non-Traditional Security". In *Non-Traditional Security Issues in North Korea*, edited by Kyung-Ae Park, 75–99. Honolulu: University of Hawai'i Press.

Kondoch, Boris. 2012. "The Responsibility to Protect and Northeast Asia: The Case of North Korea". *The Korean Journal of Defense Analysis* 24 (4): 433–448.

Lee, Hayoung, Courtland Robinson, Jaeshin Kim, Martin McKee, and Jiho Cha. 2020. "Health and Healthcare in North Korea: A Retrospective Study among Defectors". *Conflict and Health* 14 (41). https://doi.org/10.1186/s13031-020-00284-y.

Manning, Robert. 1993. "The Asian Paradox: Toward a New Architecture". *World Policy Journal* 10 (3): 55–64.

Milani, Marco. 2019. "The Evolution of the North Korean Nuclear Program: From Survival Strategy to Ideological Legitimization". *On Korea* 12: 99–111.

Moon, Chung-in, and Chaesung Chun. 2003. "Sovereignty: Dominance of the Westphalian Concept and Implications for Regional security". In *Asian Security Order: Instrumental and Normative Features*, edited by Muthiah Alagappa, 106–137. Stanford: Stanford University Press.

Nebehay, Stephanie. 2021. "North Korea Measures to Stem COVID-19 Worsen Abuses, Hunger: U.N. Expert". *Reuters*, 3 March. https://www.reuters.com/article/us-northkorea-rights-idUSKBN2AV1B2 [accessed 27 January 2022].

Park, Seo-Hyun. 2017. *Sovereignty and Status in East Asian International Relations.* Cambridge: Cambridge University Press.

Pollack, Jonathan D. 2011. *No Exit: North Korea, Nuclear Weapons and International Security.* London: The International Institute for Strategic Studies.

Song, Jay, and Benjamin Habib. 2020. "Typhoons and Human Insecurity in North Korea". *The Diplomat*, 21 October.

Snyder, Scott A., and Brad Glosserman. 2015. *The Japan-South Korea Identity Clash: East Asian Security and the United States*. New York: Columbia University Press.

Tow, William T., Ramesh Thakur, and In-taek Hyun. 2000. *Asia's Emerging Regional Order*. Tokyo: United Nations University Press.

Index

Printed and bound by CPI Group (UK) Ltd, Croydon, CR0 4YY
14/12/2022
03172689-0005